Patrick Chabal,
Peter Skalník (Editors)

Africanists on Africa

Patrick Chabal and Peter Skalník

(Editors)

Africanists on Africa

Current Issues

LIT

for the University of Hradec Králové

This publication was supported by a Specific Science Grant of the Faculty
of Arts, University of Hradec Králové
Scientific reviewers: Prof. PhDr. Josef Kandert, CSc.; PhDr. Ladislav Venyš, CSc.
Cover design: Veronika Jezdinská
Technical editorial work and index: Mgr. Jan Prouza
Printed by HRG, s.r.o., Svitavská 1203, Litomyšl, www.hrg.cz

Bibliographic information published by the Deutsche Bibliothek
The Deutsche Nationalbibliothek lists this publication in the Deutsche Nationalbibliographie;
detailed bibliographic data are available on the Internet at http://dnb.d-nb.de

A catalogue record for this book is available from the British Library

ISBN 978-3-643-10682-7

LIT Verlag Dr.W. Hopf Berlin 2010
Fresnostr.2 D-48 159 Münster
Tel. +49/ (0)251-620 320 Fax +49/ (0)251-922 60 99,
e-Mail: lit@lit-verlag.de http://www.lit-verlag.de

Distribution:
In Germany: LIT Verlag Fresnostr.2 D-48 159 Münster
Tel. +49/ (0)251-620 320, Fax +49/ (0)251-922 60 99
e-Mail: vertrieb@lit-verlag.de

In Austria: Medienlogistik Pichler-ÖBZ Gmbh & Co KB
IZ-NÖ, Süd, Strasse 1, Objekt 34, A-2355 Wiener Neudorf
Tel. +43 (0) 22 36-63 53 52 90, Fax +43 (0) 22 36-63 53 52 43, e-Mail: mlo@medienlogistik.at

In Switzerland: B + M Buch- und Medienvertriebs AG
Hochstr. 357, CH-8200 Schaffhausen
Tel. +41 (0) 52-643 54 30, Fax: +41 (0) 52-643 54 35

In the UK by: Global Book Marketing, 99B Wallis Rd, London
Phone: +44 (0) 20 8533 5800, Fax +44 (0) 1600 775 663 http://www.centralbooks.co.uk/html

In North America by: e-mail: orders@transactionpub.com
Transaction Publishers   Tel.: (732) 445-2280
Rutgers University   Fax: (732) 445-3138
35 Berrue Circle   for orders (U.S. only)
Piscataway, NJ 08854   toll free (888) 999-6778

Contents

FOREWORD

Viva Africa 2009, held in Hradec Králové, was an opportunity for Western and Eastern European scholars to think critically about the condition of Africa half a century after the advent of independence. The questions raised by an examination of the African continent fifty years after the end of colonial rule are many but they all boil down to the issue of poverty, violence and development. Why is it that the countries of Africa have not fared better since they gained their freedom? Generations of (African and non-African) Africanists have addressed this question and their answers have depended partly on their expectations and partly on their reading of the situation on the ground at the time. In this respect, one can identify three main periods: the first decade after independence; the long decade that followed the 1973 oil crisis; and the period since the late eighties and early nineties.[1]

During the first period, in which optimism reigned, a combination of state-led development policies and the priority given to consolidating national unity resulted in one-party states, which Africanists deemed historically appropriate vehicles for the rapid modernisation of the former colonies. When the 1973 oil crisis made clear that development had not taken root and that the politics of the one-party state had resulted in the creation of vastly inflated and unsustainable authoritarian states, the Africanist consensus shifted along with the new Western liberal ideology. The state was now seen as the main impediment to development and Africanists concentrated their attention on how African societies might be mobilised. This fuelled a wide range of studies on the specificities of the social, economic and political links that conditioned relations between the state and society in Africa. Previous assumptions about the relatively simple path of development Africa might had been expected to follow were questioned. There was renewed interest in colonial and pre-colonial history.

Since the eighties, the agenda has been firmly fixed on the importance of 'democratisation', both as a way of giving Africans an opportunity to express themselves freely and as a framework for development. Domestic discontent and outside pressure have combined to introduce multi-party elections throughout the continent. These have now become established, almost routinised, though there is debate as to whether they have made politics more 'democratic' and, more importantly, whether they have brought about systemic change in the way power is exercised. Naturally, the work of Africanists has been sensitive to these changes and much research has gone into the analysis of the impact of such electoral transformation. In particular, there has been great emphasis on the development and role of civil society.

Although there is no consensus yet on whether 'democratisation', as it has evolved on the continent, has made it more likely that sustainable development will (finally) emerge,

---

[1] This chronology applies to those countries that became independent between 1957 and 1964; it differs for those that decolonised later, though the broad argument still applies.

there is broad agreement on the key importance of the state. So the question has become one of understanding the complexities of the African state and of explaining why so many have failed or are failing. Here there is a wide range of conclusions that tend to cluster around two main types of explanation. One is that the state does not possess the resources and capacity to implement development plans – and hence needs more support to build up capacity. The other is that political elites, when they are not corrupt or abusing their positions, are beholden to social, economic, political and cultural constraints that hamper their development efforts. Whatever the reasons, Africanists are confronted with the harsh consequences in today's Africa of the absence of development.

The papers published in this volume cover a very wide range of topics, most of them not directly concerned with the state or with issues of development. However, most of them raise questions about the social, economic or political situation in Africa that refer to the fact that people face difficult living and working circumstances on the continent. Many of the chapters point to the extraordinary resilience and inventiveness of Africans as they adapt and seek solutions to the daily problems they confront. Others raise issues of individual and collective agency. But, implicitly or explicitly, most of them are set within a context where poverty, deprivation and the lack of economic opportunities stifle ambition and reduce achievement. Of course, there are huge differences between African countries, as the papers show, and for this reason it is clear that it is difficult to generalise about current problems and possible solutions. There is thus no conclusion to the book, except a refinement of the type of questions it is profitable to ask.

The role of Africanists is to deploy their skills to study, analyse and compare different settings. Viva Africa 2009 provided an opportunity for students of Africa hailing from different countries to discuss and contrast various approaches to similar questions. The papers published in this volume reflect the diversity of interest, approach and methodology to be found within the community of (Eastern and Western) Africanists. Together they serve to highlight the strengths, but also the limitations, of the research carried out by those who do not live in Africa. They reflect the different ways in which Africanists go about identifying the questions that matter and how they attempt to provide plausible answers to these questions. It should be a rich reference source for all those interested not just in contemporary Africa but in the work of non-African Africanists working in an Eastern European environment in which research had long been hampered by political and ideological considerations.

Patrick Chabal
King's College London

INTRODUCTION:
THE PRIMACY OF THE STATE IN POST-COLONIAL AFRICA[1]

Peter Skalník
University of Hradec Králové

The Ramifications of African Studies

The fifty years since the Year of Africa have exhibited several periods. After the euphoric years of inebriation from independence when the achievement of political kingdom was believed to provide all other benefits, came the years of coups whereby the military and police expressed their dissatisfaction with the emptiness of the promises by the founding fathers. It is intriguing that the dissatisfaction was the reaction to both Marxist-leaning regimes and the pro-capitalist ones. The vicissitudes which African societies had to go through in the decades preceding 1990 were closely connected with the instability of the post-colonial state. The latter as a by-product imported from Europe with colonialism was deemed to be unstable by virtue of its implantation into African societies, which were functioning according to a different logic. By the 1990 when Africa declared itself ready to follow the democratic path taken by the rest of the world, various authors came with a conclusion that the state in Africa has been the source of corruption, was criminalized, bewitched and thus unable to embrace democracy of the Western type (Bayart 1993; Bayart, Ellis and Hibou 1998). This negative assessment was alternated by pragmatically optimistic views that Africa in spite of this works (Chabal and Daloz 1999; Skalník 2001). During the last decade, however, the Africanists, both African and foreign, have arrived gradually to the conclusion that the post-colonial state in Africa is not as unstable as was deemed. It is rather an expression of inventive response of African political elites to the challenges of a post-colonial situation, which is characterized by the hegemony of the state in societies that are unstable as a result of both radical changes and a lack of those changes, which the population expected (Chabal 2009).

African studies have emerged as an integral part of colonialism and originally were practiced almost exclusively by academics from former colonial metropolitan countries. Later other countries with interests in Africa also joined in (USSR/Russia, USA, Canada, Japan, other European countries, India, Australia, etc.). If there were African Africanists at the moment of independence these were Europe- or America-trained scholars working according to the precepts worked out by non-African Africanists. Only gradually, as a result of Africanization of existing research and teaching centres in Africa and more equitable cooperation between African, European and American Africanists, new generations of African Africanists emerged which try to balance the numbers and influence of Africanists from countries outside of Africa. Production of knowledge

---

[1] This chapter is a result of the research supported by the Grant No. 407/09/0387 of the Grant Agency of the Czech Republic "Political Parties of Africa, Asia, Latin America and Oceania."

about Africa and the authority of academic texts concerning the continent have, for too long, been dominated by non-African Africanists. The "we know better" attitude is now over and it is high time to listen to the Africans and what they have found out about their continent, especially concerning its current developments.

Almost all contributions gathered in the present volume were written by non-Africans. Most of them were presented at Viva Africa 2009 international conference, held in the Czech city of Hradec Králové. What is their legitimacy as to presenting research based on outside, usually time-limited, research? How can they compare with the researchers who have a lifetime of experience living in Africa, but combined with the complexities of gaining livelihood which often make social research an experience of suffering, struggle for basic funds if not impossible at all? The answer is that research carried out from outside with outside funding is needed, is useful and is important. The exploration of the unknown has hardly any limits and the expansion of knowledge should not be curbed by politically correct exhortations. But this research by mostly non-African Africanists will have to be open to criticism by African researchers. Besides, research on Africa reflects itself in the research of other continents. By learning more about Africa we also learn more of Europe, etc. Study of Africa by non-Africans should serve as an inspiration for African researchers to study other continents than their own.

A specific case is African researchers who work and live outside of Africa. They feel an obligation and even right to speak for Africa, but in effect their absence from Africa puts them on almost the same footing with non-African Africanists. If we take into consideration circumstances under which the production of knowledge about Africa takes place the ensuing dialogue will be productive for all participating in it. Moreover Africanists hailing from formerly communist-ruled societies have also a specific position as their experience invites them to carry out comparisons of African development, often informed by Marxism, with Marxism-powered accelerated modernization in their countries. Thus the present volume is a contribution to the inter-continental exchange.

The Theme and the Chapters

The common denominator of the contributions to this book is the state--the state in Africa with its specific ability to play multiple roles of mover, mediator and controller, facilitator and impeder vis-à-vis the society. This specific position of the state when the inner and outer correctives are hardly available attracts the researchers because the state is not just a power structure put above the society. The well-known rhizome idea suggested by Bayart (1993) is useful here because it operates with interpenetration of the state and society. After all, society is not a passive object of manipulation by the state; it is also present in the state because the personnel of state agencies bring in the attitudes, structures and beliefs of the society's members. When Patrick Chabal in his chapter presents data supporting the thesis about the political causes of crisis in Africa, he thereby suggests that 'money and creed' coming from outside of Africa are not the solution. Those who promote development as part and parcel of outside economic intervention would have had booked some success by now. Instead, their underestimation of the political factor postponed the solution indefinitely, or at least until the full cognizance of the decisive role of politics is implemented in both theories and practice of social and economic change. Chabal clearly shows that there is no causal relation between statism and the lack of development in Africa. The policies of structural adjustment, also imposed from outside of Africa, perhaps managed to reduce state expenditures but unfortunately there where the state is needed most, e.g., infrastructure, security, reduction of the poverty of the poorest. Without legal, infrastructural and financial means guaranteed by the state there can be no market, no development.

What state do we expect to promote development and economic growth? How do we build democratic states in Africa? What is the meaning of civil society in African conditions? These are crucial questions, which Chabal, Arseniev and other authors try to answer in their respective chapters. There is little in the mechanical procedures of such programmes as Millennium Development Goals that could lead to effective governance. Therefore Chabal stipulates the minimal prerequisites for the state worthy of its name. Very briefly, the state must guarantee law and order, functioning administration, infrastructure, health, business preconditions including banks. The problem of Africa is that even the mechanisms of the bureaucratic state do not function properly. 'Good governance' is not necessarily morally good but it must work efficiently. Along with a degree of economic efficiency the state must care for a sufficient degree of cultural compatibility. This includes respect for and inspiration from the values coming from the past, original African institution of chiefdom included (Skalník 1996a, 2004).

The state is the concrete expression of power relations in a society. Therefore Chabal strives for a better understanding of the exercise of power. If politicians behave as patrons and their supporters as clients, there is no real distinction between the public and private spheres and the bureaucratic state is not possible because it is personal, good to some but not to all. Those countries in Africa, which managed to survive without coups, have apparently balanced the formal and informal governance with the expectations of the clients. The ruling political party built on the state supporters from among all population groups then also ensures that inevitable grievances never spill over and destabilize the status quo. In those states where these balances are not maintained, change of regime inevitably follows. The neo-patrimonial state in Africa has been comparatively successful because the home scene was decisive, informal politics satisfied. Once compared with the Western bureaucratic state model, the African informal state was of course unsuccessful. Chabal rightly shows that the neo-patrimonial state could not indefinitely satisfy its clients at home and be a good client to the international aid donors. Informal mechanisms prevailed and the state was privatised while political pluralism was introduced. The state as a bureaucratic system ceases to exist. No development policies are possible. The state officials do not disappear but privately collect fees for the services they clientelistically disburse. Foreign aid, indeed the whole sphere of development, becomes the source of income for the office holders.

3

To overcome the vicious circle of bad governance in Africa Chabal suggests thinking in a new way about informal politics and economics, about the traditional factors in politics that affect the accountability of politicians. 'Traditional' forms of political accountability are to be recognized, admitted and thus made more transparent. African politicians should decide and reveal what is good governance according to them. Western criteria of efficiency and political success will have to be replaced by African criteria, but this shift will have to be accompanied by the new thinking about development. Success in development is, after all, what no politician in Africa would deny as being crucial to her or his political longevity. Development is what Africans desire even though the definitions of it may differ. As Chabal suggests, African politicians will have to formulate their own vision on development based on African understanding of responsibility and accountability towards the people.

Informal/traditional constraints on the exercise of power should not only be defined but operationalised and harnessed for improvement of the state's governance. Of course a new brand of accountability does not guarantee development. African governments would have to devise new ways of improvement economic and social lot of the populations they govern. It appears that regular multiparty elections do not lead either to development or accountability. It is patently clear that neo-patrimonialism is in the long run not advantageous for both those in power and those ruled by it. People can vote but governance is not better, rather the bad governance is confirmed by a democratically executed election under international supervision! An informal approach to politics returns like a boomerang as people see no better ways of improving their lot. But what is needed most in Africa are African, not European, American or Asian policies that overcome the neo-patrimonialist cul-de-sac.

Vladimir Arseniev in his contribution is no less resolute as about the need to abandon imposed models on Africans and their political and social life. The state is the key to improvement but decentralization is not the right way. Arseniev asserts that the state in Africa has not fully developed as it is only identified with the self-serving political class. The state as a servant of the people, as a mechanism of public obligations, is an unknown entity in Africa. But Arseniev wants to take Africa into broader contexts. He finds the demise of the Soviet Union not positive for Africa. On the other hand the present economic crisis and the disaster, which took place in New York on the 11th of September 2001, spell out the possibility of decline of capitalism. If that is true, the future of Africa might be more complex than previously thought. Is Africa to join those countries which are ever more critical of the West, is Africa to change masters and become dependent on those opponents of the West? Or will Africa be able to shake off both dependencies and wrestle for itself a truly independent position, which would leave behind the post-colonialist nightmares? Arseniev is right when he sides with the vision of a multi-polar world in which Africa will have her opportunities. Much will depend on players such as the European Union, China, the Moslem World and Russia. He asks pertinently whether the return of the state as decisive force in handling the economic crisis will also affect Africa.

Chabal's analysis speaks for the growing power of the state as the main factor in development. Special relations, whether partnership or association, between the European Union and the African Union have its logic as these two continents are close to each other geographically, economically and historically as well. Arseniev, however, does not forget the mass immigration of Africans to EU countries and can imagine future severance of relations between Europe and Africa. If Europe indeed cuts its relations with Africa, the future of African states, indeed societies, might hang in the balance. A 'return' to a natural economy and local mechanisms of power with marauding armed groups reaping 'booty' from the peasants will not be a fantasy but reality. The state as we know it will have no place in such scenarios.

Arseniev maintains that the neo-colonial project has thus far been most viable in independent Africa but the state there will have to be adapted to the needs of broad populations. The three African building blocks further are Anglophone, Francophone and Lusophone spaces with their respective links to the metropolis. But the links will have to be put on more equal footing, which would enable Africa to profit more from the relationship.

Vlastimil Fiala's contribution deals with political parties in Africa with special emphasis on Lusophone countries. The theory of political parties has thus far been developed in reference to data about Euro-American politics. While the political parties in developed democracies are practical expressions of the principle that people are the source of power (both in the society and the state), African political parties derive their existence from the colonial and post-colonial state. In a very few African states there used to be regular competition between the government and the opposition so common in especially Western European countries. Thus as a rule the victorious party was actually no party because it was the whole; i.e., the whole and only power in the state. As is well known 'state-parties' have been quite common in Communist states and many Asian, African and Latin American countries. The main problem today, when pluralist models of political life are spreading into the non-Western world, seems to be how to ensure that competing political parties are not self-indulging clubs but collective builders and guarantors of democratic governance. Fiala's analysis is historically and typologically oriented. It has its advantages because the data are readily available on the origin and emergence of political parties. Typologies are useful because they are closely related to the state regime in which this or that party functions. Especially important is to realize the variety of political parties in countries where there were none before. This is the case of Lusophone countries of Africa. Probably due to delayed liberation and the need to quickly overcome the backwardness caused by Portuguese colonialism, all of them chose state-party Marxist-type regimes.

Now the need to harness the newly formed political parties into the building of accountable democratic states is even more urgent. Therefore the positive experience of Cape Verde in this respect, juxtaposed to that of Guinea-Bissau as discussed in the contribution by Jan Klíma is so important. Whereas the case of Ghana, a country with a relatively long experience with party pluralism, allows for a more refined analysis of the functioning of political parties and their relation to the society in the Fourth Republic. Jan Prouza's chapter is clear evidence of this. It deals with the key function of political parties, namely the selection of candidates for parliamentary and presidential elections. By way of the analytical framework of G. Rahat and R.Y. Hazan, he examines how concretely the selection of candidates takes place and to what extent the main Ghanaian political parties are open to citizens and segments of the society.

The same country, i.e., Ghana, has been the field of study of another political factor, which only marginally touches on political parties. However, one could argue that chieftainship has been a special 'super-party' in Ghana with direct bearing on the colonial and post-colonial state. The question, not far from Arseniev's and Chabal's questions, is whether the existence of chiefs and their specific powerless power such as *naam* in the chiefdom of Nanuŋ could contribute to the building of accountable governance. A balanced combination of the features of original African institutions such as chieftaincy and the modern state might be part of the answer. Peter Skalník's contribution shows this in the case of the role of paramount chiefs in development.

In Sierra Leone, where the state almost collapsed during the civil war, it is the 'traditional' mechanisms of reconciliation (rituals of cleansing and healing) that among other help to restore the trust of the population in the state as an impartial instrument for advancement of all. The promotion of peace among groups that were at war, aptly described by Kateřina Werkman, opens not only local scenes for development but also gives chance again to the reconstructed state of Sierra Leone to prove to its citizens that it can guarantee not only basic tolerance but also cooperation and development.

Richard Bradshaw and Ibrahim Ndzesop offer a vast comparative picture of the phenomenon of mercenaries in Africa and other continents. Again the centrality of the state for the understanding of the omnipresence of mercenaries in the past and present is evident. The authors bring ample evidence of the proliferation of mercenaries in times when the state is relatively unstable or weak. On the other hand however some states used mercenaries abundantly for the implementation of their expansionist policies. The problem is closely related to the degree of the monopoly on the use of force. Mercenaries are on one end of the continuum of violence that ends with pirates and terrorists. However, corruption, especially if it is generalized, can be equally dangerous for the states.

Isak Niehaus shows in South African field data how corruption becomes legitimised through political processes while taking place in secret. The career of the present president Zuma can serve as a precedent for patronage and lack of transparency within both the ruling African National Congress and the state structures alike. South Africa as a state is of course interested in her good image, both at home and abroad. Tourism and heritage, Africanism and 'rainbowism' are concepts and phenomena, which Hana Horáková employs in her chapter on nation-building. A reified concept of culture is used to prove that South African-ness is possible and happening. The question remains: can unity be created from above, by the state and its cultural policies?

South Africa obviously attracts a lot of interest because of its economic, political and moral importance. Deep insights by field anthropologists are invaluable testimonies of substantial changes in this country. The cases analyzed in the chapters by Vendula Řezáčová and Stephné Herselman respectively have seemingly little to do with the state. However, it is apparent that labour migration from Venda to the industrial core of South Africa, as studied by Řezáčová, has been coordinated by the South African state. If spirit possession is the result of prolonged absence of the marginalized migrant from home, then the healing process involves looking for a new distance from the source of illness.

Herselman describes what could be dubbed as the political economy of poverty in South Africa by way of a detailed analysis of the microcredit industry. Of course there are pitfalls in everything but microcredit helps exactly those whom the neoliberal state does not. The state, on the other hand, could and should be able to ensure that the functioning of money lending is as fair as possible.

Jan Záhořík and Alemayehu Kumsa's chapters on Ethiopia and Somalia respectively introduce comparative data on the seeming decentralization and de facto disintegration of the state. Ethiopia introduced a model, which if genuine would give its large ethnic groups more autonomy, possibly even the right to secession. Somalia, constitutionally a unitary state, broke down into at least three distinct polities. Somaliland works well but is not internationally recognized, Puntland lives out of piracy while the rest of Somalia is nominally ruled by a government, which however has not enough power to implement its claim to rule. Warlordism is the solution, at least for the moment. Too much of the state, too little of it, these are the extremes in the Horn of Africa.

Philip Kilbride's chapter concerns neighbouring Kenya. Street children are not potential criminals contrary to what the Kenyan state would like to assert, but they are according to his finding working children, children who want to survive and do as much as possible for the success of this aim.

Finally this book contains two chapters based on West African data. Seemingly dealing with spheres of activity which have little to do with the state, they are in fact predicated on the state's proper functioning. Daniel Künzler shows in Benin's case how the institution of apprenticeship is important for employment and the economy. Still based on the colonial model, it needs state's support to function better. In the southern oil-rich part of Nigeria the struggle for resources between the state and the militants has contributed to the general lack of security. As Jana Bayerlová vividly describes in her chapter, even 'private' activity such as dating of young people is both influenced by generational social control and the overall tense political atmosphere in the Oil States of Nigeria.

Conclusion

The book, which truly begins after this introduction, is evidence about multifaceted issues facing current sub-Saharan Africa. As I have tried to show by brief characterizations of individual chapters, the underlying theme of it is the centrality of the state. The authors show that the post-colonial state in Africa is far from withering, but at the same time it is often not capable of successfully tackling many of those problems, which in African conditions no one other than the state can resolve. Thus a host of social, economic, legal and other problems remains unresolved. To find the right balance, which would enable the state to do what Africans in each country and together expect from it, i.e., responsible and transparent governance, will take some more time and effort.

The aim of the authors has been to contribute with this book to a better understanding of current issues in Africa as seen by professional Africanists. The fact that in Africa the urgent need for development is contrasted by persisting poverty constitutes a major challenge for Africanist research. The specific role of the state agencies and political parties in Africa, especially in one-party regimes with radical programmes of reconstruction and development, supported by revolutionary ideology, can be profitably studied by Africanists from formerly communist ruled countries. As shown in this introduction, this volume's case studies and broader topics are dealt with against the general background, namely the decisive power of the state. It is hoped that the present volume will enhance our knowledge of the issues that are considered salient in current Africanist research. The authors hope that the book will find its critical readers both in Africa and elsewhere. Figuratively speaking, we believe that the dialogue between researchers and interested public is the salt, which decides the taste of the pudding.

WHY THE STATE MATTERS IN AFRICA:
REFLECTIONS ON DEMOCRACY, DEVELOPMENT AND AID

Patrick Chabal
King's College London

Recent thinking on development in Africa has been marked by the widespread recognition that the African crisis was political rather than economic. Or, to put it another way, that the lack of development was primarily due to political, rather than economic, factors. The emphasis has been on good governance and democracy. This was a huge shift since it had always been assumed in development circles that what was missing were the financial and technical means to enable Africa to reach the critical 'lift-off' stage of economic growth. For years the focus had been on the delivery of aid to support the investment that would encourage development and the emphasis had been placed on structural adjustment programmes (SAPs).

At its heart the decision to introduce SAPs derived from a double observation about the relationship between politics and economics in Africa. The first was that, despite the promises of the early years of independence, there had been no substantial development in post-colonial Africa. The second was that the rapid move to one-party states during that period had led to the excessive dominance of a state that had become both plethoric and ineffective. Since the state in Africa had taken charge of the economy, often by means of nationalisation and the creation of parastatals, the conclusion was drawn that there was a logical connection between these two factors. It was the state, and statism more generally, that was responsible for the absence of development.

Structural adjustment thus had simple aims which, under the guise of financial and monetary targets, had serious political implications. Above and beyond the measures for better financial and budgetary management, which made good economic sense, the intention was to reduce the scope of the state. This was to be achieved in two ways. One was to impose a vision of the economy that relied on the 'free market'. The assumption was that an economy less controlled by the state would more readily respond to market pressures and incentives. This would encourage the development of a business mentality that would lead to the form of capitalist competition, which fosters economic growth. The other was to force drastic reductions in the number of state employees and in state expenditures. The reasoning here was that the state was wasting vast amounts of resources, which were either corruptly diverted or were invested in state enterprises that were unprofitable. A leaner state would mean a better state.

The results of structural adjustment programmes were more complicated than many suppose but they were mixed. The push for more efficient and transparent budgetary and financial management was not in vain, even if it was rarely implemented as devised. However, this in itself did not respond to the needs of the countries concerned. By and large, it failed to spur the development of a strong private sector with which to drive development. It also resulted in catastrophic cutbacks in state expenditures and subsidies, which often led to increased poverty, reduced social services and the degradation of the infrastructure. Those countries deemed by the World Bank to be making progress on structural adjustment were rewarded with increased aid. But the bulk of Africa either failed to conform or prevaricated in the hope that half-measures would satisfy the donors.

There are many views on why structural adjustment did not have the desired effects, with clear divergences between the World Bank and African governments. The one is often the mirror of the other. I concentrate attention here on the consequences, for donors and for Africa, of the manifest failure of structural adjustment to bring about any notable development. African governments became adept at 'playing' the SAP card. To the World Bank they would argue they were doing their best but that the consequences of reduced state expenditure were dangerous. To their own constituencies they would explain that decline in standards of living were caused by the SAPs. For their part, the donors realised *both* that SAPs had nefarious costs, and so agreed to introduce social safety nets, *and* that they could not in conscience cut off aid to governments that failed or refused to implement the adjustment programmes. The result was a slow but significant dilution of the SAP agenda.

It is at that stage that the political aspects of economic development began to surface more clearly. The World Bank eventually recognised that it had been wrong in its analysis of the role of the state. If in principle it seemed a good idea to cut public wastefulness, in practice it turned out that SAPs weakened the state dangerously. In view of the terrible consequences of state failure, as witnessed in countries such as Liberia, Sierra Leone, Zaire, and Somalia, the donors began to fear further reduction of state power in other countries. The World Bank now put forward a plan that returned the state – albeit an enabling rather than controlling state – at the centre of development. The idea here was the classical notion that the state must provide the means – legal, infrastructural and financial – to make possible the unhindered operation of the market. Development would be market-led but it required a relatively organised and effective state.

At the same time, there began the process of 'democratic' reforms, which was to sweep Africa in the last decade of the twentieth century. Partly because of the failure of structural adjustment, partly for ideological reasons and partly because of the worsening socio-political situation in Africa, the West now deemed that 'democracy' would set the continent on the right path. This new set of political 'conditionalities', which came eventually to be enshrined in NEPAD, had two main aspects: one having to do with elections, the other with the role of civil society. But what do we mean when we speak of democracy and civil society?

Although these concepts are rarely discussed explicitly in the literature, which itself is a problem, there is an implicit consensus in Africanist writing. *Democracy* is essentially conceived in procedural terms: a constitutionally sanctioned system of multiparty elections in which there is freedom of political participation and competition; where elections are (reasonably) free and fair; where presidential and government changes are directly the result of the elections; and where these transitions take place peacefully and in an orderly fashion. *Civil society* is most often defined as those societal organisations that are not competing directly for political office and whose aims are charitable, developmental or advocatory. Accordingly, a vigorous civil society is one in which civil society organisations (or CSOs) are seen to be free to form, act and operate without fear of intimidation or violence.

The new political agenda sealed a remarkable move from a primarily 'economic' vision of development to an acceptance that politics was at the core of the process whereby countries achieve economic growth. The assumption now was that democracy was a pre-requisite to development. For this reason, aid became predicated on the holding of multiparty elections and the involvement of civil society in setting policy objectives. There was a shift from Structural Adjustment Programmes (SAPs) to Poverty Reduction Strategy Papers (PRSPs). This meant that the focus was now on the political and institutional framework whereby African governments would seek to put in place policies to facilitate development, reduce poverty and strengthen the mechanisms of the market. This new programmatic injunction was enshrined in the Millennium Development Goals (MDGs), NEPAD and the 2005 G8 Gleneagles Meeting that promised financial assistance.

So this is where we are today. The assumption now is that if we identify and work to solve institutional problems, we shall be in a better position to implement these objectives. But can more insistent calls for good governance result in more development-oriented policies? Is the question primarily that of the refinement of good governance or are there other political issues that affect the way in which politics in Africa impinges on development-oriented policies? Before I address these questions more systematically, let me step back and ask what good governance actually is. In its most basic definition, which is the one commonly used by international organisations, good governance includes accountability, transparency and formal institutional rule.

These are certainly key features but I would add what I think to be the key ingredient – that is an *effective* state, by which I mean states that manage actually to implement the policies they devise. On this issue, there has long been debate about whether the role of the state is that of 'enabler' or 'manager'. Whatever the case, there is little doubt that there are some minimal features of the state that are necessary for the running of a society in which economic activities can take place that are likely to contribute to development. These are to be found across the globe, in Europe, Asia and South America – even and this is important, in countries where political systems differ widely, from democratic to authoritarian.

Of these, the most important would include the following:
- The state must guarantee a minimal degree of order and peace, other than strictly by repressive measures *and* uphold the rule of law, which requires a functioning legal framework and a working judiciary.

11

- It should maintain a basic administrative organisation capable, at the very least, of underpinning the regulatory and enabling mechanisms that make it possible for economic activity to develop over time.
- It needs, either directly or indirectly, to ensure that there is in the country sufficient, and sufficiently operational, infrastructure – of which the most important components are: communication, transport, electricity and fuel.
- It ought to provide, or make possible, the provision of basic health, social and education and, if possible, the expansion of appropriate higher, and particularly technical, training – now recognised, at least in the experience of Asian countries, as being crucial to economic growth.
- Finally, the state needs to ensure that there is in the country a financial and banking infrastructure, able to make and implement business decisions other than for political reasons.

It will be immediately apparent that these features are in the main the hallmark of the modern bureaucratic state – many of which did characterise the colonial state – *and* that these are the very features that have been seriously eroded in Africa today. What is less obvious, but perhaps equally important, is that these characteristics do no not depend on political ideology. They are to be found, admittedly in unequal measure, in countries such as Sweden, Switzerland, Singapore and South Korea – countries ranging from social democracy to authoritarian presidential systems. They constitute what I would call 'good' (meaning here *effective* rather than morally palatable) government.

Because of this, it would seem possible to draw a few lessons from the experience of those countries that have achieved the highest rates of economic development in recent decades: the so-called Asian Tigers. These lessons are relevant to the discussion of what is called 'good governance'.

One is that an efficient government is fundamental to economic growth. Another is that state directed investment is critical. A third is that successful access to the world market is important in several aspects: achieving comparative advantage in trade and sharpening the economy's competitiveness. A fourth is that economic growth depends heavily on investment in human capital. The last is that culture is important – although not always in obvious ways: for instance, over the years, Confucianism has been identified as a pro- and anti- development 'belief system'. The same argument rages about African culture.

Therefore, the question is why the state politics of Africa have not been conducive to development? There are many reasons but I believe politics is the key and I thus want to focus here on the way in which power has been exercised since independence.

The African political order is best conceived as one in which the formal and the informal overlap. Hence, rulers are 'patrimonial' – meaning simply that they are primarily accountable to their followers and that their legitimacy derives from their ability to deliver resources to them. Consequently, politicians and bureaucrats are expected to behave in office as representatives – meaning in effect, patrons – of their clients. Therefore, there can be no meaningful distinction between the public and private spheres. As is immediately apparent, the logic of such a system is entirely at variance with that of the impersonal public Western bureaucratic state, which is supposed to preside over the destiny of *all* citizens and work for the improvement of the general well-being of the country *as a whole*.

A functioning neo-patrimonial state, such as was to be found in a number of African countries in the sixties and seventies – of which the paradigmatic examples were probably Houphouët-Boigny's Côte d'Ivoire and Kenyatta's Kenya – managed to blend the logics and integrate the workings of the formal and informal spheres successfully. What this meant in practice was that the ruler and his officials ensured the bureaucracy operated as efficiently as was compatible with the demands of the informal political order.

Government, firmly controlled by the presidential single party, would seek to balance the clientelistic demands of the widest possible constituency – with a marked preference, nevertheless, for the incumbent's own – *and* the rigours of state responsibility. Thus, the state would endeavour to maintain a minimal working infrastructure and sustain reasonable health, education as well as a modicum of social provisions. The one-party configuration of power required of the ruler that he seek to placate a wide range of ethnic, regional, religious and economic interests. The most successful politicians used the relatively efficient operation of the bureaucratic (formal) state to deliver wisely to the largest possible numbers the resources afforded by presidential control.

It is important to understand that the success of the neo-patrimonial state was measured *domestically*, by both rulers and ruled, in terms of how well it performed according to the criteria relevant to the workings of the informal political sphere. *Outside* Africa, however, achievement was gauged in terms of how the state performed according to the criteria applied to its modern Western bureaucratic equivalent. Whilst African politicians attempted to placate both domestic and foreign (particularly donor) constituencies, their ability to do so rested on their being able to fulfil utterly divergent demands.

To secure their legitimacy as rulers they used the revenues garnered by the state to deliver benefits to their clients. To obtain the resources they needed, they had to meet the donor's criteria of 'good' governance – broadly defined as the capacity to operate a state along Western management, bureaucratic and financial lines. So long as such criteria could be met, donors usually turned a blind eye to the informal practices taking place – especially since within the Cold War context, Western countries often sought African states as ideological allies, or clients.

But the demands of formal and informal governance were ultimately incompatible and neo-patrimonial governments reached their limits once state resources began to decline. Unable to put in place policies that would foster economic growth and favour long-term productive investment, African politicians were locked into an ever more frantic search for revenues. This meant that African governments became increasingly

13

dependent on donors, whose programmes varied according to the vagaries of Western domestic politics and changes in international relations. Once the Cold War was over, the scope for foreign aid diminished drastically and the ability of the West to impose stricter control on meeting the goals for which aid was given grew. Since by then foreign debt was out of control (in part because borrowing was so easy in the late seventies and early eighties), aid became more difficult to get.

Diminishing resources spelled the end of the functioning neo-patrimonial state, which made it impossible for politicians to continue successfully to balance the demands of formal and informal politics. While officially, African states continued to behave according to the norms of the former, in effect the informal came to predominate. This had serious consequences. State capacity was reduced, corruption increased, and competition between politicians for power grew more acute. Politics became an increasingly violent zero-sum-game in which the aim of those in power was to exploit the resources of the state before rivals did. In this context, the move to multi-party politics and the privatisation of state (or parastatal) enterprises contributed further to the frenzied use of the formal sphere for informal purposes.

Although there is today in Africa some considerable difference between the better (Botswana) and worse (DRC) states, there is generally an overall process of decay. All countries suffer from the same problems, to a greater or lesser extent, when it comes to the overall decline in resources and the inability to induce higher rates of economic growth. The recent 'success' stories – chiefly Ghana, Uganda, Mozambique – are countries that had all but collapsed and where progress today, though rapid, has not yet made up for the consequence of previous breakdown. Undoubtedly, some countries like Mali and Benin have also made headway, but again only relative to very dire antecedents. Overall, however, there is no gainsaying the trend of a decline in state efficiency, or 'good' governance. So why are we where we are? And can this be reversed?

Some analysts stress external factors, arguing that the structure of African economies and their place in world trade made them vulnerable to the vagaries of the market and impeded the long-term growth required for development. Others point to the structural weakness and political instability of African polities. The latest thinking identifies the failure of the state as the primary reason for the current situation. Whatever one may think for the reasons of state decay, there is ground for thinking that such decay may be even more serious than at first imagined and that reversing the trend will be more difficult than we think. This is for two main reasons.

The first is that state decline does not have gradually negative effects: below a certain *threshold* the efficiency of the state falls off rapidly, until it ceases to have much governance capacity, other than strictly clientelistic. The second is that such decline is more than mere administrative corrosion. It means the domination of the informal over the formal, thus contributing to the ever more rapid destruction of the modern bureaucracy so painstakingly established at independence.

There is frequently an assumption in aid circles that (de- or re-) institutionalisation is merely a technical, or administrative, question. It is clear, in fact, that such would only be the case in a situation where there is still relatively effective governance. Here, one can conceive of forms of practical assistance that would help to improve bureaucratic efficacy. Where, however, state decline has gone through a *threshold* of minimal 'efficiency', there may no longer be scope for repairing the damage by 'technical' means. Whatever its formal appearance, the state is then liable to cease existing as bureaucratic organisation, insofar as it is no longer able to discharge those responsibilities identified above as critical to development.

Below a given threshold, therefore, it is not just a question of the state working less well; it is a question of the state not working at all. The state no longer serves any substantive administrative, technical or regulatory purpose. The functions it used to fulfil either come to an end or they become the arbitrary preserve of individuals and groups.

The danger is when the informal fully invests, or takes over, the formal structures of the state. What this means in concrete terms is that politicians and functionaries increasingly neglect their formal duties in order to exploit the state for their own particularistic, clientelistic, ends. In effect, this entails the plundering of public resources for patrimonial purposes. When this happens, there is a rapidly accelerating and self-reinforcing spiral of state decay, which results in the increasing inability of governments to function. In extreme cases, bureaucrats begin to 'privatise' the business of dispensing public services, charging 'fees' for performing their duties.

Politicians, for their part, seek above all to appropriate transfers from outside, which become in this way a rent on their holding office. In this enterprise, of course, they must do battle both with their domestic competitors and with foreign donors, who insist on attaching conditions to the disbursement of aid. But here, those who control the state have an immense advantage over all others: they clutch the symbols of sovereignty. Since on the whole foreign donors and businesses must continue to conduct their affairs with the official representatives of the state – in part because of their own domestic (legal and political) constraints – they have no choice but to go through local political leaders.

So, how will it be possible to improve the quality of governance so as to give development a chance? Are African countries locked into a vicious circle of 'bad' governance that casts a curse on their peoples? Certainly not, but the way forward may not be what is presently being envisaged either in donor circles or even within NEPAD. To begin at the beginning, the search for an effective approach will demand a new *conceptualisation* of the relations between the politics and economics of accountability. And that will require an acknowledgement of the role of the informal, or the so-called 'traditional', which so far is missing in all the blueprints agreed between donors and recipients.

The first step, it seems to me, would be overtly to recognise the ways in which the formal and informal influence the work of government, instead of pretending there is no such thing as the informal. To do so would be to bring into the open the so-called 'traditional' factors that affect accountability between politicians and those who are or who are not their clients. It would also force politicians to make explicit the criteria that guide their actions and the pressures they experience because of such 'traditional' forms of accountability. This is an area that I develop at great length in my new book, *Africa: the politics of suffering and smiling.*

The second would be to invert the current way of formulating and implementing the good governance agenda. Today, the agenda is conceived and conveyed by Western donors and institutions. It consists of a programme of governance that seeks to replicate the key tenets of political accountability and transparency in the West. What should happen is the reverse. African politicians should be asked to explain how the realities of representation, legitimacy, accountability and responsibility in their own countries can be reshaped to serve a more vigorous developmental agenda. In other words, policy makers should be looking to conceptualise and operationalise the so-called informal and 'traditional' constraints of the exercise of power – with a view to strengthening the state's ability to govern for all. This will not happen if it is not attempted.

The third, therefore, would be for African governments to construct their own blueprints rather than work merely to show how they accept and will implement the donors'. The experience of East Asia shows clearly that their governments went about defining for themselves the parameters of accountability, transparency and efficiency they deemed essential to their developmental plans. These may or may not have accorded with those advocated by the West. In particular, it is clear that many regimes continued, and some still continue, to be corrupt and authoritarian. However, this was offset by the fact that they achieved levels of economic growth, which eventually made possible a type of development beneficial to the majority. Corruption, as it were, was channelled into national developmental purposes.

The fourth step, therefore, would be for African governments to devise, and publicise, the ways in which their commitment to accountability can, very concretely, contribute to the improvements of the lives of the population. Today's practice of committing to the governance agenda of donors at a formal level while continuing to practice politics according to informal demands and constraints is doomed to failure. The cynical view is that it does not matter because official acceptance of the West's conditions secures aid transfers. This is true but, ultimately, it is a self-defeating policy, which only serves to maintain Africa in fragile state of un-development. Lack of development feeds political violence because of a perennial lack of resources for clientelism. Political violence destroys the state.

For this reason, it seems to me that accountability is the key to making progress in governance. African politicians need to be convinced by their own peoples that a continuation of neo-patrimonialism will in the end rebound on all, rulers and ruled alike. In the Washington consensus parlance, this accountability is translated into a system of multiparty elections. But it is clear that multiparty elections have not brought about the type of accountability that would favour a developmental agenda. More often than not, it serves as an exercise in legitimising governments that have already failed in this respect.

In the process, democracy is further devalued since it is obvious to ordinary Africans that it has not either changed governance or brought about development. This in turn gives more credibility to the informal modes of accountability, which alone provides the means to survive. And so on.

The mechanisms for accountability and transparency advocated by the West are but instruments to an end. It is the end that matters and if the instruments are found wanting, they must be changed. Although I would not want here necessarily to advocate the type of accountability that is found in Somaliland, I would like to point out that it is home-grown, indigenous as it were, and that it works. It has brought about an end to violence, the reconstruction of a basic infrastructure, the organisation of a functioning administration and the establishment of a system of political representation that appears to be congruent with the realities of formal and informal politics. It is therefore a great paradox that the international community refuses to recognise either the country or the regime. The contrast with what is happening in Somalia is brutal, if not gross.

This example suggests to me that the way to better governance and more development can ultimately *only* be found in the *actual* commitment of politicians, civil servants, NGOs and policy makers to use the local notions of legitimacy, representation, accountability and transparency for development rather than clientelism. Outside pressure to abide by the Washington consensus or to make NEPAD a carbon copy of 'best practice' will make no dent on the problem until those who exercise power in Africa, and those who advise them, face up to the task of translating such an agenda into policies that can overcome neo-patrimonialism.

It would be a tragedy if this required greater catastrophe on the continent before politicians delivered such policies. The example of Somalia does not suggest that violence on its own can lead to the emergence of locally progressive policies. But it is well to notice the recent spate of books arguing that aid is counter-productive in respect of development and that nothing will change until aid reduction, or even the end of aid, begins to focus the minds of those politicians who presently run their countries. It is a tough challenge but there is no choice. Only those who benefit from disorder and aid would wish to continue on the same fruitless path.

.

AFTER THE CRISIS:
REDEFINING AFRICA'S PLACE IN WORLD AFFAIRS

Vladimir Arseniev
Museum of Anthropology and Ethnology of the Russian Academy of Sciences, Saint Petersburg

In theory, post-colonial independence has placed the fate of the peoples of Africa in their own hands. By the term 'people', I mean the population, the inhabitants of the continent in their various groups, distributed across the territories in distinct societies. This reality is currently organized in the form of states, whose contemporary form has its origins in the colonial period. And this separation into etatic, territorial and human spaces is a product of nothing more than artificial frontiers whose formation corresponded to the interests of colonial administrations and the balance of power between the dominant European states.

It is not only possible to surmise that colonialism itself, a phase in the history of industrial society which we are accustomed to treat as the foundation of the current state of affairs in Africa, was not a spontaneously occurring phenomenon of the end of the 19th century, but was conceived of as a project. It was a romantic, missionary, prophetic project in the beginning, a project inspired by Enlightenment mentality, bringing peace, knowledge, civilization, and finally, well-being into the non-European world, which was considered 'backward' and 'retrograde'. Although this was a myth, it was at first believed, in order to create, promote, put it into action, and, ultimately, to exploit it for ends which became more and more pragmatic.

In any case, the inhabitants of Africa were forced by the European powers on the continent to follow the logic and the evolutionary process of Europe during the colonial period, and also after the end of direct foreign rule. Even the socialist alternative of the USSR and its allies continued to encourage the same principles of evolution and of development along industrial lines.

This is a timely moment to re-evaluate our own certainties, our cultural system and world-view, that is, European and Eurocentric ideas on social evolution. These ideas only envisage a single unidirectional, evolutionary progression of society. Such beliefs are inevitably conditioned by the idea of progress which encourages an accelerated, even forced updating of our material environment, of production, of knowledge. It rules out the ideas of return, of countdown, rest, about turns, circular movement. All this makes perfect sense if one merely sees physical time as a linear vector, a view which is evident and unchallengeable in European culture, but not by any means as clear in the cultures of the Orient, and, equally in African world-views. But this transfer of core values continues and ultimately has an impact on all the questions which touch on modernization in the shorter, and especially, the longer term.

From the beginning of the colonialist project, one of its primary aims was the creation of a market founded on limited local production, fostered by an adaptation of European models, the setting up of the interaction of money and goods, produced locally and imported from Europe. But this idea contradicted the natural system, which had been based on limited production and consumption, weak monetary exchange, a tendency towards thesauration (turning all money mass into treasures), of all units of exchange which might appear, by deliberate introduction into the system, or by spontaneous appearance, adapted to their environment by the force of events and circumstances. There are principles fundamental to the traditional way of life which cannot be shifted without their destruction, without sapping to the very roots all the natural order of things inherited from generations of ancestors, and thus became sanctified, guaranteeing the survival of the population. Were the actors of the colonialist project aware of this at the inception?

Of course not! African studies were not even in its infancy at that time. There was in effect no experience of studying and understanding Africa. Prejudices and illusions existed about 'cultural differences' concerning that what was not European. But more importantly, through the European experience of social and industrial revolution, with the faith brought by the Enlightenment in the mentality of Europe, and in the human spirit and intelligence, there was a sincere conviction that everything could be changed if the will existed and if the means and energy were available. So much so for the 19th century, and even for the 20th century. But will the 21st century be the same?

These convictions were mere illusions. Neither the colonial period, nor fifty years of independence have managed to produce a stable economy or social structure which was organic and self-replicating and thus capable of replacing the old order of the traditional system. This is difficult to admit, but must be acknowledged rather than avoided. It is better to speak this truth to ourselves and to the people of Africa, in order to understand what to do about it.

We must stop looking for scapegoats, accusing the colonisers, praising the heroes of the resistance whilst feeding the myth of a probable paradise on earth in Africa, which would have existed if colonialism had never happened. What has been has been! Even the President of France has publicly acknowledged the wrongs of colonialism. But nothing has moved on in Africa since the Dakar speech of 2007, except for the ever wilder criticisms of Nicolas Sarkozy, of the colonial period in its entirety, and of the neo-colonialist politics that came after. And nobody suggests anything new, except for pro-independence slogans.

However, a very important fact has made itself noticed since independence, since it became clear that in general nothing had fundamentally changed in the African countries since the colonial period and that the era of liberty and sovereignty was only valid in the conditions of global strategic confrontation between 'East' and 'West'. Geopolitics and geostrategy aside, one may observe more success from the neo-colonial project than the pro-independence project. And this latter, on the grand historic and especially on the economic scale, has only served to camouflage the absorption of African spaces and peoples into the global economy – integration, but only in a servile and auxiliary role.

In my opinion, in spite of the limitations and advantages of political correctness, the Africanist community has a vocation, and should before all else use its expertise, and thus only speak of realities, not of myths, be they pleasant or bitter. And in the same vein we should be talking about the state as a general and even universal phenomenon as well as in the current context in Africa, because in this challenging situation of recent developments on global level and within the African continent, the state as a social institution remains a major actor in the regulation of those processes which people have to live through and confront.

At this point, to counter any false accusations which might be made of a lack of respect for the sovereign states of Africa, I must reiterate that this paper is academic and scientific, and not political. I am well aware of the importance of the modern state in Africa, of the great responsibility incumbent on it and of the expectations placed upon it by its population. It is in this very context that I find that the policy of decentralization of the state in Africa - imposed on the African countries as a condition of the cooperation and assistance of the countries of the 'rich North', moving in accordance with the liberal stratagem of the 1990s, and with the developments the world is undergoing in the 21st century – this very policy is becoming malign and destructive to entire societies and populations. In conditions of instability and its concomitant uncertainty, in the context where the market and the international political situation are going off the rails, this decentralizing of the state, of the system of direction, guidance and protection of the nation makes society open and vulnerable to exterior influences and to breakdown from within.

This is also an invaluable moment to highlight a fact which is often passed over in silence but is no less objectively true or well-known for all that. This is not only a question of the weakness of the state in Africa. Strictly speaking, the state in Africa is not a fully accomplished reality. It is rather an appliance, a superstructure imposed on the population, but it does not reproduce itself using the systems of production, of social organization, of customs and traditions of the population. In a sense, the state in Africa is a political class, a small and self-interested minority, monopolizing all power except, perhaps, economic power. True, this pseudo-class seeks fusion with and incarnation as small-scale entrepreneurs and bankers, in short, as the evolving petit bourgeoisie. But as long as the state exists, it has public obligations. And when it is strong, the state enjoys more possibilities of fulfilling its public duty in adverse conditions.

The progress of events has been more or less obvious and inexorable, from the end of the 1980s until the present day. For some twenty years, against a background of weakening and demise of the Soviet bloc, the loss of all alternatives to neo-colonialist politics, the steady disappearance of anti-capitalist ideologies, expressed in actions or in words, Africa fell into the hands of the 'rich countries' and became a mere arena for the race for mineral resources, for merchandise, for containers to store toxic waste. If it were not for the 're-conquest of the cities by the former colonists', or the immigration into Europe of hundreds of thousands of citizens of the former colonies which had been favoured at the beginning of their independence, but later demonized, the 'rich North' would never have taken any interest in Africa. The 'street revolution' of 2005-6 provoked some thought, more on the part of Europe's governments than her citizens. The Elysée palace in particular began to speak of a 'new partnership between France and Africa' and during the Lisbon summit of December 2007 the EU put forward this idea in another form, as 'an associate relationship between Europe and Africa'.

This idea met with little response when it was launched and it advanced, for better or worse, with the speed of a tortoise. What was striking in this situation was that clearly change was wanted on both sides, but nobody knew quite what or how. I had the opportunity of observing this phenomenon in February 2009 in Paris during a round-table discussion on French politics in Africa. Nevertheless, one might say that in comparison with four or five years ago, things are beginning to move!

However, let me pass to the main subject of this paper; what I have said above can be considered a preamble, a preliminary outline.

In late October-early November 2008, the global economy was declared to be in crisis. It is not possible to discuss the nature and causes of this crisis here. But as on the night of 11–12 September 2001, the world's best analysts began once again to speak of a turning-point in civilization, of inevitable and radical changes in development levels, of revolutions in values and priorities. Eventually economists and politicians began to speak of the decline of capitalism and the monetarist model of market regulation, of the nationalization of the principal branches of the economy, of banks, etc. In any case, all that had been predicted from Marx onwards and rejected with the fall of communism suddenly came back into play, to be taken into account and factored into plans of action once again. Several months on, a certain relaxation of emotions and attitudes can be observed. However, the ground is henceforth staked out!

In this context, we should note a significant, or rather, symbolic event. This is the death of Samuel Huntington, father of the concept of the 'clash of civilisations', a vision of the future of the process of universal globalization based on Judaeo-Christian culture. Whatever the outcome of this prediction, it is clear that tectonic movements in the depths of the modern world are at work before our eyes, and that in this context the destiny of Africa is more difficult to comprehend. At the moment, the new configuration of international relations has passed out of the hands of intellectuals, researchers and ideologues; now it got into the lists of measures to be taken and problems to be solved by statesmen, politicians, administrators. Science has come to the end of its allotted time.

And, it has to be admitted, without any great success! This is yet another manifestation of the post-modern state of civilization. There are no Great Ideas, no Grand Projects, such as socialism, which was at its height as a concept at the end of the 19th century and the beginning of the 20th, before it was ever put into action.

Earlier in this essay, I sought to demonstrate that Africa found herself isolated from the world's great economic and political currents. Contrary to Huntington's assertion, Africa had few opportunities to create a special geopolitical and economic space for herself in the new world order, if ever that were to come about. It is pretty much obvious that the landscape of power politics is going in the direction of multipolarity. But the cultural unity of the new spaces seems to have a rather uncertain basis in religious unity, or a traditional dominance of what may be called 'local cultures'.

There are grand geopolitical projects such as IBS or G3 (India-Brazil-South Africa) or BRIC (Brazil-Russia-India-China). Nor should the G20 project, put forward by France when the global crisis had already broken out, be neglected. In terms of revival, there is also the "FranceAfrique" project, with its new agenda taking into account the interests of the concerned parties. Similar projects could be put forwards for the UK and Africa, America-Africa, China-Africa, Russia-Africa, etc. Nevertheless, we should not rule out the development and expansion of Islamism, which has already become a substitute for secular initiatives for a large part of the population of the savannah and West Coast of the continent. But the importance of consolidation of the large geographical areas, as well as of large populations, cannot in my opinion be overstated. Explanations based on bare geopolitical principles are not sufficient any more. Considering the recent initiatives undertaken by Europe, it appears that the Europeans do not want to let processes involving Africa take their natural course, or a course controlled by other sources of influence already in place (for example, the growing influence of Islamic states, China, etc.).

It is quite reasonable to suppose that the interplay of these various sources of influence, whether their effects in Africa are still latent or already obvious, is more or less constant over time. One might reasonably compare this situation, or this probable arrangement, to a layer cake or club sandwich. Each layer represents only one unit among others – Africa in general, or a particular African state. This state, without excluding other entities – organisations, other large elements, might form a part of the unit alongside other entities. This rather cramped situation could last a long time, until the arrival of a new balance of power and centres of influence on the global scale. Of course, these centres of influence may be in mutual competition, especially as far as Africa is concerned. – a situation already seen during the East-West confrontation (in particular, during the Cold War).

During that period, despite everything, Africa constituted a sort of ideological, geopolitical and (un)economic playing card for the two opposing blocs. Since then the economic aspect and especially the race for mineral resources became the focus of the 'dance' of great and small powers alike, especially of the multinationals. We seem during the present crisis to be witnessing a return to the importance and values of the state, at least in the 'rich North'. And if beforehand, during the period 1980-2000, the state withdrew from a dominant role in the economy, now during the crisis, and doubtless for some time to come, we will see the rebirth of the state. Could this also be true for Africa? We shall see…

We are brought back to the explanation of this phenomenon of the return of the state by an idea which seems highly probable in the current global context, as well as in the broad view which seeks to interpret tendencies which show themselves in everyday life. That is, if the world in general is realigning itself, if henceforth we will no longer have either the former bipolar system, nor the sole dominance of the United States or another great power, known or not. If other centres of influence are to show themselves in the near future, it is quite clear that Africa will have little chance of staying intact. Europe, which declares itself to be a new power, a new source of influence in world politics, advocates partnership and even association with Africa. Yet at this moment we should also be aware who are the greatest advocates of these projects, namely France and Portugal. And we may also note the strange absence of the United Kingdom in this initiative. There were even rumours about offers made to France by her partners in the EU to be a mediator in relations between Europe and Africa.

Before coming to the end of these brief and preliminary reflections, I must mention a possibility which is entirely theoretical but which nevertheless must be foreseen in order to be avoided. This is the improbable (put not impossible) sidelining of Africa from the mainstream of world affairs, of its elimination, by external forces, or even by voluntary or involuntary internal forces from global relationships. Under current circumstances it is not possible in real terms, but how far will the crisis take us? To the limits! Given that the state in Africa is most often only a mechanism, or a 'political class', and that it works to connect the country, its population and the whole world, the international community would do well to safeguard its functions and its links with the outside world. But what if the outside world, within the foreseeable circumstances does not think of these interests? If the problem of African immigration into Europe were only to be resolved by a rupture with Africa, the future of the African state would be utterly uncertain. In this fictional situation, we might anticipate long-lived and bloody linkages between the elites in power, their groups and supporters in power and near the centres of power, fighting over the spoils acquired and accumulated through the system of 'world civilisation'. This could last through the lifetimes of two or three generations with the deterioration, or even the destruction of all which reflects, or belongs to civilisation, with not only the loss of wealth and knowledge but even of large numbers of the population. But in the end, everything comes back to natural systems of production and the slow re-establishment of stability and the return to ancestral systems; the state as mode of organisation, a machine saturated by its constituent workers, would probably disappear. Let us remember, however, that this dismal picture is only an unpleasant imagining, though what has happened in Sierra Leone, Liberia, and elsewhere, has sometimes come near it. I do not think that social relations would break down on a global scale. However, we must not rule anything out!

In my opinion, it is much more relevant to hypothesise another series of events, which will largely depend on the foresight and willingness of the leaders in power in politics, the economic sector, and the media. Here I will return to the key ideas expressed above. That is to say, that the future world will be multi-polar, but its spatial organisation will not follow the lines of Huntington, who saw it in terms of the great pre-twentieth century civilisations. Rather I would envision a sort of renaissance of the colonial empires, but with different foundations from those of their formation at the end of the 19th century.

As long as the contemporary world remains unprepared for a conscientious and thorough rethinking of its way of life, as long as even the possibility of change remains unwished for by humanity in general, it would be rash to move towards the total destruction of the patterns which already exist. In this respect, we should not forget the miserable experience of ill-prepared reform undergone by the USSR and its doubtful consequences for the balance of international relations. Thus, if the multi-polar world is essential for a peaceful future for humanity and is already on its way, we must formulate a system which is accessible and better adapted to the expectations of the current population. We need a model which enables us to avoid those confrontations which are inevitable when radical and brutal changes arise, changes which affect fundamental practices of human life. Nor must we forget that 'civilisation' (here I mean the industrial civilization) is far from being exhausted, let alone dead. It has the reserves for survival, and it will defend itself.

For example, we might say that in the large areas of Africa where so-called European 'post-industrial' culture (in the sense of 'civilisation') coexists with 'Islamic' culture, the search for a single identity would lead to civil wars and large-scale massacres. It would also bring about a reconfiguration of frontiers and states. These things must be avoided, nipped in the bud. Our great Civilisation, 'post-industrial' culture, strives for survival. And in real life, it will survive, because at the moment, all alternatives are ephemeral.

Without forgetting my earlier remark that until now, the neo-colonialist project has proven that it is the only real and successful one in Africa since decolonization, nevertheless this should be adapted to a state more balanced and more in line with the interests of Africans – this means with the entire population, not merely the elites. The population in general is alienated from the state, but remains used to it, and no doubt would like to align itself more closely with a state which represented civil society and guaranteed it not only survival but a positive role within the framework of the state.

At the moment, the former colonial empires are linguistic and cultural spaces (Anglophone, Francophone, Lusophone), which continue to follow a trend dictated by older principles aimed at incorporating Africans into the life of the metropolitan milieu. These spaces continue to exist in economic and particularly in financial terms. At the same time, these spaces are, in legal terms, more or less homogeneous. With the former metropolitan groupings, the old colonies formed quite discrete and reasonably stable entities. To make them viable again, much effort and mutual will is needed.

In these new conditions of global crisis, the consolidation of these spaces on the basis of equality and mutual interest within a privileged partnership would be highly advantageous, both for the older urbanised centres of the EU, and for Europe as a whole, which delegates initiative and responsibility for this cooperation back to the older centres. But those who stand to gain most must be the countries and peoples of Africa, who, after sixty years of independence and amid universal questioning of the processes of globalization across the board, continue to lose out.

THE ORIGIN OF POLITICAL PARTIES IN AFRICA:
THEORETICAL AND METHODOLOGICAL RESEARCH PROBLEMS [2]

Vlastimil Fiala
University of Hradec Králové

Introduction

Modern general theory of political parties in the past decades was primarily based on the experience provided by the foundation, development and activities of European and American political parties. Most contemporary general theses on political parties and systems are thus based only on detailed knowledge of the parties in the so-called Euro-American society, while the situation in other continents, Africa, Asia and practically all of Latin America, only appear occasionally in general treatises of political parties and party systems.[3] Many of the foremost political scientists openly admit this shortcoming and when they deal with some theoretical issues linked to political parties they openly resign at any attempt at an analysis of political parties in the underdeveloped world.[4]

Their arguments are mainly based on the prevailing undemocratic character of these political systems, the practical non-existence of any clear social stratification in these societies,[5] when most of these countries have not yet passed through the stage of an industrial revolution. Moreover, the now classical lines of conflict cannot be easily applied to underdeveloped countries,[6] because these lines refer to the generally known types of European political parties. Another frequent argument is that of the unstable political situation with the dominant position of the military, which often interferes with the domestic political issues and thus prevents a continual development of political parties and party systems. Occasionally it is argued that societies (civilizations) based on different cultural values and religions cannot be compared.

And yet, as Huntington points out in his book *The Clash of Civilizations* (Huntington 2001), the world political system does not consist only of European countries and the USA. There are scores of states on other continents, which strive to achieve an equivalent

---

[2] This chapter is a result of the research supported by the Grant Agency of Czech Republic, grant No.407/09/0387, project "Political Parties in Africa, Latin. America, Asia and Oceania".

[3] From the last large theoretical works on political parties and party systems perhaps the only exception is the work of Alan Ware (Ware 1996). He too, however, depends on random cases from South Africa, Rhodesia, Zambia and Mexico. A special chapter deals with Japan, but that is outside the scope of underdeveloped countries. Latin America is a certain exception in the underdeveloped world, mainly because it is anchored in Euro-American civilization. See, e.g., Mainwaring and Scully 1995.

[4] In Czech political science see, e.g., Fiala and Strmiska 1998: 30–32.

[5] The dominant role in most underdeveloped countries is played by politically active peasants. Peasants in the countries of Africa represent 60–90%, in Asia 60–70% and in Latin America 20% of the population.

[6] The so-called cleavages, i.e., conflicts centre vs. periphery, church vs. state, urban vs. rural areas, and class conflicts. See Lipset and Rokkan 1967 or Rokkan 1970.

27

place in world politics and economy. Disregarding political processes in these regions and underrating their political structures and political culture is no longer feasible. Modern political scientists must abandon the prevailing Euro-American approach to the analysis of political development, political systems and institutions in those countries and should pay greater attention to the special features in their local historical, political, social and economic development.

In this connection we ask the fundamental question whether it is correct to apply to Asia, Africa and partly Latin America the current black-and-white Euro-American concepts of evaluation of political processes, according to which there are, in general, on the one side democratic political systems and the other side undemocratic political systems. The former are clearly defined by generally accepted criteria,[7] while when one of these conditions is not met (in particular in the sphere of human rights and limitations in activity or downright ban of political parties, no or irregular and not free elections) these systems are called undemocratic. In recent studies of democracy in Africa, the importance of the role of the institutionalisation of political parties and party systems has been increasingly emphasized.[8]

Still, Robert Dahl in his theory of polyarchy points out that there is no ideal democratic state in the world, although modern democratic countries are doing their best to come as near as possible to this ideal, which, however, at least in Dahl's opinion, can never be reached (Dahl 1971: 3–20). If Dahl's principle thesis is applied to Africa, the first question to be asked is where the present-day African states are heading and what they want to achieve. From the Euro-American aspect there is no simple answer: the only variant is the road to democracy. Nevertheless an examination of world history reveals that Euro-American democracy has evolved into a particular society and culture and has gone through a very long development, in most countries lasting several centuries, during which their inner conflicts (national, ethnic, social etc.) were solved and national unity was achieved.

As a matter of fact, the development of democracy in the countries which have not yet reached national unity, was made doubtful 35 years ago by Dankwart Rustow (Rustow 1970), who rejected the earlier attempts to list the required conditions for the functioning of a democracy and who clearly formulated the single criterion: the removal of all kinds of conflicts and the establishment of co-operation of the main political elites, i.e., the achievement of national unity. Meeting this condition can lead to the development of democracy, which Rustow believes has both internal dynamics and a distinct periodization.[9]

---

[7] For example see Dahl (1995) or Sartori (1993).

[8] See, e.g., Sandbrook 1996: 76, Olukoshi. 1998 or Randal and Svasand (2002: 30–52), and many more. In recent years fundamental monographs were written on the development of democracy in Africa, among them Bratton and Van de Walle 1997 or Gyimah-Boadi 2004.

[9] D. Rustow mentions three fundamental phases: preparatory phase, phase of decisions and adaptation phase. In Czech political science Rustow's periodization was discussed in detail by Jiří Kunc and Vladimíra Dvořáková (Dvořáková and Kunc 1994: 18–21).

It is true that in the last few decades the social processes tended to accelerate but the arguments about enforcing the introduction of democracy in Africa is premature.[10] Why shouldn't we ask whether the Euro-American world still continues its favourite colonial policy of spreading so-called civilization, and in good faith, in the name of human rights and liberties, tries to "enforce or speed up"[11] democratisation of those countries where democracy has so far been an unknown category, with no meaning for the substantial part of the population.

One of the most prestigious American political scientists, the late Samuel Huntington, while generalizing the fundamental tendencies in the political development of the world speaks of several waves of democracy. He put the beginning of the, thus far the latest, third wave, of democratisation in the middle of the 1970s in connection with the fall of undemocratic regimes in Portugal and later in Spain (Huntington 1991). He believes that this wave of democratisation culminated with the fall of the Communist system in Eastern Europe at the end of the 1980s and in the early 1990s, and then spread to Asia and especially to Africa.[12] It appears, however, that in Asia and Africa this "democratisation" has specific forms.[13]

Considering the issues mentioned above we have to ask how contemporary political theories respond to problems of Africa and Asia. Do the most fundamental, general

---

[10] There is no doubt about the development of democracy in the early 1990s, but the present political situation in some African countries (e.g., Zimbabwe, Ivory Coast, Togo, Cameroon and Angola) also indicate reverse trends, while democratic consolidation remains incomplete in other countries (South Africa, Mauritius, Senegal, Benin and Ghana). This is discussed in great detail by E. Gyimah-Boadi (Gyimah-Boadi 2004: 9–13).

[11] It will certainly be interesting to see how political scientists, after several decades, will put into a wider framework of democratization the American military effort in Afghanistan an Iraq. Outwardly, it both cases the chief result was the removal of an undemocratic system. In both cases the U.S.A. and allies attempt the holding of free elections and the establishment of a democratic government. The first phase was successful due to the overwhelming military strength of the U.S.A, the second phase will be much more difficult and in my opinion in spite of the early success (under direct „supervision" of the allied forces) the establishment of democracy in these two countries will not last because Rustow's condition, a national unity, was not fulfilled.

[12] One of the main trends is especially the abandoning of the thesis of Afro-communism (Guinea-Bissau, Mozambique, Angola, etc.) and the democratization of political systems in the Republic of South Africa, Namibia and other countries. On the origin and development of Afro-communism, see e.g. Ottaway and Ottaway 1981, Rosberg and Callaghy 1979 or Keller and Rothchild 1987.

[13] Political scientists who try to squeeze African and Asian countries into a general theory of democracy use various names for specific types of democracy, only to show that democracy in these continents is developing. See e.g. O'Donnell 1994; Zakaria1997. A detailed analysis of democratic reforms in African countries is given by Gyimah-Boadi 2004, especially in the first chapter, *Africa: The Quality of Political Reform*, pp.5–28. In Czech literature it is possible to refer to a short chapter, *Hybridní demokracie* (pp.285- –296), in Hloušek and Kopeček 2004.

[14] Many contemporary recognized political scientists, such as Juan Linz (Linz 2000), try to unite Euro-American experience in classification of political systems with the development in countries of Asia, Africa and Latin America, but even his new detailed typology of undemocratic regimes shows that classification of political systems in the underdeveloped world is far from simple.

theories of political science hold in the underdeveloped world or were they formulated only for the needs of the more or less democratic Euro-American societies? This difficult question can only be answered by a detailed analysis and comparison of political processes, systems and institutions that will include the socio-economic and political reality of the underdeveloped world.[14]

As stated above, the existing general theories of political parties and party systems essentially avoid the facts and experience of politics in the underdeveloped world.[15] In some of the latest monographs references may be found to some political parties and party systems, especially in Asia (e.g., India, Japan), but African experience in the formation of political parties and party systems continues to be largely ignored.[16] As a matter of fact while examining political structures especially in Africa we encounter numerous methodological problems connected with the existence of specific political parties and the more or less non-existence of operating multi-party systems. In only a few cases can we speak of more or less liberal democratic systems (in the 1990s especially Botswana, Gambia, Mauritius, Senegal, Cape Verde, Saint Thomas and Prince Islands and a few more), while in the rest of the African countries, from the Euro-American perspective, various forms are found of more or less semi democratic or undemocratic regimes. Still, these problems should not discourage us from basic research and especially from making comparisons.

When we adopt the generally accepted thesis that scientific theories are only correct when all the starting points and postulates are correct, then modern "partyologists" cannot leave without notice the origin, development and activity of political parties and party systems in the underdeveloped world. When we start from the presumption that the general theory of political parties and party systems holds for all existing political parties and party systems, we can no longer avoid an examination of political parties and party systems in the underdeveloped world, the comparison of regions, continents and the whole intercontinental (intercivilizational) reality.

Political scientists studying political parties and party systems soon will have to deal with the fundamental issue of how to define the political parties in Africa, Asia and Latin America and how to treat their development, ideology, functions, classification and typology.

---

[15] Pioneering works on political parties begin to appear in the 1980, e.g. Randall 1988.

[16] The only exception is perhaps Nigeria, with which deal many comparative studies written in the last few years. So far I cannot understand why general political scientists so often discuss Nigeria. The main reason may be the fact that political parties and the party system in Nigeria is one of the most studied themes in African Studies, especially due to the monumental work of Richard Sklar (Sklar1963). In 1983 Princeton University Press published the 2nd edition of this seminal work and in 2004 Africa World Press, Inc. participated in the 3rd edition.

The following presentation is one of the first attempts, at least within the Czech political science, at an analysis of the origin of political parties in sub-Saharan Africa.[17] The study is restricted to the analysis of and generalization about those political parties, in the formation of which the local people took part,[18] and when many of these political parties formed both before and in particular after political independence was achieved and when *one-party state system* was abolished. The study will rely mainly on an analysis of the development of political parties in Lusophone Africa.[19] In this analysis of the formation of parties, the character of the political system will be put aside.[20] The study will mainly focus on the manner of the formation of African political parties, that is how they arose and which general models can be applied to them. The author, however, especially in the theoretical analysis, will touch on several further issues, especially why and under what conditions political parties in Africa have developed.

At first sight it may appear that the selection and number of the countries is not fully representative, but during the 20th century for instance only in the countries of the former Portuguese colonial empire more than 100 various political organizations came into existence. The author understands that due to the limited number of countries his general theoretical conclusions will be somewhat limited but he will attempt to document the various types of development of African political parties based on the instances of further political parties from other African countries. The space restrictions would prevent this analysis from dealing in detail with most political parties in any case.[21]

This study is based on the theoretical principles of the establishment of political parties in Europe and America, as they were formulated by the leading classics of political parties, Maurice Duverger, Sigmund Neumann, Giovanni Sartori, Jean Blondel, Klaus

---

[17] Only a few Czech Africanists have dealt with the issue of African political parties. Worth mentioning are some older works by Vladimír Klíma, Zdenek Poláček and the present author.

[18] Left aside are all political parties in the origin of which colonizers took part, including all branches of metropolitan political parties in the colonies. The present study only refers to those white political parties, which, at least for some time, "survived" and became involved in the formation of African party systems.

[19] Angola, Mozambique, Guinea-Bissau, Cape Verde Islands and Saint Thomas and Prince Islands.

[20] With some distortion it can be said that in Cape Verde Islands, Saint. Thomas and Prince Islands, in Mozambique and Guinea-Bissau since the 1990s a democratic transition is going on and in each of these countries a system of several political parties evolved. In Angola, from 1975 torn by civil war, according to the peace treaty concluded in Lusaka in 1992 democratic elections were held, with participation of 18 political parties, but UNITA failed to recognize the election results and renewed the civil war. The situation became calmer and the twenty-year-long civil war ended only at the end of the 1990s. See Bratton and Van de Walle 91997: 116–1220 or Chabal et al. (2002: 170–184).

[21] In my estimate, in various periods more than 1,000 political parties were founded in sub-Saharan Africa. T. Hodgkin in his book *African Political Parties* of 1961 mentions 189 political parties, movements and fronts, and this number need not be complete (Hodgkin 1961: 210–217). From the 1990s two more survey works are important: East and Tany 1993 and Vysotskaya, Geveling, Kosukhin, 1998.

von Beyme, Joseph LaPalombara, Myron Weiner, Alan Ware, etc.[22] The author does not restrict himself to examples of the formation of political parties in African "democratic" countries only, he is interested in the development of parties in undemocratic systems as well. Since this is an introductory study,[23] the foundation of all African political parties is not covered but we believe that the general models of development presented below could be applied on other African political parties as well.

In African Studies the problem of parties has been studied for several decades. A rapid development of African Studies took place especially after 1960, when a majority of African countries achieved political independence – that year is often called the Year of Africa. Among the first major pioneers in the field of the study of political parties in Africa was the British Africanist Thomas Hodgkin, whose not very large monograph, *African Political Parties*[24] (1961), offered the first general hypothesis about African political parties. Soon after few general theoretical studies of political parties in various language regions were published (e.g. Morgenthau 1964) and there were also biographies of parties included in more general historical and political science works.[25] In the 1950s and 1960s existing political science journals[26] published relatively numerous articles analysing various aspects of the origin and development of political parties in each African country.[27] T. Hodgkin moreover could use biographies of African leaders, such as Kwame Nkrumah, Sékou Touré, Léopold Sédar Senghor, Habib Bourguiba and Nnamdi Azikiwe[28] and at the same time received detailed data from his numerous visits to African countries. Hodgkin's study not only presents the first theory of political parties in Africa,[29] but in its supplement entitled "The Main African Political Parties in 1945–1960," classified according to the countries, Hodgkin put together much that is still relevant to the beginnings of political parties in African countries.

Over the next few decades, in addition to detailed biographies of political parties and party systems in each African country, several comprehensive theoretical studies were

---

[22] Duverger 1954; Neumann 1956; Epstein 1967; Sartori1976; LaPalombara and Weiner 1966; Ware 1996, von Beyme 1985; Blondel 1978.

[23] The study is a preliminary version of a chapter from a monograph on African political parties and part systems that is being prepared by the author.

[24] Hodgkin authored several more works of importance. Here I refer especially to his *Nationalism in Colonial Africa*. London 1956 and *Nigerian Perspectives*. London 1960.

[25] Apter 1955; Coleman 1958; Ezera 1960; Raweliffe 1954 and many more.

[26] E.g. *West Africa* (London), *Africa Digest* (London), *Afrique Nouvelle* (Dakar), *Africa Report* (Washington), *Africa To-day* (New York), *Marchés Tropicaux et Mediterranéens* and several more. Publication of Africanist journals has been intensified especially from the second half of the 1960s. A high-level journal is *Africa Research Bulletin*, oriented at detailed reporting of political events in Africa.

[27] Their list would be fairly long, here only the major ones are given: Lewis, I. M. 1958, Lloyd 1955, Bennett 1957.

[28] E.g. Nkrumah 1957; Touré 1959; Azikiwe 1957.

[29] The structure of the work is as follows: Introduction, The Setting, The Origin of Parties, Types of Parties, Party Organization, Party Activities, Party Objectives and Concluding Hypotheses.

written. Here in the first place the work *Political Parties and National Integration in Tropical Africa* by James Coleman and Carl Rosberg should be mentioned (Coleman and Rosberg 1966). Works dealing with the foundation and development of countries with one ruling party appeared in the same time (e.g. the major work *African One-Party States*, edited by Gwendolen. M. Carter, was published in 1961.

In writing this study the author used his own research in political parties and party systems in African countries while he was attached to the Africa Department of the Oriental Institute of the Czechoslovak Academy of Sciences (Fiala 1984, 1987, 1989a, 1989b).

The study consists of two main sections. In the first part the author attempted a brief summary of contemporary theoretical principles relevant to the foundation of political parties in Europe and America and defined the main types of African political organizations. The second part is an analysis of political parties in African countries and offers the principal models and then applies them on the general classification of the foundation of political parties.

The study does not aim to be an exhaustive study of the problem. The author is conscious of some methodological problems and the risk of premature theoretical conclusions. As I said above, this is one of the first attempts at a generalization of the issue and I know that my thesis will have to be confirmed by further research and presenting further examples from African (Asian, Latin American) political practice. Its aim is not only to verify the theories of the foundation of political parties on a sample of select African countries, but also open a discussion on this issue, and expand the range of questions about the origin, development, abolition, functions and types of political parties. The amount of data available on political parties in underdeveloped countries will reopen the discussion on some fundamental theoretical issues. This study thus hopes to be a small contribution to the future discussion.

The Foundation of Political Parties

The classics of political parties usually connect the main cause of the origin of political parties in Europe and America with the extension of suffrage and the advantages of the parliamentary system based on democratic competition of political subjects. Most of them agree that the nuclei of political parties are to be sought in parliaments (the so-called dignitaries, pressure organizations) and finally even outside parliament, due to the transformation or integration of various special-interest organizations.

Until the middle of the 19th century due to the election census, decisions about deputies were taken in a narrow elite group of society ("dignitaries"). Thus there was no need to establish any major specific political organizations. Small special-interest groups, usually called election committees, were able to win sufficient support for the election of each deputy among the rather small number of persons with voting rights.

The situation began to change at the turn of the 19th and 20th century, when many people from various social groups obtained the right to vote and the deputies had to look for new ways of addressing and winning the new voters. The original election committees expanded their ranks, obtained new agitators, all over the country new branches were established, a program was sought, an ideology which addressed potential voters. Maurice Duverger in his classical work *Political Parties. Their Organization and Activity in the Modern State* speaks of this type of formation of political parties as parties originating in elections and parliament (Duverger 1978).

Duverger claims that the roots of these political parties derive from parliament, generally from deputies with identical views or attitudes, and that from there they later move to an existence outside parliament.[30] Another step towards the establishment of a political party is the linking of these groups of deputies with election committees, whose main role was to secure the re-election of a deputy. (Duverger 1978: xxiv-xxv). Very typical of this method is the development of British political parties, especially the Conservative and Liberal Parties, which with the gradual extension of the voting right after 1832 were obliged to transfer their activity from Parliament to outside that institution, which brought the need of building up the party structure, gain members and address the voters.

The second type of the development of political parties is seen by Duverger in parties founded outside the elections and parliament. Here he speaks especially of the activities of extra-parliamentary organizations, such as philosophical societies, workers' clubs, groups of intellectuals associated around daily newspapers, etc. (idem, pp. xxx). Duverger says that the number of similar organizations and groups is very large and it is impossible to register all of them. As a general example he names the activities of trade unions, which gave an impulse to the foundation of Socialist and Social Democratic parties, and he refers to the history of Labour Party in Britain. Similarly, various peasants' associations stimulated the foundation of agricultural political parties, which were strong especially in Scandinavia, Central Europe, Switzerland, Australia, etc. Political parties often arose from the initiatives of intellectuals (e.g., Jean-Paul Sartre and his attempt at the foundation of a leftist Revolutionary Democratic Party), students (left-wing parties), freemasons (especially radical and liberal parties in Europe) or even business and finance circles.

---

[30] Duverger deals in detail especially with the origin of French, British and partly German political parties. On the example of French parties he shows that the first impulse need not be shared views and attitudes (ideology), but for instance geographical predetermination or the wish to defend some special-interest and professional groups. Duverger believes that the original local groups adopted an ideology only later. As an example he gives the French Constitutional Assembly of 1789, in which the so-called Breton Club was formed. Deputies from this region met in a special room in one cafe in Versailles and there tried to unite their attitudes both to regional issues and the fundamental issues of national policy. Later the members of this regional club became generally known as the Jacobins, and in a similar way the Girondists were formed. The deputies in the French Constitutional Assembly of 1848 were also divided according to ideology. The moderate republicans met in the Palais National, Catholic monarchists in Rue de Poitiers, left-oriented deputies in Rue de Castiglione and Rue des Pyramides. A similar situation was in the Frankfurt Parliament (Duverger 1978: xxiv-xxv).

In the process of forming various political parties a major role was played by the Church. Thus in the Netherlands the Calvinistic Anti-Revolutionary Party was founded to be in opposition to the existing Catholic party, and similarly in Belgium religious authorities initiated the foundation of the Catholic Conservative Party. The influence of the Church is also seen in the establishment of European Christian-Democratic parties in the 20th century. Likewise unions of war veterans were present at the foundation of fascist parties in Italy and France (Duverger 1978: xxx-xxxiii).

Duverger gives one more example of political parties originating from various leagues and secret societies and illegal groups. As soon as the state calls off the ban on their activity or when conditions are created for their legalization, these secret societies or illegal groups tend to change into political parties. For instance, after the First World War some resistance groups turned into political parties, and Duverger in this connection refers to the Russian Communist Party, which from illegality passed straight to power. (Duverger 1978: xxxiii)

When we generalize Duverger's classification of the manner of development of political parties, then his main, determining criterion is the place of origin so that he divided the parties into those which developed in or outside parliament. On the other hand, from Duverger's analysis and examples other methods of foundation may be derived, though he did not try to classify them according to logical criteria. One of these criteria may be the development from the centre, i.e., from a single place – this is the case of a centralized party, which afterwards establishes its lower structures, and the club of deputies then plays a dominant role in the party structure. Or the parties developing from local interest groups, who become associated, create a party structure from below with the aim of gaining political power in the elections. This is a decentralized party (e.g., socialist, social democratic, agrarian parties), and if this party succeeds in the elections, its central committee plays a much more dominant role than the club of its deputies (Duverger 1978: xxxv).

Duverger in hints follows even the foundation of parties according to conflict lines in a society (e.g., the Dutch political parties); Stein Rokkan and Seymour Lipset developed this theme much later.[31]

Our study will finally show that with the passage of more than fifty years since Duverger's work,[32] his institutional theory of the origin of political parties only holds

---

[31] Petr Fiala is right in pointing out the fact that the real discoverers of conflict lines were not the two authors but the Dutch political scientist H. Daalder, who formulated the „cleavages lines of the party system" one year earlier than the two authors. (Fiala and Strmiska 1998: 58, note 11). Similarly H. Daalder was the first to come with the main theses of the polarization of the society in The Netherlands, which later became the principle of Lijphart's theory of consociational democracy. It seems that H. Daalder has ceased to be the author of two most important theories of modern political parties.

[32] First published in French in 1951.

for some countries in Europe, whereas in other European countries, in America and of course in the underdeveloped countries[33] it completely abandons its main theses.

Among Czech scholars Duverger's theory of political parties is fairly strictly accepted by Miroslav Novák who in his main work, *Systémy politických stran* (Political Party Systems, 1997), says that Duverger's theory should be complemented by a third way of development, i.e., merging or splitting of existing parties (Novák 1997: 36). At the same time Novák points to the necessity of supplementing Duverger's theory in some places in order to apply the results of latest historical and political science research.[34] As show further theories discussed below and as we shall see on the example of the development of political parties especially in Africa, not even the third type is sufficient for a revitalization of Duverger's Institutionalist Theory. We are also going to demonstrate that the thesis of the "development of political parties in the majority of underdeveloped countries simultaneously with the state in a sort of institutional vacuum" (Novák 1997: 37) does not correspond to political reality in the underdeveloped world. It should be said right in this place that research into parties in a majority of underdeveloped countries reveals that political parties (or their roots) existed for decades before the country acquired political independence. Thus it is logical that non-white political parties in the colonial period could not have their origin in parliament, but on the other hand their establishment agrees with the second thesis of Duverger, namely, that various social organizations, cultural and educational circles, groups of intellectual, etc. can be at the origin of the parties.

Many interesting stimuli for the theory of the origin of political parties were brought by Stein Rokkan and Seymour M. Lipset, when on the basis of the *historical-conflict approach* they came forward with the principal thesis that the foundation of political parties is linked with the existence of social conflicts in various historical stages of development. (Lipset and Rokkan 1967; Rokkan 1970) They believe that in the period of national revolution a conflict arises between the centre, which defends national culture, and the periphery, which can differ from the centre in ethnicity, language and religion (cleavage Centre – Periphery). At the same time in the national revolution a conflict arises between the national state, which supports centralization and unification, and the church, which supports historical privileges (cleavage State – Church). Another major social division,

---

[33] It should be said in Duverger's defence that when his book was published in the first edition, there were hardly any works available on the origin and development of political parties in underdeveloped countries.

[34] In connection with the development of American political parties he points out the necessity to expand Duverger's thesis on the presidential system (not only parliamentary) and notes that in some countries Duverger's thesis on the development of parties due to introduction and expansion of general suffrage does not hold because in Norway and Sweden political parties were founded long before the introduction of general suffrage, while in Denmark and France it was only several decades after it (Novák 1997: 36). As Petr Fiala notes, referring to the historical research of J. Malíř, a similar situation is to be found in the Czech lands in the period of the Austro-Hungarian Empire. (Fiala and Strmiska 1998: 55–56)

when new political parties are born, is the industrial revolution, which brings a conflict between rural and industrial interests (cleavage Town – Country), and simultaneously a conflict goes on between the group of owners and employers and the group of workers and other working people (cleavage Workers – Working people). (Lipset - Rokkan 1967:14) Rokkan believes that these cleavages are linked to the development of new political parties (liberal, conservative and radical vs. workers' or communist parties; Christian-Democratic vs. radical parties; centralist vs. federalist, autonomist or separatist parties; agrarian, agricultural and ecological).[35]

Rokkan based his theory mainly on the study of the origin and historical development of political parties in Europe. So far we have not encountered any serious attempt at application of this or a similar historical-conflict theory to underdeveloped countries. A mechanical application of Rokkan's theory is not possible in underdeveloped countries because some African countries have not yet finished the national revolution, not to speak of the industrial revolution. A major methodological problem is the inclusion in Rokkan's theory of the so-called national liberation revolution (NLR); nearly all former colonies have passed through it in various forms. During the NLR a clear conflict line arises – the colonial power vs. the independent "national" state.[36] This conflict results in the development of political parties, on one side moderate, wishing to preserve the status quo or a certain form of "autonomy," on the other side nationalist parties, national liberation movements and fronts, whose main goal is achievement of political independence.

A successful conclusion of the NLR is linked with the proclamation of political independence, followed by sometimes short, sometimes long periods of national revolution, which are characterized by usually fierce ethnic or tribal conflicts, civil wars linked with genocide of whole nations and ethnic groups, military coups, etc. In general these conflicts could correspond to Rokkan's cleavage centre vs. periphery, but the second cleavage characteristic of the national revolution, state vs. church, which influences the foundation of corresponding political parties, is more difficult to document.[37] Rather there is the conflict state vs. traditional society. Quite controversial is, however, the existence of parties, which in Rokkan corresponds to the period of industrial revolution. Although in the majority of countries in Africa and Asia NLR did not take place (they continue to be agrarian countries with backward agriculture); Socialist, Social democratic

---

[35] J. Kunc and V. Dvořáková attempted an application of Rokkan's cleavages on Czech parties (Dvořáková and Kunc 1996: 133–145).

[36] „National" only in the sense of gaining political independence for a certain internationally recognized historical state formation.

[37] Religion in these regions plays a much more important role than in Europe but religious conflicts are usually part of ethnic and tribal conflicts. For example due to the strong position of Islam in Arab countries (often 99,9 %) it is unimaginable that any radical parties could develop there as a contrast to the Islamist political parties.

and even Communist parties, and also liberal, conservative or radical parties commonly exist in those countries. The reason for their development is to be sought in other historical developments rather than an industrial revolution.

In the middle of the 1960s, David Apter wrote his major work, *The Politics of Modernization* (Apter 1965) in which the American political scientist dealt in detail with the modernization of societies outside Europe. In Chapter 6, Apter discussed in detail the political parties, which he holds to be the most important tool for modernization of society. "In the area of political modernization," D. Apter wrote, "no single role is of greater importance than that of party politician. This is because political parties are themselves historically so closely associated with the modernization of Western societies and, in various forms (reformist, revolutionary, nationalist), have become the instruments of modernization in the developing countries" (idem, p.179). Apter finally examines in detail the role, position and function of political parties and comes to the conclusion that their role in underdeveloped countries is markedly different from the position of parties in industrial countries. Parties in underdeveloped countries usually get mass support, require strict discipline, create the political hierarchy of power and prestige, and express the fundamental segment of the modernizing society (idem, p.222).

Political parties in underdeveloped countries, moreover, meet specific functions (administrative, educational, police, social welfare, etc.). In countries in which political parties are in power, it is sometimes hard to distinguish what is the function and responsibility on one side and what is the role of the government and state administration on the other side (idem, p.187) Unfortunately, Apter practically ignores the issue of the development of the parties. The modernization theory is partly accepted by other contemporary political scientists, such as Joseph LaPalombara a Myron Weiner.[38]

Another major German political scientist, Karl von Beyme, in the early 1980s tried to generalize the existing analyses of the origin of political parties and came forward with three partial theories relevant for the development of the parties.[39] The first institutional theory starts from Duverger's conception and its substance is the birth of parties on the basis of the development of parliamentary systems and election mechanism in connection with the expansion of voting rights. The second theory is based on Mair's theory of critical situations, which makes the parties the result of the proclamation of independence of new states or is linked with the collapse of the constitutional system (e.g., France in the 1950s, Italy in the early 90s). Finally, the modernization theory is based especially on some social and economic factors in the development of parties, which were mainly analysed by S. Rokkan, J. LaPalombara and M. Weiner.

The development of political parties in the underdeveloped world aroused the interest of many Marxist as well as non-Marxist political scientists who tried to generalize the

---

[38] Especially the chapter *The Origin and Development of Political Parties* in LaPalombara and Weiner 1966: 3–42.

[39] Cf. Beyme (1985).

increasing factual material after 1960. Although both groups took up different ideological positions in a bipolar world, which was most observable in the description and evaluation of the parties, the orientation and ideo-political orientation; however, in the matter of the mechanical development of the parties they shared the same position. When we leave aside the ideological overtones on each side, the period 1960–2004 brought a great many views, conceptions and classifications of the development of political parties in the underdeveloped world, which remain of value to this day. However, before we start with our own classification we have to conclude the discussion of the terminology in order to understand these processes.

African Studies, like other related fields, in order to understand and explain the new processes and trends in the underdeveloped world sought for less often used terms. In particular in the countries, which were able to win political independence only after a prolonged national liberation fight, inclination toward leftist ideas appeared. Many historical examples show that leftist radicalism was very common in transitory periods after major social crises (e.g., the wave of revolutions in Europe after the World War I, the increased power of Communist and leftist parties after the World War II or the rise of Socialist parties after the fall of the Portuguese dictator Marcelo Caetano or the death of Generalissimo Franco in Spain in the middle of the 1970s, etc.). In many underdeveloped countries there was a pronounced trend to form parties with a socialist programme.

Soviet Bloc Africanists usually used the terms "national democrats", "revolutionary democrats" and "African Marxists" for the leftist intellectuals of various orientations, who after the proclamation of independence became leaders in many African countries.[40] On the basis of the characteristics of these political elites, labels were created to characterise the new parties as national democratic parties, revolutionary democratic parties, vanguard parties of the working people, etc.. The new terms were to illustrate the differences in social, cultural and especially political structure of the underdeveloped countries. East European Africanists believed that the penetration of ideas of scientific socialism into the underdeveloped world was reflected in the logic of the formation of the parties. National democratic parties turned into revolutionary democratic parties, which after adoption of scientific socialism could turn into vanguard parties of the working people, which were to become the basis for the foundation of communist parties.

After the collapse of the communist system in Eastern Europe, the popularity of socialist ideas has declined even in the underdeveloped world. Unlike the political systems in Eastern Europe, at the turn of the 1980s and 1990s no major changes in political elites

---

[40] It is a pity that no one has yet attempted a serious comparative analysis of the influence of university education in Eastern and Western blocs on intellectuals from the underdeveloped countries. I would not be surprised to find that intellectuals educated in the Eastern bloc were later far less revolutionary (Marxist) than the graduates of Western universities.

took place in African countries,[41] but the leftist orientation is weakened or abandoned. For example the thesis of the leading role of the party in the class struggle disappeared from the party programmes,[42]. Many political scientists speak of an intensification of the third wave of democratisation, which has a great influence on the development of new parties and the formation of multi-party systems.

Similarly, Western Africanists during that period had to react in their terminology to the leftist radicalisation in the underdeveloped world after gaining political independence and so they commonly used the terms *communist parties, Marxist-Leninist parties, vanguard parties, Afro-communist parties* as comprehensive labels for parties in USSR-oriented regimes.[43]

The first attempt at a generalization of the origin of political parties in Africa can be found in the work of the British Africanist Thomas Hodgkin, who in his survey of African political parties mainly relied on Duverger's theory of political parties. Because of the various interpretations of the term African political party and the use of various names for political organizations, such as nationalist movements, fronts, congresses, parties, Hodgkin tried to define the African political party as an organization that formulated in detail its goals as a political programme, and which adopts a certain ideology, builds a formal democratic structure, usually based on local branches and individual membership, wants to compete regularly with the other parties in elections with the aim of controlling the government and has a greater flexibility in its strategy, reacting to the topical needs, especially in the realization of political power (Hodgkin 1961: 51).[44]

On the basis of Duverger's approach, Hodgkin arrived at the conclusion that an absolute majority of African political parties developed outside of parliament. The historical development of most countries in Africa shows that this was in fact so. Further, Hodgkin and Duverger agreed that these outside-parliament parties were mainly formed from various associations and groups with the aim of achieving political power (Hodgkin 1961: 46).

---

[41] For example in Lusophone Africa political elites changed only in Cape Verde, where in 1991 the central-rightist Movement for Democracy gained power. In Mozambique, Angola, Guinea-Bissau and Saint Thomas and Prince Islands the former „Afro-Marxists" continued to stay in power.

[42] Here it should be said that the so-called leading role of the party was typical not only of the leftist systems but appeared even in pro-capitalist countries, which called themselves one-party states (e.g., Zambia, Senegal, Ivory Coast, etc.).

[43] Political scientists thinking in black and white preferred the term communist parties/Marxist-Leninist parties for all leftist parties in underdeveloped countries but many others such as David and Marina Ottaway, Carl Rosberg, Barry Munslow and many more American and European Africanist scholars tried to distinguish between leftist parties. See, e.g., Fiala 1989a.

[44] Unfortunately the definition applies only to the countries that tried to introduce a democratic regime. Besides these parties, perhaps hundreds of political parties may be found in Africa, for which democratic competition and establishment of a democratic structure were only empty words, with no meaning whatsoever.

As in Europe, these proto-party organizations and groups were cultural, educational and student organizations: groups of war veterans, trade unions, religious associations, sporting organizations, tribal unions and many more. In Hodgkin's opinion, the rapid spread of these associations in the interwar period and after World War II helped in the formation of parties in three various ways:

1. Many leaders of these associations, originally, for the most part, non-political, later began to lead nationalist organizations, which thus actually prepared the new nationalist elites.
2. These associations created new types of loyalty, not always necessarily national but certainly wider than were the loyalties of family or village relationships, and thus they enabled the nationalist leaders to mobilize and direct important sections of the population.
3. In various regions, these associations created the main blocs of popular support, which later became important for the foundation of mass political parties (cf. Coleman 1958: 47–48).

After a study of various sources and his first partial analyses of African political parties, Hodgkin proposed the following classification of the development of African political parties:

1. Change of Earlier Associations

In Hodgkin's view, some political parties were formed from existing organizations, which only were given the label of a political party and political function, although, at least in their initial phase, no major change took place in their structure, leadership or ideology. As a classic example he uses the *Northern People's Congress* in Nigeria, which arose in December 1949 as a pan-northern cultural organization with a dominant membership of conservative Malams, which later became defunct and re-emerged in 1951 in the middle of an election campaign as a political party uniting conservative nationalists and members of the *Fulani gida* (the traditional ruling class of the former realm of Fulani).

2. Evolution from a "Congress"

Hodgkin defines the congress as a political organization of a specific type with several principal features. Firstly, wide nationalist goals (especially abolition of the colonial system) and secondly, a free structure, usually consisting of local functional associations formed around the central organ, which fully controls the policy. He says that congresses usually express the idea of representation of all people and adopt an active strategy, the cause of which is a lack of constitutional mechanisms for the realization of their nationalist goals.[45] Along with the definition of the congress, Hodgkin analyses the so-called fronts, which originate in revolutionary situations (he refers to the FLN in Algeria) and like the congresses try to unify all existing organizations and streams in order to

---

[45] Description of the main political organizations is in each author different. See, e.g,. Coleman 1958.

achieve a complete transformation of political and social structures, while using means outside the constitution rather than means based on elections. Hodgkin says that fronts rather resemble political parties, especially mass parties because of their more closed structure based on party cells rather than on branches, strict discipline and definition of their goals. He also says that in practice pure forms often do not exist, "congresses during the process are transformed into 'political parties,'" and, conversely, "'political parties' keep some features of 'congresses' or adopt the character of a revolutionary front." (Hodgkin 1961: 52)

Hodgkin thinks that the change of a congress into a political party is manifested by accepting a new and much more efficient structure, which is based on loyalty branches or cells, consists of individual members who contribute or intend to contribute to party funds. It is a gradual process, and sometimes the exact date or deadline of the transformation is fixed.

3. Secession from Congresses and Parties

The development of new parties by seceding is one of the most common ways of foundation of African parties. Progressive fractions get into conflict with conservative or moderate groups and the result is their leaving the congress and foundation of their own political party. In this way, e.g., in Ghana the *Convention People's Party* (CPP) was formed, which in 1949 seceded from the *United Gold Coast Convention* (UGCC), or in Senegal where the *Bloc Démocratique Senégalais* split off in 1948 from the *Section Française de l'Internationale Ouvrière-Fédération du Sénégal* (SFIO).

4. Integration of Political Parties and Groups

The reverse of the above model is integration of several political parties and groups into a single political organization. So, e.g., the Ghana Congress Party was born in 1952 by unification of one part of the UGCC, the conservative *National Democratic Party,* and a group of the so-called CPP rebels. African political practice contains many similar examples of integration of parties. Thus for example arose the Front for the Liberation of Mozambique (*Frente de Libertação de Moçambique* – FRELIMO) or the People's Movement for the Liberation of Angola (*Movimento Popular de Libertação de Angola* - MPLA.).

5. External Influence

Hodgkin noticed an interesting fact, namely that many African political parties arose because of some external influence. In colonies the so-called administrative parties were established with the assistance of the colonial administration. Their main aim was the creation of a particular political alternative to the existing nationalist parties. Besides these administrative parties, however, socialist and communist parties appeared in Africa, usually in co-operation with leftist parties in big cities. That is, e.g., the origin of the SFIO in Senegal in 1936 or, at the congress in Bamako in 1946, the *Rassemblement Démocratique Africain* (RDA) with branches in nearly all French colonies.

An interesting view of the formation of African political parties was brought by David Apter in his study on Ghana, a major work on political parties in Africa in the second half of the 1960s (Apter 1955).[46] Using the historical approach he attempted a generalization of each phase in the establishment of political organizations in Ghana, which would be theoretically valid for the development of other African political parties as well. He thinks that the morphology of the development of the parties can be divided into five main groups:

I. Ethnic and pressure groups (1870–1940)
1. Ethnic associations
2. Protective organizations
3. Progressive associations and various clubs of people of the same convictions
4. Literary and discussion groups

II. Fraction coalitions with political goals (1920–1950)
1. Local coalitions
2. National coalitions

III. Representative political parties (1945–1956)
1. Conservative nationalist parties
2. Radical nationalist parties

IV. Solidarity parties (1957–1960)

V. Fractions within monoliths
1. Conservative wing
2. Radical wing
3. Intellectuals (Socialist radicals and opportunists (Apter 1966:261)

A comparison of the two classifications reveals that they overlap. Apter in his study clearly says that the roots of Ghanaian political parties are closely linked with ethnic and pressure groups. He speaks of the pre-political phase, when these groups put pressure on

---

[46] A group of leading world Africanists specialising in political science (Aristide R. Zolberg, Victor T. Le Vine, David Apter, Immanuel Wallerstein, René Lemarchand, Richard L. Sklar, Thomas Hodgkin, Ruth Schachter-Morgenthau and several other) headed by James S. Coleman and Carl G. Rosberg published in 1966 the book *Political Parties and National Integration in Tropical Africa*, the chapters of which, in territorial case studies, tried to generalize the main trends in political development in select African countries from the aspect of foundation and activity of the parties. The major contribution of this collective monograph are not the case studies but the interesting comparative analyses of the attitudes of political parties vis-f-vis voluntary organizations, trade unions, traditional structures of African society, and the role of students in national integration (Coleman and Rosberg 1966).

the colonial administration; some of them formed coalitions with the goal of achieving greater legitimacy. The next step in the political organization in Ghana was the creation of representative political parties, which defended from various positions the national interests of the whole population of Ghana (*United Gold Coast Convention, Convention People's Party*). Apter takes note of various fractions too, which led to the formation of new political parties (Apter 1966:261–262). Basing ourselves on Hodgkin's classification we find in Apter and the Ghana example practically most of models of the development of parties.

An interesting book *Političeskie partii Afriki* (African Political Parties) was published in the Soviet Union in 1970 (Solodovnikov 1970), which attempted, from the Marxist-Leninist point of view, an analysis of African political parties. Leaving aside the usual ideological ballast of that day, we find that Soviet Marxist scholars arrived at practically the same results as African Studies in the West. The authors avoided a concrete classification of the development of parties but like T. Hodgkin and D. Apter they sought the roots of the political organizations in the 19th and early 20th century in various educational, cultural and pressure groups. In their interpretation of the origin of the 20th-century parties they depended on the Marxist-Leninist thesis that political parties are a reflection of the existence of social classes and express their interests (Solodovnikov 1970: 7). Subsequent historical survey offers a list of African social groups and their political expression in the form of political parties. National bourgeoisie, intellectuals, representatives of feudal and tribal societies, clergy, students and proletariat, these were in the opinion of Soviet authors the main initiators of the organization of the first political parties in Africa. As I mentioned above, the authors failed to deal with the ways of origin of political parties, with the exception of the first part of Chapter 5 where they discussed the influence of outside factors (Solodovnikov 1970:34–42). The rest of the book dealt with the party types: revolutionary democratic, Marxist-Leninist, bourgeois and pro-bourgeois (Solodovnikov 1970: 66–307).

One of the latest works on the theoretical problems of political parties in Africa is *African Political Parties* (Salih 2004). In the introduction to his book, which in addition to several theoretical chapters contains case studies from several African countries (Zambia, Tanzania, Sudan, Ethiopia, Namibia, Ghana, Kenya, Botswana and South Africa), M. A. Mohamed Salih briefly discussed the birth of political parties. He did not come forward with any applicable theoretical classification but obviously under Hodgkin's influence he subdivided the introduction into several sections according to the way of formation of the parties. In the first section he deals with those parties, which have remained in power since the colonial days (*Sierra Leone People's Party* - SLPP, *United National Party, Socialist Party of Senegal* and *Rassemblement National Démocratique*), most of which are follow-ups on various educational, cultural and other associations. The next section deals, using the examples of the MPLA in Angola, the FRELIMO in Mozambique, the Mozambique National Resistance (*Resistência Nacional Moçambicana* – RENAMO), *South West Africa People's Organisation* - SWAPO in Namibia, *African National Congress* – ANC in South Africa and the *Zimbabwe African National Union – Patriotic Front* – ZANU-PF, with the transition from mass organizations to political parties. Salih only admits the development of those parties, which resulted from organizational activities of military rulers. As an example he chose the military regimes in Sudan, Ethiopia and Nigeria (Salih 2004: 19).

There is no doubt that M. A. Mohamed Salih is familiar with the fact that African political parties arise in different ways as well (especially by integration and disintegration, due to external factors), but only the three ways referred to above are probably held by him to be of key importance and decisive. As a matter of fact, in the conclusion to the last chapter of the introductory part he says that "the evolution of African political parties is neither linear nor homogenous. African states have not only adopted different political-party systems..., but they have also developed unique African party systems." (Salih 2004:27)

From all these definitions and classifications it is evident that modern political scientists meet many methodological problems in their formulation of modern theories of African political parties. The most fundamental problem is an exact definition of all forms of organizations both in the history of Africa and in the present of the continent.[47] Definitions are needed for the following organizations, which stood at the birth of African political parties:[48]

1. Special Interest and Pressure Groups
In special-interest and pressure organizations I include the various cultural, educational, sporting and other associations, clubs, trade unions, unions of veterans, religious organizations, etc., which at their birth were non-political, but gradually became more radical, demanded the abolition of colonialism and were the first organizations that educated the political leaders of the future. Congresses/fronts and, in some cases, proto-political parties or political parties were formed upon their foundation.

2. Congresses
Congresses are understood as organizations, which usually speak on behalf of the whole population (ethnic group, tribe) with the aim of removing the colonial system. The congress structure is amorphous, it relies on various associations, action groups led usually by a small group of intellectuals who from the centre formulate the main goals and the strategy. A congress is usually without ideology though at times its programme may contain allegiance to African nationalism, Panafricanism or various forms of African socialism. These are, however, not very detailed. Unlike the fronts

---

[47] By the term organizations in this context I mean all types of African non-political and political special interest and pressure groups, congresses, fronts, proto-political parties and political parties.

[48] I leave aside the term nationalist movement, which is commonly used as the most general term expressing the effort of Africans at liberation from colonial oppression, while this meaning does not represent any type of organization. Hodgkin includes various institutional forms, including congresses, parties and fronts (Hodgkin 1960:50).

referred to below, congresses prefer non-violent forms of struggle and try to achieve their objectives within the constitution (for example Kwame Nkrumah's campaign for 'positive actions,' proclaimed in the Gold Coast in 1949). Another classical example is the non-violent struggle of the Indian National Congress with Gandhi at the head, aiming at the independence of India).

3. Fronts

Usually they are organizations that were forced by historical development to wage a campaign for national independence, generally in the form of a long national liberation struggle (e.g., MPLA, UNITA and FNLA in Angola, PAIGC in Guinea-Bissau, FRELIMO in Mozambique, the ANC in South Africa, etc.). They have a clear, detailed programme, a firm structure, strict discipline and often accept some type of ideology. They differ from political parties mainly by the use of non-constitutional forms of political struggle because in their countries only whites or select sections of the population can vote so that the main political objectives (especially the proclamation of independence) could not be achieved within the regular election struggle.

4. Proto-political Parties

They are predecessors of African political parties, which in the colonial period were usually founded in deep illegality, had a firm structure and a strict discipline. Their main goal was the removal of colonialism and achievement of political independence; their programme often contained some ideology, with an emphasis on what makes Africa specific. They mainly differed from the classical African political parties by their small membership (usually a small group of intellectuals) and their small or meagre means to achieve their political goals. These proto-political parties can often be defined as political discussion clubs. They differ from special-interest and pressure groups by their political character and political programme. Proto-political parties usually become parts of congresses or fronts, after achieving independence, or after the installation of a multi-party system they may be transformed into political parties.

5. Political Parties

They are political organizations with a more or less clear structure and distinct party hierarchy and usually have individual membership and accept a particular ideology. In their activity they are guided by a pragmatic, short-term or long-term political programme and other party documents (e.g., the statutes). Party members regularly meet at their congresses where usually a ballot takes place to confirm or renew the party leadership. Unlike most Euro-American parties, not all African parties that speak of democratic competition in the political struggle prepare legal conditions for it (one-party systems,[49]

---

[49] After long discussions, the view came to be gradually accepted that one-party states cannot be automatically regarded as totalitarian regimes. See, e.g., Zolberg, 1966 and Carter 1962. I am increasingly convinced

control of mass media, use of state power and means in the election campaign, etc.), so that their declarations are often only verbal.

When studying the origins of African political parties it is necessary to examine at first the character of the organization and find out whether it is a real political party or some other type (special-interest or pressure organization, congress, front or political party). This analysis is often very difficult because one party carrying the same name can pass through all these types and it is often next to impossible to say when a pressure organization changed into a congress or front, and a congress and front into political party, etc.

Classification of the Origin of African Political Parties

1. Classification and its scientific import

On the basis of the theoretical approaches to the development of political parties, as they were referred to above, and after a summary of the existing research on this issue one can present a classification based on a single criterion, the way/mechanism in which they were formed. This author leaves aside Duverger's institutional theory and especially his criterion of place and way (parliament, outside parliament, from above, from below) of origin because unlike Europe this is of marginal importance in Africa. Due to its history an absolute majority of political parties originated outside the parliament. However it cannot be denied that with the democratisation of African society in the early 1990s, which was manifested especially in the abolition of the system of the *one-party states*,[50] there was a massive growth in new political parties as well as return of formerly banned, illegal or exiled political organizations.

For our classification not even Mair's theory of critical situations is suitable because it rather points out the causes or favourable conditions for the development of the parties (proclamation of independence, collapse of the constitutional system). In Africa it seems that critical situations were rarely a nursery of political parties. This thesis can be partly confirmed by the period of proclamation of political independence and

---

that *one-party states* in Africa are/ were one of the necessary stages of development in the African party system, during which the multi-ethnic state became consolidated, rules of the political game were set and fundamental conditions were created for the subsequent democratization of society and the introduction of the party system. For greater detail see my forthcoming study *Origin and Development of Party Systems in Africa.*

[50] The sympathisers of Duverger's theory will argue here with the development of the parliamentary system, while the second prerequisite , the broadening of voting rights, was usually fulfilled immediately after the gaining of political independence. Thus not the broadening of voting rights, but democratization (from the point of view of Duverger's theory of 'development') of the Parliamentary system led to the increase in the number of African political parties. Nevertheless from the point of the view of classification we, along with Duverger, still only move at the level of conditions of the creation of political parties and not how these political parties came into existence.

the organization of the *founding election*,[51] but the incidence of other critical situations (collapse of the constitutional system) usually leads to civil wars. See, e.g., the latest developments in Somalia, the Democratic Republic Congo, and Ivory Coast and, in the past, in many other countries, where a crisis of the constitutional system brought about military regimes.[52] Similarly there no help can be found in the modernization theory based on some social and economic factors in the origin of the parties because this is again turning to the causes rather than the birth itself of the parties.

As stated above, this is the first classification of this type. It could be tested by further analyses and eventually corrected or expanded to include other types of development of the parties in Africa. Experience from the foundation of parties in Asia, Latin America and Europe shows that a similar classification could be applied to their political parties.

Principal Theoretical Models for the Development of Political Organizations

- Transformation of Non-political Organizations into Proto-political/Political Parties
- Transformation of Proto-political Parties into Political Parties
- Transformation of Congresses and Fronts into Political Parties
- Detaching a Political Party from a Congress or Front

Integration of Non-political and Political Organizations

- Integration on the Basis of Individual Persons (usually intellectuals sharing an ideology)
- Integration of Special Interest and Pressure Groups into a Proto-political / Political party
- Integration of Special Interest and Pressure Groups and Proto-political Parties into Political Parties
- Integration of Political Parties
- Joining of Special Interest and Pressure Groups, Proto-political and Political Parties to Another Political Party

Disintegration of Political Organizations

- Disintegration of Congresses, Fronts and Political Parties
- Splitting Off from Congresses, Fronts and Political Parties

---

[51] This is the case of the first Parliamentary election following the gain of political independence, often under the supervision of the former colonial power or the U.S. Compare, for example, Bratton and Van de Walle 1997: 114–116.

[52] We will allow ourselves here one provocative statement that in a number of cases of the introduction of military regime was the only way how to renew laws, rights and safety in African countries, it often led to the removal of African totalitarian and tyrannical governments. Without these military coups the democratization that followed would have never taken place in a number of countries. I would even go as far as to use, in some cases, the controversial term: democratic military coups.

Political Parties Established by Decree

- By a Decree Issued by a Totalitarian/Authoritative/Authoritarian Group (mostly army representatives who want to strengthen the legitimacy of political power after a military coup)
- By a Central Decision about the "Transformation" of Fronts and Congresses into Political Parties

Foundation of Political Parties by an External Impetus

- By a Decision of the Colonial Government, Foundation of the 'Administrative Political Party'
- Foundation of Political Parties as Branches of Metropolitan Political Parties (usually African socialist or communist parties, etc.)
- Development of Political Parties under the Influence of a Global Policy (e.g., environmental parties)

At first sight our criterion and our classification does not seem to have any scientific value. The principal question is how the models of the development of parties can help in the identification of the role, position and functioning of political parties and party organs? In my opinion, scientific research on these models can be based on the following arguments:

Historical Arguments

From the aspect of the history of society the manner of the development of a political party and the generalization of these models is of the same importance as the study of all the other aspects of the activities of political parties. The main objective is a detailed knowledge of a concrete historical phenomenon and its generalization for the subsequent political science research.

Sociological Arguments

The manner of the foundation of a political party usually depends on individuals (politicians, major personalities in the society) or groups (political, economic and cultural elites, the military, feudal circles, party factions and various social and national-ethnic groups, etc.). The model can tell a great deal when it is based on the wide consensus of various social groups or, on the other hand, it may be an outcome of a decision made by an individual person or a small power group. The detailed knowledge of the mechanism of the origin then predetermines the position and role of those individuals, elite groups or other social groups within a political party, can incline toward the installation of a charismatic leader – founder, can represent oligarchic tendencies of an elite group or can bring balanced decisions made by various social groups into the power structure of political parties.

Political Science Arguments

For political science, models for the development of political parties are not only a technical matter. Each model has encoded the causes (personal, ideological, power, etc.), which are often reflected in the subsequent structure of membership (oriented toward various social, national or ethnic groups) and organization (centralized, decentralized, local, national, etc.) of political parties, ideologies, activities, goals, etc. The manner of the foundation can directly influence the inner party non-democratic mechanisms or behaviour within the party system. There are no doubts about the influence on the coalition potential. The parties that arose, e.g., through disintegration (collapse, splitting-off), usually cannot find enough room for political consensus, especially when the cause of disintegration was personal, ideological or ethnic.

Our classification need not cover all models for the foundation of the parties and should presently be regarded as a as working hypothesis, which has to be confirmed by further research. Each of the types of the development has many variants in the political practice of sub-Saharan countries and often it is not easy to identify the type exactly. It is for instance difficult to subdivide variant Detaching a Party from a Congress or Front and Central Decision about the 'Transformation' of Fronts and Congresses into Political Parties. Were the Party-Front for the Liberation of Mozambique (Partido FRELIMO) and the People's Movement for the Liberation of Angola – Labour Party (MPLA-Partido Trabalho) formed in the first or the second way?

Similarly it will be very difficult to say when some changes took place, especially in types of the first category. Is a proclamation of the leaders about the transformation of a front/movement into a political party sufficient or is it a long-term process during which it is necessary to study changes in the party documents, especially the programmes, to see what role is played by ideology, how the change is reflected in the organization and membership structure (number of members, social distribution) and especially whether the practical activity of the party corresponds to the original proclamations or whether only after the confirmation of this transformation one can speak of a new type of the party. In the next subchapters we shall deal with the classic cases of the foundation of an African party, especially in Lusophone Africa.

2. Transformation of Non-political and Political Organizations

The process of transformation of cultural, educational, student and other organizations was fairly common in Africa, especially in the post-WWII period. Obviously in each African country varieties of this evolution can be found. *Action Group* was established in Nigeria in 1951; the beginnings of its organization were linked with the cultural Yoruba organization *Egbe Omo Oduduwa*, which was historically linked with the *Nigerian Youth Movement* (Sklar 2004:101–103). Students from the *Nigerian Union of Students* had a share in the foundation of the *National Council for Nigeria and the Cameroons*, established as an organization of the congress type in 1944 (Sklar 2004: 55–57). At first a northern cultural organization, the *Northern People's Congress* (NPC) was established in 1949, which in October 1951 turned into a political party (Sklar 2004:93–96).

Many similar cases may be found in Lusophone Africa. Transformation of non-political organizations into proto-political or political parties took place mainly in Angola and Mozambique in the interwar period and in the 1940s and 1950s. For example, the student organization *Núcleo dos Estudantes do Moçambique* stood at the birth of the political organization National Union of Mozambique Students (*União Nacional dos Estudantes do Moçambique* – UNEMO), and many of them later took part in the foundation of the FRELIMO (Mondlane 1969: 114).

The transformation of the amorphous Committee for the liberation of St. Thomas and Prince Islands (*Comité de Libertação de São Tomé e Príncipe* – CLTSP) into the Movement for the Liberation of St. Thomas and Prince Islands (Movimento de Libertação de São Tomé e Príncipe – MLSTP) are also in this category. Transformation of proto-political parties in Lusophone countries is less frequent but it includes the transformation of the St. Thomas People's Alliance (*Aliança Popular* – AP) into the St. Thomas Labour Party and the Christian Democratic Front (*Frente Democrata Cristão* – FDC) into the FDC – Party of Social Unification, and the Reflex Group into the Party of Democratic Convergence *(Partido de Convergęncia Democrática* – PCD-GR).[53]

The history of the *Partido da Luta Unida dos Africanos de Angola* – PLUA, one of the four political organizations that in 1956 stood at the birth of the MPLA, is connected with the cultural organization *Angola Negra a Comissão de Luta das Juventudes contra o Imperialismo Colonial em Angola* (Chilcote 1973: xxxiv).

Transformation of congresses and fronts into political parties is quite common in Lusophone Africa when we include the transformation of the national liberation fronts FRELIMO, PAIGC, PAICV, MLSTP and MPLA into political parties. In some of these movements it is difficult to specify the date of the transformation even though some of them tried to reflect this change in a change of their name (e.g., MPLA- Labour Party, Party FRELIMO and MLSTP – Social Democratic Party).

David Apter, a foremost specialist in Ghana, linked the roots of the parties in Ghana with ethnic fractions and pressure groups from 1870–1940. In his generalized conclusion he differentiated four main groups: ethnic associations, e.g., *Fanti Confederacy*, protective associations such as *Aborigines' Rights Protection Society*, the so-called progressive associations and clubs, such as the *Young Men's Free Mutual Improvement Society* and literature and discussion clubs, as *Achimota Conferences* (Coleman and Rosberg 1967: 261).

Transformation of cultural, educational, student, trade union and other organizations into political organizations was very common in Africa. As in many European countries it is linked with the growth of nationalism and renaissance of African culture, even though this process is not limited to the period before achieving political independence.

---

[53] Another transformation from PCD-GR into PCD only had the character of simplifying the name of the party.

3. Integration of Non-political and Political Organizations

The second integration variant appears to be without problems but even here we face a lack of information and sources on the practical steps taken during the development of the parties after their usually proclamative statements of the foundation of these parties by way of integration of individuals, pressure and special-purpose groups, proto-political parties, movements, fronts and political parties. Unlike the dating in the preceding cases, here the official proclamation of the creation of a political party is accepted as point zero. Some variants are difficult to prove (e.g., II.3 integration of proto-political parties in a political party).

The history of African parties contains many instances of integration of various political organizations. Hodgkin gives several examples, e.g., the formation of the *Ghana Congress Party - GCP*, which arose by unification of the remaining part of the *United Gold Coast Convention* – UGCC, the conservative National Democratic Party and the group of 'rebels' from the *Convention People's Party* – CPP. GCP never became a mass party and in 1954 for practical reasons it merged with the *National Liberation Movement* –NLM. When, however, the CPP government banned ethnic and regional parties, NLM merged with the *Moslem Assication Party, Northern People's Party* and *Togoland Congress* in October 1957, which gave rise to the *United Party*. (Hodgkin 1961:56) This example demonstrates how one political party within three years (1954–1957) underwent three integration processes, each having its own specific character.

Another example of the development of a party by integration of special interest and pressure groups and proto-political parties is the *Parti Démocratique de la Côte d'Ivoire* (PDCI), established in April 1946, which gradually became the dominant political party in Ivory Coast.[54] PDCI was formed when the proto-political party *Bloc Africain*[55] merged with the *Syndicat Agricole Africain*, which defended interests of small African owners of cocoa and coffee plantations (Zolberg 1969:68–77).[56] PDCI is another example of the merging model because in 1960 it swallowed most opposition parties while the rest were forced by the Government of this one-party to terminate their official activities.

Most St. Thomas parties established after the introduction of the multi-party system in the 1990s are based on integration of major politicians most of whom left the ruling

---

[54] PDCI became the only reigning party in Ivory Coast after gaining independence in 1960 and its Chairman Félix Houphouët-Boigny became the President for Life (he died in 1993.) Compare, for example, Le Vine 2004:.206–213.

[55] *Bloc Africain* (a party by the same title existed in Senegal) was created in August 1945 in Abidjan and it unified the local educated Africans supporting democracy (Morgenthau 1964:182). This was in its essence an antipolitical party with a narrow circle of members with a nationalist program.

[56] The agricultural organization *Syndicat Agricole Africain* (SAA) was created in September 1944 with Félix Houphouët-Boigny in its lead. The SAA defended the interests of African growers vis-f-vis French competitors (Zolberg 1966: 66–67). We have to refuse Le Vine's claim that the SAA was at its birth a political party. Compare Le Vine 2004: 207.

MLTSP. In this way, e.g., the People's Alliance (Aliança Popular – AP), the Independent Democratic Action (*Acção Democrática Independente* – ADI), the National Union for Democracy and Progress (*União Nacional para a Democracia e o Progresso* - UNDP), headed by Abubacar Baldé, Party for the Restoration of Democracy (*Partido da Renovação Democrática* - PRD) and the National Progressive Party (Partido Popular do Progresso – PPP) were formed.

Otherwise, in Lusophone Africa relatively few instances may be found of the foundation of a party by integration of special interest and pressure groups and proto-political parties. Among their examples are the Coalition of the Democratic Opposition (*Coligação Democrática da Oposição* – CODO), formed by the merging of the National Front of Resistance in St. Thomas and Prince Islands (*Frente de Resistência Nacional de Sâo Tomé e Príncipe* – FRNSTP), the League for Democracy and Independence of St. Thomas and Prince Islands (*União Democrática e Independente de Sâo Tomé e Príncipe* – UDISTP) and the National Democratic Action (*Acção Democrática Nacional de Sâo Tomé e Príncipe* – ADNSTP), because all three organizations were pressure groups rather than political parties.

FRELIMO should be included in this group, which arose by the merging of three political organizations, the Mozambique National Democratic Union (*União Nacional Democrática de Moçambique* – UDENAMO), the Mozambique African National Union (*Mozambique African National Union* - MANU) and the African Union for Independent Mozambique (*União Africana de Moçambique Independente* – UNAMI). From the theoretical aspect it is interesting to watch the establishment of the MANU, created in February 1961 in Mombassa in Kenya by a merging of several Makonde cultural and self-help organizations with the Tanganyika Mozambique Makonde Union (*Tanganyika Mozambique Makonde Union* – TMMU) (Marcum 1968: 196–197).

The foundation of the People's Movement for the Liberation of Angola (MPLA) is no exception, where, as Marcum says, four minor political organizations merged, i.e. *Partido da Luta Unida dos Africanos de Angola* – PLUA, *Partido Comunista Angolano* (PCA), *Movimento de Libertação Nacional* (MLN) and *Movimento de Libertação de Angola* (MLA) (Marcum 1969: 28-30). A similar process of unification was undergone by the *Front pour la Libération de l'Enclave de Cabinda* (FLEC), which united three organizations: *Comité d'Action d'Union Nationale des Cabindes* (CAUNC), *Alliance de Mayombe* (ALLIAMA) and the *Mouvement pour la Libération de l'Enclave de Cabinda* (MLEC) (Chilcote 1973:593).

Many instances of integration may also be found in Nigeria. In R. L. Sklar's book, *Nigerian Political Parties,* a great many are mentioned. One example is the United Middle Belt Congress, established in 1955 by the merging of the conservative Middle Zone League and the radical Middle Belt People's Party (Sklar 2004:346–347).

Integration of political organizations is obviously the most frequent form of the creation of political parties in Africa (like the disintegration discussed below). Various historical cases reveal that integration can have several political reasons. The most frequent one is integration of small opposition parties to stand up to the dominant large national party. No exception, however, is a complete integration of the majority of political organizations in a particular country, often with the aim of creating national unity in the period of the struggle for political independence. Integration is frequent between a big dominant party and a minor party, which represents an ethnic section of the population, with the aim of achieving representation of various sections of the population and thus enhances its legitimacy.

4. Disintegration of Political Organizations

The third disintegration variant seems to be without problem. Congresses, fronts and political parties can break up into several new political groups. This variant appears very frequent when from an existing political organization a fraction splits off to found its own party, often with a similar programme and ideology. Another frequent cause of disintegration is a conflict between the radical and the conservative wings. In this way the *Convention People's Party* (CPP) was founded in Ghana, which seceded from the *United Gold Coast Convention* (Coleman and Rosberg 1967:273). Later a radical group seceded from the CPP and founded the *National Liberation Movement*.[57] Similarly, from the *Nacional Council of Nigeria and Cameroons* (NCNC) in 1953 a group of expelled ministers seceded to found their own party, the *National Independence Party* (later renamed to *United National Independence Party* - UNIP) (Sklar 2004:124). In Sierra-Leone from the dominant *Sierra Leone People's Party* (SLPP) two fractions seceded and later founded the parties *United Progressive Party* and *People's National Party* (Hodgkin 1961:55).

Quite common in Lusophone countries is the seceding of individuals and fractions from congresses, fronts and political parties. For example, on St. Thomas and Prince Islands the disintegration model is fairly popular and common in political practice. In this way the Christian Democratic Front (*Frente Democrata Cristão* – FDC) was established, which seceded from the National Front of Resistance on St. Thomas and Prince Islands *(Frente de Resistência Nacional de São Tomé e Príncipe* – FRNSTP). The Movement of Democratic Forces for Change (*Movimento Democrático Força da Mudança* – MDFM) took the same road when the chairman of the Independent Democratic Action (*Acção Democrática Independente* – ADI) Carlos Neves left this party with several of his supporters and founded the MDFM. In 1962 FRELIMO underwent the same process when the original founding organization MANU seceded from it, and in 1963 a fraction seceded to establish the party UDENAMO-Moçambique.

Similarly, various secessionists from the ruling Movement for the Liberation of St. Thomas and Prince's Island (MLSTP) gradually founded political parties, which in the end

---

[57] A very detailed description of the Ghana's political parties formation is found in Apter 1955, in particular chapters 9 to 14.

found a firm place in the party system on St. Thomas and Prince's Island. This is certainly the case of the Party for Democratic Convergence (*Partido de Convergencia Democrática –* PCD-GR) and the ADI (the party of the founder of MLSTP, M. Trovoady). In the birth of other political parties, such as FRNSTP, People's Alliance (*Aliança Popular –* AP) and the National Progressive Party (*Partido Popular do Progresso –* PPP), many former high representatives of the MLSTP can be found.

Disintegration as a model for the establishment of political parties is very frequent in other Lusophone countries as well, and it holds in general that it is highly represented in other African countries.

5. Ordering of Political Parties by Decree

Some problems with the fourth variant were already indicated above, where it was shown that the decisive force in the foundation of a party by a central decree need not always be the military but a traditional tribal or royal authority (e.g., Swaziland). Still the most important model cases are associated with the military trying to make its power legitimate and further strengthen it.

A classical example is the formation of the *Worker's Party of Ethiopia –* WPE, behind which was the military government of Mengistu Haile Mariam. The Ethiopian army, which in 1974 carried out a national democratic revolution and dethroned Emperor Haile Sellasie, at first did not think of establishing a political party but during that year the army became differentiated, with the result that Derg's[58] position and the legitimacy of the army became weaker in Ethiopia. The decision to establish a political party was linked to the effort of involving the population in politics and in the end to stabilize the power of the army.

In 1977 Mengistu Haile Mariam as chairman of the Derg announced that the core of the future party would be five unofficial political organizations, which previously took part in the Ethiopian revolution jointly with the army. After this decision, in June 1977 the Union of Ethiopian Marxist-Leninist Organizations (UEMLO) was formed, the basis of which were the organizations Revolutionary Blaze, Workers' League, Marxist-Leninist Revolutionary Organization and the Pan-Ethiopian Socialist Movement (Irchin 1981:136). This attempt to establish a united party by a decree failed in the late 1970s due to differences in opinions between the groups (Fiala 1986: 84–89).

The failure of the UEMLO made Mengistu Haile Mariam decide to create a *Committee to Organise the Party of the Workers of Ethiopia -* COPWE), which was to become a school "where its members can gain experience in party work and in practice demonstrate their ability to be a member of the party that is being established" (Fiala 1986: 90). The decree of the provisional military administration council No. 174 of 18 December 1979, "On

---

[58] The temporary military managing/executive council (Derg) was a body comprising of military representatives of all Ethiopian military units.

the establishing of the COPWE", specified the Committee's goals and structure and defined the relation of the COPWE to state organs and social organizations, specified the rights and the authority of the leading organs and the duties of the rank and file members of the COPWE.[59] The constituting congress of the Party of the Workers of Ethiopia (WPE) took place in September 1984 in Addis Ababa with the presence of 1742 delegates from the whole of Ethiopia.[60] In 1969 the Congo Labour Party and in 1975 the Party of the People's Revolution in Benin were established in a similar way.

In Lusophone Africa The process of the development of a political party by a decree issued by authoritarian groups has not occurred. As stated above, controversial remains the transformation of the MPLA into the MPLA-PT and of FRELIMO into the Party FRELIMO, which can be regarded as a culmination of the transformation of a front into a political party rather than by administrative decree.

6. Foundation of African Political Parties by an External Impetus

The modern development of the party system in Africa may make some critics reject this model because they are not sure whether this variant is still topical and relevant. History speaks in favour of keeping this variant for some parties, which are active to this day and have a firm place in the party systems. Experience from French, British and other colonies make us regard this category as an equivalent model variant of the development of political parties in Africa.

Many institutions could have a share in this development: colonial administration, local white population, political parties in big cities, trade unions, churches and religious groups, etc. Hodgkin calls the parties that arose with the support or stimulus of the colonial government 'administrative parties.' Thus, e.g., the French colonial government tried to counterbalance the influence of the interregional *Rassemblement démocratique africain* (RDA), associating African nationalists from most francophone countries in Africa, by founding administrative parties in almost all French colonies.

For example, in Ivory Coast the French colonial government supported as many as five political parties against the local RDA section operating under the name *Parti Démocratique de la Côte d'Ivoire* (PDCI) and headed by Félix Houphouët-Boigny, the later president. Among the ethnic group of the Baulé an opposition to the PDCI was formed by the *Union des Indépendants de la Côte d'Ivoire*, the party active among Muslims was *Entente des Indépendants de la Côte d'Ivoire*, with Sékou Sanogo at the head, in the southern part of the country the party called *Bloc Démocratique Eburnéen* became active while led by Senator Djaument. Two more parties existed from 1946: Progressists among the

---

[59] The Ethiopian Herald, 19 December, 1979.

[60] To the incessant power control of the COPWE testifies also to the fact that 79 from 123 members of the central committee of the COPWE were soldiers or police officers. The members of the Derg controlled the main administrative posts of the Ethiopian public administration (12 out of 14 main regional officers were members of the Derg), the ministries and regional administration (cf. Salih 2004: 22-24).

Agni, and Socialists among the Bété (Morgenthau 1964: 188). In Chad the party *Union Démocratique Tchadienne* had a similar role. The British colonial administration supported moderate parties, e.g., the *Northern People's Party* in northern Ghana, and the *Northern People's Congress* in northern Nigeria.

Besides the administrative parties there were parties established with the assistance of the Church: the Roman Catholic *Democratic Party* in Uganda and the *Liberal Party* in Sudan (Hodgkin 1961:60-61). Another type, co-founded in the colonies by European settlers, is political multi-national party. One example is the *United Tanganyika Party*, alleged to have had 10,000 members, of which two thirds were Africans.

The last category is political parties, at the birth of which stood big city parties, especially Socialist parties. That is the origin of the *Section Française de l'Internationale Ouvričre* (SFIO) in Senegal. In literature, RDA is regarded as an African movement with roots in African society, but in practice until the end of 1950 it was closely linked with the French Communists (Le Vine 2004:76–77).

Moreover it is easy to imagine that there may be (or has been) an 'export' of some global themes (e.g., ecology) to Africa and this is then reflected in the development of ecological movements and later ecological parties.

The foundation of political parties by an external impulse is not clear in the former Portuguese colonies even though some parties established before independence could have that character. With the exception of the Communist Party of Angola we are unable to document the influence of Portuguese (East European) communists or socialists on the launch of political parties in Portuguese colonies.[61]

As the more or less random cases from several African countries quoted above show, both the past and the present political practice in Africa brings hundreds of instances of various models for development of parties. African studies and general political science face a major task to devise their exact classification.

At present there are many fundamental theoretical works on the formation of African parties (Hodgkin 1961; Segal 1961; Carter 1962; Morgenthau 1964; Coleman and Rosberg 1966; Zolberg 1966; Solodovnikov 1970; Randal 1988; Olukoshi 1998; Salih 2004; Le Vine 2004 and many more) and numerous detailed studies for each country (Apter 1961, 1963; Sklar 2004; Coleman 1958; Le Vine 1964; Zolberg 1966; Marcum 1969 ; 1978, etc.). Most of these studies, however, analyse the formation of political organizations before the countries achieved political independence or from the period following soon afterwards. For the period of the democratisation of African states after

---

[61] We will leave out the indisputable influence of the USSR on the creation of the so-called avantguard parties of the workers (ASP) in Angola and Mozambique, which is very difficult to prove. The Angolan and Mozambique revolutionary democrats studied with interest the activities of the Eastern European Communist parties and the creation of the ASP was to be the first step towards the building of similar Marxist-Leninist parties in their countries. Compare, for example, Zotov 1985.

1990, no detailed analyses of the development of new parties have been available so far.[62] Since in many African countries up to four democratic elections were held in the past 20 years, it is possible to concentrate on the study of the formation of party systems.

Conclusion and the Future Tasks of Political Science

The above classification should be regarded as a working conception. It has to be confirmed by further analyses of the origin of African parties and thus supplemented or altered in order to generalize the majority of variants found in Africa. It cannot be a mechanical analysis, which would focus on technical issues in the development of political organizations. It is absolutely necessary to examine the causes and reasons for the formation of the parties. Besides traditional causes, such as the struggle for national liberation and independence, the struggle for political power and others, scholars should concentrate on the specific features of African society. Great attention should be paid to the social structure of African society, in particular to the issue of how a traditional African society reflects the political organizations, but also what are the ethnic, tribal and religious influences.

In Africa, unlike in Europe and America, there is a much stronger influence by charismatic political personalities and various ideological conceptions of African nationalism and African Socialism. Since the development of African parties took place especially during the Cold War, African Studies and political science will have to consider the effect of outside factors.

Very difficult issues will have to be dealt with in connection with the fact that after gaining political independence, the majority of African countries passed to the stage of the *one-party state*, which undoubtedly influenced the party systems in Africa. It is possible to deliberate about a parallel with the stage of the colonial period, and political scientists should study in depth whether within the *one-party state* the initial stages of the formation of political organizations were repeated, i.e., whether cultural and social organizations, movements and illegal proto-political parties developed, which after the introduction of a multi-party system were transformed into political parties. Scores of parties turned up during the third wave of democratisation in the early 1990s in various countries and they did not rise of their own accord; instead they have roots in the one-party state system and most probably reflect the subdued existence and activity of various political fractions in the ruling mass political parties.

Another step to be taken by political scientists is a comparison of the development of African political parties with their counterparts in the underdeveloped world (Asia and Latin America) and with parties in Europe and America. In this way political science

---

[62] In this context we can draw attention to several more significant periodical studies in Party Politics, Journal of Democracy, Journal of Modern African Studies, African Affairs, etc. See the literature list. The works of Salih 2002 and Le Vine 2004 are the first more serious attempts at generalizing the creation and development of political parties in the last 15 years.

should return to the general theory of the formation of parties and include in it the theory of the formation of parties in the underdeveloped world.

This short analysis of the theory of the formation of parties shows that now we no longer can do with the theoretical conclusions of M. Duverger, J. Blondel, G. Sartori, A. Ware and other political scientists who specialize in the study of political parties. Of course they can help to start our research, but the vast amount of, as yet, uninvestigated and ungeneralized facts and data on the origin, development and functions of political parties in the underdeveloped world makes us inspect the theory of parties from the viewpoint of these regions.

Some of the earlier basic postulates of the theory of parties may stand their ground in this confrontation, though more likely there is the need of a theoretical modification, "opening" or expansion of some of the existing definitions so that they could be applied to theoretical examples from the underdeveloped world.

These tasks are time consuming,[63] and especially as methodology is concerned, because political scientists will have to consider in greater depth the specificity of the historical development of each country, its ethnic and social structure, the level of social development and relations between social groups, and many more factors that make the underdeveloped world different from the Euro-American civilization.

---

[63] For a number of African, Asian and partially also Latin American countries at present there is a lack of quality analysis of political parties and party systems of individual countries, which could become the basis for appropriate comparisons. One of the first most important steps is creating detailed territorial bibliographies, which will include publications and articles about political parties and party systems. The main aim of these territorial bibliographies is to indicate the gaps in the research of political parties and party systems in developing countries or insufficient basic researches.

SELECTION OF CANDIDATES IN THE MAIN POLITICAL PARTIES OF GHANA[64]

Jan Prouza
University of Hradec Králové

Introduction

Political parties form an integral part of a representative model of democracy, because they organise elections and in accordance with the electoral results the parties then recruit members of representative bodies. Elections in this manner give citizens, via the free competition of political parties, the opportunity of political participation (even if it is limited, as we will mention below) and are therefore without a doubt the basis of democracy.

Consequently, if elections form the basis of democracy, then their preparation is an essential function in the life of political parties (Katz 2001: 277). They enter elections with certain candidates and with certain programs through which they try to aggregate the interests of the majority of citizens – and therefore voters. Whilst parties' programs are a matter of rather normative or declarative character and their (non)compliance depends on a range of other circumstances, lists of candidates serve as factual and concrete outputs of political parties, which in itself mirror both tendencies and preferences inside parties and also the preferences of their voters.

Simply put, if a party wins an election, it must put together an appealing electoral program for voters and select suitable candidates for its presentation (both are influenced by the financial possibilities of each party). But according to what kind of method does this selection of candidates take place? Who is included in this selection process and on the contrary who is eliminated from it? If we project these questions into the context of an election, we find out that their answers can provide us with information about the level of the intraparty's democracy. Because our electoral preferences during an election are limited only to pre-selected candidates, which means, that we vote from a selection that was made by individual parties over which we have no influence unless we are party members.

However, do at all ordinary party members have a real opportunity to influence the selection of candidates? Where does the real crux of the matter of decision-making about the composition of the Legislature and the Executive lie?

The submitted chapter focuses on the issue of the selection of candidates for the presidential and the parliamentary elections in Ghana because this country is largely perceived as a „microcosm of social, political and economical processes in Africa. Ghana's predisposition to experimenting transformed Ghana into a real laboratory for

---

[64] This chapter is a result of the research supported by Grant Agency of Czech Republic, project „Political Parties in Africa, Asia, Latin America and Oceania", no. 407/09/0387.

the testing of distinct approaches to endemic African problems " (Pellow and Chazan 1986: 209–210). The subject matter of our analysis is the two main political parties of Ghana – the *National Democratic Congress* (NDC) and the *New Patriotic Party* (NPP). During the Fourth Republic of Ghana both political parties alternate in power and the selection of their candidates is thus crucial for the occupancy of posts within the Legislature and the Executive.

The text is divided into four main chapters – the first chapter foreshadows the contextual framework of the party and electoral system in Ghana. The second chapter then describes the selection process of candidates which the third chapter subsequently analyses and compares within the scope of both researched parties. The findings of this analysis are summarized in the final chapter which we use to verify our research hypothesis:

H1: *The more Members of Parliament (M.P.s) a party has got, the more closed its selection process will be and the less M.P.s a party has got, the more open its selection process will be.*

Because of the separation of elections for the Executive and the Legislature, it is theoretically possible that one party wins the parliamentary (legislative) election, whereas the other party wins the presidential (executive) election. In practice however it has never happened, and therefore we consider the strongest party in the Parliament to be the governing party and the other party to be the opposition.

A governing party is under more pressure in terms of its cohesiveness – the party must vote and act as unanimously as possible so that it is able to fulfil its program. Primaries, if not otherwise monitored by the party leadership, can lead to the creation of a double loyalty for M.P.s, whereby the local party is more important to them than the central party, and that is why governing parties try to select candidates more exclusively and with regard to their future loyalty to the Government.

This hypothesis applies to two aspects – (1) the issue of loyalty of M.P.s who are dependent on a process through which they were selected; and (2) whether parties try by means of a greater openness and democratic nature in the selection of candidates to increase its chances of winning the next election. These two aspects do not differ in independent and interchangeable values (the first operates with possibilities: Government versus Opposition, the second with possibilities: Winner versus Loser), but in point of view – whilst the first one is concerned with the governing party, the second one is concerned with the strongest[65] opposition party.

H2: *The more a party claims a left-wing focus, the more decentralised a form of selection of candidates it uses.*

---

[65] Only with this strongest opposition party it is likely that it was in power in the past and that consequently by reason of defeat, that brought it into opposition, it aims to strenghten the openness of candidates in order to win government opposition again.

This hypothesis takes into consideration the influence of the ideology of candidates, and assumes that left-wing ideology puts greater emphasis on controlled decentralisation of the selection of candidates (especially with regard to women) than the right wing, which prefers free competition among candidates.

H3: *The greater party continuity with the previous non-democratic regime, the lesser intraparty democracy.*

The third hypothesis assumes a relationship between the creation of a party and the level of its internal democracy. Parties with a great level of personal continuity with a previous non-democratic regime are threatened by the tendencies of its leaders to use the same practices used during the previous non-democratic regime, despite having new constitutional and legislative measures of a democratic character. This hypothesis is in a larger sense concerned with whether a party can, within the scope of a democratic system, keep a non-democratic character, or whether the strengthening of democratic institutions and the trust of its citizens in democracy will lead to its democratization.

The main research method of this work is an analysis of the pertinent literature, documents of the two political parties and interviews with their representatives that were acquired during our stay in Ghana. We subsequently applied the analytical framework of Gideon Rahat and Reuven Y. Hazan to the conclusions of this analysis. The essence of their analytical framework forms four questions: (1) *Who can be selected?* (2) *Who does select candidates?* (3) *How are candidates nominated?* (4) *Where are candidates selected?* Answers to the first three questions are then transferred to the axis, its opposite poles are *inclusiveness* („*openness*" – a situation when all citizens participate in the selection process) and *exclusiveness* („*exclusiveness*" – the opposite situation when only party members participate in the selection process, and have to follow other conditions and restrictions). Answers to the last question are placed on the axis with poles of *centralisation* and *decentralisation*. Under this dimension the authors further differentiate two levels of analysis: *functional* (concerns itself with (non)representation of social groups and sectors in the selection process) and *territorial* (influence of regional and local party organization). Tools that both authors suggested for this analysis are easily applicable to the selection of candidates that takes place in a single-phased and uniform manner (with the same conditions for everyone). In reality however candidates generally face various selective bodies (selectors) and restrictions, different nomination processes or various types of placements on the list of candidates. That's why Rahat and Hazan recommend differentiating complex systems into (1) *mixed methods of selection of candidates* (various candidates are selected by various selectors, according to various restrictions, in various places) and (2) *multilevel methods* (all candidates must face more than one selector). Each complex method should then be simplified, with the help of certain modifications, so that it can be compared with a single-phased and uniform method. That is why the analytical framework of

63

Hazan and Rahat enables us to compare various systems for the selection of candidates (on a national and international level), without any considerable distortions.

1. Contextual framework

The Constitution of the Fourth Republic introduced a presidential system following the American model, which it supplemented with elements of a Westminster system, and in many respects originated a problematic hybrid, its greatest weakness being insufficient separation of the executive and the legislative branches.

The highest executive power is a directly elected President, who for her/his election must obtain an absolute majority of votes. If none of the candidates gets 50 % plus one vote in the first round, a second round takes place, in which Presidency is contested by the two most successful candidates from the first round. In accordance with Article 62, the criteria for becoming President are (1) must be a native citizen of Ghana, (2) is over 40 years old, (3) fulfils the rest of the eligibility criteria for members of Parliament. Article 64 further specifies a limit of a maximum of two electoral terms of four years. Following her/his election the President appoints members of the Cabinet that serve the President as an advisory body. Overall the system resembles a presidential model, but on the other hand more than half of the Ministers must come from the Parliament which must also approve every appointed Minister. This weakens the role of the President (Article 78 of Ghana's Constitution).

The legislative power is made up of a single chamber Parliament, which currently consists of 230 M.P.s[66] elected for four years. M.P.s are elected in single-mandate constituencies by a simple majority election (Article 50 of Ghana's Constitution). The eligibility conditions set out in Article 94 of the Constitution are as follows: a candidate can only be (1) a Ghana's citizen over 21 years of age who is a registered voter, who has (2) reported permanent stay in the constituency for which he/she runs; or has been residing there for a period of at least 5 years in the last 10 years preceding the election, in which he/she runs; or must originate from that constituency; and who (3) has dutifully paid all taxes or undertook appropriate steps satisfactory to the relevant bodies for the payment of all taxes. A parliamentary mandate is not restricted by a maximum number of terms, unlike the presidential one. The focus of the parliamentary power lies in the legislative activity, because every law and amendment must pass through the Parliament. In addition it is also concerned with drafting the budget and appointments to high posts (in accordance with Articles 76, 82 and 155 of Ghana's Constitution).

The legislative framework of political parties is defined (1) in common protective provisions on the freedom of assembly; (2) in Article 55 of the Constitution and (3) in Act 574 regarding political parties (*Political Parties Act of 2000*).

---

[66] The number of M.P.s is dependent on the population of Ghana, which since independence (1957) is continuosly growing. That is why in the year 2004 the number of M.P.s increased from 200 to 230.

Criteria for the registration of political parties is also defined in Article 55 paragraph 7 of the Constitution, in accordance with which every party that wants to be registered must first provide a copy of its Statutes with names and addresses of its national representatives to the Electoral Commission. It must also convince the Electoral Commission that it fulfils the following conditions:

1) in every constituency there is at least one citizen (or there registered voter), who belongs to the founding party members;
2) the party has got branches in every region of Ghana and furthermore has got its organizations in at least two thirds of its constituencies;
3) the name, emblem, colour, motto or other party symbol has not got any ethnic, regional, religious or particularistic meaning („sectarian connotation") or shows in any other way that its activities and interests are restricted only to a particular part of Ghana.

By these provisions the Constitution tries to prevent the establishment of ethnic-regional parties. Although this system means the parties are *de jure* nationwide and non-ethnic, *de facto* it is not so. This is not only due to the behaviour of some representatives of political parties, but mainly because of the perception and attitudes of the average citizen, above all the part of the population that is illitrate.

The Constitution and Act 574 also states that political parties must fulfil the conditions of internal democracy, specifically Article 55 paragraph 5 of the Constitution states: "The internal organization of a political party shall conform to democratic principles and its actions and purposes shall not contravene or be inconsistent with this constitution or any other law." (Article 55, pararaph 5 of the 1992 Constitution).

In agreement with the Constitution, Act 574 regarding political parties in section 9 states as follows: "The Electoral Commission shall not register a political party under this Act unless the internal organization of the party conforms to democratic principles and its actions and purposes are not contrary to or inconsistent with the constitution." (Act 574 regarding political parties from the year 2000: chapter 9).

Nevertheless, the reality is often different. Above all the question that raises the maximum dissatisfaction concerning the selection process of candidates among ordinary party members and even more among unsuccessful applicants for candidacy is that their failure does not derive from an election defeat but from a decision by the party leadership. This happened for example in 2000, when the NDC decided not to hold primaries[67] and to support the mandate of the incumbent M.P.s instead (for more see Nugent 2001); or in the NPP in 2004 when accusations of corruption and plotting took place due to the influx of careerist people into the then governing NPP Party (The Open Society Initiative for West Africa and AfriMap 2007: 79).

---

[67] The selection of candidates in the NDC and NPP is classified by the parties as *primaries*, although in the strict sense of the word they cannot be called primaries, because candidates select delegates and not ordinary party members.

2. Parliamentary elections
2.1 Characteristics of the selection of parliamentary candidates
National Democratic Congress (NDC)

The selection of candidates in the NDC went through a number of changes. Although not too many sources exist about the selection process for the first election in 1992, it is possible to assume that in the view of the political-cultural setting and the way by which the NDC originated (by transformation from the military Provisional National Defennce Council), the selection process took place under the control of the Central Office. Until that time, the military were interested in staying in power even under the conditions of an emerging democracy. The character of this first Parliament could be described as a „rubber stamp", meaning that it only passed governmental proposals, more accurately those of the President J. J. Rawlings. On the other hand, thanks to the opposition's boycott of the election, the NDC had a 94 % mandate and amongst such a high number of M.P.s there were logically a number of rebellious M.P.s, who were more loyal towards their constituencies than towards the Central Office. As it appeared, their number was not negligible, and so the Parliament immediately placed a veto on Rawling's six proposals to the Ministers (Lindberg 2008: 9).

For the second election (1996), the NDC decided to transfer the selection of candidates to the constituency level (Öhman 2004: 109). A consequence of this was that in many places votes or whole nomination conferences were being bought, which caused protests at the national level (Nugent 2001: 415). The party leadership was also concerned that M.P.s, instead of working in Parliament spent their time in their constituencies, where they carried on campaigning (Öhman 2004: 110). Overall the selection process of candidates for election in 1996 was carried out with the dissatisfaction of the Central Office, which decided to restrict the influence of the constituency organizations and to strengthen its own influence.

Before the third election (2000) the NDC's Central Office decided that instead of primaries it would introduce a new method which would favour the incumbent M.P.s. The Secretary general of the NDC described it as follows „... *a consultative method, that will get appreciation and consensus, because it covers a wider spectrum of opinions than primaries, in which a few of the delegates decide for the majority.* " (The Ghanaian Times, 7th July 2000). The method drew from the experience of the British Labour Party, where M.P.s are appraised before an election, and on the basis of the results of these appraisals they are then either allowed or not allowed to stand as a candidate again. In the case of the NDC, this procedure was carried out by M.P.s alone and in places where the NDC did not dispose of any mandates, then the best candidate was chosen by the party leadership (Öhman 2004: 111). The results of the appraisal method are logically dependent on those who carry out the method. If M.P.s appraise themselves, it is more likely that the results will be influenced by their aspiration to retain a very profitable mandate for herself/himself. The possibility of new faces arriving into the parliamentary system is therefore considerably reduced.

On the other hand many M.P.s were restricted by interference of Natioanl Executive Committee (NEC), which decided to hold primaries in some constituencies (mainly in those, where the NDC faced a strong opposition candidate), to transfer candidates to other constituencies (Nugent 2001: 416), or not to confirm some candidates from primaries or the last election and instead nominate its own candidates. This behaviour of the party's leadership considerably worried some NDC's M.P.s[68] as well as members on a local level, because in practice it allowed them to appoint to a candidate's post whoever they wanted and not to take into account the constituency organizations and members' opinions. The appointment of candidates regardless of the opinion of constituency organizations had a negative effect straight away – firstly it maintained corrupt politicians in office for the next four years and secondly it pointed out a democratic deficit that ruled inside the NDC. Both of these factors then played their role in the NDC's election defeat (Nugent 2001: 407).

From the lost election in 2000, the NDC learnt its lesson, and for the next election in 2004 it incorporated official rules for the selection of candidates in its Constituion. Until then the selection process was defined in such a vague manner that it could apply both to primaries (1996) and to the leadership nomination (2000).

These rules were agreed at a party congress in 2002 and remained valid for the election in 2004 as well as for the election in 2008. On their basis a person can only be accepted for nomination to stand for the NDC if (1) members of this party, who have been its members for (2) more than two years, (3) have paid all their party contributions, (4) are active, and (5) have a good character (Abubakar 2009).

The selection process for candidates in the NDC takes place two years before the election. The setting of a time table depends on the National Executive Committee (NEC), which subsequently announces it to all of the Regional Executive Committees (REC), which in turn announces it to the Constituency Executive Committees (CEC). The CEC then announces it to all of the NDC branches in a constituency, which then start to collect candidate applications.

Applications are then sent back to the CEC, which registers all candidates from its constituency until the moment that the CEC sets as a deadline for the submission of applications. Afterwards, the CEC in conjunction with the REC, creates a special committee for the reassessment and vetoing of applicants and subsequently places a veto on those who do not fulfil the criteria. This first *filter* is followed by a second one that takes place on the national level, because all nominated candidates must be approved by the NEC. In cases where, even after the first filter, there are still doubts

---

[68] Uncertainty is well illustrated by a parliamentary discussion in July 2000, during which the Speaker of Parliament asked those M.P.s who were not nominated for the next election not to despair, because that is a part of a democratic process. Afterwards he noted that even he himself does not know whether he will be a candidate in the next election and so he asked the Majority Leader about his future, which caused laughter in the House of Parliament (The Daily Graphic, 31th July. 2000, cited in Öhman 2004: 113).

about the legitimacy of a certain candidate, the NEC will establish a commission, which will investigate controversial candidatures, and will either definitively approve, or dismiss them (Abubakar 2009, NDC 2002: 38–39).

When nominations and the veto processes are closed, the real selection of candidates starts. This selection begins by the election in **constituency conferences** (CC), in which two deputies from each branch who were elected during a branch assembly, participate. In order for an ordinary member to become a voter, he/she must (1) be a branch member for at least two years, (2) have paid fees and (3) be elected to this post as part of her/his branch. Except these (a) chosen voters, whose total number must not exceed 280, (b) all CEC members; (c) the REC members, who come from a given constituency as well as (d) the NEC members also participate in the selection process (Abubakar 2009).

If after the primaries are completed new doubts arise about the suitability of a candidate, the NEC can again summon an investigation commission. The commission can eliminate a controversial candidate if it proves, that the candidate has a criminal record, had won in the primaries due to unfair practices or other breaches of the election criteria. If this happens the NEC will declare new nominations and a new election in a given constituency.

A new nomination and a new election can be declared by the NEC even in the case when it is shown that a candidate is not able to lead her/his election campaign. This kind of case happened before the last election in 2008 and was caused by the interference of the NEC (i.e. the centre) into the results of primaries in the constituencies. The candidate in question was S. Mensah, who won the primaries but was looking in vain for a sponsor for his campaign. The NEC therefore decided to pay Mensah's expenses for his campaign during the primaries and to open a new round of nominations followed by intraparty election. In these elections the winning candidate was a person who was placed fourth in the initial primaries and whom now unsuccessful Mensah was helping with the election campaign (Abubakar 2009).

New Patriotic Party (NPP)

The selection of candidates in the NPP proceeded with the same principle of a *primary election* in all of the elections during the Fourth Republic as the NDC. In reality, however, we cannot talk about a primary election in the strict sense of the word, because the candidates are being selected by a Conference of Delegates on a constituency level (an *Extraordinary Constituency Delegates Conference – ECDC*).

Before the first election in 1992, the NPP had – much like other opposition parties – only a short time for the preparation of primaries and the election campaign. The selection of candidates proceeded in haste, and accordingly in several constituencies only a single applicant applied for a candidacy (Öhman 2004: 116), who was then approved by the ECDC in accordance with Article 12 paragraph 7 of the NPP's Articles of Association. However, in the end the NPP boycotted the election and thus none of the selected candidates took a seat in parliament.

For the election in 1996, the NPP decided to collaborate in the framework of a pre-election coalition with the *People's Convention Party* (PCP) and to form a joint list. That of course meant that the NPP had to give up some constituencies in favour of the PCP. Difficulties in reaching an agreement between the NPP and the PCP resulted in several lost seats by selecting PCP's candidates in constituencies which were clearly dominated by the NPP, as for example in the Kwaho South constituency. The selection of candidates within the coalition made clear that the leadership cannot effectively intervene in the selection process in all constituencies. The leadership of the NPP and the PCP declared that they would nominate a common candidate for the constituencies. However in some constituencies the local NPP decided to nominate its own candidate, who then competed with the PCP's candidate. This led to a lost seat in the Birim North constituency (Frempong 2007: 147).

In the election of 2000 the NPP stood alone and therefore the scope for the selection of candidates was extended. The NPP was aware that it might win this election (in light of a planned Rawlings' exit), and that is why it recommended the constituencies' selectors to confirm the incumbent M.P.s (Daily Graphic 30th October 1999), who had greater popularity and the means for a succesful campaign. The election took place in the atmosphere of a call for change and the NPP's M.P.s could utilize their longstanding parliamentary criticism to weaken the NDC. Naturally, it was a recommendation that was in some places met with the support of the constituencies' conferences and in other places it did not get support. (Öhman 2004: 120).

In the next election in 2004, the NPP had a real advantage because it had been in power for four years. To be in power is indeed an advantage for an election campaign, on the other hand, it attracts opportunists into the party. As a consequence of this, many accusations of corruption and manipulation of the selection process of candidates and the dissatisfaction of ordinary members and unsuccessful candidates appeared that weakened the party. For these reasons three M.P.s, who lost in controversial primaries, left the NPP, and became independent. In the next election however they did not defend their mandate (The Open Society Initiative for West Africa and AfriMap 2007: 79). Similar problems were faced by the NPP in the last election in 2008, when the buying of votes and other unfair practices in the primary election used to happen. As a consequence of this, the NPP's leadership decided to reform the process and to bring it closer to the ordinary members by means of introducing *closed primaries*, primaries for which all party members select candidates. The public relations officer of the NPP Kwabena Essem stated, „to bribe 40 to 100 voters is possible, but to bribe around 40.000 voters, therefore all members off the NPP in a constituency, that's impossible. " (Essem 2009). The NPP will decide about the reform of primaries during a National conference of delegates at the end of May 2009 and hence its form at the time of writing this chapter is not known. Therefore we will concentrate on the description of the current selection procedure of candidates for the parliamentary elections, according to which candidates were selected for all elections held in the Fourth Republic.

Candidates for the NPP must be members of the party, who fulfil the criteria set out in the Constitution and the NPP's Articles of Association which make a candidacy conditional upon (1) two-years service in the NPP (there is an internal party discussion about the meaning of „service" and its difference from „membership"), (2) the payment of all contributions, (3) a fee in the amount of 500 Cedi (approx. 300 EUR), (4) the signing of an undertaking of parliamentary candidates („Undertaking of Parliamentary Candidates"), (5) good character and (6) good standing in the party (the payment of extraordinary contributions) as well as in a constituency.

The NEC announces primaries a maximum of 30 months before the election that are held every four years in December. Nominations can be made a maximum 29 months before the national election. After the lapse of this time, the NEC collates all applications and sets dates for primary elections for individual constituencies and afterwards it does not excessively interfere with the selection process. The selection of candidates for the parliamentary elections is then in the hands of the constituency selectorate, that may listen to the leadership preferences, but is not formally bound by them (Essem 2009).

On a constituency level, the CEC summons a *Vetting Committee* that judges all applications for candidacy and tries to disqualify those applicants who do not fulfil some of the stated criteria. The Vetting Committee consists of the CEC officials as well as a few supervisory officials on the regional and national level, who must prevent unfair prejudice or on the contrary the backstairs influence of certain applicants. The Vetting Committee is the only body and there is no appeal against its decision. This also became a centre of criticism after the last election (Essem 2009).

The approved applicants then take part in the primary elections that are held a maximum of 26 months before the national election (Article 11 of the NPP's Articles of Association). Primary elections are held on the level of individual constituencies, where an **Extraordinary Constituency Delegates Conference (ECDC)** is in session. The ECDC consists of the CEC members as well as delegates from individual election constituencies that are selected by their Boards of Executives (*Polling Station Executive Committee* – PSEC). Every constituency selects one delegate, who most often is the Chairman of the local Board of Executives, but theoretically a delegate can also be an ordinary member of the NPP. The selection numbers between 40 and 110 delegates – the size is dependent on the support of the NPP in a given constituency. The election proceeds with the help of the FPTP (*First Past the Post*) formula – a candidate will become that applicant who gains the most votes (Essem 2009).

2.2 The analysis and comparison of the selection of parliamentary candidates

In this section, we apply the analytical framework of G. Rahat and R. Y. Hazan to the selection of candidates in the NDC and the NPP. This enables us to determine and compare the level of inclusiveness (openness) and (de)centralisation in both parties. The section is therefore divided into four parts, where each one is dedicated to one dimension from the above stated analytical framework that is first briefly characterised and then applied to the researched subjects.

Candidacy: Who can be selected?

This question can further be divided – do any restrictions exist for candidature? If yes, then how strict are they? Do they notably restrict the nature and size of the group of candidates?

The level of detected restrictions for candidature are transferred to the continuum according to how they contribute to *exclusiveness* (exclusiveness – is a status where the selection is shared only by party members with other limiting requirements and restrictions in force), or to the *inclusiveness* of candidature (inclusion – is a status where the selection of candidates is shared by all citizens).

Candidature for the NDC and the NPP is both restricted to party members who have been members for more than two years and have paid members' contributions. The NPP, in addition, requires that each candidate is not only a party member but also that it serves the party, which amounts to the payment of extraordinary fees. Parties also accentuate the activity of applicants and their moral credentials (criminal record, etc).

Diagram 1 – Candidacy (1ˢᵗ dimension)

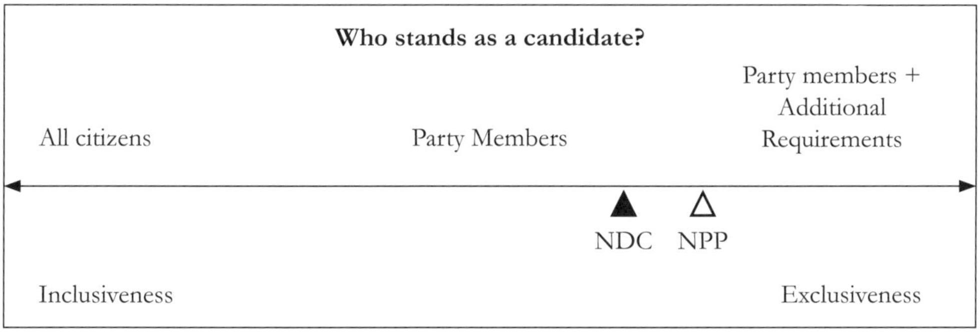

Who stands as a candidate?		
All citizens	Party Members	Party members + Additional Requirements
	▲ △	
	NDC NPP	
Inclusiveness		Exclusiveness

Source: *Adapted from Rahat and Hazan 2001: 301*

The NPP, in addition, introduces other criteria – the payment of candidate's contributions (300 EUR) and the signing of parliamentary obligations that oblige candidates to support the NPP in the Parliament.

Both parties in the context of the continuum of *inclusiveness – exclusiveness of candidacy* have doubts in its more exclusive part, because both enable a candidacy only to party members, who in addition fulfil certain criteria. Candidacy in the NPP is considered more closed, because it introduces more fees for candidates and candidates are obliged to support the NPP in advance.

Selectorate: Who selects the candidates?

Do any restrictions exist for participation in the selection process of candidates? How do they influence the nature and size of the selectorate?

An selectorate is any party body, which selects candidates. Its composition reflects different levels of inclusion – from an individual or a narrow group (exclusiveness), through to a good-sized group to as far as all voters (inclusiveness)[69]. According to the composition of an selectorate we can therefore transfer the process of candidate selection to the continuum in accordance with the level of inclusiveness and exclusiveness, in terms of individual categories of selectorates we can differentiate more sub-categories.

In terms of the second dimension, parties show greater differences. Whilst in the NDC a veto precedes on the constituency level and afterwards more on a national level (NEC), in the NPP only the constituency commission vetoes candidates. From the existence of a two-level control of applicants in the NDC a more tightly controlled selection process comes about, nevertheless we do not consider the Vetting Committee as a deciding selectorate, but more as a means of setting criteria for a candidature. That's why the deflexion of the NDC towards the pole of exclusiveness caused by a double veto is small.

We consider a key selectorate for both parties to be the nomination conferences that are organised on the constituency level.

In the NDC, the candidates are selected by a Constituency Conference (CC), that consists of (a) two deputies from each branch from each NDC branch in a constituency (their number must not exceed a total of 280), (b) all 18 members of the CEC, (c) the REC members and (d) the NEC that comes from a given constituency. The selectorate is thus sizable (it numbers a minimum of 300 members) and the overwhelming majority is directly elected by ordinary members in primary party organisations (branches). The distance between members and the selectorate is therefore small, because in order for a member to become a delegate, it is enough for him to win a single election in its branch (however he must have been a member for at least two years and have paid the contributions).

The NPP selects its candidates at an Extraordinary Constituency Delegate Conference (ECDC), from which every Executive Committee of an election district elects one delegate. This is generally its Chairman, but it can also be an ordinary member. The NPP's selectorate numbers between 40 and 110 voters (depending on the NPP's strength in a constituency) and is thus a minimum three times (maximum more than seven times) smaller than the NDC's selectorate. We also consider the distance between a delegate and an ordinary member of the NPP to be greater, because in an overwhelming majority

---

[69] Near the pole of exclusivity according to Rahat and Hazan would be an Israeli ultra-orthodox party Degel Ha Torah, where the composition of candidature is decided by only one Rabbi. On the contrary the closest to the pole of inclusivity are primaries in some American States, where registered voters can vote for candidates who are not necessarily party members (Rahat and Hazan 2001: 301-303).

of cases the delegates are the Chairmen of an Executive Committee in an election constituency. Delegates must therefore be firstly elected at an Election Conference of an election constituency (to become a Chairman) and then again elected (delegated) by an Executive Committee of an election district.

Diagram 2 – Selectorate (2nd dimension)

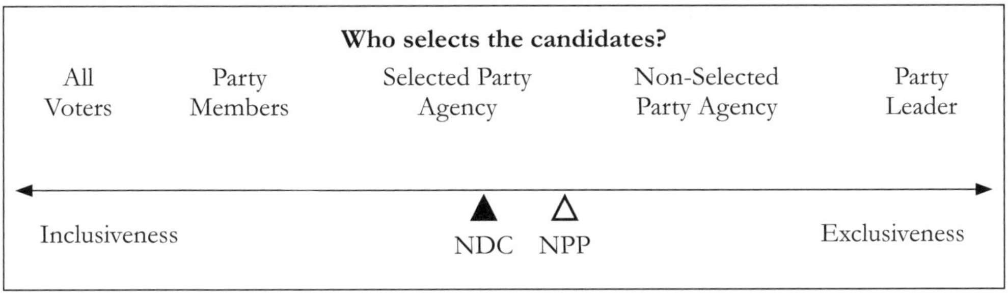

Who selects the candidates?

All Voters	Party Members	Selected Party Agency	Non-Selected Party Agency	Party Leader

◄───►

Inclusiveness   ▲ △   Exclusiveness

NDC NPP

Source: Adapted from Rahat and Hazan 2001: 301

The NPP and NDC also differ as far as the (non)existence of a corrective mechanism is concerned. Whilst national bodies of the NPP do not have power to review the results of primaries, in the NDC it is the opposite case. The National Executive Committee of the NDC can – if doubts arise about the correctness of the results – cancel the results and announce a new round of elections in a constituency. The NEC can also announce a new round even after a longer period of time, if it is shown that the selected candidate is unable to run the campaign. Although those cases are rare (in the last election in 2008 only one interference by the NEC into the results of primaries occurred) we must look on the possibility of interference by the NEC in the overall evaluation.

We place both parties into the category of selected party bodies, therefore bodies that consist of delegates. The mutual position of the parties is given by the size of an selectorate (Rahat and Hazan (2001: 302) and its distance from a member (Linek and Outlý 2005: 10). The NDC has got a much greater selectorate and an ordinary member is separated from a voter by a single sieve (instead of two in the NPP), and that is why we consider the NDC's selectorate as more open. The level of inclusiveness is restricted by the NEC's possibility to cancel the results of a primary election, but this power is not pro-active, but reactive, and the NEC moreover cannot see its own candidate through. That is why its shift towards exclusiveness is not so important.

Decentralisation: Where are candidates selected?
This dimension consists of two mutually interconnected parts – territorial and functional (de)centralisation. Whilst the first one deals with the question - where does selection take place? – the second one explores the influence of an applicant's status on being selected.

The selection of candidates in both researched parties proceeds on a level of an election constituency, which within the scope of a diagram of the third dimension we compare to a local level. The equality of representation of all branches of both parties is assured in each constituency, because each nominates the same number of delegates (one or two delegates in the case of the NPP or the NDC). The selection in the NDC and the NPP is therefore considered as territorially decentralised, although the NDC is closer to centralisation, with regard to the NEC's possibilities (at a national level) to cancel the results of primary election in the constituencies.

Functional decentralisation in Ghana is much discussed in relation to gender and ethnicity. Whilst both main parties adopted an agenda of equality of gender, the issue of the influence of ethnicity is generally denied, because in accordance with the Constitution ethnically or religiously based parties are forbidden (Article 55 paragraph 7).

Women representation is according to both parties very important, however real empowerment of women in politics still lags behind proclamations on this topic. It is interesting that in its election program the NPP promises „to drastically increase women representation in the government – especially at ministries and district assemblies ...“ (NPP 2008: Chapter 7 section 4.7 Promoting Gender Quality), but it does not mention an increase in the number of women M.P.s.[70] Equally the NDC promises in its program only „...to strengthen the position of women and substantially increase their number in senior governmental posts ...“ (NDC 2008: 74).

Table 1 – Women representation in the NPP and the NDC during the 2004 and 2008 elections

PARTY	ELECTION	CANDIDATES			PARLIAMENT	
		NUMBER	WOMEN	%	WOMEN	%
NPP	2004	227	27	11,89 %	20	8,70 %
	2008	226	22	9,73 %	14	6,09 %
NDC	2004	212	16	7,55 %	5	2,17 %
	2008	226	13	5,75 %	5	2,17 %

Source: Electoral Commission of Ghana

According to the NPP's public relations officer the low women candidacy is caused above all by their lack of interest in politics (Essem 2009). This shows itself in a reluctance to stand as a candidate (In the NPP's case, 12 % of candidates were women in 2004 and

---

[70] According to the Constitution (Article 78) most Ministers must be M.P.s, however it is also possible to nominate non-M.P.s into the Government, who fulfil the eligibility criteria for M.P.s. That is why it is possible for the NPP to fulfil this promise even without increasing the number of women in the Parliament.

10 % in 2008). If we compare the success of candidates, then we find out that women have a greater chance to be elected than their male colleagues (Table 2 – Women success in the NPP and the NDC during the 2004 and 2008 elections).

Table 2 – Women success in the NPP and the NDC during 2004 and 2008 elections

PARTY	ELECTION	CANDIDATES		M.P.S		SUCCESS*	
		M	F	M	F	M	F
NPP	2004	200	27	108	20	54 %	74 %
	2008	204	22	93	14	46 %	64 %
NDC	2004	196	16	89	5	45 %	31 %
	2008	213	13	109	5	51 %	38 %

Source: Electoral Commission of Ghana

* „Success" is measured as a quotient of elected M.P.s (respective women M.P.s) to all candidates (respective women candidates) of a given party. In a case, that success equals for example 33 %, every third women standing as a candidate was elected and so on.

The NDC puts the issue of women representation more strongly – women should gradually form at least 40 % of delegates at conferences and party congresses (NDC 2008: 75) and after the election President Atta-Mills also pledged to appoint at least 40 % of women into the position of *District Chief Executive* (DCEs). This promise however meets with resistance in many places and so its fulfilment is uncertain (Daadu 2009).

In terms of real life women representation during a candidacy to become an M.P. and then subsequently in the Parliament, we must state that substantially more women stood as candidates and were selected for the NPP than for the NDC (Table 1 – Women representation in the NPP and the NDC during the 2004 and 2008 elections). This result can be determined by the nature of an selectorate, because the NPP's voters (predominantly literate urban citizens) have possibly got a greater understanding of women equality than the predominantly illiterate NDC's voters, living in rural areas, where the male position is more dominant.

Ethnicity plays a more important role during a candidate's selection than gender. An election body is in the main very sensitive as to the character of a candidate, mainly in the case of the NDC. As stated by a representative of the NDC's national organization, Awudu Arif Abubakar, a party must nominate in constituencies those candidates who are members of a local majority ethnic group (Abubakar 2009). That is true especially in the regions where the NDC holds a strong position (the Volta region and the three northern regions Upper West, Upper East and Northern). Exceptions however exist where the NDC selects candidates from a minority ethnic group. For example, it is so in the Ejura-Sekyedumase constituency (Ashanti region), where immigrants with northern ethnicity form a third of the population, especially Dagarti or Fulani (Asante 2006: 235). In this constituency, the NDC always nominates a candidate of northern ethnicity, and this candidate (in the last two elections Alhaji Pangabu) wins here. That by the way confirms that the Akan ethnic groups are less dependent on the ethnic influence in their decision making than the northern ethnic groups or than the Ewe and the Ga[71].

The ethnic influence on the selection of candidates in the NPP is weaker, because its election body (predominantly of the Akan ethnicity) is not so dependent on ethnicity in its decision making. The party therefore is not so motivated to exploit the ethnic affiliation of candidates to mobilise the selectorate.

The final position of both researched parties on the vertical axis above all takes into account the role of ethnicity in the selection of candidates. Although the ethnic influence in the NPP is noticeably weaker, its position near the NDC reflects a relatively high level of success for women candidates in this party.

Diagram 3 – Decentralisation (3rd dimension)

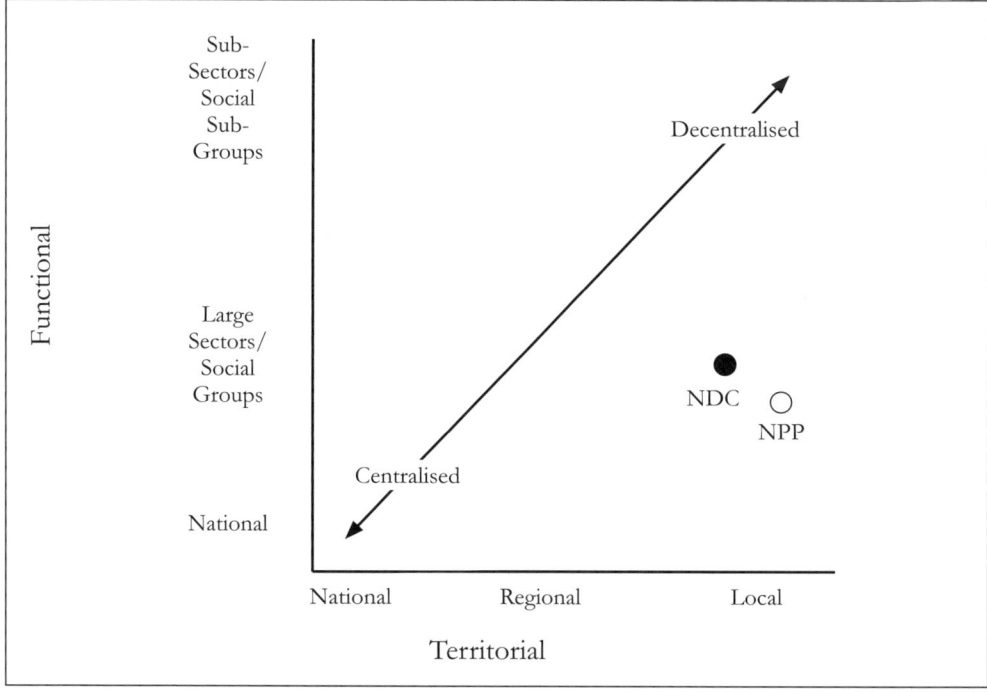

Source: *Adapted from Rahat and Hazan 2001: 305*

---

[71] From this conclusion comes a simple idea – if the NPP's voters were really to vote only according to ethnic affiliation (in concrete terms an affiliation to the ethnic Ashanti), then in a constituency where the Ashanti form about 70% of citizens, a non-Ashanti candidate could not win.

Election versus appointment: How are candidates nominated?

The extreme position of this dimension is *a pure appointment* (a situation, when a candidate is selected exclusively by a single appointing party committee), versus *a pure election* (where all selected candidates win party elections and no other party body has got the power to change the selected candidature composition).

This dimension, in the case of both studied parties, is unambiguous because the NPP as well as the NDC use a majority single-round system for the selection of candidates (FPTP). That however does not mean that both parties are in the same position. In the NPP's case, if only one applicant puts down their name for a primary election, the NPP approves this applicant without an selectorate having to vote for him. The applicant is in this way merely nominated not elected. On the contrary, in the NDC an selectorate must approve even a single candidate by voting, in which a candidate must get an absolute majority of votes. That is why we have to place the NPP nearer the pole for appointment. In view of the fact that the share of nominated candidates does not exceed 5 % (Essem 2009), the deviation of the NPP towards the system of appointment is not too significant.

Diagram 4 – Election versus appointment (4ᵗʰ dimension)

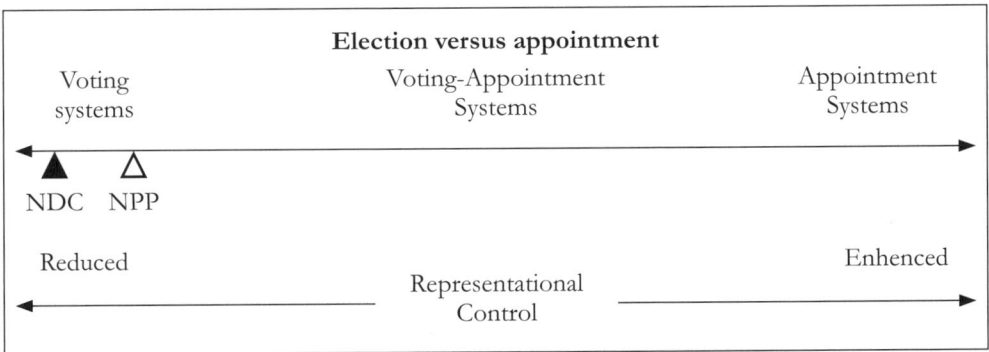

Source: Adapted from Rahat and Hazan 2001: 307

2.3 Summary

The selection of candidates for the parliamentary elections was at the beginning slightly different in both parties, because the NDC struggled with a lack of internal democracy and clearly given rules – it was a party of a single man, its founder J. J. Rawlings.

Since the preparation for the 2004 elections it adopted clear rules for the selection of candidates – as well as the party organisation – and since then its method of selection shows considerable similarities with the NPP in all four researched dimensions.

Both parties make it possible to stand as a candidate only for party members who have been in the party for more than two years. Through this measure the parties try to restrict opportunists who would enter the governmental party with a view to gaining quick access to governmental or other well-paid posts (Essem 2009). On the other hand, the membership conditions restrict the possibility for citizens „... to participate in political activities with the aim to influence the government composition and politics", that Article 2 of the Act 574 regarding political parties guarantees. Although individuals have the possibility to stand as candidates independent of political parties, their chances are not great[72], because a lot of money is needed for a campaign and the citizens of Ghana have a very strong affiliation and loyalty to political parties[73]. Overall, the candidacy for the NDC and the NPP for citizens of Ghana is fairly closed, and lowers the possibilities of them actively participating in the political process.

On the other hand the selectorates of both parties are in the middle of the continuum of *inclusiveness – exclusiveness*, because Nomination Conferences, which in terms of a number of members are quite large, select the candidates. In the next election, both parties will with the greatest probability be even nearer the pole of inclusiveness. Particularly it applies to the NPP which plans to introduce closed primaries, i.e. primaries for all party members.

Decentralisation is shown best in its territorial form, since the selection happens on the level of election constituencies. Functionally the selection is more centralised, especially in connection with women representation which is very low in both parties. On the other hand, the selection is partly functionally decentralised thanks to the influence of the ethnic nature of candidates, and so the final position of parties is approximately in the third of the axis of *centralisation – decentralisation*.

The similarity in the last dimension is to a great level influenced by the election system – it is understandable that for the FPTP system in the parliamentary elections the parties do not select candidates by a proportional system. In addition, the FPTP method is quite easy to evaluate and is established in the parliamentary elections. In both parties therefore candidates are being selected through elections – delegates at conferences have got one vote and the winner will be the applicant who gets a simple majority of votes. An exception is a situation, when only one applicant stands as a candidate in the NPP. In that case, an election does not take place and that candidate is nominated without voting, that is why the NPP is nearer the pole of *an appointment* than the NDC.

---

[72] In five of the elections held so far, only 11 independent candidates gained a parliamentary mandate (Electoral Commission of Ghana).

[73] According to the Afrobarometer, 57% of the population showed parties' support in 2002 and 69% of the population in 2005 (Afrobarometer 2005).

3. Presidential election
3.1 The characteristics of the selection of presidential candidates
NDC

The selection method for the NDC's presidential candidate has gone through quite a number of changes. At the beginning it was not *stricto senso* a selection, because the position of the „founding father" J. J. Rawlings was unshakeable, not only because of his status as the founder or his popularity among part of Ghana's population, but also thanks to the control of the armed forces. The NDC thus was at the beginning a party of only one man who did not have a challenger. Primary elections were therefore not needed.

Rawlings' position in the party illustrates the selection of a presidential candidate for the election in 2000, in which he alone – according to the constitutional restriction of a repeated candidature – could not take part in[74]. The selection happened in reality before the election in 1996, when Rawlings decided that his running-mate (i.e. candidate for a vice-president) would be the completely unknown John Atta-Mills, whom until then Rawlings allegedly had never seen (Nugent 2001: 413).

He decided to select J. A. Mills despite the fact that J. A. Mills was a completely unknown university law teacher who did not have any position in the party and therefore no power base. The reason for Rawling's decision was probably based on a conflict of business interests between his former favourite and protégé from the times of the PNDC, Goosie Tanoh, and Rawling's wife, Nana Konadu Agyeman Rawlings. (Although Rawlings supported his wife in this conflict, at the same time he destroyed her own plans to stand as a candidate in the next presidential election by announcing his support for Mills in June 1998.) Having understood, that without Rawlings' support he did not stand a chance, Goosie Tanoh left the NDC and established his own party, the NRP, regardless of the fact that the Election Congress that was to select the next presidential candidate, did not take place until half a year later – that meant December 1998 (Nugent 2001: 415).

Incidentally, the strong position of J. J. Rawlings in the NDC is apparent even today – in the central office of the NDC, we see his portraits on every step of the way[75] and Rawlings even has influence on J. A. Mills. His Presidency in no way strongly objects to Rawlings' criticism towards the conduct of his present Government. This Government, according to the former President, acts too sluggishly, because it did not immediately arrest former NPP Ministers, whom Rawlings publicly criticised as thieves and traitors of the nation (Gyebi, 7th April 2009). On the contrary Vice-President John Dramani Mahama,

---

[74] Despite the fact that the constitutional restriction of a repeated candidature was introduced by more African countries, cases where a President would abide by them are not very common.

[75] On the basis of the author's personal experience from his visit to the central office at Ringway Close 641/4, Kokomlemle, Accra on 30th April 2009.

publicly protested against Rawlings' criticism on several occasions even before election. For example, he opposed the „founding father", who accused the previous government (i.e. government of NPP) of distributing weapons to supporters to unleashed mayhem ahead of the December polls (Think Ghana, 26th September 2008). The straned relations between Rawlings and Mahama could be traced in the Vice-president primaries for 2008 election – Rawlings would have preferred Mrs. Betty Mould Iddrisu and therefore he ordered "NDC apparatchiks" to front her, however, the big wings of NDC picked Mahama against his will (The African Executive, 23th April 2008).

In the last two elections (2004 and 2008) the selection of a presidential candidate proceeded according to given and approved rules, although even in these Rawlings kept a certain influence via a Senior Council.

According to these rules, that are incorporated in Article 43 of the Articles of Association, an applicant for the presidential candidacy must fulfil (1) the eligibility criteria given by the Constitution (Article 62 of the Constitution), according to which a President has to be a native citizen of Ghana and more than 40 years old, who also fulfils the other eligibility criteria for election to the Parliament as stated in Article 94 of the Constitution and (2) the NDC criteria – at least two years membership, regularly paid all contributions and activity. At least one member from each of the 230 election constituencies of Ghana must confirm an application for candidacy. (In constituencies where the NDC is strong – the Volta, Upper East and others – a candidacy must be supported by two members). A list of candidates who have gained the prescribed support will then be assessed by the party's Vetting Committee. The committee will further eliminate candidates about whom it finds out, that despite their declarations, do not fulfil some of the stated criteria (Abubakar 2009).

The selection of a presidential candidate proceeds via an election at a **Party National Congress**, its delegates are (a) delegates of constituency conferences (five delegates per constituency, from which at least two must be women); (b) the NEC members; (c) the President and the Vice-President, if from the NDC; (d) the NDC's Ministers; (e) all members of the NDC's parliamentary club; (f) the founding members; (g) the district Governor's for the NDC; (h) the Regional representatives – regional organizers, propaganda secretaries and representatives of youth and women from regions and others. It is a relatively large selectorate, because delegates from constituency conferences consist of 1150 voters and on top of that the NDC wants to double this number for the next intra-party election (Abubakar 2009).

If only one candidate enters the *primaries*, he must be approved by an absolute majority of votes (50 % + one vote). If that does not happen the NEC will call for a new round of nominations, after which the next round of elections will happen. In the case that at least two candidates compete, the one who gets a simple majority of votes will win.

Primaries for the election in 2008 were held on 22nd December 2006 and the winner was John Evans Atta-Mills, who thus repeated his victory from the years 2002 and 1998 (then however he was not elected, but only appointed by J. J. Rawlings).

Table 3 – Results of presidential primaries in the NDC in 2006

NAME	VOTES	VOTES (%)
John Atta-Mills	1 362	81,4
Ekow Spio-Garbach	146	8,7
Alhaji Iddrisu Mahama	137	8,2
Eddy Annan	28	1,7
CELKEM	1 673	100,0

Source: Electoral Commission of Ghana

The selection of the NDC's presidential candidate after the election in the year 2004 proceeds on the basis of given rules, according to which the party national congress, composed of delegates from constituency conferences, selects a candidate. As show by the election results, there is not a great deal of competition for the candidate post in the party, because only four candidates applied, amongst whom Atta-Mills did not have a serious competitor.

NPP

The selection of the NPP's presidential candidate proceeded during the whole Fourth Republic in accordance with the same rules which are incorporated in the Articles of Association. The NPP differs from the NDC in that it selected its candidates in accordance with unclearly defined rules, and on top of that the rules changed from election to election (Öhman 2004: 111).

In accordance with Article 12 of the NPP's Articles of Association a presidential candidate must be (1) an active party member with a membership of more than 5 years, who (2) is of good character and (3) has a good reputation, (4) paid a fee for the presidential candidate (25.000 Cedi, approx. 15.000 EUR), (5) is approved by the Vetting Committee, (6) has signed an obligation of a presidential candidate and (7) has gained written consent of at least 10 credible members from each of the 10 regions (Article 12 paragraph 4).

The fate of every candidate is decided by the Vetting Committee that consists of nine members – six members are appointed on the basis of their function (Chairmen of other professional committees of the NPP's National Council) and the remaining three are subsequently selected by them. The Vetting Committee will judge an applicant and will reject or recommend its candidature. It will provide the reasoning for its decision to the applicant and the NEC. If an applicant is not satisfied with its verdict, he has the right to appeal against it to the NEC that will decide his candidature with final effect (Article 9 paragraph 5 para f) of the NPP's Articles of Association).

The National Congress (NC) then decides about the approved applicants, it consists of (a) 10 delegates from each constituency, one representative from (b) the founding

81

members and (c) patrons/sponsors from each region and finally (d) one representative from each overseas branch of the NPP. So the maximum number that can meet at the congress is 2323 delegates, it is possible to regard this selectorate as quite large.

Its greatest part (2300) consists of constituency delegates, who are selected at the ECDC (Extraordinary Constituency Delegates Conference). From the total of 10 delegates from each constituency, six must be ordinary members without any party function and the remaining four are constituency officers (Article 6 paragraph 18 of the NPP's Articles of Association).

In the case that only one applicant is applying for the post of a presidential candidate, the Congress no longer votes for him and only approves his candidature. If more than one applicant applies, then the Congress must vote for a winner. Each delegate has got one vote and the winner will be the applicant that gets 50 % + one vote. If nobody manages to get an absolute majority a second round will be held, into which the two most successful candidates from the first round will proceed (Article 12 paragraph 7 of the NPP's Articles of Association).

Although in the first round of primaries no candidate has got an absolute majority of votes, Alan Kyerematen decided to leave the election and admit the victory of Nana Akuffo-Addo.

Table 4 – Results of presidential primaries in the NDC in 2006

NAME	VOTES	VOTES (%)
Nana Akufo-Addo	**1 096**	**48.0**
Alan Kyerematen	738	32,3
Aliu Mahama	146	6,4
Yaw Osafo Marfo	63	2,8
Dan Botwe	52	2,3
Papa Owusu Ankomah	34	1,5
Hackman Owusu-Agyeman	28	1,2
Kwame A. Addo Kufour	22	1,0
Prof. Mike Oquaye	20	0,9
Jake Obetsebi-Lamptey	20	0,9
Dr Konadu Apraku	19	0,8
Prof. Kwabena F. Boateng	12	0,5
Boakye K Agyarko	10	0,4
Kwabena Agyepong	9	0,4
Felix K. Owusu -Adjapong	9	0,4
Dr. Barfour A. Barwuah	6	0,3
Dr. Kwabina Arthur Kennedy	1	0,0
TOTAL	**2 285**	**100**

Source: Electoral Commission of Ghana

As in the case of primaries for the parliamentary elections, the NPP also plans a change to the selection process for the presidential candidate. According to the new method, a presidential candidate should be selected by 330,000 voters for the election in 2012 (The Statesman, 15th May 2009).

3.2 The analysis and comparison of the selection of presidential candidates
Candidacy

The greatest differences in the applicant conditions between the NDC and the NPP can be seen above all in the requirement of the NPP to pay quite a high fee for the presidential applicant (15.000 EUR) and in the length of required membership (five years in the NPP versus two years in the NDC). On a lesser level it concerns the provision about the necessary support from a number of regions (NPP), respective constituencies (NDC). The NDC requires the applicant to gain at least 230 signatures (a minimum of one each per election constituency), whereas the NPP requires only 100 signatures – 10 each from 10 regions.

Whilst the first two differences are considered as strongly limiting the openness of the NPP, the third difference does not give candidates from the NDC greater problems (one can assume that it is also thanks to corruption). The position of the NDC nearer exclusiveness is influenced – except the above mentioned requirement of constituencies' support – mainly by the condition of a two year party membership.

Diagram 5 – Candidacy (1st dimension)

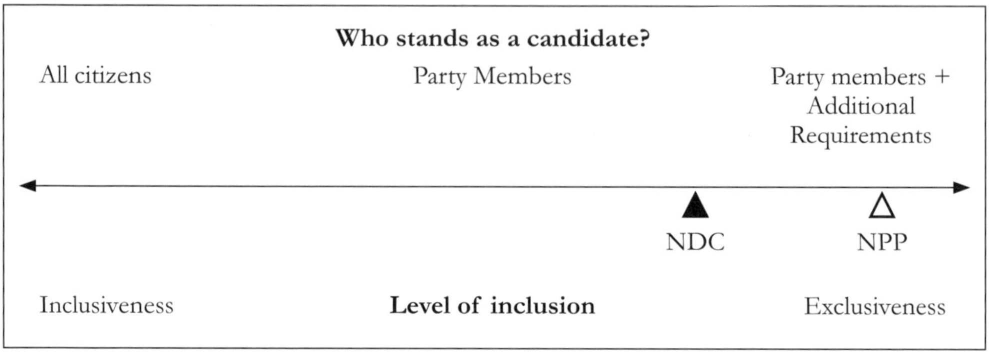

Who stands as a candidate?

All citizens	Party Members	Party members + Additional Requirements

◄───►

               ▲   △

         NDC   NPP

Inclusiveness	**Level of inclusion**	Exclusiveness

Source: Adapted from Rahat and Hazan 2001: 301

In both researched parties, the applicants must first appear before the Vetting Committees that will decide whether they fulfil the prescribed criteria. As in the case of the parliamentary election, we do not consider these committees to be selectorates, and therefore we won't deal with them in our analysis.

The NPP as well as the NDC select their presidential candidates at their National Congresses. There are, however, major differences in their composition and size. Whilst in the NDC five representatives stand as candidates per constituency, in the NPP there are twice as many representatives. Consequently the final size of an selectorate also differs – in the last primaries the difference was 612 delegates in favour of the NPP.

Almost a third (523 delegates) of the NDC's Congress consists of party officers, who delegate on the basis of their function (the NEC members, ministers, members of parliamentary club and others), whereas the NPP's selectorate nearly exclusively consist of constituency delegates. The NPP moreover determines that a majority (six) delegates from each constituency must not hold any other party function, through which it strengthens the role of ordinary members in the selection of its presidential candidate.

Both parties fall within the category of *selected party bodies*, because they select their candidates at congresses. Congresses consists of delegates who are delegated

Diagram 6 – Selectorate (2nd dimension)

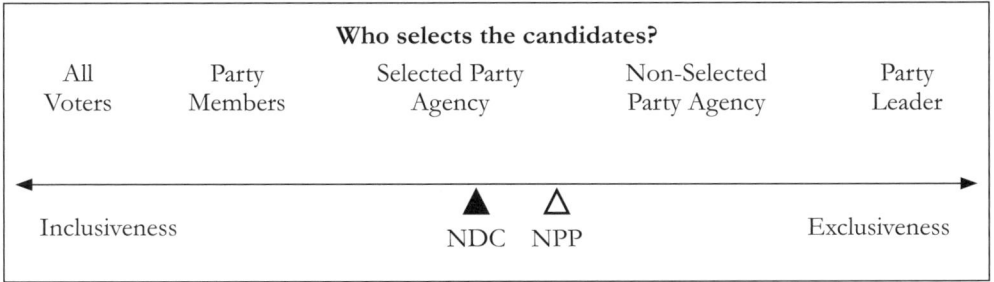

Source: *Adapted from Rahat and Hazan 2001: 301*

by constituency conferences. Congress delegates therefore must undertake a double selection – (1) at a constituency conference and subsequently (2) at a national congress. The distance between an ordinary member and a delegate is therefore greater by one selection round, which moves both parties towards the pole of exclusiveness. The NDC's selectorate is considered – in view of its size and composition - more closed that the NPP's selectorate.

(De)centralisation

For the selection of a presidential candidate neither functional nor territorial decentralisation plays such a role as it would in the case of parliamentary primaries.

The selection of candidates is unambiguously territorially centralised because candidates are being decided on a national level.

Functionally the selection is centralised, above all in relation to gender – women are not in any way advantaged and therefore there was not a single woman among the applicants for a presidential candidature in the last election (Electoral Commission of Ghana 2007).

The influence of ethnicity is more problematic, because its examination is restricted by constitutional restrictions against a parties' ethnic character as well as by the lack of cases. The selection of a presidential candidate in the NDC for the first three elections (1992, 1996 and 2000) practically did not take place and in the next election the role of J. J. Rawlings was very important.[76]

In spite of that, it is apparent that ethnicity does have an influence, because it is difficult to imagine – in view of the election results and the overall form of relations

---

[76] The extent to which Rawlings influences the possibilities of the NDC's applicants will be shown after the next election. In the last two elections the NDC's candidate stood in opposition, and therefore Rawlings had no need – or reason – to criticise the Presidential candidate. Nowadays, however, Atta-Mills is in power and Rawlings has criticised his behaviour many times, and so it is possible that he decides to support another candidate in the next primaries.

Diagram 7 – Decentralisation (3rd dimension

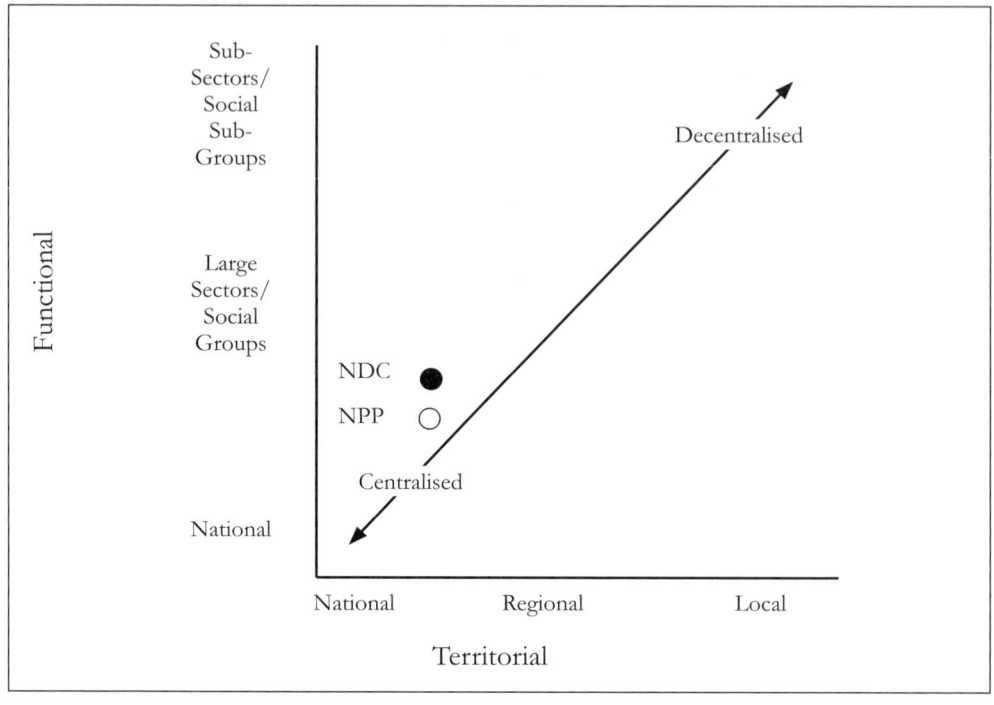

Source: *Adapted from Rahat and Hazan 2001: 305*

among ethnic groups – that for example an Ashanti stood as a candidate for the NDC or on the other hand an Ewe for the NPP. The influence of ethnicity can also be seen in the nomination of Atta-Mills as a presidential candidate in the year 1998. The fact that Rawlings nominated Mills from the ethnic Fanti group meant that he desired to establish a second *world bank*[77] from the Central region (Frempong 2001: 149). In this region the Akkan not the Ashant ethnic group is dominant (Asante a Gymiah-Boadi 2004: 10) and Rawlings mistakenly assumed that Fantis would blindly vote for candidates of the same origin – for a son of the soil.

To date, the NDC considers ethnicity to be a key motive in the decision-making of its voters and the selection of its candidates is subordinate to it (Abubakar 2009). On the contrary, the NPP tries – at least according to the words of its public relations officer – not to prefer any ethnic group and not to use ethnicity for the mobilisation of voters (Essem 2009, Frempong 2006: 163–165), although in reality it often did not succeed (compare with Frempong 2001: 153).

---

[77] That is what the Volta region is called in Ghana, where the NDC completely dominates.

The position of both parties on the horizontal (*territorial*) axis reflects the national character of selectorates (congresses) of both parties. However, the provision about equal representation of all constituencies in these selectorates moves both parties slightly towards decentralisation.

The vertical (*functional*) position reflects the absence of any quotas or other formal advantages for women (or other large sectors and social groups), which balances out the influence of ethnicity. Overall it is possible to consider the selection in both parties as centralised, therefore one where candidates are being selected in a national competition. The openness and equality of opportunities is however restricted by the influence of ethnicity that can discriminate/advantage candidates on the basis of their origin.

Election versus Appointment

The NPP as well as the NDC (usually) use different systems of a majority election for their elections. The NDC uses the FPTP system for the selection of a presidential candidate – the winner is the candidate who gains most votes. But if there is only one aspirant applying for a candidate post, a congress must approve him by 50 % + one vote – that means by an absolute majority.

The NPP's Congress selects its candidate through an election system of an absolute majority with a second round (*run-off*). A winner then becomes that candidate who gains 50 % + one vote. If nobody reaches this quorum, a second round takes place, into which the two most successful candidates will go through and in which a simple majority of votes is enough to win. In the case that only one candidate applies for a candidate post in front of the congress, an election will not happen and the applicant automatically becomes the winner – the same as in the case of parliamentary primaries.

The position of parties on the diagram of 4th dimension differs from the parliamentary primaries. Although parties use the same election systems, in the case of parliamentary

Diagram 8 – Election versus appointment (4th dimension)

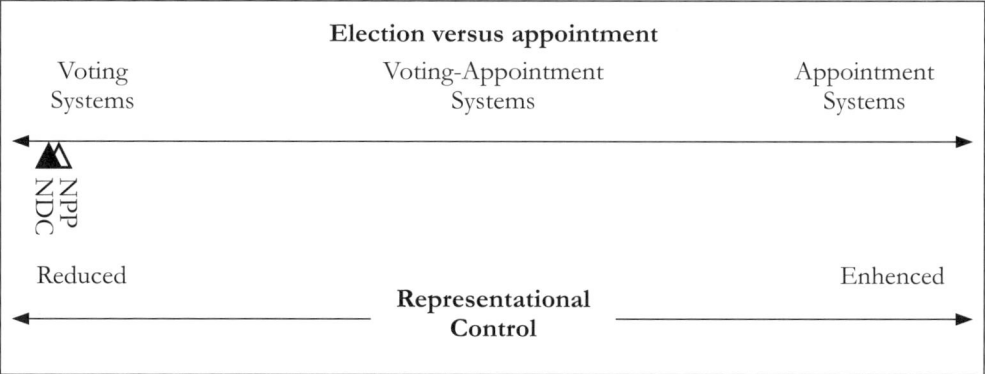

Source: Adapted from Rahat and Hazan 2001: 307

primaries a decision, thus far, has always been made by an election. That is why the NPP is placed in the same position as the NDC.

3.3 Summary

The selection method of presidential candidates in the NPP and the NDC was initially considerably different, because the NDC de facto did not vote for its candidate – J. J. Rawlings position in the party was in debatable. A change occurred during the preparation for the election in 2004, for which the NDC was selecting its presidential candidate on the basis of formal rules that can be found in the party's Articles of Association. On the contrary, the NPP selects its candidate for all elections in the Fourth Republic on the basis of the same mechanism, towards which the NDC moved closer to after 2004.

A candidature, the same as in the parliamentary election is considerably restricted – it applies only to party officers with a long standing membership (two years in the NDC and five years in the NPP). Candidates from both parties must also show that they have got support across all regions. The NPP further determines the possibility to stand as a candidate, by the requirement to pay a considerable fee, and that is why a candidature for this party is very closed and inaccessible for an ordinary citizen.

The selection itself proceeds in the NPP as well as in the NDC at the National Congresses. Here delegates from all 230 election constituencies are represented. Both selectorates are slightly more closed than the process for the parliamentary primaries, because for an ordinary party member it is more difficult to become a voter. On the other hand, both congresses are quite large. It is also worth mentioning that compared to the parliamentary primaries selectorates do change their positions and the NPP is the more open party.

As we stated, the selection proceeds on a national level and is therefore territorially centralised. Functionally, it is also rather centralised, but as in the parliamentary primaries, the ethnic origin of voters plays an important role by slightly decentralising the selection of candidates. This shows itself to a greater degree in the NDC.

The parties noticeably differ in the election system – both parties use a majority method, but while the NDC uses a simple majority, the NPP on the contrary uses an absolute majority. That is true except in the situation where only one applicant stands as a candidate, whom the NPP approves without voting, however the NDC decides about his (non)approval by an absolute majority of votes.

Conclusion

The aim of this work was to introduce to the reader the selection process of candidates for the parliamentary and the presidential elections in the two main political parties of Ghana. On the basis of an analysis of these problems we can now proceed to the verification of the three following hypotheses that we set out at the beginning.

H1: *The more M.P.s a party has got, the more closed its selection process will be and the less M.P.s a party has got, the more open its selection process will be.*

This hypothesis applies to two aspects – (1) the effort of the leading party to strengthen the loyalty of M.P.s; and (2) the effort of the opposition party to increase its chances to win the next election by means of a greater openness and democratic character in the selection process of candidates.

The verification of the first aspect of this hypothesis is partly made more difficult by the unclear mechanisms that the NDC used for the selection of candidates in the elections of 1992, 1996 and 2000. The very fact that there were no formal rules shows the non-democratic spirit of the candidate selection process, because it gives a space for non-formal influences that push intraparty democracy to the side lines. As we have shown, the position of J. J. Rawlings in the NDC was so dominant that in reality he decided who would be selected as a candidate and who would not. In the elections of 1992, 1996 and 2000 we consider this hypothesis to be valid. The NDC lost the elections in the year 2000 partly due to the very exclusive and non-democratic way in which it selected its candidates, because it brought about the anxiety of ordinary members, a number of who separated from the NDC and established their own party.

Following the defeat in the 2000 election, the party adopted new rules that entrusted the power over the selection process into the hands of a constituency conference. Although it allowed interference by the central office, in reality this hardly happens. It is therefore possible to consider the selection as an open one, which also confirms our hypothesis, because after the election in 2000 the NDC had a fewer number of mandates.

On the contrary, the NPP adopted rules for the selection process when it was founded in 1992 and since then it has markedly not changed them. This invalidated our hypothesis, because since 2000 until 2008 it was the governing party.

Table 5 – The NDC's and the NPP's results in the elections of the Fourth Republic

	1992	1996	2000	2004	2008
NDC	189	133	92	94	115
NPP	0	61	100	128	107

Source: Electoral Commission of Ghana

The second aspect of this hypothesis was confirmed – following the defeat in 2000, the NDC introduced a more inclusive selection at the constituency conferences for the next election. The same as the NPP following its defeat in 2008 it will in most probability adopt a new and considerably more inclusive form of candidate selection at the end of May 2009 (closed primaries for all party members in the constituency).

Overall, we consider this hypothesis to be valid, most of all in respect of its second aspect. Nevertheless, we realize its restricted basis that deserves to be expanded on by a comparison with small opposition parties.

H2: *The more a party claims a left-wing focus, the more decentralised form of selection of candidates it uses.*

On the basis of a comparison of both researched parties – the right-wing NPP and the social-democratic NDC – in the dimension of (de)centralisation of selection of candidates, we must declare this hypothesis invalid.

Table 6 – Women representation in the NPP and the NDC during elections in 2004 and 2008

PARTY	ELECTIONS	CANDIDATES			PARLIAMENT	
		NUMBER	WOMEN	%	WOMEN	%
NPP	2004	227	27	11,89 %	20	8,70 %
	2008	226	22	9,73 %	14	6,09 %
NDC	2004	212	16	7,55 %	5	2,17 %
	2008	226	13	5,75 %	5	2,17 %

Source: Electoral Commission of Ghana

Although the NDC is placed nearer the pole of decentralisation, it is mainly thanks to the influence of ethnicity that a more pragmatic effort emerges to take advantage of the ethnic group to gain a mandate, than from any particular ideological focus.

Women representation is far more important for the verification of this hypothesis, in which NDC shows much worse results than the right-wing NPP.

H3: *The greater party continuity with the previous non-democratic regime, the lesser intraparty democracy.*

This hypothesis assumes a relationship between the origin and the level of intraparty democracy, but also the democratic influence of institutions on political parties.

Whilst the NDC, which originated from the transformation of the military PNDC, shows a considerable lack of intraparty democracy since the election in 2004, the NPP which originated in a standard way, still keeps a normal level of intraparty democracy. We consider it important that the NDC changed after the departure of J. J. Rawlings, who personifies the military origin of this party. It ensues from the election results, that the NDC was gradually losing electoral support, which we ascribe to the consolidation of democratic relations, specifically to a continually greater level of electoral competition and greater freedom of the press. Following this defeat, the NDC decided to substantially strengthen intraparty democracy, which we consider to be a confirmation of our hypothesis about the democratic effect of institutions on the party, which due to its non-democratic character puts off no small number of voters.

The findings from this hypothesis might not seem surprising in the context of the Czech Republic[78], but in the context of African countries, they contribute to the opinion that the establishment and the maintenance of democratic regimes is possible through the support of democratic institutions, which is also the aim of the European Union and the Czech Republic.

The selection of candidates, that we consider to be a key indicator of intraparty democracy, gives us grounds for optimism. Especially the procedures laid down in the Articles of Association, that enable the transparency of the whole process, and also the whole level of its inclusiveness, that is in the middle of the continuum. Although the candidature is very closed (it applies only to party members, who also have to fulfil other criteria) and the possibility to stand as a candidate in the election independently of the party only partly compensates this, we consider the predominant election system to be positive as it enables delegates to realistically influence who will stand as a candidate. On the other hand, the possibility of nominations could be used to strengthen women representation (for example by nominating women in constituencies, where a party is clear to win), which is still very low in the Parliament (8 %).

The overall development of party political systems in Ghana represents a promising perspective. We are encouraged in this belief, especially by the fact that the importance of ethnic dividing lines is falling (even though very slowly) and at the same time the justice and competition of elections is increasing. Both of these factors made it possible for Ghana to change its governing party for a second time by elections, which in the context of previous „bloody" elections in Zimbabwe or Kenya gives hope to other African countries that are yet to prepare for elections. Also Ghana's elections are a good signal for European donors and institutions, which participated and are now participating in the development of Ghana's democracy.

We consider the Electoral Commission, which showed great professionalism and bravery and also support from the public, to be a very important elements in the strengthening of election transparency and justice. Other important elements are a free press and political parties that show a greater level of tolerance towards its competitors. Tolerance is however still dangerously low and politicians, the same as party members and voters, perceive politics to be a zero sum game.

In spite of this promising perspective, Ghana faces a number of calls for change. On the party political level it is above all the dominant ethnic dividing line and also a strong town versus country divide. Furthermore, we must mention a high level of corruption and unequal possibilities of political parties that result from the absence of state funds,

---

[78] In this respect it could be interesting to compare it with the Czech Republic, where the KSČM (*Communist Party of Bohemia and Moravia*), a follower of the nondemocratic KSČ (*Communist Party of Czechoslovakia*) showed a substantially greater level of inclusivity than the ODS (*Civic Democratic* Party) or ČSSD (*Czech Social Democratic* Party) during the selection of candidates for the election into the European Parliament (Linek and Outlý 2005: 18).

91

the insufficient control of party finances and the overall inter-relationships of parties with the state. On a basic level, the insufficient separation of the executive power from the legislative power and the judicial power remains a large problem. This situation will with the greatest probability remain the same in the future, because better separation and strengthening of judicial power is not in the interest of the political parties.

CHIEFS AS DEVELOPERS AND POLITICIANS IN NANUŊ CHIEFDOM OF NORTHERN GHANA[79]

Peter Skalník
University of Hradec Králové

Abstract

The paper explains the role in politics and development of the paramount and divisional chiefs of Nanuŋ, a medium-sized chiefdom in Northern Ghana. I will start by discussing the oscillating dynamics of chiefly politics during the different regimes of independent Ghana. Especially the use of violence by Nanumba chiefs differed in dependence on alternation between democratic and military regimes of the 1970s and 1980s when economic malaise prevailed in the former British protectorate. The conflicts were more likely to erupt when democracy was restored and state force was less likely to be used. The conflicts were more latent or in a stalemate while the power of the state was more genuine, i.e. when the military took over. In the end it was non-governmental Nairobi Peace Initiative and its Ghana assistants who managed to restore „peace" in the mid-1990s. The well-known conflict between the Nanumba chiefly polity and Konkomba 'acephalous' tribesmen centred on the political, judicial and developmental powers of chiefs. The gradual economic improvements during the Rawlings and Kuffuor eras have contributed to the increase of the power of the state in the provinces and consequently limitations on the power of the chiefs. But the resulting decrease of inter-ethnic tensions was in the case of Nanuŋ overshadowed by chieftaincy succession conflict. Even the latter have been heavily influenced by economic growth and interests. The paper will point in the direction of more refined and complex analysis of the dynamics between the relative erosion of the state monopoly on the use of violence and the ability of chiefs to influence local politics and development.

Introduction

During two last decades chiefs, chiefdoms and chieftaincy in Africa (and other parts of the world) have received less negative assessment than in the preceding periods. It has to do with the persistent crisis of the modern imported state on the one hand and with the quest for African identity on the other. Chiefs, chiefdoms and chieftaincy, irrespective of numerous succession conflicts, have been looked upon with respect, awe and hope (Boafo-Arthur 2001). Some studies have indicated that the new wave of democracy in Africa can and should be connected with new prestige of chiefs and institutions such

---

[79] This chapter is a result of the research supported by the Grant Agency of the Czech Republic, „Political Parties of Africa, Asia, Latin America and Oceania", Project No. 407/09/0387. An earlier version was presented and discussed at the 3rd European Conference on African Studies, Leipzig 2009.

as chiefdoms and chieftaincy (Fisiy 1995; Rouveroy 2000; Chabal, Feinman and Skalník 2004; Fokwang 2005, 2009; Skalník 1996a, b, 2004, 2007).

The interest in the developmental role of chiefs and institutions surrounding them goes back to the work of Isaac Schapera in what is today Botswana. Schapera established that Tswana chiefs had been active innovators and one could ask today whether that fact has had impact on the success Botswana recorded in post-colonial decades (Schapera 1970). My own work in northern Ghana started also as a study of the role Nanumba chiefs played in development but soon expanded into the research on their political status and their handling of armed conflicts with the Konkomba (Skalník 1981, 1983, 1986, 1987, 1989, 1992a, 1992b). Another impulse for the study of the chiefs as politicians and developers has been the South African transition which released the chiefs from the stain of collaborators and stooges of European imperialism (Skalník 1988).

Nanuŋ chiefdom

Nanuŋ is a medium-sized chiefdom located in northern Ghana. It has existed for several hundred years judging from the genealogies of the paramount chiefs or *naanima* (sing. *naa*) of Bimbilla. Nanuŋ is the chiefdom (*naam*) of the Nanumba people but their territory has also been inhabited by 'strangers', i.e. Konkomba, Dagomba, Gonja, Ashanti, etc. while Konkomba who came as refugees in the 1940s have become a clear majority due to their massive influx and higher demographic curve. While Nanuŋ has been a minor player in the politics of the savannah and Sahel regions of West Africa, it has never been unimportant and at some periods even rose to become a key player in the regional politics. Located between more known polities of Asante, Gonja and Dagboŋ it has had oral traditions testifying that Nanumba chiefs and their armies played sometimes a crucial role in armed conflicts among chiefdoms and kingdoms of what had been referred to as the pre-colonial period. Although Dagboŋ was Nanuŋ's immediate northern neighbour and sometimes considered as hegemonic, most traditions attest to the independent existence of Nanuŋ as the youngest of three southern Mole-Dagbane speaking chiefdoms. Although reconstruction of independent history of Nanuŋ is a fascinating research topic, in the present paper I am concerned with the role of chiefs in the colonial and post-colonial period.

Nanuŋ was conquered by Germany in 1896 as part of the Second Reich's Togo adventure. Whereas Dagboŋ was divided between the British who founded Tamale as their administrative stronghold for the Northern Territories of the Gold Coast and the Germans who occupied Yendi, chiefdom's capital, Nanuŋ was incorporated in its entirety into the German Togo. However, it was located in the north-western corner of the Togo colony and hardly anything of the 'Musterkolonie's heralded achievements had been imprinted onto it. What we know about the moment of the conquest is that prior to the Adibo battle which sealed the history of independent Dagboŋ, the Nanumba were forced to resist the German military party. Actually there were three armed contingents in Nanuŋ, one located in the military villages around the capital of Bimbilla, one around

Nakpa and one around Dakpam, the 'gate' towns of the two alternating chiefly houses from where the Bimbilla Naa or paramount chief of Nanuŋ usually originated. I shall not dwell on details about the alternating rule of succession in Nanuŋ but will just point out that the existence of three armies in Nanuŋ shows that the chiefdom was not a polity which had one centre of monopoly of the use of physical force against an external enemy and coercion vis-à-vis the subjects. Hierarchy of village chiefdoms and 'divisional' chiefdoms, i.e. the mentioned 'gate' towns, was also hierarchy of threat of use or actual use of force. The violent meeting of German army and Nanumba warriors has demonstrated two strikingly different political cultures. The colonizing power relied on the hegemony of its armed force whereas the Nanumba responded by vain defence. The utmost care of the latter was to keep the *kali* (custom, tradition) as untouched as possible under the changed conditions.

The colonial conquest drastically limited the scale of action for chiefs (Callaway 1974). Though not abolished, the chiefs in Nanuŋ were no more able to continue in their usual range of activities. They lost political and military sovereignty to the newly formed colonial state. Nevertheless they were allowed to continue to practice their rituals, and play their usual role in the administration and judicial process of the chiefdom. German, later British and still later Ghanaian authorities harnessed the chiefs as interpreters of the modern centralized policies to their subjects and to some extent also as presenters of subjects' interests to the administrative institutions of the colonial and postcolonial state. At the same time chiefs were not supposed to jeopardize the supremacy of colonial authorities by entering into disputes about succession and other 'traditional' matters. Nor were they allowed to participate actively in political life of the colonial state. But early into the colonial era it was the German colonizing power that intervened into the usual traditional practices by interning Bimbilla Naa Salifu and tried to enstool a new Bimbilla Naa. The colonizers showed ignorance of the logic of *naam* (chiefdom, chieftaincy) which does not allow enskinment of a new paramount before the previous chief dies. In fact *naam* does not know anything like the destoolment of southern chiefs, impeachment or expiration of office period in western type of states.

Within the policy of Indirect Rule which the British implemented starting from the 1920s, the chiefs enjoyed limited autonomy in the matters of tradition but had to be fully obedient as far as the central administrative and later development policies were concerned. Some of the chiefs, and here I mean especially the paramount chiefs such as the *naanima* of Bimbilla, were active players within the framework of the indirect rule while others only passively reproduced the decisions from the region and the capital. The two alternating chiefly houses seemed to follow a contrastive pattern: whereas the Baŋyili chiefs followed actively the path of education and development, the Gbuxumayili chiefs could be seen as adhering to a conservative approach. During the rule of Bimbilla Naa Natogmah (for Baŋyili from 1945 to 1957) his younger brother Mr Attah, one of the first Nanumba literates, became active in the party of Kwame Nkrumah, the Convention People´s Party. He became the Member of Parliament and shortly before the 1966 coup against Nkrumah even served as deputy Minister of Defense. Thus with Mr Attah in the state politics, Baŋyili-led chiefdom of Nanuŋ was pro-CPP. Bimbilla Naa Natogmah was credited with progressive attitudes because during his reign a number of development projects were realized from the development finances received by the local government no doubt and because Mr Attah was an influential CPP member the Bimbilla Naa was clearly pro-CPP. As a recognition of his role in the development of Nanuŋ Naa Natogmah was decorated with Queen´s Medal for African Chiefs in 1956.

In contrast, during the long rule his successor from the Lion´s House, Bimbilla Naa Dasana (1959–1981), the development work slowly subsided until it was standstilled. The first seven years coincided with the CPP rule in the country and therefore the influence of Mr Attah. The subsequent Ghanaian regimes were either short-lived or they were economically detrimental for the development in the whole of Ghana, Nanuŋ not excluded. When I first met Naa Dasana in 1978, most public services and their buildings were dilapidated, the paramount chief was known to have indulged in alcohol abuse. He limited himself to dutiful reception of each government official who called on him. It should be noted that these visitors considered their duty to show respect to the Bimbilla Naa.

My fieldwork was conducted mainly in the years 1978–1983, with returns in 1986, 1994, 1997 and 2003. I had opportunity to follow two times the alternating succession to the *naam* (paramountship) of Bimbilla and thus the passages of the high office from Gbuxumayili (Lion's House) to Baŋyili (Bangle House) which took place in 1981–1983 and from Baŋyili to Gbuxumayili (1999–today). The first succession was ramified by the open armed conflict between the Nanumba and the Konkomba that rocked political stability of Nanuŋ and its chiefly institutions. Actually according to various informants the not natural death of Bimbilla Naa Dasana in May 1981 followed the first armed clash in April not by chance but because the chief felt guilty for the humiliation which involved not only to numerous Nanumba dead but most importantly the loss of Kpasaland, a Nanumba hunting territory predominantly inhabited by Konkomba settlers. Blaming himself for the first clash and defeat in Kpasa was allegedly connected with his failure to perform ritual bath prescribed by tradition to each Bimbilla Naa (Skalník 1986).

The death of the paramount made easier if not prompted the decision of radicals to attempt to reconquer Kpasaland which followed in June 1981. However this adventurous military campaign ended in a fiasco: Nanumba forces were routed by the well-organized Konkomba warriors who then approached the Bimbilla town and only a contingent of Ghana Army averted the catastrophe. The enskinment in 1983 of Bimbilla Naa Abarika, the younger brother of Bimbilla Naa Natogmah, heralded more active political and hopefully also developmental involvement of the paramount. The chief has tried to find a solution to the stalemate with the Konkomba by negotiation but to no avail.

When later, in 1994, a much more serious armed conflict broke out and seven districts were dragged into it, about 2000 people died and hundreds of compounds were burnt out, the Bimbilla Naa joined forced with other northern Ghanaian chiefs in search for a lasting solution. For example in his memorandum for the Permanent Committee on the Northern Conflict which was established by the Government of Ghana, Bimbilla Naa Abarika mentioned that the chiefdom of Nanuŋ was established long before the colonial conquest and that the Nanumba never had to share their land with the Konkomba. The paramount stressed in the memo the welcoming attitude of the Nanumba towards the first Konkomba settlers. But as other strangers Konkomba when received in Nanuŋ agreed to the customary duties stipulated by Nanumba custom (*kali*). In 1981, explained the Bimbilla Naa, the Konkomba waged war against the Nanumba because they did not want to fulfil these customary duties any more. They ignored the duties ever since. Konkomba settlers in Nanuŋ also wanted more Konkomba chiefs to be enstooled for them even though the custom stipulated one chief for each foreign ethnic group settled in the chiefdom. The 1994 conflict was seen by the Bimbilla Naa as a continuation of the 1981. He relates the escalation of violence to the establishment of the Konkomba Youth Association in 1975. This organisation, he believes, is intended to eject the Nanumba from their legitimate land. The Bimbilla Naa branded the Konkomba as aggressors and saw a further coexistence of the Nanumba with the Konkomba as impossible. The document stated the resolution that "we shall never stay with the Konkombas in Nanun is final and not negotiable" (Skalník 2002). However, within two years, through the sustained efforts of Professor Hizkias Assefa and his Nairobi Peace Initiative[80] the Kumasi Accord on Peace and Reconciliation between the Various Ethnic Groups in the Northern Region of Ghana was achieved in which Nanumba and six other ethnic groups involved in the 1994 conflict obliged themselves not to resort to violent means in resolution of mutual conflicts. The Nanumba, for their part, signed by their three representatives that from then onward the Konkomba will be treated by them as "brothers in development" and not as mere alien tenants. Even though the Konkomba will have to respect Nanumba customary law and usage as the Nanumba were recognized by the Accord as "the sole owners of the land in Nanun". Nanumba had to admit that their accusation that the Konkomba sought to take their land from them was untrue and thus invalid (Skalník 2003). When I saw Bimbilla Naa Abarika last time, in 1997, he was still fairly sceptical about the Kumasi Peace Accord but he admitted that it holds.

The Bimbilla Naa died in 1999 and the peace accord still holds, probably also because the Ghanaian state is more careful to distinguish between "chieftaincy quarrels" and interethnic clashes or even wars. The latter is an anathema for the postcolonial state as it is directly undermining the political system, threatens with secession, nay disintegration of the modern state. Peculiar is that Nanumba-Konkomba relations have improved, even it happened in Nanumba electoral constituencies that Nanumba and Konkomba candidates stood for the same party. Wienia describes the "calm" tension in Nanuŋ in mid-2000 which culminated in new clashes around chieftaincy in early 2007 (Wienia 2008).

---

[80] Martijn Wienia offers a detailed description of Assefa´s activities, see Wienia 2008.

The conflict potential shifted from the Nanumba-Konkomba relations to the conflict about succession to the Bimbilla skin which flared up openly after the *naakuli* (ritual funeral) of Bimbilla Naa Abarika in 2003. There was no quarrel about alternation as it was clear to everyone that it was Gbuxumayili's turn after the funeral of the Baŋyili paramount. The problem was however who from the Lion´s house should become the new Bimbilla Naa. The evident successor was the Nakpaa Naa Salifu Dawuni, a great grandson of Bimbilla Naa Dawuni. He became the chief of the Gbuxumayili gate town of Nakpaa after being an incumbent of Bakpaba *naam* which became a notorious chieftaincy when three predecessors on Bakpaba skin died under strange circumstances. Standing against him is Andani Dasana, eldest son of Bimbilla Naa Dasana. Andani has never been a chief; he studied for an engineer and worked as such in Tamale until 2003. The complication is in the fact that six out of nine electors have sided with Andani. Most powerful among the pro-Andani electors is the Wulehe Naa, an influential yam trader living for decades in Accra who was enskinned as the Wulehe Naa by the *gbonlana*, Naa Abarika´s eldest son. Thus a party called by me "progressives" because they respect business efficiency more than tradition has tried to enforce Andani as the new Bimbilla Naa referring to "democracy" of majority and not to traditional Nanumba principle of consensus of all electors. Under the conditions of chaos two Bimbilla Naanima were enskinned and the Ghana court resolved that these enskinments were invalid. Obviously also Nanumba tradition would disagree with two parallel courts and two paramount chiefs. This resembled the situation which for years has prevailed at Yendi (Skalník 2008).

Conclusion

The main actor in the dispute was of course the modern state, whether colonial or independent, which intervened whenever it felt that violence might break out. Ostensibly declaring that 'traditional' matters are to be resolved by the parties concerned, the modern state could not allow the breech of its monopoly of the use of force and thus allow the existence of a state within the state. Chiefdoms such as Nanuŋ may have own political culture but it should never disturb the internal sovereignty of the imported state. Thus it was the modern state which intervened in the traditional politics rather than chiefdom such as Nanuŋ competing with the modern state.

TRADITION-BASED RECONCILIATION CEREMONIES AND RITUALS IN POST-WAR SIERRA LEONE

Kateřina Werkman

Charles University, Prague

Index words: Sierra Leone; reconciliation; tradition/traditional; conflict management; cleansing/purification ceremonies/rituals; reintegration; child soldiers; peace building; Truth and Reconciliation Commission (TRC); Fambul Tok; Revolutionary United Front (RUF)

Sierra Leone was torn apart by a violent conflict that lasted for over a decade between 1991 and 2002. As with other societies emerging from war, one of the major challenges it faced in its aftermath was to find ways for the people to live together again – the combatants and civilians, victims and perpetrators. Two critical questions needed to be answered in this respect – how to reintegrate the combatants back into the communities and persuade the civilians to accept them and how to foster reconciliation and peace while delivering at least a degree of accountability for what happened.

It is mainly in response to these challenges that the use of traditional conflict management practices has been discussed and advocated. It is believed that traditional methods and institutions contain within themselves a great potential that can be put to use in the process of restoring war-torn societies and building peace. Throughout Africa, there are many examples of traditional practices being explored and adapted for the challenges of post-war reintegration and reconciliation. In Mozambique, traditional cleansing and purification ceremonies have made a contribution to the reintegration of ex-combatants into their communities. In Rwanda, the traditional gacaca courts have been adapted to deal with the backlog of perpetrators and bring about justice and reconciliation. Also in South Africa, Burundi, Uganda and elsewhere traditional concepts, practices and institutions were used in post-war contexts.[81]

This chapter is structured as follows. It firstly considers the general arguments about the major strengths and weaknesses of the African tradition-based approaches in the context of contemporary post-war reconciliation and peace building efforts put forward in the theoretical and empirical literature on the subject. It then moves on to discuss three instances in which the local traditional practices were put to use in post-conflict Sierra

---

[81] For Mozambique, see for example Honwana 2006. The *gacaca* courts in Rwanda belong to the most widely cited adaptations of traditional practices and also to the most problematic. See for example Le Mon (2007) or research by Susan M.Thomson. Allen (2006) brings a critical discussion of the Mato Oput ritual in dealing with the LRA combatants in Northern Uganda and a detailed discussion of the traditional justice among the Acholi and the ways they have been used in reintegrating former rebels can be found in Baines et al .(2005). The bashingantahe institution in Burundi is discussed for example in Ntahombaye et al (1999).

Leone. After a brief background to the armed conflict itself, the child ex-combatants reintegration programmes, the Truth and Reconciliation Commission and the Fambul Tok grass-roots initiative are explored in more detail.

Several issues need to be addressed before the discussion can commence. First, the terms 'tradition' or 'traditional' are rather ambiguous[82] and often bear 'Eurocentric connotations that tend to view such institutions and practices as "patterns followed from 'time out of mind' in static political and social circumstances" (Alie 2008:133). Tradition is not something inert, unaltered or archaic. Rather, it is 'inspired by a group's past' but being continually updated, adapted and adjusted to respond to the changing political, economic and social circumstances as well as able to incorporate external influences in order to survive (Stovel, 2008; Alie, 2008; Zartman 2000). It is in this sense that 'tradition' is used in this article.

Second, any attempt to discuss the general features of traditional conflict management practices in Africa faces the dilemma of finding a balance between the universal and the particular in these practices. On the one hand, traditional practices and institutions are always context specific – in fact 'the contextual embeddedness in itself is a decisive feature of the traditional approaches' (Boege 2006:6). They are rooted in the culture and history of the particular people and are in one way or another unique to each community. On the other hand, they also show many similarities across the many African societies. Lending, borrowing and fusion of different cultural traits might have gradually occurred as a result of frequent population movements across ethnic boundaries for the purpose of inter-regional trade, inter-marriage, conquest or else (Apollos and Yakubu 1999:5). A certain degree of generalization seems therefore justified although at the same time it remains tentative.

African Traditional Practices in Post-War Situations

The debate on the role of traditional conflict management practices and institutions in modern post-war situations is not a new one and can be observed both in the theory and practice since at least the early 1990s. In the conflict resolution field, an emphasis on more culturally sensitive approaches came with the concept of transformative peace building. John Paul Lederach suggests that "peace building initiatives and solutions [...] must be rooted in the soil where the conflict rages and must be built on contextualized participation of people from that setting if reconciliation is to be sustained" (Lederach 1997:107). Similarly, in practice the traditional mechanisms and ceremonies have been part of government and civil society considerations in designing post-war peace building strategies at least since the end of the civil war in Mozambique (Stovel 2008).

Every post-war society faces a distinct mixture of challenges stemming from the different history and nature of the conflict, which to an important extent influences the possibilities and limits of using and adapting the traditional practices. Some of their

---

[82] For an important discussion on tradition see Hobsbawm and Ranger 1983.

general characteristics can nonetheless be identified that make them highly relevant for post-war states, societies and communities – most importantly their orientation toward reconciliation and their participatory nature.

Reconciliation and restoration of relationships and social harmony are the principal goals of traditional practices as opposed to retribution and punishment. The conflict is viewed less in terms of a problem between two parties but rather understood as one occurring between an offender and the community. Consequently, rather than proving individual innocence or guilt, the ultimate purpose of the conflict management process is mending the broken relationships, reinforcing social solidarity and restoring order and harmony in the community (Ngwane 1996:52). In fact, reintegration of the offender into the community is implied by the demand to restore social harmony as punishing the offender would be "harming the group a second time" (Faure 2000:158).

Another potential merit lies in the participatory nature of the traditional mechanisms. Participation of whole communities is crucial in post-war peace building as it contributes to the sustainability of the process. Traditional mechanisms are usually public and inclusive. Not only the parties to the conflict have the opportunity to tell their story but also people from extended family, neighbours and other members of the community can take part. This results in an agreement, which reflects the consensus of the entire community as inclusively as possible. Herein the belief is embodied that "the whole group always has some responsibility for what people do, or do not do, as it plays a central role in the education of its members and the position they later on occupy" (Faure 2000:159) while at the same time every individual is a part of the communal body and therefore his action affects the well-being to the whole community. Thus the individual and the community are inseparable and everybody has to take responsibility for the solution and restoration of harmony. This is well represented in the case of the Rwandan traditional gacaca courts, an informal, community-based ad hoc meeting convened to resolve disputes among its members. It is attended by the disputants as well as the affected community and chaired by a wise and respected elder who leads the hearings and discussions. The achieved settlement must be acceptable to all participants. The goal of gacaca is thus to "sanction the violation of rules that are shared by the community, with the sole objective of reconciliation" and to restore harmony and social order and re-include the perpetrator (OAU 2000).[83]

Traditional practices also make use of different methods of healing and purification, performed by traditional healers or other spiritual authorities that serve to appease the spirits and the ancestors and also play a critical role in the mental and spiritual rehabilitation of victims and perpetrators (Boege 2006:15). Singing or dancing together also plays an important role. In the current practice, such ceremonies are often used as

---

[83] The adapted gacaca tribunals set up to deal with the perpetrators of the 1994 genocide are however very different from the traditional ones. In fact, they are much more strongly focused on legal retribution rather than restoration of harmony and reconciliation.

part of reintegration of former child soldiers. "The performance of these ceremonies as rituals of integration create a spiritual tranquillity in the people while individuals living in communities see themselves (feel) protected and capable of confronting any situation which the integration of children involved in armed conflict might bring about" (Bennet 1999).

A further supposed advantage concerns the traditional institutions and authorities. Some believe that while the legitimacy of the state institutions in many African states has been shaken by years of misconduct, corruption and conflict, involving traditional institutions in post-war peace building and reconciliation "takes into account that in general people on the ground have a desire for peace building and perceive respective endeavours as positive, whereas state-building is often perceived as irrelevant for peace and order and [...] even seen as negative" (Boege 2006:14).

There are however several reasons for caution when contemplating the potential of traditional mechanisms and practices. First of all, traditional institutions and actors are not always as detached from the state as an idealised perception of traditions as something 'preserved from the better days' might imply. Many post-independence political leaders have used traditional authorities to mobilize and sustain popular support for the regime. Osaghae beliefs that "relevance and applicability of traditional strategies have been greatly disenabled by the politicization, corruption, and abuse of traditional structures…which have steadily delegitimized conflict management built around them in the eyes of many, and reduced confidence in their efficacy" (Osaghae 2000:215).

Furthermore, these mechanisms are based on a set of social normative values that make up the ground for their effectiveness and are therefore limited to the contexts of small local communities (Faure 2000:165). "African traditional management techniques depend [...] on the existence of a community of relationships and values to which they can refer and that provide the context for their operations" (Zartman 2000:224). The lack of such common ground can be observed in the case of young ex-combatants who are often deeply alienated from their communities, traditional values and ways of life, so that using traditional practices to reintegrate them into these communities might just be ineffective (Boege 2006:16). Protracted armed conflicts, population shifts, urbanization or intermarriage may too have decreased the appeal and influence of traditional practices. In Uganda, forced displacement and decades of life in the Internally Displaced Persons (IDP) camps caused that "many people today no longer automatically know their Rwot [anointed chief], nor what his role should be" (Baines 2005:21). As traditional ways of transmitting the cultural norms have been restricted in the IDP camps, many Elders also observed they didn't command the level of respect they once did from their communities, and particularly from the youths (Baines 2005:22).

Lastly, traditional methods and institutions are often very conservative and inflexible in the values they aim to protect and may contradict universal human rights standards. In many practices, it is the village male elders who play a central role while women and young men tend to be excluded from the councils.[84] Women can often be victims of the resolutions under customary law – swapping women or giving girls as compensation are not uncommon (Boege 2006:6).

The War in Sierra Leone

The following part presents a brief insight into the history of the war in Sierra Leone.[85] The civil conflict erupted in March 1991 when rebels of the Revolutionary United Front (RUF) led by a former army corporal Foday Sankoh and numbering initially just over a hundred men, entered from Liberia the Kailahun and Pujehun districts in the south-eastern parts of Sierra Leone.

The attacks were preceded by several decades of deteriorating political, economic and social conditions in the country as a result of bad governance and abuses of power, bad economic policies, plundering of the country's rich mineral resources and rampant corruption. Since the introduction of one-party system in 1978, power and resources were fully in the hands of the All People's Congress (APC) government in Freetown while the upcountry rural areas were very marginalized or completely neglected – especially the opposition Sierra Leone People's Party (SLPP) strongholds in the eastern and southern parts of the country. Abuse of power was not limited to central government. Especially in the provincial areas, local government officials and chiefs who retained an important role in interpreting customary law used their authority to "reinforce hierarchies of class, gender and age and to silence or marginalize those who they perceived as a threat" (Stovel 2008). It was mainly young men who suffered most from this abuse. Compounded by poor educational and employment opportunities this led to the alienation of young men, many of whom left their villages for diamond mines or big towns. The disgruntled youth then formed a ready pool of recruits for the armed factions when the war broke out (Alie 2008; Hoffman 2003; TRC 2004).[86]

The rebels achieved initial success and enjoyed some support from the population as they tried to capitalize on people's frustration to present themselves as liberators. The first phase of the war until November 1993 was a "conventional 'target' warfare" with head to head fighting between the RUF and the Sierra Leone Army (SLA) (TRC 2004). After the military coup by a group of young army officers in April 1992 and setting

---

[84] In Sierra Leone, some truth-seeking mechanisms are headed by women. There is however no place for young men. See Alie 2008.

[85] This is a very short introduction of some of the important features of the conflict. For a more detailed account of the war, see e.g. Adebajo 2002 or Keen 2005.

[86] While the root causes of the conflict are largely internal, the conflict became highly internationalized with many outside parties intervening to support either side in the civil war which probably contributed to prolonging and intensifying the war. Liberia and Burkina Faso supported the RUF, motivated mainly by economic opportunism (mainly diamonds, but also bauxite and rutile), the government was supported by the Nigeria-dominated West African peacekeeping force ECOMOG as well as several private military companies intervened.

up of the National Provisional Ruling Council (NPRC), intensive military operations were launched that brought the RUF to the verge of defeat in November 1993. The NPRC was also seen by many citizens as the desired regime change which detracted the initial sympathy for the RUF. It was at this point that the RUF announced the reversion to 'jungle warfare' that relied on ambush and terror tactics against both soldiers and civilians, and used abductions, mainly of children, as a main means of recruitment. By making the lives of the people unbearable by using large-scale violence that commonly included murder, amputations, rape and torture as well as the systematic destruction of property, the RUF aimed at forcing the government to negotiate a power-sharing deal (TRC 2004).

Successive military and later democratically elected governments waged war against the rebels but were unable to decisively defeat them. In reaction to the RUF scare tactics, the government forces often adopted 'irrational responses' and also committed many serious crimes (TRC 2004). After a rebel offensive on Freetown in January 1999 that left many casualties and half of the city was burnt in its wake, a peace agreement was finally signed in Lomé in June 1999.

At least two provisions of the comprehensive peace agreement are important for the following discussion. Firstly, a blanket amnesty was granted to all the rebels under the deal.[87] Second, and related to the previous, it envisaged the establishment of a Truth and Reconciliation Commission as an accountability mechanism tasked with "address[ing] impunity, break[ing] the cycle of violence, provid[ing] a forum for both the victims and perpetrators of human rights violations to tell their story, get[ting] a clear picture of the past in order to facilitate genuine healing and reconciliation" (Lomé Peace Agreement 1999:Art.XXVI).

Traditional Conflict Management and Reconciliation Practices in Sierra Leone

Most ethnic groups in Sierra Leone have complex social, cultural and belief systems that include methods and practices to deal with crime and punishment, compel truth-telling and promote reconciliation. Responsible for administering justice and resolving conflict in the communities are the local authorities. At the top of their hierarchical structure is the Paramount Chief who chairs the Council of Elders[88]. The disputes they usually deal with include land and marital disputes, arson, theft, incest and other sexual offences, etc.[89] One issue pointed out as problematic with respect to the use traditional practices in the current post-war situation is the lack of mechanisms to deal with the kind of atrocities

---

[87] Later however the Special Court was set up to prosecute the major offenders for serious war crimes.

[88] Some of the groups view the Paramount Chief as an incarnation of the ancestors which gives him important political as well as spiritual powers while in others he is seen more as just one of the members of the Council of Elders with much less influence.

[89] For more on the systems and practices of customary law in Sierra Leone see e.g.. Manifesto 99 (2000). This article only outlines some of the aspects of the conflict resolution practice and community reconciliation.

that were routinely committed during the war such as amputations and abductions, as well as the high occurrence of otherwise rare crimes like murder or rape, which were often dealt with outside the realm of customary justice (Manifesto 99:36).

The process of conflict resolution itself consists of questioning of the victim, the suspect and the witnesses, giving testimony and oath taking. Once the truth is established, the elders may order the culprit's family to pay in money or goods or some other form of restitution or compensation (Jabarti Interview; Manifesto 99). Ceremonial acts such as reconciliation and cleansing rituals or pouring of libations are also an important part of the process. These have their roots in the traditional belief systems – which also share some important similarities among the different ethnic groups in the country.

Fundamental to these beliefs is the belief in the supernatural. This has three main elements. The first is the belief in a supreme being. Second is the belief in spirits or natural divinities that mainly reside in the 'bush' and can be either good or bad. Third is belief in the spirits of the ancestors who continue to influence the day-to-day affairs of the living. (Alie 2008:136; Manifesto 99:31)

In this respect, the notion of spiritual pollution or contamination is important. Those who killed, participated in killings or saw people being killed are believed to have angered the spirits who – unless they are appeased – will administer their wrath in the form of health problems, poor harvests or other misfortunes at the expense of both the perpetrators and their communities. Spirits of those who were killed or mistreated in life – in Sierra Leone called 'mompilas' – have the power to hurt or haunt those who cause their death or suffering (Gbla 2003:186). Not only killing but also having sexual intercourse or rape in the bush are a serious crime and could upset the ancestral spirits. "If a woman is raped on a farm, the food will spoil. So you have to offer a sacrifice to the ancestors on the farm and cleanse the girl on the farm..." (Stark 2006:214). Certain crimes like rape, incest, defilement of the bush, shedding blood or murder therefore require cleansing rituals to take place to deal with the spiritual pollution. Similarly, acts like pouring of libation are performed to appease the spiritual world (Manifesto 99:34).

Cursing or swearing bad deeds or crimes which no one admits is another traditional practice that is widely shared among most of the groups. The type of swearing or curse depends on the type of crime and differs from one ethnic group to another but the central aim is the same – the curse is meant to bring punishment in the form of misfortune, disease or death to the offender and his family and thereby motivate him or coerce him to come forward and admit to his crime in order to avoid the consequences of the curse. Among the Mende, for example, stealing is punished with the Sasa curse that inflicts bronchitis upon the offender, while adultery and sexual offences are associated with the Ngegba curse that brings death by thunderbolt (Manifesto 99:31–32). A suspect may be ostracised by his family and the whole community who will be afraid to share his faith, which may add another incentive for the offender to admit to his wrongdoing (Manifesto 99:31–33). When he does so, the curse is not valid.

Traditional belief systems and customs still play an important role in the lives of people and communities in Sierra Leone, including the field of conflict resolution and reconciliation (Manifesto 99; Caulker Interview; Williams Interview). The war has however impacted critically on traditional institutions and practices in Sierra Leone. The rebels often specifically targeted the traditional leaders whom they saw as part of the structures they were trying to topple (Alie 2008). The combatants also desecrated or devastated places in the bush where many such ceremonies used to occur and destroyed ceremonial objects, all of which led to a decrease in their prestige and relevance (Alie 2008:140; Jabarti Interview).

Cleansing and healing ceremonies and the reintegration of child soldiers

Traditional cleansing and reconciliation ceremonies were probably most widely used across the country as part of reintegration programmes for child ex-combatants implemented by national and international agencies and NGOs like UNICEF, International Rescue Committee, Caritas Makeni, Children Associated with War and others.[90] As mentioned above, children were abducted – or in some cases joined voluntarily – to fight for the RUF and also fought in the ranks of the army and the local civil defence militias. Exact numbers are not known but UNICEF documented 8466 children as 'missing' between 1991 and 2002 (Williamson 2006). According to demobilization figures, approximately 6787 children were formally demobilized between 1998 and 2003 (Denov 2007).

As mentioned earlier, ancestral spirits and other spiritual forces play an important role in the socio-cultural settings of Sierra Leone both in the well-being of the community as well as of the individuals. The returning children were believed to be polluted by the spirits of the dead and cleansing ceremonies were therefore performed to appease the spirits and bring peace to both the child ex-combatants and to their communities. At least two roles of these rituals are critically important in the reintegration process. Firstly, they are gestures of acceptance of the children and of community reconciliation. Caritas Makeni, for example, decided to make use of these ceremonies because "for the people to be able to receive the children wholeheartedly... acts like washing feet, joint dancing, drumming... shows that people forgave and are willing to accept those kids" (Williams, interview). Secondly, they can be seen as symbols of a spiritual transformation of the individual children for which it is an opportunity to put the past behind and feel better and more acceptable (Williamson et al 2002:29).

The ceremonies took various forms in the different communities. In a cleansing ceremony carried out for a 15 year old ex-RUF returnee in northern Sierra Leone, "the elders in his family... took the boy to the bush where a hut had been built using grass... On entering the hut, Amadu [the ex-combatant] was asked to undress himself, that is, to take off the clothes he used to put on while with the RUF. The hut and the clothes

---

[90] These programmes included many other aspects too like community sensitization, Interim Care Centres, school or skills training, counselling, etc. See Williamson 2006.

were then set alight while an adult relative helped out the boy quickly. The burning of the hut and the clothes and everything else that the boy brought from the war symbolically represents his sudden break from an evil past. Immediately thereafter, a chicken was sacrificed to the spirits of the dead and the blood smeared around the ritual place" (Gbla 2003:188).

Cleansing ceremonies also played an important role in some NGOs' programmes in helping young women associated with the fighting forces as well as those who had been subjected to rape or other forms of sexual abuse to return and be accepted in their communities. Girls and young women were largely left out in the official disarmament, demobilization and reintegration programmes and received only little attention despite being one of the hardest hit groups.[91] Upon their return, girls and young women were often stigmatized, discriminated against or rejected by their families and communities because they were seen as impure and polluted as result of the sexual abuse. The spiritual contamination was believed to impact on many aspects of the girls as well as community lives. Cleansing ceremonies then had similar effects as in the case of child soldiers and facilitated the girls' reintegration as well as improved their self-perception and psychosocial health (Stark 2006).

Although all these cleansing ceremonies were part of larger externally-driven interventions, which may raise suspicion that the demand for them may be outside-driven, much evidence confirms that this is not the case. In the communities where Caritas Makeni worked is was requested that the rituals be a part of the reintegration programmes (Williams interview). Similarly, Stark's study found that carrying out the cleansing ceremonies for the girls was either desired by the girls themselves or by their families, with the decision mostly supported by both parties (Stark, 2006:213). In addition another study confirms that the rituals and ceremonies were in some cases arranged by the families and communities themselves with the NGOs only helping them to obtain the items needed for such ceremonies (Williamson 2006:196).

Truth and Reconciliation Commission

The potential involvement of the traditional institutions and use of traditional conflict management practices were some of the key issues discussed in the preparatory phase before setting up the TRC. The TRC Act gives the Commission the right to "seek assistance from traditional and religious leaders to facilitate its public sessions and in resolving local conflicts arising from past violations or abuses or in support of healing and reconciliation" (TRC Act 2000:III.7). To this end the UN Office of the High Commissioner for Human Rights funded research by a local NGO Manifesto 99 into the practices among the country's different ethnic groups. The study recommended that

---

[91] Of the above mentioned UNICEF estimate of 8466 'missing' children, as many as half of these are believed to have been girls.

the TRC should make use of traditional beliefs and customs of the local communities in order to reinforce people's ownership of the reconciliation process – an opinion endorsed by many others (Caulker Interview). Importantly, the belief in swearing and cursing was suggested to be seriously considered by the TRC as it could facilitate the processes of confession, and subsequently granting a pardon and forgiveness (Manifesto 99:25).

The Commission's public hearings commenced in April 2003 and lasted just over four months. During this period, the TRC travelled to each of the country's districts for week-long sessions. Traditional and religious leaders were present at the public hearings but their most important role was at the closing ceremonies on the final day of each district hearing. These official ceremonies on many occasions drew from the traditional rituals of forgiveness and reconciliation for those perpetrators who showed repentance and asked to be publicly forgiven, such as in Kailahun, Makeni or Tonkolili (Kelsall, OHCHR Report). They differed from place to place and often also included setting up symbolic monuments or memorials in places of important events or mass killings to mark the reconciliation, like in Bo and Kenema (OHCHR Report).

In Tonkolili in northern Sierra Leone, the closing ceremony was inaugurated with Christian and Muslim prayers after which the ex-combatants were invited to come forward and ask for forgiveness. "The perpetrators sat in a row of chairs behind the lectern... They looked nervous. One by one, they were invited to apologize. Base Marine, the local commander of the RUF, got up and said he was sorry... [His] face was hard, but he spoke with gravitas. He knelt at the table before the paramount chief and the three leaders touched his head. ...After the confessions, the Bishop brought together Base Marine and the witness who had impugned him. They smiled and embraced to applause." Afterwards traditional leaders gathered in the front of the hall, "intoned a mantra, clapped and poured libations of whisky on the floor" (Kelsall 2005:378–380).

Although it makes more sense to talk about these ceremonies as tradition-inspired rather than traditional, in many places they did seem to have an important symbolic value and reconciling effect. Kelsall observed "an emotionally charged atmosphere that succeeded in moving many of the participants and spectators, ... and which arguably opened an avenue for reconciliation and lasting peace" (2005:363). In Bo, the ceremony also included the acknowledgement of the harm done, prayers, pouring of libations and a symbolic renaming of a so-called 'Soldier Killed Rebel Junction' to a 'Peace Junction' and created a 'deeply moving atmosphere' which had a visible 'healing effect'. On the contrary, the conciliatory effect of the closing ceremony in Kailahun was much more ambiguous as the harm caused was not acknowledged by all sides. (Personal conversation with Laura Stovel, see also Stovel 2006).

On the whole, the TRC did not make as much use of the traditional practices and rituals as was expected or hoped for. There may be several explanations for this. Firstly, the Commissioners did not always have enough trust in the traditional authorities because of their association with the political and state structures and problems with corruption. The TRC was also wary as it received many complaints about violations committed by many of the Chiefs during the conflict "for which they neither as a group nor individually expressed remorse or offered any explanation to their communities" and made the Commissioners feel uncomfortable relying on the traditional structures to foster reconciliation (TRC 2004). Some of the traditional practices were also considered by the Commission as backward and contradictory to universal human rights standards (TRC 2004). Particularly the decision not to use swearing and cursing to encourage confessions and truth-telling is seen by some as a wasted opportunity (Alie 2008; Kelsall 2005), especially in a situation where a blanket amnesty meant the perpetrators had little motivation to come forward and tell the truth.

Community Reconciliation: Fambul Tok

With the publication of the TRC Report in 2004 and end of the reintegration programmes around the same time, problems of reconciliation largely disappeared from public sight. However, many communities both in the rural areas and in towns remain deeply divided (Caulker interview, Jabarti interview). While the top-down initiatives like the TRC have been limited in reaching the communities outside the major district centres, these have been so decimated by the war that it has so far been too difficult for them to find their own way to deal with the problems (Caulker interview). In response, a local NGO Forum of Conscience launched a nationwide initiative called Fambul Tok in 2008. Over the course of the coming years, reconciliation events will take place in the local communities across the whole country.

'Fambul Tok' means 'family talk' in Krio and is a symbolic expression of the effort to involve all the members of the local communities across the country – victims, perpetrators or witnesses – to participate in rebuilding mutual trust and respect and draw everyone 'back into the Sierra Leone family' (Fambul Tok 2008). This is to be achieved through traditional reconciliation ceremonies that the communities themselves will identify as appropriate. By giving an opportunity to the victims and perpetrators to tell the truth in front of the whole community about what had happened and ask for and offer forgiveness when ready, these ceremonies give an opportunity to the communities to reflect on the past, acknowledge the wrongdoings and empower them to deal with it (Hoffman, 2008:132). Groups of villages in each chiefdom set up reconciliation committees – in which not only elders and religious leaders but also women and the youth had a representative – that then design and prepare the reconciliation ceremony based of their specific local practice.

Fambul Tok launched its work in Kailahun district in the east of Sierra Leone which was one of the most affected by the war. I was given the opportunity to witness one of these ceremonies in a village in Kissy-Kama chiefdom, just a few minutes walk from the country's border with Guinea. The ceremony started with a joint meal of traditional rice and cassava leaf for everyone. In Sierra Leone, sharing a communal meal is an important event and a can also be an important gesture of reconciliation (see also Stark 2006:213). A bonfire was then lit and the chiefs started the ceremony. First, the truth-telling – a young man told a story of the death of his family members after they had been discovered in their hide-out in the bush. He then pointed at another man who he knew had been responsible for committing these murders. The perpetrator then came forward to face the victim and the community. He admitted to the killings, apologized and asked for forgiveness, which he was given and the men shook hands. They were one of four victim-perpetrator pairs that shared their story that evening. After that, a possessed diviner spoke to the ancestral spirits about sacrifices they needed to appease. On the next morning, people were singing and dancing accompanied by drummers, awaiting in a celebratory atmosphere the elders, chiefs and the Paramount Chief who slowly gathered in the village to take a goat and kola nuts to a sacred place to offer them to the ancestors (to where no women or children were allowed to follow them). The ceremony was then concluded with another joint meal.

While it is too early to judge the reconciliatory effect of these ceremonies, it seems the Fambul Tok is filling in several gaps left in the reconciliation process to date. Firstly, they reach out to the remotest places in the country where the TRC had hardly had any impact. Secondly, the consultative nature of the initiative and the participation of the local communities in designing their own ceremonies raise the prospects giving them a sense of ownership over the whole process and thus improve its sustainability. And thirdly, it offers space to engage the adult ex-combatants who previously had little motivation or opportunity to come forward, confess and ask for forgiveness.[92] There is already some evidence of this, as about 90 % of those who testified at the Kailahun ceremonies so far were ex-combatants (Hoffman 2008:136).

Conclusion

Two challenges in the post-war situations – reintegration of the combatants and reconciliation were identified in the introduction as areas where traditional institutions and practices could play an important role. This article focused on three instances in which reconciliation and cleansing ceremonies – as a specific feature of traditional practices – have been used in Sierra Leone. Cleansing ceremonies made important contributions mainly to the successful reintegration of child soldiers back into their families and communities, although arguably not just on their own accord but complementary to other measures implemented by national and international agencies and NGOs. In the same way, the cleansing ceremonies where carried out they improved communities' acceptance of the victims of rape and sexual violence. There is no evidence, however, that such ceremonies were used outside these official programmes or that adult ex-combatants would take part in any reconciliation or cleansing rituals upon return to their home or other communities.

---

[92] An important factor in their reluctance to do so in the past (and even at present) is the fear of being arrested and prosecuted by the Special Court for Sierra Leone as there is little knowledge up country about the role or jurisdiction of the Court.

Traditional reconciliation rituals also stood as an inspiration for the closing ceremonies that marked the ending of each district hearing of the TRC. The most important body of transitional justice in Sierra Leone arguably did not make the most of the traditional practices. Particularly the use of the practice of cursing and swearing as tools to compel perpetrators to confess seems in many respects a lost opportunity as it may have brought more confessions – and more truth-telling.

There is now certain hope that the Fambul Tok-supported ceremonies in the villages across the country will in some places push forward the reconciliation process that has so far gone only half way – as people in Sierra Leone are now able to live together in peace but much distrust persists in the local communities. It is important to bear in mind that traditional ceremonies and rituals should be seen as important but mainly symbolic expressions of reconciliation. 'True' reconciliation is better understood as a long journey in which the traditional conciliatory practices can only complement other efforts and processes.

Interviews: (March-June 2008)
John Caulker (Forum of Conscience)
Raphael Williams (Caritas Makeni)
Mohamed Jabarti
and personal conversation with Laura Stovel

THE PROLIFERATION OF MERCENARIES IN PRECOLONIAL AND POSTCOLONIAL AFRICA IN WORLD HISTORICAL PERSPECTIVE[93]

Richard Bradshaw and Ibrahim Ndzesop[94]
Centre College, Danville, Kentucky, U.S.A. and Université Paris I, France

The presence of mercenaries in Africa during the last half century has provoked a great deal of concern (Beshir 1972; US Congress 1976; Thomas 1984; Mockler 1987; Bernales 1997; Adams 1999; Musah and Fayemi, 2000; Nduru 2004; Francis 2005; Venter 2006; Roberts 2006; Dunnigan 2008) but there has been no effort to place this phenomenon in a long-term, comparative perspective. From a world historical perspective, the proliferation and reduction of mercenary activity in Africa has been closely linked to state-formation and disintegration, in other words, to the imposition and loss of monopolies on the use of force. The use of mercenaries reached an all time high in Africa during the 19th century, declined dramatically once European colonial rule was well-established, and then increased again during the postcolonial and post-Cold War eras (Bradshaw 2007). Contrary to the oft-repeated claim that the use of mercenaries all but disappeared in the wake of the American and French Revolutions (Urban 2007; Avant 2000; Thompson 1994; Percy 2007), the employment of mercenaries increased not only in Africa but in most parts of the world during the 19th century. This fact undermines the claim that an anti-mercenary norm resulted in a decrease in mercenaries after the American and French Revolutions (Percy 2007).

Anti-mercenary norms have never had any significant long-term impact on the use of mercenaries. Instead, increases and decreases in the use of mercenaries throughout world history have been linked to the rise and fall of states and empires and the expansion and contraction of trade. The use of mercenaries usually diminishes quickly when states and empires establish near-monopolies on the use of force but rises rapidly again during civil wars or the fragmentation of states and empires (Bradshaw 2007; Bradshaw and Ndzesop 2008).

Studies of mercenaries or freelance soldiers-for-hire have generally been limited by a Eurocentric perspective which associates certain types of military manpower with three stages in European history: knights in the Middle Ages, mercenaries during the Early Modern Era and citizen-soldiers or conscripts in the post-Napoleonic Era (Kümmel 2006: 423). Such studies usually ignore the long history of mercenary use in other parts of the world and the ineffectiveness of anti-mercenary norms. This study exams evidence from all major regions of the world in order to place Africa's current security crisis in world-historical perspective.

---

[93] An earlier version of this paper was published online in the first issue of *Afrika Nipashe* 1 (2009).

[94] Send comments to Richard Bradshaw at rick.bradshaw@centre.edu or Ibrahim Ndzesop at University of Paris I, France: ibrahimndzesop@malix.univ-paris1.fr

China

Chinese philosophers have long been preoccupied by the "proper relationship between the soldier and the farmers who made up the vast majority of the population," and the idea of what this relationship ought to be has been "reformulated many times" throughout Chinese history (Graff and Higham 2000: 10). From at least the time of Confucius (c. 500 BCE), many philosophers and government bureaucrats in China have favoured the idea of farmer-soldiers and therefore there has been an anti-mercenary norm among many of the educated elite in China since antiquity.

Nevertheless, all attempts to maintain a military system based on the conscription of farmers ultimately failed, and many dynasties turned increasingly to the use of mercenaries to defend their borders, expand their empire, or crush rebellions. During the Spring and Autumn Period (722-481 BCE), aristocratic elites were the main actors in warfare (Graff and Higham 2000: 10), but mercenaries were also employed. The Ba people of western China "were prized as mercenaries throughout their history," from the Spring and Autumn Period until the Han Dynasty Era. One Ba subgroup, the Bashun, had a reputation as fierce warriors, often served as mercenaries, and "were also known for martial song and dances, which became a staple of the official repertoire" (Kleeman 1988: 4, 45, 53). Thus the use of mercenaries was very common even during the Spring and Autumn Period which Confucian philosophers usually depicted in an idealized manner.

Several major Chinese dynasties attempted to develop armies of conscripts, military colonists or hereditary soldiers, but each of them eventually came to rely increasingly on mercenaries. The Han dynasty (202 BCE – 220 CE) implemented universal conscription, established government-sponsored farms with colonies of veterans, and used criminals as well as conscripts for garrison duty on the Wall of China, but by the Later Han Period mercenary forces came to prevail, which were often paid with money raised by a tax imposed on those not performing compulsory military service (Morton and Lewis 2005: 56). From the 8th century CE on, long-service mercenaries rather than farmer-soldiers "tended to predominate, even as scholars sang the praises of the sturdy (and inexpensive) yeomanry of earlier times" (Graff and Higham 2000: 10).

Mercenaries became common at the end of the Tang Dynasty (589–907 CE) and the Song dynasty (960–1279 CE), when conscripts were replaced by mercenaries. During the last Chinese dynasty, the Qing (1644–1911), the Manchus initially relied on Banner troops and families of hereditary soldiers but in the 19th century, when faced with the Taiping Rebellion, the government, provinces, landlords and urban merchants turned increasingly to the use of mercenaries (McCord 1993; Carr 1995).

Sun Yatsen, regarded as a national hero in both mainland China and Taiwan, repeatedly employed groups of mercenaries in his many failed attempts to overthrow the Manchus, and when he established a base in southern China, he again relied heavily on mercenaries before finally turning to the assistance of the Soviet Union (Bergère 1998). The use of mercenaries thus reached its peak in China in the late 19th and early twentieth centuries and it was not until the Communist victory of 1949–1950 that a new monopoly of force was imposed and the market for military labour collapsed.

Despite anti-mercenary arguments advanced by mandarin elites throughout Chinese history, mercenaries have frequently been employed in China by local lineage leaders, merchants, feudal lords, regional strongmen, rebel leaders, warlords, emperors, and even modern nationalist heroes in the post-Napoleonic era.

Southeast Asia

The first record of mercenaries in Southeast Asia may be in the bas-reliefs of the temple complex built during the 12th century CE at Ankgor Wat in Cambodia, in which the *Siam* or Thai people are mentioned for the first time in inscriptions. These Thai "are pictured as mercenaries of the Khmer army" (Briggs 1949: 62). The Portuguese conquered Malacca in 1511 with the help of six hundred Malabari mercenaries (Cady 1964: 75). Between 1511 and 1814, the Portuguese and the Dutch as well as many local rulers in Southeast Asia frequently employed mercenaries but their use increased in the 18th century and then peaked in the 19th century. In the 18th century, waves of Bugis migrants from southern Salawesi "served as mercenary fighters," and became "involved in the various struggles between rival princes… and virtually controlled the trade of the Malay peninsula during the major part of the eighteenth century" (Saw 1988: 37).

Source: (SarDesai 1997: 88)

During the 19th century, however, after the end of the Napoleonic Wars, the Dutch began consolidating their control over the East Indies (now Indonesia) and needed additional military manpower, so they set up a mercenary-recruiting center which was nicknamed "the sinkhole of Europe." Between 1814 and 1909 more than 176,000 mercenary soldiers were employed at this center, most of whom (106,000) were Dutch volunteers. Others were from Belgium (24,000) and Germany (23,000), but there were also about 7,500 French and almost the same number of Swiss (Wesseling 2004: 37).

In 1800 the Dutch only controlled a small part of what is today Indonesia (see map). But between the early 19th and early 20th centuries, they expanded their control over the whole archipelago and imposed a near-monopoly on the use of force, after which the number of mercenaries decreased dramatically in the early 20th century.

In Vietnam, during a prolonged war between the Tây Son dynasty and the Nguyẹn dynasty for control of the country, both Nguyẹn emperor Nguyẹn Áhn Gia Long (r. 1782–92) in the south and the Tây Son emperor Quang Trung (r. 1788–92) in the north used many mercenaries. Nguyẹn Áhn employed Thai, Chinese, Malay, French, and other mercenaries (Wilcox 2006). Once Nguyẹn Áhn succeeded in imposing his rule, the use of mercenaries declined sharply in Vietnam until the French began to conquer the region. Once the French established a monopoly on the use of force, a relatively small standing army suppressed dissent and rebellion, but after World War II, when France attempted to reconquer Vietnam, it began to employ *montagnard* or 'mountain' mercenaries such as the Hmong who were also used extensively by the United States after the French pulled out of the country (Hamilton-Merritt 1993; Quincy 2000). It was not until Vietnamese communists imposed a monopoly on the use of force that mercenary use dramatically declined.

Many Vietnamese mandarins versed in the Confucian classics no doubt idealized the citizen-soldier and reluctantly resorted to the use of mercenaries, but from the time of the French Revolution until the Vietnam Wars of the mid-20th centuries, mercenaries were often employed when states and empires were in the making, and their use declined rapidly when states enjoyed near-monopolies on the use of force.

Latin America

Mexico is named after the *Mexica* nomads who, after arriving in the Valley of Mexico in the 13th century, worked as mercenaries for the city states there which were in constant conflict among themselves. The class structure of the nomadic Mexica developed as its emerging nobility "gained land for themselves as reward for their efforts in the Tepaneca wars" (Bakewell 2004: 26, 340).

Throughout Latin America, the Spanish, Portuguese, Dutch and French all used local Amerindian mercenaries as well as hirelings from other continents during their conquests. The activities of Amerindian mercenaries have been studied under the label "ethnic soldiering" (Whitehead 1990; Lechner 1990: 47–48). The employment of mercenaries gradually declined as these Europeans powers imposed monopolies on the use of force in their colonies, but in the early 19th century, the Spanish empire in Latin America disintegrated as many local states fought for their independence, and these local states employed many foreign mercenaries during the Wars for Independence (Rodriquez 2006; Brown 2007; Lynch 2006: 121–30; Hasbrouck 1969). Mercenaries were also used to penetrate the interior of states like Brazil, where *bandeirantes* and Indian mercenaries were often employed to defeat and eliminate hostile Indians (Morse 1965).

Even after Latin American countries gained their independence, competing factions often labeled Conservatives and Liberals but always involving struggles for power among local strongmen-*caudillos* (Scheina 2003) with private armies, kept many gunslingers employed during much of the 19th century. In Mexico, this continued during the Mexican Revolution and its aftermath, into the 1930s (Taylor 1986, 1993). Many Mexican leaders, such as Francisco Madero, were initially ideologically opposed to the employment of mercenaries, but various "practical considerations compelled Madero to modify his policy" (Taylor 1986: 30). No anti-mercenary norm stopped Madero and his fellow rebels from hiring many 'Yankee' American and other mercenaries.

After the Mexican Revolution, conservative groups and local strongmen continued to hire mercenaries during the 1930s to intimidate and murder local school teachers and others who attempted to spread the socialist ideals of the revolution (Hamilton 1975: 100). In the 1940s there was stability and the employment of mercenaries fell sharply and remained low until Mexican drug cartels began hiring mercenaries in the 1990s (Farah 1997). The Mexican state was able to impose a near-monopoly on the use of force for only a little more than half a century, between c. 1940 and 1995.

In Latin America, the use of mercenaries did not decline after the French Revolution but rather increased as the Wars of Independence and a century of Conservative-Liberal conflicts between *caudillos* provided enduring employment for mercenaries.

South Asia

Indian mercenaries have found employment at home and abroad since antiquity. In the *Arthasastra* (Science of Politics), believed by many to have been written or compiled from ancient texts by Kautilya in about 300 BCE. This 'first great political realist' wrote that the army "was rooted in the treasury. In the absence of the treasury the army goes over to the enemy or kills the king" (Boesche 2002: 66). Kautilya suggested that "hereditary troops were better than hired troops," but he wrote that kings could conquer enemies by "hiring heroic men," and when Kautilya's patron King Chandragupta conquered much of India and established the Mauryan Empire, he did so with the help of many mercenaries, including *montagnards* from the Himalayas. From the Mauryan to the Mughal Empires, mercenaries were often used in India, and the market for military reached its peak during the 18th century. Millions of soldiers were available for hire by numerous competing states as well as local landlords, merchant princes and caravan leaders (Gordon 1969; Gommans 1993; Kolff 2002). The army of the Mughal Empire was not centralized but consisted largely of units of mercenary soldiers recruited by military entrepreneurs. As the Empire fragmented, successor states competed for military labour which was often employed, as under the Mughals, by military entrepreneurs.

> As the news of the Mughal collapse spread and the consequent opportunities gradually became known, soldiers and mercenaries of all manners descended into the Deccan Plateau and Gujarat. These included Arabs from Hadhramaut, but also Europeans of different nations and their Indian offspring, Pathans and Rohillas from what is now Afghanistan and the Northwest Frontier

Province, and Baluchis from Baluchistan. A smaller number of Sikhs, Rajputs, Sindhis, and Siddis (Africans) completed the picture of free-lancers available for hire in the chaos following the fall of the Mughal Empire (Khalidi 1997: 70).

Numerous Indian states employed European mercenaries to train their troops in the late 18th and early 19th centuries. The ruler of the Sikh Empire, Ranjit Singh, first hired a European mercenary in 1809. By 1822, after the Napoleonic Wars, he had over 50 European mercenaries (Ness and Stahl 1977: 2–29) and he eventually had 200 (Docherty 2008, 198). By this time, however, the British East India Company (BEIC) had expanded its rule over much of India. The Company used local *sepoy* soldiers to conquer India and to establish a near-monopoly on the use of force in the region. By c.1820, the Company employed only about 350,000 *sepoys* (Bayly1990: 68) to rule an area "six times larger than Texas" and "eighteen times larger than the United Kingdom" (Farwell 1989: 18). Although many mercenaries worked for the hundreds of Indian states that continued to exist under British hegemony, hundreds of thousands of mercenaries who had previously been employed by Indian states were put out of work. In 1841 a British officer estimated the Company was using only about 10 percent of the available military manpower. "The nine-tenths, who have been disbanded," he wrote, "remain…in a state of painful transition, longing for some change that may increase the demand for soldiers" (Sleeman 1841: vi-vii).

Britain never completely 'pacified' the Indian subcontinent, and mercenaries working for Indian princes or wealthy landlords sometimes acted as bandits (James 2000: 319). As was the case with the Manchus in China, the British Raj tolerated a good deal of local violence as long as it was not directed against the regime. Bandit gangs continued to operate in India right through the Raj and Independence until the present, but after about 1820, the number of mercenaries in South Asia was small compared to the number of soldiers-for-hire during the disintegration of the Mughal Empire. The Indian princes were pressured to gradually diminish the number of their often mercenary retinues (James 2000: 319). Even after World War I, British India, with a population of 300 million and growing nationalism, had an army of only 206,000 soldiers, about a third of whom from Great Britain.

North America
U.S. mythology emphasizes the role of citizen-soldiers in the Revolutionary War and yet George Washington suggested the employment of Amerindian mercenaries and the Continental Congress approved their use even before the Declaration of Independence was issued (Davis 1887). Washington also welcomed the assistance of many European mercenaries and French assistance played a critical role in the defeat of the British. But it was in the 19th century that the U.S. gained a reputation as "a filibustering nation" (May 1991: 857). Filibusters were soldiers who joined unauthorized military expeditions to foreign countries, who were often promised money and land as a reward for their service. As the U.S. expanded westward to the Pacific and gobbled up much of Mexico, American

filibusters and mercenaries were particularly active in Latin America. They did not have the official approval of the U.S. government, which often attempted to stop filibustering expeditions, but these American adventurers were often regarded as national heroes even though they were defying American neutrality laws (May 1991; May 2002).

The U.S. government also employed mercenaries and privateers, however. During the First Barbary War (1801–1805), President Thomas Jefferson authorized the employment of mercenaries to join an expedition to attack Tripoli in an effort to stop North African pirates from capturing, enslaving or ransoming Americans (Zacks 2005). During the War of 1812, the British navy outnumbered the U.S. navy by nearly ten to one, so the U.S. Congress gave the president authority to "issue to private armed vessels of the United States commissions or letters or marquee and general reprisal, as such form as he shall think proper, and under the Seal of the United States" (Armstrong 2007, 169). The U.S. government even offered a $25 bounty for every British prisoner brought to the States. Many Amerindians also assisted the Americans against the British during the War of 1812, and continued to assist the U.S. army throughout the 19th century (Dunlay 1982).

American mercenaries fought for both sides in the 1826–28 war between the United Provinces of Rio de la Plata (now Argentina) and Brazil. In the late 1830s and early 1840s American 'scalp hunters,' including Delaware and Shawnee Indians, worked for Mexicans killing Apache and Comanche Indians (Smith 1999). In 1849, the president of Yucatan in Mexico attracted 200 American mercenaries with promises of "eight dollars a month, a new suit of clothes every three months, and a gift of 320 acres of land" (De Armond 1951).

In 1851, during a rebellion in Chile, 21 Californians left an American vessel and joined the rebels (Scheina 2003, xxviii). During the American Civil War, many foreigners fought on both sides. More than 500 young males from Denmark alone left their country to join the Union army, motivated by "excellent pay for the soldier." (Burton 1998). In the 1870s, about "50 officers from both sides of the American Civil War" worked as mercenaries in Egypt (Dodenhoff 1969). In 1893, when Brazil's President Floriano Peixoto faced a naval officer's revolt and rebellion in Rio Grande do Sul, New York businessman Charles Flint assembled a squadron of ships with American sailors which came to the rescue of the 'Iron Marshal.' The U.S. government not only allowed this mercenary assistance but even sent several navy cruisers to provide an unofficial escort (Topik 1998). At the turn of the 20th century, American mercenaries joined both the Boers and the Brits during the South African War (1899–1902) and the U.S. employed mercenaries in the Philippines during its efforts at 'pacification' after the Spanish-American War (Meixel 2006). The numerous opportunities for mercenaries during this period is illustrated by the mercenary career of General Henry MacIver, whose autobiography, *Under Fourteen Flags* (L'Estrange 1884) did not include the last four governments he fought for. Thus, throughout the 19th century, American mercenaries were very active in many parts of the world.

The U.S hired many mercenaries to fight in many locations around the world in the 20th century and is of course using 'military contractors' from many countries in

Iraq at present. Anti-mercenary sentiments expressed by Americans from the time of the Declaration of Independence to the present have not been able to prevent the employment of mercenaries when their use was deemed expedient by the government, and filibusters usually received more public sympathy than moral condemnation.

Southwest Asia and Islamic States

The employment of mercenaries in Southwest Asia thousands of years ago was so common that stories about mercenaries are found in the Bible as well as in many other sources. The story of King David, whether literally true or not, provides a paradigm of how mercenaries were involved in state- and empire-building. In exile, David is joined by professional soldiers and then he takes employment as a mercenary for the Philistines, and eventually he conquers Jerusalem with the help of his mercenaries. When his son revolts against him, David's mercenaries remain loyal to him and help him return to power (Halpern 2001).

In the 14th century CE, the Muslim scholar Ibn Khaldun developed a theory about the rise and fall of dynasties. Ibn Khaldun himself recruited mercenaries for the Marinids of Fez, but then he spent several quiet years writing "a narrative of human aggregation" in which he describes an *asabiya* force that integrates supporters and provides the cohesion of a dynasty. It matters little, a recent revisionist argues, "if this *asabiya* is composed almost exclusively of kinsmen….or of a mixture of kinsmen, mercenaries, freedmen, allies and others, as in the case of the fully constituted state, and more elaborately in the oecumenical state" or empire (al-Azmeh 2000).

This is an important corrective to those who distort Ibn Khaldun's idea to mean simply that dynasties are founded by 'tribal kinsmen' with *asabiya* and dynasties fall due to 'mercenaries' without *asabiya*. As in the case of King David, whose initial band of fugitives included a few of his kinsmen and various social discontents, mercenaries often join the 'human aggregation' which, if it develops *asabiya* fervour and cohesion, often leads to the establishment of new dynasties. A dynasty which comes to power often depends upon several distinct military groups – kinsmen, allies, fief-holders, mercenaries – who are all initially held together by *asabiya* (al-Azmeh 2000). But over a period of four generations, Ibn Khaldun argues, this *asabiya* becomes weaker as luxury and rising taxes to support new effective soldiers undermine the cohesion and strength of the dynasty. As the story of David suggests, dynasties are often destabilized by the competition of kinsmen, who often prove more disloyal than mercenaries. Rivals often try to strengthen the *asabiya* aggregation by hiring mercenaries and so both the start and end of cycles are times when military labour markets thrive.

During Ibn Khaldun's lifetime a new Islamic dynasty, the Ottomans, was expanding.

The *ghazis* who initially expanded the empire were often filled with religious fervour but they were also attracted by the prospects of plunder and land. The Ottomans relied for a long time on Janissaries, *sipahis*, and various types of irregular cavalry and infantry, but the Janissary corps was destroyed in 1826. In the early 19th century the

Ottoman Empire, with territories in Europe and Africa as well as Southwest Asia, began to fragment, and it began to rely on mercenaries more than ever (Uyar and Erickson 2009: 124). The *sipahi* commanders recruited and maintained their own troops and thus *sipahis* consisted of 'irregular military corps under military contractors' or mercenaries recruited by military entrepreneurs. Irregular troops included *akinjilar*, bands of raiders stationed on the Ottoman borderlands, and *bashi-bozuks*, or freelance fighters who joined bands recruited by military entrepreneurs all over the Empire. After the destruction of the Janissary corps, the Ottoman army was very small and the Empire relied heavily on irregular soldiers such as the *bashi-bozuks* (Reid 2000: 105–06).

Many tribal chiefs or local notables acted as military entrepreneurs to provide a certain number of their kinsmen or followers to fight in wars, but once a chief had presented his retainers to the Ottoman authorities, he often left most of his tribal contingent or retainers at home and hired *bashi-bozuk* bands or substitutes known as *bedel*. The military unit a chief provided was often known by an ethnic name, but in fact was often composed of a motley mix of mercenaries from many different ethnic backgrounds. Poor *bashi-bozuks* expected less in the form of reward than the chief's kinsmen did (Reid 2000: 132, 154). Again, kinsmen could be more greedy and disloyal than mercenaries.

The Arabian Peninsula was only nominally under Ottoman control during this period and various tribal chiefs or warlords strove to carve out states in the region with the help of mercenaries (Rosenfeld 1965; al Rasheed 1992). Many Arabs, particularly from Hadhramaut in the southern part of the Arabian Peninsula, went abroad to India and elsewhere to serve as mercenaries (Khalidi 2000).

In Ottoman parts of southeastern Europe, including Greece, there were many soldiers-for-hire available after the French Revolution . The British poet Lord Byron traveled to Greece and searched for a band of mercenaries he could hire to assist the Greeks in their war for independence against the Ottomans (Reid 2000: 122). In 1823 Byron wrote that

> A soldier may be maintained on the Mainland for 25 *piastres* (rather better than two dollars a month) monthly…or for five dollars, including his paying for his rations – therefore for between two and three thousand dollars a month … I could maintain between five hundred and a thousand of these warriors for as long as necessary (Reid 2000: 122).

In October 1823 Byron wrote that "every man that can command or pay from one hundred to a thousand Gillies is independent – and seems to act for himself" (Reid 2000: 122). Though the use of mercenaries diminished within western Europe after the Napoleonic Wars, soldiers-for-hire were clearly available in large numbers in parts of eastern Europe such as Greece.

Thus, the use of mercenaries was on the rise throughout the Ottoman Empire in the 19th century, including eastern Europe and northern Africa. This was linked to both the fragmentation of the Ottoman state and the imperial expansion of Egypt, under Muhammad Ali and his successors.

121

Europe

The idea that use of mercenaries declined dramatically after the French Revolution is derived from several myths – that the *levée en masse* (mass conscription) of the French Revolution was a great turning point after which mercenaries were replaced by citizen-soldiers; and that mercenaries were not much used in subsequent European wars or by European nations. The enthusiasm and patriotism of the soldiers called up during the *levée en masse* of the French Revolution has been greatly exaggerated (Moran 2003; MacKenzie 1997). There was widespread resistance to conscription (Forrest 1989) and growing reliance on impressed foreign subjects and mercenaries during the Napoleonic Wars (Dempsey 2002; Gould 1995).

> Revolutionary France was no more able than earlier states in history to keep over 1 per cent of her population under arms for any prolonged period of time....France reached a peak of 750,000 soldiers in 1794 only at the price of economic mayhem, and numbers fell to around 400,000 the year after, where they remained until the end of the decade. In 1805 the French army numbered only about 300,000 men...a host of satellite states supplied troops to the imperial army at their own expense, doubling its size during the Empire's zenith...the whole of western-central Europe was harnessed to support imperial France's might (Gat 2006: 502–503)

As for France's main rival, Britain:

> Costs and manpower figures continued to spiral upwards during the Napoleonic Wars, when Britain was able to match the French revolutionary and imperial might with the proceeds of burgeoning industrialization...Subsidies to her Continental allies during the final campaign (1812–15) [paid]... for nearly 500,000 allied troops, mostly Russian, Prussian and Austrian (Gat 2006: 503)

Thus both France and Britain grew more dependent on foreign military manpower as the Napoleonic Wars progressed and the final outcome was not a victory of the French 'nation-at-arms' but rather of Britain and its heavily subsidized allies and foreign fighters. Victory went to the side that could secure and support the most skilled, best-armed foreign manpower.

In 1814, when Napoleon abdicated, six Swiss regiments were incorporated into the revived Royal Army. These were not disbanded until January 1830, when a wave of republican enthusiasm swept over France, but in March 1831 the Foreign Legion was established for service outside of France. Seven battalions of foreigners from many countries were enrolled (Mockler 1987: 21). The Legion was used to protect and expand the French colonial empire during the 19th century but it also fought in European wars, including the Carlist War, the French intervention in Mexico, the Franco-Prussian War and both World Wars.

In June 1835 Queen Christina of Spain hired the French Foreign Legion during the First Carlist War. Queen Christina's rivals, the Carlists, also raised a foreign legion. In June 1837, the French Legion and the Carlist Legion "almost obliterated each other while the Spaniards on both sides paused to look on" (Mockler 1987: 22). Thus, the first civil war in Western Europe after the French Revolution was fought by mercenary armies employed by rivals for the throne. During the Franco-Mexican War (1862–1866) the French used the Foreign Legion as well as Sudanese soldiers provided by Egypt (Hill and Hogg 1994). During the Franco-Prussian War, after the French Imperial Army was defeated at Sedan and the Third Republic was created, France desperately needed trained soldiers and so the Foreign Legion was brought in. On 11 October 1870, two battalions landed at Toulon and attempted but failed to lift the Siege of Paris (Porch 1991).

The anti-mercenary sentiment which prohibited foreigners from enlisting in the French army did not prevent the establishment of a Foreign Legion (conveniently based in Algeria), nor the use of foreigners during France's subsequent wars. When states find themselves in desperate need of skilled military manpower, they frequently resort to the employment of mercenaries, regardless of widespread suspicion of and hostility to the use of mercenaries.

Mercenaries also fought in World War I, World War II, and during the disintegration of Yugoslavia (Koknar 2003). In short, during the 19th and 20th centuries European soldiers fought as mercenaries in many regions of the world, and soldiers from many parts of the world fought for Europeans as mercenaries.

Africa

The first evidence of mercenaries in Africa comes from Egypt in the third millennium BCE when Egypt began expanding southward into Nubia and northward into the Levant. Like mining companies today, the Egyptian elite wanted gold and other resources and penetration into the Sudan eventually led to the employment Nubians as guards and policemen (Spalinger 2005; Hamblin 2005). In the Sixth Dynasty (2345–2183 BCE) of the Old Kingdom, Nubians from five distinct ethnic groups (Irjet, Medjay, Yam, Wawat, and Kaau) were used in campaigns against the 'sand-dwellers' of Canaan (Málek 1992: 98–99). This was a common imperialist tactic of using peoples from one frontier to defeat the people of another frontier. Other Egyptian dynasties employed, among many others, Sherdans, Kehek, Meshwesh, Carians, Greeks, Phoenicians, Cypriotes, Aramaeans, Jews and 'Sea Peoples' as mercenaries (David 1999: 40, 127, 231, 240, 264; Kaplan 2003)

During the First Intermediate Period (2181–2055 BCE), the employment of mercenaries proved to be an important factor in determining the outcome of the power struggle that emerged from the collapse of the Old Kingdom (Seidlmayer 2000: 130). When Egypt began expanding its influence into Nubia again during the Middle Kingdom (2040–1640 BCE), its rulers used some Nubians very effectively to defeat other Nubians (Hamblin 2004: 382–83).

Mercenaries increased during periods of imperial expansion and state disintegration in Egypt all the way to the 19th century, when Muhammad Ali and his successors employed a wide variety of mercenaries to assist them in their imperialistic expansion into Sudan and adjacent areas of northeast Africa. Turks, Albanians, Circassians, British, French, Swiss, Italians, Germans and American veterans of the American Civil War were being employed by the 1870s (Dunn 2005). When British General Wolseley took 25,000 troops into Egypt to crush the Urabi rebellion, they included Indian troops, but once the British occupied Egypt and imposed a near-monopoly on the use of force, the new Egyptian army they formed consisted of only 6,000 men (Raugh 2004: 303). This was less than even the 7,000 *bedouins* that Khedive Ismail is estimated to have employed as border guards, constables, scouts and raiders (for Ł1 a month) before 1882 (Dunn 1996: 128), not to mention Ismail's regular and auxiliary troops. After World War II, Egypt hired former Nazi officers as military advisors. These German officers were allowed to stay and continued training and advising Egypt even after Nasser took power (Lee 1999: 23–24).

Between the late 15th and early 19th centuries Europeans often served as mercenaries for Africans and Africans for Europeans, particularly along the coastal regions of Africa (Thornton 1999: 45, 49, 77, 81, 108, 150; Smith 1989: 57, 63, 91, 128, 146; Newitt 1981: 42, 87, 70, 72, 77, 82, 152, 158, 208, 217; Newitt 2004: 15, 49–50, 111, 114, 238). Portuguese mercenaries fought in Benin, Kongo, Ethiopia and southeast Africa in the 16th century. But even in the interior, Bornu employed Turkish mercenaries and the Arma along the Middle Niger hired Tuareg mercenaries (Collins and Burns 2007: 17). When Dutch, English, Prussian and Danish soldiers manned forts along the Gold Coast in the 17th century, they sometimes fought for African rulers (Thornton 1996: 81).

In the 19th century, international commercial networks began to penetrate almost all regions of Africa and the use of mercenaries increased dramatically as ambitious new leaders attempted to gain control over trade and resources (Bradshaw and Ndzesop 2008; Bradshaw 2007). Thus "merchant adventurers…relied less on citizen militias than on alien mercenaries, small bands of ruffians scarcely more numerous than the colonial troops by whom they were later defeated" (Lonsdale 1985: 711). Plundering *ruga-ruga* bands hunted ivory but were "ready to follow any ambitious chief in need of soldiers of fortune" (Oliver 1963). If this suggests some striking similarities between the 1870s and the 1970s in Africa (Curtin, Feierman, Thompson and Vansina 1978), the employment of mercenaries in postcolonial Africa pales in comparison to their use prior to the Partition when they were found in every region of Africa

In eastern Africa, Bunyoro King Kabarega hired Nilotic mercenaries; Bulamoga kings hired Teso mercenaries; Zanzibar sultans used Arab, Baluchi and British mercenaries Masai warriors served as mercenaries for local African and later European colonial armies; Batwa forest foragers served King Mwami as bodyguards and warriors (Low 1975; Nicolini 2006; Horton and Middleton 2000; Lamphear 2005; Mazrui 1975); the Galla ruler Abba Jifar I and his successors had "1,500 mercenaries from such northern regions as Shoa, Wollo, Gojam, and Gondar" until at least 1882 (Lewis 2001: 103).

In southern Africa, bands of mercenaries became very common in the late 19th century. Venda served as mercenaries for the Shona; the Zulu, Rolong, Korana, Tlahping, Tatlou, Rapulana, and others employed Boer mercenaries and often lost land as a result. The Mfengu helped the British defeat the Xhosa, and half the troops who defeated the Zulu were Africans. Former slaves led by an Indo-Portuguese contractor named Matteus sold their services as mercenaries to the Portuguese; in the Congo basin

Chokwe hunters and others served as mercenaries; in the northeastern Congo, the Mangbetu King Nabiembali had a royal bodyguard composed of mercenaries as well as relatives and dependents of the king (Smith 1983: 181: Mavunga 2003; von Oppen 1993: 85; Shillington 1985: 140; Meredith 2007: 149; Isaacman and Isaacman 1977; Vansina 1990:177).

In western Africa, Dahomey's King Behanzin employed mercenaries from Togo and Germany; the Aro in the Niger Delta employed many mercenaries. In Sierra Leone, 'buying war' was prevalent among both Africans and Europeans; the Fulani *jihad* in northern Nigeria used mercenaries; when Sir Garnet Wolseley led an attack on the Asante, chief Gbanya sent mercenaries to help the British; and when the Asante ruler Mensa Bonsu was no longer able to procure a steady supply of slave soldiers in the 1880s, he recruited European mercenaries, West Indians, and Hausa who deserted British units (Person 1985; Hill 1987: 752; Lovejoy 2000: 85–86; Sibthorpe 1906; Spitzer 1974: 94–97; Smith 1989: 59; Abraham 1975: 124; Aidoo 1977: 24).

In the Volta River region, many communities specialized in warfare; in the Senegambia region, Mandingo kingdoms fought over control of profitable trade in slaves and manufactured goods and "anyone holding sufficient wealth to hire mercenaries could further enrich himself and move up the political ladder" (Mendonsa 2002: 156). The regions of western and southern Mauritania came "under the hegemony of Arabic-speaking nomadic groups" who "were specialized warriors." From the mid-1840s, some of these Arab chiefs began to rely increasingly on 'tributaries' "who "changed sides often, selling their support to the highest bidder" (Taylor 1995: 419); in Gambia, royal armies of slaves and mercenaries were resented (Klein 1972; the Serahuli and Jola served as mercenaries during the Soninke-Marabout Wars (Hughes and Perfect 2008: 121, 211), and the *mansa* of Niumi increasingly employed mercenaries who "rustled cattle, plundered traders, and harassed Muslims in their enclave villages" (Wright 2004, 146); Mandinka chiefs hired Tucolors and Turkanos mercenaries in Gambia and Loma mercenaries in Guinea (Højbjerg 2007, 85).

These are only a few of the many documented instances of the use of mercenaries in Africa during the 19th century (Bradshaw and Ndzesop, forthcoming). In the area of almost every state of modern Africa, mercenaries were prevalent by the beginning of the Scramble for Africa. During the Partition, Europeans employed mercenaries to defeat rival African armies and eventually imposed near-monopolies on the use of force in their colonies. Once this process was essentially completed –there was much resistance and many revolts against colonial rule of course – European powers were usually able to rely on a small standing army to maintain their control, in large part because their subjects knew that they could muster a much larger forces by drawing on forces in their other colonial territories and the metropole. European colonialism thus led to a dramatic decrease in the employment of mercenaries, and their replacement by small standing armies which were backed by the threat of the use of massive force, if necessary. In Northern Rhodesia (now Zambia), for example, the British maintained only one battalion or 800 African troops, commanded by just 30 British officers and NCOs (Hack and Rettig 2006: 55). This is only a very small fraction of the soldiers that were employed in the region prior to the establishment of colonial rule.

During the decolonization of Africa European powers rapidly or gradually lost their monopoly on the use of force in Africa and mercenaries began to appear again. Where neo-colonial influence was strong, as in many former French colonies, the threat of the use of force by the colonial power still remained for some time, but this began to erode more rapidly after the end of the Cold War. Today the world's most powerful nations are reluctant to intervene in many conflicts in Africa, and many African states have failed in the sense of being able to provide basic security for most of its citizens. The presence of mercenaries with a variety of skin colors will almost certainly continue to be prevalent in Africa until strong local states or empires are established which are able and willing to impose monopolies on the use of force.

Conclusion

The growing or declining presence of mercenaries is best explained in relation to such cyclical phenomena as the establishment and disintegration of states and the expansion and contraction of commerce, not by progression through stages of history culminating in nation-states employing citizen-soldiers. Mercenaries did not virtually disappear in the 19th century, as has often been claimed, but in fact proliferated in most parts of the world, and anti-mercenary sentiment or norms have never had any long-term impact on the presence or absence of mercenaries. Mercenaries proliferated in Africa in the 19th century just as they did in many other parts of the world.

Calls to curtail the activities of mercenaries in Africa or to create new courts to deal with mercenaries may seem important but are not likely to contribute in any significant way to the solution of the security crisis that needs to be addressed in many parts of Africa. It is difficult to even define mercenaries in a way that is universally accepted, much less prosecute them effectively. What may be needed is a well-trained international force which is capable of restoring security and stability in areas where bandits, gangs and other armed groups have made life insecure for so many Africans (Francis 2005). Who might best recruit, organize, train, command, deploy, and control such a force are questions which need to be addressed.

ETHIOPIAN FEDERALISM REVISITED

Jan Záhořík

Charles University, Prague

Introduction

The paper focuses on the contemporary problems of federalism in Ethiopia since 1994 and it follows my previous studies dealing with questions of ethnicity, the Ethiopian constitution, and general issues in regard to federalism. Ethiopia has undergone huge changes since the existence of the Ethio-Eritrean federation of 1952–1962, and we can see a new configuration of state where all major ethnic groups have their own province/ state after the new constitution of 1994.[95]

Since the new constitution we can see a somewhat problematic discussion concerning the Ethiopian federalism, rather filled with political activism and emotions than with a serious academic debate. This paper will examine these various and very often mutually discordant opinions from within Ethiopia as well as from the diaspora and academic circles. A special focus will be given to issues which seem historically determined. These do not relate to the contemporary character of the Ethiopian federalism as they relate more to the historical position of the Amhara, Oromo, Somali or Sidama people.

The study is based on fieldwork in Ethiopia (2008 and 2009) and an analysis of a representative amount of literature and basic documents which are available in regard to the discussed topic. What seems to be one of the major characters of this topic is the rising role of Ethiopian diaspora in these discussions (mainly the Oromo and the Somali). On the other hand, researchers tend to be more moderate and balanced while pointing at an increasing voice of political activism within these debates. Nevertheless, Ethiopian ethnic policy has become a fragile place and a very sensitive arena where many critical voices tend to be heard ranging from those most radical calling for the independence of Oromia to moderate ones hoping for truly democratic Ethiopian state.

It seems that contemporary discussions on the Ethiopian federalism very often include some aspects of what I call "an image of the Ethiopian state", which can be external as well as internal. The internal image, as I call it, embraces the historical topics of colonialism, oppression, nation-building, marginalization, exploitation, violence, Ethiopianisation/Amharization, etc. In the following study, I will try to underpin two main aspects of contemporary tensions in Ethiopia based on the Ethiopian constitution; it is the right to secession and the "territorial principle" of ethnicity.

---

[95] The study is a result of my postdoc research project *Separatism, conflicts and seats of tensions in Africa* (GA 409/09/P061) financed by Grant Agency of the Czech Republic. I am indebted to the Grant Agency and the Institute of Near East and Africa, Charles University, Prague for allowing me to conduct the fieldwork in Ethiopia.

African Multi-Ethnic States

Since the main topic of contemporary debates concerning the Ethiopian politics is ethnicity and ethnic-based federalism, we should put the Ethiopian case into a comparative perspective. The vast majority of African states is said to be composed of multi-ethnic and multi-lingual countries with a high percentage of ethno-linguistic minorities (Batibo 2005). In the process of decolonization and independence, African states had to decide which constitution and which approach towards accommodation of ethnic diversity would be the best solution for the given country. An accent on the right for self-determination and human rights could be seen as the most common feature of African constitution, at least in theory while in practice many constitutions have been violated by different regimes claiming to defend African values or unity of the state (Verdirame 2000).

Several countries can be regarded as problematic in terms of ethnicity and implementation of minority rights. These would include mainly the Sudan, Congo/Zaire, Congo-Brazzaville, Angola, Ethiopia and some other countries (Ismagilova 2000). Ethnicity is in these states seen in various spheres of life including cultural, social, political and military. A huge number of political parties that have been created since independence stemmed from ethnicity or ethnic principle. The best example could be seen in Congo-Kinshasa where this kind of ethno-political diversity resulted in a civil war and the brutal regime of Mobutu (Haskin 2005).

Ethnicity has played a significant role as a heritage of colonialism and in many places as a result of quick decolonization which has allowed some ethnic groups to take control over economic and political sources while others were destined to stay in the marginalized position. In certain cases, the role of colonialism in ethnic conflicts is beyond doubt as, for instance, in Rwanda (Mamdani 2001). Some African states have been forced to redefine their political systems and constitutions after bloody, long-lasting civil wars as for example in Rwanda, the Sudan, Nigeria, Congo/Zaire, Angola or in Ethiopia. Secessionist or separatist movements and tendencies have occurred in relatively rich as well as poor countries (including Nigeria on one hand and Ethiopia on the other), which have led Donald Horowitz to make an analysis of backward regional economies and advanced regional economies in various countries of the world being affected by secessionism due to various reasons (Horowitz 2000: 234).

Common features of these conflicts can be described as follows: lack of good governance, socio-economic marginalization, unequal distribution of incomes, political oppression, dominance of one party or one ethnic group, etc. Although many African constitutions have reflected ethnic diversity of states, no progress in equality politics was usually made until a revolution or a civil war forced the governments and the political actors to create a new political climate which would respect a multi-ethnic character of these countries. As pointed out by Ismagilova (2000: 217), "ethnic problems are too delicate. That is why some countries try to avoid even mentioning them and prefer to use such term as 'regionalism.' Instead of ethnic pluralism they prefer to talk about multiculturalism."

While some countries have stopped using the term "ethnic origin" in the population census, Ethiopia has gone a rather different way and ethnicity or ethnic origin has increased its importance since the 1990s. In the following part I will try to define the main problems of the contemporary Ethiopia which are rooted in its constitution of 1994.

Federal Constitution and its Interpretation

Ethiopia is a complex society composed of dozens of minorities which have had only a limited sense of a united nation since most of the territory south of Addis Ababa had been conquered during the 19th century. The 20th century was characterized by strong assimilation tendencies rooted in the centralized state system based on the long-lasting Amhara hegemony. The emperor had been the central point of unification as Article 4 of the Imperial Constitution of 1931 stated the following: "By virtue to His Imperial Blood, as well as by the anointment which He received, the person of the Emperor is sacred, His dignity is inviolable and His power indisputable."[96] Article 1 stressed that the "Empire of Ethiopia comprises all the territories, including the islands and the territorial waters, under the sovereignty of the Ethiopian Crown. Its sovereignty and territory are indivisible. Its territories and the sovereign rights therein are inalienable. All Ethiopian subjects, whether living within or without the Empire, constitute the Ethiopian people."[97] The existence of the constitution thus mixed the traditional with the modern (Markakis 2006).

This situation prevailed until 1974 and in a certain sense continued until the Derg regime which, according to Abadir Mohamed (2008: 59), "had to pretend that Ethiopia was a Nation-State blind to the diversity inherent in the ethnic, linguistic and cultural communities inhabiting the country." As added by Aberra Dagafa (2008: 1), a lot of people "feared that multiculturalism would lead to the disintegration of the State and that assimilation would serve as the best instrument for the creation of national unity." In terms of ethnic and minority rights, the new Ethiopian constitution of 1994 is usually presented as an innovation (Dirar 2000: 237) though other scientists stress the fact that, despite some positive aspects, the constitution is only a theory, neglected or often rather violated in practice (Kumsa 2006: 25).

While the Ethiopian history has been outlined as a continual process of "Amhara thesis", "Oromo anti-thesis" and "Ethiopian synthesis" by Donald Levine (1974), others, as e. g. Merera Gudina (2006) talk about perspectives of colonialism, nation-building and national oppression. From its very beginning, the Ethiopian state has been challenged by a historical heritage which has formed its political system until nowadays. As obvious, especially the Oromo case has become one of the central points of discussions and

---

[96] The Imperial Constitution of 1931. http://www.angelfire.com/ny/ethiocrown/Constitution.html (downloaded on 10 April 2009).
[97] Ibid.

129

debates throughout academic forums but also because of numerous individuals of the Oromo diaspora, who are active in presenting and examining the Oromo history and culture.

The Right to Secession

In our previous study, Wondwosen Teshome and I discussed (Teshome and Záhořík 2008) some crucial points of the Ethiopian Federal Constitution which might cause potential political clashes including the right to secession as the most visible one. We also discussed numerous opinions on the Ethiopian federalism ranging from those arguing that it is a good experiment to those warning against "re-tribalization" of Ethiopia (Teshome and Záhořík 2008: 9).

Federalism in Ethiopia is, in its theory, based on Article 1 of the Ethiopian Constitution, which "establishes a Federal and Democratic State structure. Accordingly, the Ethiopian state shall be known as The Federal Democratic Republic of Ethiopia".[98] The Constitution is based on the principle of equality, where all "Ethiopian languages shall enjoy equal state recognition" (Article 5) and where all "sovereign power resides in the Nations, Nationalities and Peoples of Ethiopia" (Article 8).[99]

Although there are some articles on the character of the Ethiopian Federalism, none of them considers Article 46 as the crucial point of the contemporary debates and tensions in Ethiopia. Article 46 claims that "states shall be delimited on the basis of the settlement patterns, language, identity and consent of the people concerned".[100] As already mentioned, one of the most discussed issues is the right to secession supported, for instance, by Article 47 which gives the right to form a state if some of the five stated demands is fulfilled,[101] and thus it follows Article 39 (1) declaring the right to secession. The Ethiopian constitution with its ethnic-based federalism needs to be seen in the context of previous constitutions stemming from highly centralized regimes calling for a unified nation preventing minorities from decision-making processes. As underpinned by Asnake Kefale (2003: 11), the "adoption of federal system of government in multinational Ethiopia is the logical outcome of the failure of the centralized state. Federalism is thus recognition of the importance of a decentralized administration that recognizes

---

[98] *The Constitution of the Federal Democratic Republic of Ethiopia.* Addis Ababa, 1995, p. 77.

[99] Ibid., p. 78-79.

[100] Ibid., p. 102.

[101] Article 3 (a): When the demand for statehood has been approved by a two-thirds majority of the members of the Council of the Nation, Nationality or People concerned, and the demand is presented in writing to the State Council; (b) When the Council that received the demand has organized a referendum within one year to be held in the Nation, Nationality or People that made the demand; (c) When the demand for statehood is supported by a majority vote in the referendum; (d) When the State Council will have transferred its powers to the Nation, Nationality or People that made the demand and (e) When the new State created by the referendum without any need for application, directly becomes a member of the Federal Democratic Republic of Ethiopia.; Ibid. pp. 103-104.

cultural heritages of diverse ethnic groups of Ethiopia". Some authors even claim that the constitution itself is based on a contradiction as it aims to foster deterministic self-determination on one hand and to maintain Ethiopian statehood on the other (Praeg 2006: 238).

One of the main specialists on the contemporary Ethiopian federalism, Asefa Fiseha, is of an opinion that by "establishing regional governments whose boundaries coincide with at least some of the major nationalities, the federal system has served as a conflict-regulating device, by creating more homogenous states" (Fiseha 2006: 135). It is not common to see the constitutional incorporation of the right to secession. Christophe van der Beken compares the Ethiopian constitution to that of the Soviet Union whose constitution of 1977 declared the same right, but as added by van der Beken (2003: 16), only "as a theoretical principle".

Federalism implicates decentralization which can be in Ethiopia described in a five-level structure from federal, through regional, zonal, *wereda* to *kebele* levels of government. State functions have been formally divided between federal and regional governments though several authors conclude that the contemporary situation is not fully sufficient, or, better to say, together with Kassahun Berhanu, that federalism and decentralization are not ends in themselves, they "should be considered as political provisions having the potential for promoting self-rule, entrenching genuine popular participation in decision-making, and consolidating opportunities for peace, stability and development" (Berhanu 2007: 65). Several researches made at local levels of the federal structure show that the decentralized governance is weak and insufficient (Ayenew 2007) while others compare the present system to "Interventionism" and "Statism" of the previous regimes (Abebe 2004).

Southern Ethiopia and Oromia

Even though the constitution tried to solve ethnic problems on the local basis by declaring local *weredas* and *kebeles*, the recent political development especially in Oromia and the Southern Nations, Nationalities and Peoples' Region (SNNPR) has shown that a lot remains to be done in order to satisfy the demands of all ethnic groups and to prevent some of them from being marginalized. In these two regions there were attempts to reject the existing territorial principles in the last few years (Záhořík and Kumsa 2008: 53–54).

Various examples of conflicts stemming from ethnicity and ethnic-based federalism have been analyzed for example by Tsegaye Tegenu (2006), Zerihun Abebe (2004) and Merera Gudina (2007). Tegenu discusses the process of the so-called ethnic decentralization on the example of the Gurage people from the SNNPR. He states that the prevailing tensions in some areas of the region may have their origin in ethnicity since uneven economic development and lack of decentralization can be based on "ethnic ideology" (Tegenu 2006: 32).

Zerihun Abebe considers ethnic political processes in the Siltie area of Gurageland as a success of what he calls "Formal Ethnicism" or revivalism (Abebe 2004: 130). Abebe argues that in the history of Ethiopian political development there is no evidence of ethnic identity called "Siltie" since people speaking the Siltie language have been for centuries identified with the Gurage. After 2001, following a period of the "nation-building" process where unity can live together with diversity, the Ethiopian government supported creation of the Siltie zone which also encouraged to revive indigenous religious beliefs and local languages. On the other hand, in the so-called "frontier areas" it (the newly created ethnic identity and identification with certain values, e. g. Islam) creates an atmosphere of tensions among groups which identify themselves with, for instance, the Gurage.

The case of Oromia is very sensitive since there is no unified opinion within the academic circles on the position of the Oromo in Ethiopia's history, and the Oromo opposition is the most serious challenge to the Melese Zenawi government. As analyzed by Solomon Negussie (2008), there is a growing tendency of complaints and secessionist rhetoric especially in the case of the Oromia region. The complaints of the Oromo leaders are focused on unequal distribution of wealth throughout the country, or, in other words, the government fosters development in other regions at the expense of Oromia (Negussie 2008: 271). Oromia is well-known for its natural resources and is the main producer of Ethiopia's most wanted commodity, coffee. The problem lies also in management of business companies because most of them are strongly related to the government. Negussie (2008: 272) thus states that the more resources will be exploited, the stronger and louder the secessionist rhetoric will be.

Merera Gudina (2007) sees unequal distribution of power and resources as the main reason why the Oromo struggle against Ethiopian governments at least since the 1960s. Unlike some radical thinkers, Gudina does not call for independence of Oromia but rather seeks true democracy. In a personal interview, Merera Gudina, Chairman of the Oromo People's Congress (OPC) and the First Vice-Chairman of the United Ethiopian Democratic Forces (UEDF), has told me that the Oromo people do not wish an independent state but a truly democratic Ethiopia which would be based on mutual respect and equality. The desire for an independent Oromia, claimed by some as one of the main goals of the Oromo struggle against the Ethiopian colonialism, is rejected by Merera Gudina since, as he says, there are no clear borders of the Oromo territory (Gudina 2009a).

Due to centuries-long migrations, Ethiopian territories have witnessed waves of migrating populations which have created the current ethno-lingual climate in Ethiopia. The Ethiopian state in its present form is not a federation but rather a "Stalinist" type of state (Gudina 2009a). Tesfaye Tafesse (2007) claims that among the major political causes of conflicts in East Wollega Zone, where he conducted his research, ethnic federalism and the quest for self-determination are the main ones as he shows on the example of the Oromo-Amhara relations (Tafesse 2007: 83). While the Derg regime emphasized class as a revolutionary force, the current regime has replaced it with ethnicity. The principle seems to be the same.

Beyond Federal Politics

While the question of federalism in Ethiopia remains largely a matter of scholarly debates, Ethiopians usually perceive politics from different points of view than from the "decentralization-perspective". Basic needs such as supplies of electricity, water, food and sufficient infrastructure or job opportunities are usually taken as signs of good politics while water shortages, black-outs, bad roads, unemployment or lack of basic food is seen as a product of failed policy. In my opinion, most people in Ethiopia (especially on the so-called periphery) are interested not so much in debates concerning a formal shape of Ethiopia, but rather in practical politics in the micro-level socio-political arena which directly influences their lives. In other words, theoretical political changes and gains are not necessarily interconnected with freedoms in the state which is ruled by one party, EPRDF.

Even though federalism gave, for instance, Oromo people the right to use their own language in daily communication and at administrative level it does not say anything about the degree of decentralization and democratic gains. A number of articles have been written concerning a failure of democratic development in the Horn of Africa and reasons of this process. Only a minority of texts deal with how people at the micro-level arena perceive the political decision made at federal or state levels and which obstacles form a major barrier to proclaimed decentralized state. It is generally known that the so-called Oromo People's Democratic Organizations (OPDOs) are attached to the ruling party and are not taken as real representatives of Oromo voices.[102]

Lack of democratic and decentralizing efforts by the government may be measured by formal institutional processes including decision-making process and by informal micro-level public (dis)content with the way the government deals with public affairs in daily life. While the first can be "easily" researched and reported and there exist a certain amount of studies regarding practical politics, the second depends on interviews with people and observation in the field and demands various strategies the fieldworker may employ. First, after a short time one comes to a conclusion that people are generally afraid of talking about politics, both in formal and informal dialogues or interviews. It is thus difficult to obtain direct data; these have to be abstracted also from other than verbal signs. Second, unlike government reports and other official data, researching what people think about politics depends much more on fieldworker's interpretation and interpretative experience. Third, one has to take into account a number of variables that come into the researched problem. By these I mean age, sex, education, social status, religion, and/or political past. In this sense, my conclusions and ideas presented in this study need to be taken as illustrative rather than authoritative, as partial rather than exhaustive.

---

[102] During many visits in Ethiopia and a number of informal and formal interviews, I witnessed that OPDOs are a popular target of public debates and jokes especially among Oromos.

My research has been (and still is) originally focused on Oromo nationalism but because nationalism and contemporary politics in Ethiopia are strongly interlinked issues, a question of public discontent in Oromia and public opinion on the so-called democratic decentralization (as proclaimed by the government media) and federalism have seemed to be a necessary part of studying Oromo nationalism. I have argued before that some Oromo politicians and activists complain about unequal distribution of wealth and development at the expense of Oromia. When travelling through Oromia (or areas largely inhabited mainly by Oromo-speaking people though not officially inside Oromia federal state) one may witness several zones of development which I would divide into four categories: 1) those of strategic importance (Adama, Dire Dawa, etc.); 2) urban areas on "traditional" communications (Nekemte, Ambo, etc.); 3) rural areas (with ranging degree of development but generally underdeveloped); 4) areas of sensitive political heritage (there I include mainly Dembi Dolo as a former headquarters of Oromo Liberation Front).

In my research I focused mainly on categories 1 and 4 which mean both important centers of trade and underdeveloped localities belonging to the so-called periphery. When we compare Dire Dawa and Dembi Dolo[103] one may find many differences as well as many similarities. Both towns were established approximately one hundred years ago and both centers served as important trade crossroads during the Italian occupation.[104] While Dire Dawa is predominantly Muslim area, Dembi Dolo has been a traditional center of Protestant as well as Catholic missionaries with only a recent minor Muslim influence. Interviews have been made mostly with educated informants whose contacts with different levels of federal structure have been based on their occupation since the majority of them were teachers and traders or entrepreneurs. Some of my informants were educated (with secondary and tertiary education) but due to different reasons with little access to a sufficient jobs.

Education, trade and unemployment are three aspects of daily life which are (perhaps more than any other) dependent on governmental conditions, restrictions, assistance and decisions. Even though Dire Dawa is at first glance much more developed and railway as well as road connections with other towns have helped to develop the city into a major regional center, recent governmental interventions into a traditional commercial networks have created an atmosphere of distrust towards the government which may lead to a distrust between communities so far living in a relative peace and consensus (Oromo, Somali, Amhara, Harari, Tigray). One of my key informants told me that since the ruling party took power over business, majority of trading companies have been

---

[103] Dire Dawa lies 550km east of Addis Ababa and is an important trade center connecting Ethiopia with Djibouti and Somaliland. Dembi Dolo is located some 660 km to the west of the capital and has become visibly one of the most underdeveloped towns in Ethiopia due to its recent history.

[104] Interviews in Dire Dawa and Dembi Dolo (January/February and August/September 2009).

dominated by Tigrayan/Amhara owners while local traders are strongly disadvantaged.[105] Connection between politics and Tigray-speaking Ethiopians became evident in popular thinking as well as scientific literature which uses the term 'Tigrayan clique' to label the true ruling element in contemporary Ethiopia. Moreover, among many Ethiopians, as I observed, persuasion that politics and business is largely in hands of rich Amhara and Tigray businessmen is widespread. Ethiopian federalism is thus by some viewed as means how the 'Tigrayan clique' may use wealth of Oromia in order to develop its own region and thus to impoverish the Oromo.[106]

Public discontent and fear of politics is even (and not surprisingly) more evident in Dembi Dolo, which became famous for its resistance against Mengistu regime and then, at the beginning of the 1990s, against the Transitional government which OLF did not want to support after it became clear that visions of major actors are not compatible. For more than fifteen years, Dembi Dolo has been neglected by both Federal government as well as the government of the Federal state of Oromia. According to local narratives, Dembi Dolo was during the Haile Selassie rule regarded as a rich trading centre with first direct air connection with Addis Ababa.[107] Since the early 1990s, Dembi Dolo was a target of governmental political and economic revenge even after OLF was forced to leave the area. Still, the heritage of OLF is hot there. Despite being a homeland of former Ethiopian president, Negaso Gidada, Dembi Dolo is an extremely underdeveloped locality. No tar road connects the town with other important centers including Ghimbi or Gambella. Lack of infrastructure has a direct impact on many aspects of socio-economic and political life including education, tourism, imports and exports of goods. In Dembi Dolo, perhaps more than anywhere else, I was confronted with an absolute distrust towards the government and the state which correlates to a public fear of talking openly about politics.

This can be well documented on local development debates concerning a promised infrastructure. The federal government of Oromia plans to build a new tar road from Ghimbi to Dembi Dolo next year which would increase trade and investments in the town and neighborhood but among local inhabitants it still remains unclear. As one man told me: "Every year, our government says there will be a new road but nothing happens." In an informal speech, people usually equal the federal government and the government of the federal state of Oromia as these are "ruled by one party" and thus

---

[105] Interview with an informant, February 5, 2009.

[106] According to some informants, as long as there will be a government ruled by Meles Zenawi, there will be no development of Oromia.

[107] These reminiscences are usually reminded by local saying *Dembi Dolo bd'rri aka bokolo* (Dembi Dolo, where maize is like a bïrr)

"by one man" (meaning Meles).[108] As I have shown, state functions have been formally divided between federal and state governments but the term 'formally' needs to be stressed especially when talking about local perceptions of 'high politics'. Some people even talk about "mockery" in terms of "democratic federalism" (Gudina 2009b).

Power of EPRDF in the regions is not weaker than in the center since the ruling party-nominated politicians and coalitions govern regions as well as local *kebeles*. Atmosphere of fear and suspicion is even greater in peripheral areas, especially since the 2001 split within the TPLF/EPRDF. Absolute domination of EPRDF cadres undermines the abovementioned federal structure which now seems to be outlined only as a theoretical principle. For a micro-level daily life, local *kebele* officials are more important for people than decision made at regional or state capital because people's welfare depends on good relations with those who oversee basic services.[109] Violations of democratic principles or generally those principles prescribed by the Federal Constitution complicate the debates over advantages and/or disadvantages of the Ethiopian 'ethnic federalism' as these become useless face-to-face massive abuse of power by one political party and its tiny group of leading cadres.

Conclusion: Any Alternatives?

Of course, the Federal Constitution has both advantages and disadvantages as compared to its predecessors. One of the most common critical opinions blames the Ethiopian constitution for taking ethnic groups as brute data, as a sort of natural species with clearly defined boundaries between them (Mennasemay 2003: 90). The history of Ethiopian ethnic groups is strongly intertwined as they have not existed separately. The existence of more than 80 ethnic groups should not lead us to the conclusion that each ethnic group should be organized as a separate political entity. Claiming that the ethnic issue is the key aspect of peace and development is generally false or, as claimed by some, another African experiment (Abebe 2004; Mennasemay 2003; Praeg 2006).

Ethnic federalism is thus a certain continuation of previous attempts to declare genuine African politics such as authenticité (in former Zaire), African socialism (Guinea), ujamaa (Tanzania) and others that more or less failed (Nugent 2004; Liebenow 1986). What is, basically, a major point of criticism in regard to the Ethiopian constitution is its emphasis on 'nations, nationalities, and peoples' which means groups rather than individual citizens. While there is a vast group of critics of the contemporary political system in Ethiopia, only a minority asks for alternatives which should then replace the

---

[108] According to many observers and political opposition in Ethiopia, the Ethiopian government establishes its own opposition parties which have to weaken the real opposition and to show a „democratic nature" of the Ethiopian federal republic. That is why many people usually consider political parties which form governments at higher administrative levels as belonging to one political wing.

[109] One of the latest illustrative examples is given by International Crisis Group report No. 153, *Ethiopia: Ethnic Federalism and Its Discontents*, pp. 16–19.

existing ethnic federalism. Some scholars, as already mentioned, even deny that this political system would have the right to be called ethnic federalism while pointing at the non-democratic and centralized character of the state (Gudina 2009a).

What, on the other hand, can be regarded as a common argument is the fact that the contemporary federalism based on the Federal Constitution has created an atmosphere where ethnicity is strongly politicized? This however does not appear as the major cause of contemporary tensions. The problem lies in a rather continual character of the Ethiopian regime that becomes ever more dependent on military power which would keep potential opposition out of reach of power and resources. Decentralization, as one of the key aspects of democratization in this multi-ethnic country, is slowed down by ethnic tensions and by government interventions. One year before the following Ethiopian elections, no progress can be expected in terms of democratization or true implementation of the Ethiopian constitution. As I have shown on previous pages, even theoretical debates concerning contemporary "ethnic federalism" in Ethiopia seem to be redundant when we take into account the real structure of the Ethiopian political arena dominated by one concrete power. The so-called ethnic federalism is thus only a theoretical concept violated even by those who promoted it in order to keep political and economic power in hands of a tiny minority which does not necessarily has to be "ethnic".

TWO FACES OF CONTEMPORARY SOMALIA

Alemayehu Kumsa
Charles University, Prague

Introduction

Republic of Somalia is the first failed state in contemporary history. In this paper I will assess political history of this country in three parts. The first part will discuss the political institutions of Somali people in pre-colonial era in which the Somali people controlled their internal peace and protected themselves from outside enemies organizing themselves in blood paying groups. The Somali people were the best example of classical segmented society in the text book of political anthropology of Africa. In pre-colonial era the political system which the Somali people created for their segmented society functioned for many centuries and shielded them from expansion of Abyssinian kingdom starting from ancient time. During the colonial period the Somalis were divided into various colonial administrations, which brought to this people various colonial administrative systems, and different kinds of constitutional norms, mainly from British and Italian colonial administration. The Somalis lived almost for three generations under various political cultures which they gradually adopted as their own. In each of colonial territories they used different official languages, different traffic signs, different currencies and different codes of conduct.

During the decolonization process the British Somaliland got its independence and immediately unified with Italian Somaliland which brought about the existence of the Republic of Somalia without any agreement how to unify both entities. The new republic faced from the very beginning both internal and external problems which we will discuss in detail in the main part of the paper. The core question of the paper is why Somalia was divided into two parts in 1991 after the coordinated struggle of many opposition movements which eliminated the government of Siyad Barre, one of the worst human rights violators in contemporary Africa and not able to build viable central government of Somalia. As the topic of the paper indicates from 1991 Somalia has two faces, one face is the Republic of Somaliland which built the best democratic institutions and demonstrated peaceful life in the unstable region of Horn of Africa. The second face of Somalia is the southern part of the country which has been devastated in civil war for almost twenty years. The paper analyzes two models of state building after the demise of Siyad Barre regime, one in the north which built from the grass roots of Somali traditional political institutions without interference and help from outside world. In the southern part of the country another model of state building was tried and failed many times. It was not rooted in traditional political institutions of the Somali people.

The work is divided into three parts. The first part elucidates the historical background of political traditions of the Somali people which Professor Ioan M. Lewis, the doyen of the study of Somali politics and society, called Pastoral Democracy. The second part of the paper illuminates how the Somali territory divided into five colonial territories and how the two territories from which the Republic of Somalia emerged developed two political institutions very different from each other. The last part of the paper explains how the Somali people in the first decade of their independence tried to build a democratic society mainly based on their pastoral democratic tradition and how the military force took state power eliminating the First Republic and built the government of one clan making the other five clans its enemies. It ignited the beginning of the end of the military government. In the last part of the paper we will draft some scenarios in what direction the future of Somalia may develop.

Somalis before colonial era

The Somali people are living from the immemorial time until now as pastoral society moving from place to place according to the availability of water and pasture for their camels, sheep and goats in this part of Africa (Lewis 1999:31). There are only some Somalis who are sedentary farmers in southern Somalia especially between Wabi Shelle and Juba Rivers. The linguistic data, oral tradition and middle age records by Arab geographers certify that the origin of Somali people and other Eastern Cushitic peoples of the Horn of Africa as a group originated in highlands of south eastern contemporary Ethiopia from which first the Saho and Afar moved to the eastern lowland of Red Sea coastal region and Somalis moved to the Indian Ocean cost covering the area from Babel Mendeb to South eastern Kenya covering the largest costal region in Africa (Lewis 1966:27).

The Somalis belong to Eastern lowland Cushitic language group like other their neighbors bordering on the north with Afar on the west with Oromo. The Somali language is from all these languages very similar with the Rendille language which G. Schlee called it if this language was spoken in Somalia it will be taken as Somali dialect (Schlee 1994: 9). The Somali language has two main dialects; the southern agricultural Somali of Digil and Rahanweyn and the northern majority pastoral Somalis. The difference of these both dialects according to Ioan M. Lewis, the doyen writer on Somali politics and society, is similar to Portuguese and Spanish (Lewis 2002:5). The standardization of the Somali language by establishing Latin script in 1972 by military government of Muhammad Siyad Barre gradually eliminated the differences by transforming the known Somali oral poetry from oral to written form and extensive use of radio broadcasting enhanced the unification of the language (Adam 1983:33). Poems and songs played a great role in the development of Somali culture.

> The Somali society is geographically, culturally and historically divided into two main groups of 'Samale' or Somali proper and the Sab. The former is the largest group of Somali people and the name is accepted as the name of the nation, the Sab included. The Samale consist of four large groups of 'clan families'. These were vast confederations of kinship groups whose members claimed descent from a common ancestor some twenty-five to thirty generations ago (Cassanelli 1982: 17). The Samale clan families comprise Dir, Darod, Hawiye and Isaq all of whom are primarily pastoral nomads.

The Dir clans (Issa and Gadabursi) are concentrated in southern Djibouti Republic, Ogadeni Somali in southeastern Ethiopia and western part of Somaliland. Smaller groups of Dir are settled in the south in Merka district and between Brava and Juba River.

The Isaq clan-family mainly inhabits in Republic of Somaliland and the Region Five in Ethiopia. The Isaq mingled with the Dulbahante and Warsangeli division of the Darod in the area of Saanag which both Somaliland and Puntland claimed to be part of their territory and many times there were military skirmishes between both armies (Hoehne 2007:1).

Darod are the largest and most widely distributed of all the Somali clan families. They are the majority of the population of Puntland mainly Majeerteen clan. They are also the majority of the people in Region Five of Federal Ethiopia mainly the Ogaden clan of Darod. A part of this clan lives in North-Eastern Kenya (Cassanelli 1982:17–19).

As we mentioned above the second main sub-group of Somali nation is Sab. This Somali main group is less scattered and has only two main divisions of Digil and Rahanweyn. These both groups are inhabited in the best fertile land between Wabi Shebelle and Juba River in southern Somalia.

In addition to these main groups of Somalia there are minority groups from various origins. The numerous Somalized Bantu groups scattered in agricultural areas between Wabi Shebelle and Juba (Lewis 2002:19). This minority groups were the pre-Somali people and the freed slaves during colonialism. The best known of such groups are the Shidle, and Shabelle on the Shebelle River and Gosha and Gobaweyn on the Juba River. Other minority group who are less numerous but economically and politically influential are immigrants from Asia. These Asiatic groups are Arabs, Persians, Pakistani and Indians. The Asian immigrants were mainly occupied on the commercial sector of the economy.

Political tradition of Somali people in pre-colonial period

According to some historical written documents and oral traditions, in some parts of Somali territory some kingdoms had been developed in the coastal regions of Indian Ocean such as Zeyila kingdom which moved its centers many times from place to place until it was dismantled after the defeat of Mohammad Gragn in 1543 at the battle in Wayna Daga against Abyssinia (Henze 2001:86-90). The other Sultanates which were established in Southern coastal regions of Somalia by Swahili Arabs were not able to control large part of territory and unite Somalis under one government. As mentioned above the Somali society is divided into six big clan families. These clan families were divided hierarchically into clans, sub-clans, primary lineage, finally a dia-paying (blood compensation) groups (Lewis 1999: 5–7). The main political, social and economic activities of pastoral Somalis functioned at the *dia*-paying group level (Contini 1971). These were the smallest social units, including undefined number of families bound by closest kinship ties.

141

Dia groups take collective responsibility for their own security, as well as undertaking an obligation to compensate other *dia* groups for any harm done by any of their members(Le Sage 2005:15).

The conflict resolution mechanism in Somali society is based on their customary law called *Xeer*. This mechanism developed to settle disputes and guard peace. It is not a written legal code but rather a tradition that has been passed down orally from generation to generation. The time of origin of *Xeer* system is not known but it seems to have existed for many centuries if not thousands of years. It may be created by the agreements reached by elders of various clans that lived and migrated adjacent to one another (PDRC 2002:25). The decision making power in *Xeer* system is realized by general assembly of all adult male. *Xeer* is a single principle common to all Somali clans across the country. The generally accepted principles of *Xeer* are referred to as *Xissis adhaaday*. This is the name given for the most fundamental, immutable aspects of *Xeer*.

The main pillars of *Xeer* are as follows:

1. Collective payment of *dia* (blood compensation, usually paid with camels and other livestock) for death, physical harm, theft, rape, and defamation as well as the provision of assistance to relatives.
2. Maintenance of inter-clan harmony by sparing the lives of 'social respected groups' (including the elderly, the religious, women, children, poets and guests), entering into negotiations with 'peace emissaries' in good faith, and treating women fairly without abuse.
3. Family obligation including payment of dowry, the inheritance of a widow by a dead husband's brother (*dumal*), a widower's rights to marry a deceased wife's sister (*higsian*) and the penalties for elopement.
4. Resource-utilization rules regarding the use of water, pasture and other natural resources; provision of financial support to newlyweds and married female relatives; and temporary or permanent donations of live stocks and other assets to the poor (Le Sage 2005:32–33).

The *Xeer* can be divided into two broad categories. These divisions are called *guud* and *gaar*.

Xeer guud includes the general aspects of traditional clan law that regulate common, day-to-day interactions, civil affairs and means of dispute settlement within a clan and between clans.

Xeer gaar includes specific laws that regulate localized economic production relations for clans and sub-clans specifically involved in pastoralism, fishing, frankincense harvesting, etc. *Xeer* was not codified as written law but remained as oral law passed down through generations. *Xeer* is guarded and implemented by respected elders known as the *Xeer Begti*.

Xeer holds the entire *dia* paying group collectively responsible for a crime committed by one or more of its members.

During the colonial era British colonial administrators used the famous British colonial policy of Indirect Rule to administer the territory through the local leaders of the community. As a result of indirect colonial rule the traditional Somali political institutions remained intact. In contrast the Italian colonial rulers used entirely different policy of direct colonial rule thereby uprooting Somali traditional governance. This became one of the main obstacles for the state formation during the post-colonial era in Somali Republic.

The first Somali Republic (1960–1969) and the military government of Siyad Barre (1969–1991) tried to abolish the *dia*-paying system to make individuals responsible for crime he/she committed but did not succeed. It seems that the people rejected to abolish *dia*-paying system because it is very hard for nomadic individuals, who have too few personal resources, to pay a given obligation. In such a case, if *dia* is not paid, the aggrieved clan may opt to kill the criminal or members of that person's clan. This may lead to a war between clans and a cycle of insecurity. To avoid this violent conflict the Somalis create a common responsibility for action taken by members of *dia* paying group. Islam is present in this part of Africa starting from 9th century and 100 per cent of population of Somalia are Muslims . According to Shari'a (Islamic Law) each individual is responsible for whatever action he takes but in Somali society whenever there is a conflict between Somali customary law and Shari'a the former prevails. The Somali people's political tradition and Islam as their religion are two separate institutions which lived together and Islam did not manage to destroy this independent political system.

The Somalis under colonial yoke

The Somali nation faced similar unfortunate history like many African peoples during the Scramble for Africa when their territory was divided into five colonial territories:

- Northern part of Somali territory was colonized by France at the last part of 19th century. This was later known as French Somaliland, a base and coaling station along the long route to Madagascar and Indonesia. Through it was expressed France's desire to develop trade and participate in the competition among the powers of the time (Touval 1963:37). At the end of foreign rule the French colonial territory became the Republic of Djibouti, independent since 1977.
- Northeastern part Somaliland was colonized by Great Britain and was called British Somaliland that became independent on 26th June 1960 and joined on 1st July with Somalia Italiana to create the Somali Republic as it existed between 1960 and 1991.
- The Ogaden – conquered by Ethiopian Empire between 1887 and 1895 – became an integral part of the empire. It is now called Somali State of the Federal Republic of Ethiopia (Ethiopian Constitution, Article 47:1995).
- Somalia Italiana –colonized by Italy. After Italy's defeat in 1941, it was under British military Administration until 1948 when the United Nation gave back quasi-colonial mandate to Italy, its former colonial master. The territory was then

ruled between 1950 and 1960 by *Administrazione Fiduciar Italiana* (AFIS) before becoming independent and immediately being joined by the northern British Somaliland territory to form the Somali Republic which lasted until 1991.

- The Northern Frontier District- colonized by the British as the northeastern corner of Kenya's Crown Colony. In 1963 at the time of Kenya's independence, the new government in Nairobi refused the local Somali demands to detach from the new state and reunite with the Somali Republic (Prunier 1995:2).

The heritages of various colonial rules

In colonizing that part of Somali territory the aim of the British government was to control the other side of Aden which was already British Colony and provide meat for Aden residences and to ensure safety of the trade-routes to India. The British were not interested to invest like in Kenya or Uganda. As Saadia Touval observed "the occupation was to be as unobtrusive as possible [...]. No grandiose schemes were to be entertained; expenditure was to be limited to be a minimum, and was to be provided by the local port revenues" (Touval 1963:118). The British Somaliland administration used the known British Indirect Colonial Rule in the territory. The British established an administrative post at Berbera to keep the flow of livestock export from interior of the territory to the port and to ensure stability in the area. The British colonial administration faced a long anti-colonial war of Muhammad Abdille Hassan from 1899 to 1920 (Hess 1964:415–433). This Somali anti colonial warrior waged war against British, Ethiopian and Italians for twenty one years until he was defeated along with the end of WWI. "This London finally agreed to, and at the beginning of 1920 a carefully planned combined air, sea, and land attack was launched which at last routed the Dervishes" (Lewis 2002: 77). From this organized offensive the leader of this anti-colonial warrior escaped and finally died by natural death on 21 December 1920 in South Western Somalia.

The British colonial administration in British Somaliland did not impose its rule of law but the Somali traditional customary law of *Xeer* remained untouched (Schraeder 1999:66: 68). The colonial administration used traditional elected leaders of the community as mediators between the administration and the people. District courts as before were presided by judges known as *qadis* who dispensed a familiar blend of customary and religious laws (ICG Africa Report No.66:3).

During the Second World War the British Somaliland was occupied by Fascist Italy in its grand program of forming Italian East African Empire which included Italian Somalia, all territory of Ethiopian Empire and Eritrea. The occupation of British Somaliland by Italian army did not live long as after only seven months the British expelled Italians from their colony. In addition they occupied the Italian Somaliland and ruled it from 1941 to 1950 in the form of British Military Administration.

The Italian Somaliland was given back to Italy by United Nations General Assembly decision to administer it as UN Trusteeship for ten years from 1950 to 1960. The Italian quasi-colonial rule in Somalia was inspired by "extremely authoritarian philosophy [that] had led to the nearly complete destruction of indigenous forms of political and social control" (Prunier 1995:3).

The main problems of the unification of British Somaliland and Somalia Italiana
The dual colonial heritage of the new republic has brought many challenging questions before its new leaders. Among them were:

The administrative officials were trained under different systems of governance and each administrative staff operated under different conditions of service and on rates of pay which differed radically. This was true of all officials in every branch of government. The two regions had separate legal traditions. The northern legal system was based primarily upon English Common Status Law, and Indian Penal Code. In the south the system depended mainly upon Italian Colonial law.

In fiscal and accounting procedures the position was equally complex, for wide differences in procedure distinguished the British system in operation in the north from that introduced by the Italians in the south. In addition the existence of variations in tariffs and customs dues and in patterns of trade divided the north from the south (Lewis 2002:170).

The south used Italian as the administrative communication media and the north used English and when both regions were united the administrative officials used translation for written form of communication because there was no agreement reached which script to use for the Somali language. The Latin script was adopted for written Somali language in 1972 and declared as the official national language by military government of M. Siad Barre (Hussen and Ford 1998: 2).

There was serious lack of infrastructure link between Hargeisa and Mogadishu. There was no telephone link between both cities and the journey by road frequently took three days to accomplish. Strong clan cleavage between the north and the south was supplemented by the decline of Hargeisa from the former capital of British Somaliland to a provincial centre.

All mentioned reasons accumulated in the north and on 20th June 1961 more than half of the Northerners rejected in referendum the new provisional constitution under which the two territories had united the previous year (Adam, 1994: 21–38).

The dissatisfaction of the North was openly expressed by the short-lived and abortive military coup of December 1961 by northern soldiers who were trained in Britain and assigned in the North under an Italian-trained commander. The aim of the coup was to "break with the south and destroy the Republic" (Lewis 2002:174).

The union of former British Somaliland and Somalia Italiana was not well prepared. The Northerners did not obtained from the colonial power their independence timetable until May 1960, i.e. only one month before the Independence Day (26th June 1960). In April 1960, a delegation of British Somaliland's new leaders traveled to Mogadishu, where they accepted without modification the constitutional arrangements that had already been prepared for the independence of the Somalia Italiana (ICG Africa Report No.66:4).

The British Colonial Administration was not prepared to transfer political and economic power to the people of the territory. For example in 1957 the first Somali Legislative Council was appointed by the British governor. The replacement of expatriate government officials with Somalis started only in 1958. The empowering of the people started in 1959 when Legislative Council was reconstituted to include twelve elected representatives, and the introduction of a new constitution in early 1960 permitted the formation of an executive branch.

After five days of independence of the British Somaliland, Somalia Italiana obtained its independence on 1ˢ July 1960 and on the same day the legislatures of the two territories met in joint session in Mogadishu and announced their unification as the Somali Republic. The name of British Somaliland changed to the 'Northern Regions' and received just 33 seats of 123-member national assembly. The key government posts were filled by the southerners. For exampled the posts of President and Prime Minister were both held by southerners as well as the principal ministerial portfolios such Defense, Foreign Affairs, Finance and Interior. The command of newly established national army was overwhelmingly drawn from former Somalia Italiana army officers which was a source of frustration for British-trained military officers from the north (ICG African Report No.66:4).

Despite the integration of the two administrative systems, latent corruption has been attributed to the residual Italian influence (the 'Italian factor') in the public sector (Ismail and Green 1999:116).

With all these discontents the northerners did not lose their hope for building a unified country. The representatives of the northern regions tried to present their region's interest in the National Assembly and government. In 1967 Somaliland's independent leader, Mohammed Haji Ibraim Egal, became the first northern Prime Minister of Somalia.

Many members of National Assembly did not respect the interests of their own electors and changed their sides in the voting in National Assembly in order to gain personal advantages and corruption became an acute problem.

The first constitution of 1960 guaranteed not only the unity of two Somali territories, but also democracy and guaranteed multi-party system and freedom of expression. Political differences encouraged a proliferation of parties 'to the point where Somalia had more parties per capita than any other democratic countries except Israel.' In the last multi-party elections in Somalia held in March 1969, more than 60 parties contested (Hussen and Ford 1998: 116). Majority of these political parties are not based on any ideology than clan politics.

On 15 October 1969 during an overseas state visit of the Prime Minister Mohammed Haji Ibraim Egal a shocking event happened in Somalia. While visiting drought stricken regions in the north of the republic President Abd ar Rashid Ali Shirmarke was shot dead by one of his police guard. As this news reached the Prime Minister he interrupted his state visit and came back to organize the election of a new president. The program of presidential election was underway on 20th of October evening in National Assembly but early in the morning of 21 October 1969 the military took over the state power without bloodshed. The group of military men led by chief of staff General Muhammad Siyad Barre established the Supreme Revolutionary Council (SRC) and assisted by twenty four other officers from the rank of major-general to captain (Lewis,I.M., 2002: 207).

Somalia under military rule 1969–1991

The Supreme Revolutionary Council immediately suspended the constitution, abolished the Supreme Court, closed the National Assembly and political parties, professional associations were declared illegal.

To discourage the interminable blood feuds between lineages which had done so much to undermine national solidarity in the past the death sentence was introduced to replace blood compensation (*dia*) paid traditionally between groups.

The military government declared a new ideology as the guidance of the country on the first anniversary of the coup in October 1970. It was Scientific Socialism - 'fully compatible with Islam and the reality of the nomadic society.' Under the slogan of 'socialism unites, tribalism divides' clan and kinship ties were officially banned and new government promised to root out any reference, verbal or written, to clanship (Hussein and Ford 1998: 117). Mentioning of clan affiliation was prohibited and all Somalis were *Jaale* to each other, i.e. 'comrade ,' Asking a person's clan affiliation was an offence and could lead to persecution (Prunier 1995:3).The national campaign against clanism, corruption, nepotism, and misrule was conducted for two years and culminated in early 1971 by symbolically burning or burying in Republic's main centers.

The opposition to emerging personal rule of General Siyad Barre started from within. The most widely publicized event occurred in July 1972 when two generals (one of them vice-president) were executed on the charge of attempting to overthrow General Siyad Barre's regime. This violent action shows that within the Supreme Revolutionary Council the word of the leader could not be disputed and building of Barre's personality cult went on. State mass media machine spoke of the leader of the military government as the father of the nation whose mother was the revolution.

The core of one of the future opposition groups emerged from Islamic Conservative Centre, which led the opposition against atheist ideology and against a new liberal law which, contrary to traditional Islam, gave women the same inheritance rights as men. According to Islamic tradition daughters will get fifty percent less than sons from their father's property. The government accused the local religious leaders of preaching against new law in the mosques and in January 1975 executed ten religious personalities and twenty-three others received long prison sentences. The execution of these religious dignitaries sent a shocking message to the majority of the people who were dedicated believers. The Islamic movements of the post-Siyad Barre era originated from this grievance.

The Ogaden war 1977–1978 and the beginning of the end of Siyad Barre government

The flag of Somalia has in the centre a five-pointed star that represents five Somali territories colonized by alien forces at the end of the 19th century. Two major territories unified in the Somali Republic. Three other territories remained under foreign rule. They included the Ogaden in Eastern Ethiopia, an area the nationalists called Western Somalia, the Northern Frontier Districts in Kenya, and the Djibouti enclave which in nationalist parlance was called the Somali coast (Markakis 1987: 169). The Somali Republic's main foreign policy during the first two decades of its existence was to free these three territories and include them into Somalia. The aim of reclaiming of these areas by supporting nationalist movements and in some places by directly waging war against neighbouring states made the Somali Republic the enemy of all its neighbours. The main focus for government of Somalia and the most important of all territories under alien rule has been the Ogaden region in Ethiopia.

The origin of the inclusion of Ogaden into Ethiopia is connected with the Abyssinian colonization of its neighbouring nations by Menelik II between 1894 and1897 (Bulcha 1988:34). Menelik was equipped with arms supplied from France, Italy and Tsarist Russia (Lewis 2002:231). The conquest of Somali territory by Abyssinia coincided with the partition of Somali lands by France, Britain and Italy. The Somalis immediately organized themselves under the Somali nationalist leader Muhammed Abdille Hassan (1864–1920). The resistence lasted for twenty years (1899–1920) and consumed energies of the three colonial powers. The first gunfire targeted Ethiopian occupation force at Jigjiga in March 1900. The emancipation struggle from all colonial rule ended in 1920 by a coordinated battle of Ethiopian, British and Italian armies. If conventional war ended by the death the Dervish leader Muhammed Abdille Hassan in 1920 then guerrilla war continued until the Italian occupation of Ethiopian Empire (1936–1941). During the Italian war against Ethiopia the Somalis sided with the Italian and fought against Ethiopia. For example before the war started Emperor Haile Selassie came to Harar in May 1935 and summoned Somali notables to support Ethiopia against Italy. He told them he was the ruler of all Negroes in the Horn and urged them to join the struggle against the whites. "Given a chance to respond, the Ogadens did not mince word. Ahmad Asci, the first to speak, said he saw no reason why Somali should fight the Italians when it was Ethiopians who called them dogs, abused their women, and killed their animals"(Markakis 1987:172). After the defeat of fascist Italy by combined forces of Ethiopia and Great Britain in 1941 Ogaden was administered until 1954 by the British and it was transferred to Ethiopia the same year. The first Ogaden conflict which confronted both Somali and Ethiopian army started in June 1963 and ended March 1964 after Somali were unable to gain support from the Organization of African Unity (OAU), United Nations, the U.S. and the Soviet Union. Somali Republic lost for the time being on both diplomatic and military sides. The army of Somalia was very small compared to the Ethiopian army which was then the largest force in Sub-Saharan Africa. The Somali army was only one-fifth of Ethiopian army.

The Somali-Ethiopian war of 1977–78 had its root in the 1974 Ethiopian revolution in which the Somali military government thought that Ethiopia was destabilized by various conflicts such as that in Eritrea where almost all parts of the province except main cities was under control of Eritrean national movements, in Tigrai where Tigrean People's Liberation Front (TPLF) coordinated its war against Ethiopian Army with Eritrean People's Liberation Front (EPLF) controlling highways from Addis Ababa to Asmara, Eritrean capital. The Oromo Liberation Front (OLF) was waging a liberation war to liberate Oromiyya from Ethiopian rule and in Addis Ababa a city guerrilla war took place between Ethiopian Peoples Revolutionary party (EPRP) and Ethiopian military government in which more than 55,000 young Ethiopians were butchered by military government's killing squads almost eliminating one intellectual generation of Addis Ababa (Balsvik 2003:13). The Provisional Military Government of Ethiopia also was locked in an internal conflict about in what direction to lead the weakened Empire and how to handle the conflicts in the country. The group who wanted to solve the Eritrean question in peaceful negotiation with Eritrean Liberation Movement was eliminated from the government by the group led by Colonel Mengistu Haile Mariam who became the chairman of Provisional Military Government (PMG) leading the country in all direction to war. The group included the first two chairmen of the PMG who were executed by Mengistu Haile Mariam.

The Ethio-Somalian war of 1977–78 changed the support of superpowers in the region. During the 1960s and the first part of the 1970s, i.e. before the conflict, the Soviet Union supported the Sudanese Government and Somali Republic against Ethiopia because of the U.S. support and an American military base in Ethiopia. The Sudanese Government expelled all Soviet Union diplomats in 1971 after the failed military coup organized by Sudan Communist Party. The Ethiopian PMG declared Scientific Socialism as its ideology before the beginning of the Ethio-Somali war. In addition to this ideological shift the Ethiopian government closed American military communication base in Asmara and expelled American military advisers from the country. Mengistu Haile Mariam changed his foreign policy from Haile Selasie's pro- American to pro- Soviet Union one. To attract Soviet military support Megistu signed with the Soviet Union a military cooperation treaty for twenty years in 1977. Professor Ioan Lewis expressed this shift of superpower alignment in these words: "This move signaled the commencement of a seismic shift in superpower alignments in the Horn of Africa with wider-ranging consequences." Fidel Castro came to the Horn of Africa in March 1977 with new big socialist federal project visiting Somalia, Yemen and Ethiopia. His project was to form Socialist Federation of Ethiopia, Yemen and Somali in which the Ogaden Somalis will get local autonomy (Lewis 2002:232–33).

When Siyad Barre refused the proposal of Fidel Castro Cuba, Yemen and Soviet Union provided military assistance to Ethiopia which included well trained war-seasoned soldiers, various amounts of modern weapons. Somali Republic expelled 6,000 Soviet Union military and civilian personnel and their families were given a week to leave the country. Soviet troops moved to Ethiopia.

All superpowers including the U.S.A. opposed the occupation of Ethiopian territory by Somalian Army. Ethiopia supported by Soviet, Yemen and Cuban troops started an offensive war against Somali army and in March 1978 General Siyad Barre announced the end of the war declaring that his army left all territory of Ethiopia. In this war about 25,000 Somali soldiers were killed.

The attempted military coup and the formation of opposition fronts in Somalia

The Ogaden war inflicted devastating losses on the Somali Army which felt morally defeated. As a result senior military officers from the Majerteen clan of Darod clan family attempted a military coup in April 1978 within a month after the withdrawal from Ethiopian territory. The coup was crushed by the government but some leaders of the coup escaped to Ethiopia and formed the first opposition movement called Somali Salvation Democratic Front (SSDF) led by Colonel Yussuf Abdullahi. The SSDF got support from Mengistu Haile Mariam who aimed at weakening of the Somali government (Prunier 1995:4). The Siyad Barre government made responsible not only the coup leaders but the Majerteen clan as a group. Majerteen clan in the view of Siyad Barre became his enemy and the army targeted them by looting, raping, and murder. The government of Somalia divided Somali clans into enemy and friendly clans, supporting friendly groups and targeting those it considered its enemy. At the beginning of his military rule Siyad Barre condemned clanism and buried its symbols in city squares. However at the end of his rule Siyad Barre relied mainly on three clans: the Marehan, his father's clan, the Ogaden – his mother's clan, whose members lived mostly in Ethiopian Ogaden, and Dolbahante – his son-in-law clan known in Somalia by nickname MOD (short for Marehan-Ogaden-Dolbahante). The members of these three clans filled all key military, economic and education posts, thus attaining the top of Somali establishment. These three clans belong to one clan family of Darod, other four clan families of Somali nation were excluded from key political, economic and military positions.

The armed opposition groups were not based on Somali national identity but became the mirror of the clan policy of Siyad Barre. As mentioned above SSDF was based on Majerteen clan of Darod clan family and Somali National Movement (SNM) was established in 1981 in London and its core members and its constituency came from Isaaq clan who are inhabitants of former British Somaliland. SNM moved its headquarters from London to Ethiopia 1982 from where it launched effective guerrilla warfare against the Somali government in 1983. Relationship between Ethiopia and Somali dramatically changed in 1988. Ethiopian military leader Colonel Mengistu Haile Mariam and his counterpart Siyad Barre met in Djibouti and agreed not to support each other's opposition. After this meeting Ethiopian government instructed the SNM to cease its operation in Somalia and withdraw its forces from Ethiopian border areas. The

SNM in this terrible situation started decisive attacks in main northern towns to expel the government army from northern towns.

The United Somali Congress (USC) was founded by Hawiye clan family who are the inhabitants of Mogadishu. Between 1989 and 1990 around thirteen political organizations were formed to fight against the declining Siyad Barre government (Prunier 1995: 8–9). These armed opposition groups fought the government army from all directions. The battle in and around Mogadishu in January 1991 forced Siyad Barre to abandon the city and escape to the south with all gold and hard currency from the National Bank. The USC captured Mogadishu but immediately split into two factions on the question of who will be the president of the country. The division was based on the two clans of Hawiye clan family. The division was between General Aydeed (Habr Gidir clan) and Ali Mahdi (Abgal clan) which brought the worst conflict to Somalis in their history. The former British Somaliland which got its independence on 26 June 1960 and formed union of Somali Republic on 1st July of the same year declared its withdrawal from the union and declared its independence on 18 May 1991. The Republic of Somaliland is not recognized by any state or United Nations until now but it is the most stable country in the unstable region of Africa.

The Somali National Movement (SNM) which led the region to victory built its political activities on Somali traditional political culture. It built a new political system from Somali traditional root. The SNM started peace building from the grass root starting from inter-clan meetings; all financed by local businessmen and community leaders. The main historical conference called *beeleed* (clan conference) was held in 1993 at the town of Boorama where a peace charter based on traditional law of social conduct between clans established the basis for law and order and a national charter that defined the political structures of government (Kaplan 2008:148). This conference was attended by five hundred elders, religious leaders, politicians, civil servants, intellectuals, businessmen. The conference institutionalized the functions of clan leaders into formal government bodies. The new system of government developed from a hybrid of western political institutions and the traditional Somali system of clan representation. The Somaliland leaders established two chambers of parliament. The upper house *(Guurti)* comprising 82 members seats were distributed by clan. The Guurti is charged with maintaining peace and security in the territory. Over time the Guurti which was composed of traditional leaders or their representatives, also emerged as Somaliland's supreme moral authority (ICG Africa Report,No.66:10)

The lower house serves as a legislature. The constitutional drafting committee which comprised 45 members was jointly nominated by executive and legislature, came up with a mutually acceptable draft. The new constitution was approved by an overwhelming majority of the population in a national plebiscite on 31 May 2001. The Republic of Somaliland based on this new constitution conducted local elections in December 2002, presidential elections in April 2003, and legislative election in September 2005. The 2005 elections "were fairly unanimous in their views that (the elections) were, on the whole, the freest and the most transparent democratic exercises ever staged in the Horn of Africa"(Bradbury, Abokor and Yusuf 2006:475) The question is how to rebuild again a unified Somali state?

Conclusion

In this paper we discussed the existence of various political systems in pre-colonial era which African peoples developed throughout long history of their being as groups. One of the political systems developed in Africa which the Somali segmented system considered as classical example had been functioning for many centuries. The Scramble for Africa disturbed the Somali political, economic and economic institutions imposing on them foreign political systems, economic interests and social values. Colonial administrations did not damage Somali political institutions in the same level. The Italian Fascist colonial administration abolished the most basic of Somali social institutions in Italian Somali territory imposing cruel and authoritarian administration. The British using their known policy of indirect rule through the elected community leaders left intact the traditional political system of Somali people in their colonial territory. In the former Italian colonial territory Somali political leaders inherited the authoritarian political tradition from colonial administration which was completely different from Somali pastoral democracy which remained functioning in the former British Somaliland. These different political cultures were one of the obstacles faced the Somali politicians after independence. The Siyad Barre military rule continued authoritarian rule with dividing clans by putting them against each other. The people of the former British Somaliland after thirty one years (1960–1991) of common state opted out of the union and declared their independent state in May 1991. As Prof. I. M. Lewis suggested the problem in Somalia is not that the people of Somalia failed to build their own state but the model of state imposed on them by elite supported by foreign interest was failed. The state of Republic of Somaliland was established based on Somali political tradition of decentralization and power sharing between the center and regions. It is functioning well for nearly twenty years. These two models of state building in Somalia are a very good examples for students of political anthropology, political science and constitutional law. They show that to build on what already developed for centuries is better than imposing on the people a form of state which has no root in their political tradition.

..."LIKE SOMETHING THAT HAPPENED TO JACOB ZUMA": CORRUPTION AND CONSPIRACIES IN THE SOUTH AFRICAN LOWVELD

Isak Niehaus[110]
Brunel University, Uxbridge, U.K.

Social analysts have repeatedly been struck by the banality of corruption throughout the post colonial world (Gupta 1995; Lomnitz 1995; Reno 1995; Werner 2000; Haller and Shore 2006). Olivier De Sardan (1999) observes that in many African countries corruption has become a routine element of functioning of administrative apparatus, deeply engrained in social habits. Corruption does not correlate to any type of political and economic regime (some dictatorships are less corrupt than democracies) and though corrupt persons are frequently denounced, they are seldom subject to legal sanctions. The perpetrators, themselves, often perceive their practices to be legitimate.

These observations prompt Olivier de Sardan (1999) to contemplate whether a 'moral economy' of corruption might exist in West Africa. He suggests that a number of practices which in themselves have nothing to do with corruption, help accord it with cultural acceptability. These include the regulation of exchange by negotiation, pervasive gift-giving, the salience of solidarity networks, and the virtually omnipresent obligation to render mutual assistance to kin, neighbours and peers. In addition, Olivier de Sardan (1999) highlights expectations of predatory authority and redistributive accumulation. Those in power claim the right to proceed with various kinds of extortion. But at the same time, constituents expect them to profit, display their wealth and spread around the benefits. The permanent search for cash and the absence of any sharp distinctions between private and public affairs also facilitates corruption. Familial obligations contradict impartial, impersonal, bureaucratic procedure (Olivier de Sardan 1999:48).

Olivier de Sardan's (1999) provocative theory does not address the extreme difficulty of making any viable distinction between cultural logics that motivate corruption and cultural logics that serve as *post hoc* legitimations thereof. Moreover, Smith's (2007) detailed ethnographic study of Nigeria shows that the morality is more likely to be contested than Olivier de Sardan's model suggests. He highlights the prominence of a moral economy focused upon patron-client relations in Igbo-speaking areas, noting that power-holders face pressure to use resources to help clients, notably kin and those from the same community of origin. For example, in elections the value of a politician's purse is often more important than his message. Whilst ordinary villagers regard certain forms of corruption, such as string pulling for access to schools and universities as laudable, but

---

[110] Isak Niehaus teaches social anthropology at Brunel University in the United Kingdom. He has done extensive fieldwork on the diverse topics of population relocations, witchcraft, politics, masculinity, and on HIV/AIDS in rural South Africa.

condemn corruption that takes place in favour of individualistic accumulation. Nigerians are concerned that elites have hijacked the system of patronage. Local administrators serve as clients of the central bureaucracy; businessmen cultivate relations with state patrons to secure lucrative contracts and ruling elites create Non-Government Organizations (NGOs) not to assist the poor, but rather to gain direct control of donor funds and oil money. Powerful outsiders are complicit in corruption. Western governments accept the results of rigged elections, and international funders take inequities within Nigerian NGOs for granted. Yet Smith (2007) observes that villagers are not only victims and critics of corruption, but also agents thereof who feel compelled to navigate in corruption to attain their goals.

Drawing upon my general understanding of South African politics, and upon ongoing ethnographic fieldwork in the Bushbuckridge area of Mpumalanga Province, this chapter aims to contribute to our understanding of the murky domain of corruption, its moral economy and legitimation. I discuss the social drama that unfolded after Milton Morema, the executive mayor of Bushbuckridge, Lakios Mosoma, and two municipal officials were placed on trial for murdering political opponents in April 2008. Though potentially an extremely serious form of abuse of public office, residents of Bushbuckridge posted bail for the three officials and vocally demonstrated in their support. Like Smith (2007) I see the generality of corruption as crucial to its legitimation. He shows how young men, whose hopes for employment are frustrated, parody corruption by the country's elites by perpetrating E-Mail scams. The young men lure recipients into advancing payments, by portraying themselves as wealthy oil industry executives or politicians, in a position to transfer millions of dollars of ill gained money into foreign bank accounts (also see Apter 2003). Milton Morema drew a different set of parallels. He claimed that, like Jacob Zuma, the president of South Africa's ruling party – the ANC (African National Congress) – who also faced charges of corruption, he and his co-accused were victims of a powerful conspiracy. Such mimicry mediates between the national and the local. I suggest that such conspiracy theories have particular appeal in a hegemonic party system where political processes lack transparency. Moreover, I contend that supporters endorsed these claims, not only because they possessed an 'aura of factuality', but also because the supporters aimed to secure or retain access to the fruits of patrimonial and neo-patrimonial distributions. [111]

---

[111] Patrimonial politics refers to the 'building support through redistributing resources on a personal basis to followers (Richards 1996:34–5). Analysts sometimes add the prefix 'neo-' to denote situations where these distributions are structured along legal-rational, bureaucratic lines (Englund 2002:176).

Social Drama in the Centre: New South African Corruption

Ominous signs of corruption appeared in post-apartheid South Africa within a decade of democratic rule.[112] In 2002, 37 % of South Africans indicated that payment of bribes was necessary to obtain services from police officers, and 28 % said the same of local government officers (UNODC/SAG 2003). Discourses of corruption soon shifted towards the centre, 'where leading ideas come together with leading institutions to create an arena in which the events that most vitally affect members' lives take place' (Geertz 1983).

Several factors prevailing in South Africa facilitate the prominence of corruption. Comparative studies show that actual and alleged corruption thrives in situations of transition towards new bureaucratic orders, where institutions of government have monopolies over the supply of goods and services, powerful external legal controls are absent, and where officials have a large degree of discretion (Lovell 2005; Haller and Shore 2006). This is clearly apparent in post-apartheid South Africa. A hegemonic party system without competitive elections, in which ruling elites of the ANC are accountable to the party machine, has stifled open parliamentary debate (Good 1997). 113 Political processes take place in hidden spaces, in a manner that is conducive to suspicion about clandestine, corrupt, activities.

In this context, allegations about government's involvement in shady arms procurement deals and about Jacob Zuma's involvement in fraud and rape, is the stuff that social dramas are made of. Andrew Feinstein's (2007) personal account of working as an ANC member of parliament's Standing Committee on Public Accounts (SCOPA) contains juicy revelations. Under Nelson Mandela's presidency, he claims, the ANC's caucus room 'resonated with sound debate and discussion'. But after Thabo Mbeki assumed leadership in 1999 the caucus reflected a more 'constrained party, a party fearful of its leader, conscious of his power to make or break careers, conscious of his demands for loyalty, for conformity of thinking' (Feinstein 2007:38, 39).

While Mbeki's government claimed that anti-retroviral drugs were unaffordable, it spent about fifty billion rand (€4.5 billion) on arms. The Auditor-General's report found a litany of irregularities. Key role players had clear conflicts of interest. 'Chippy' Shaik worked as the director of Procurement in the Defense Force, whilst his brother, Shabir Shaik, was a director of African Defense Systems (ADS), a company chosen to provide

---

[112] Corruption was inscribed into the institutional materiality of the apartheid state. During the 1970s the Department of Information launched clandestine initiatives – such as investments in English language newspapers – to improve government's image. Bantustan leaders, such as the Matanzima brothers of the Transkei, reaped great financial reward from central government (Streek and Wicksteed 1981). Moreover, police regarded crime syndicates as allies in the fight against national liberation movements (Ellis 1999).

[113] Since democratization the ANC has effectively dominated South Africa's national elections. The party attained 62.65% of the vote in 1994, 66.35% in 1999, and 69.69% in 2004 (*News 24* 2009).

combat suits for ships. BAe/SAAB won the contract to provide trainer and fighter jets. Yet the tender of their Italian competitor, Aeromacchi, cost half as much and was the preferred technical choice of the South African Air Force. Bidders allegedly donated R10 million (ca. € 900,000) to South Africa's minister of Defense, Joe Modise, and R5 million (ca. € 450,000) to the ANC veterans' association (Feinstein 2007: 150–155). When SCOPA investigated these claims, senior ANC members castigated it for being 'part of a massive conspiracy to bring down the democratically elected government' (Feinstein 2007:193). Instead, government appointed a Joint Investigation Team, which exonerated the ANC executive of any wrongdoing.[114]

The arms procurement deal has tarnished the reputation of Jacob Zuma, whose exploits subsequently came to occupy centre stage in the theatre of South African politics. Born in Nkandla, KwaZulu-Natal, Zuma received only primary schooling. He joined the ANC's military wing *Umkhonto We Sizwe* as a young adult, was convicted of conspiring to overthrow South Africa's apartheid government, and imprisoned on Robben Island for ten years. Hereafter, Zuma went into exile in Mozambique and in Zambia, where he served as the ANC's head of Intelligence (Gordin 2008). Following the unbanning of the ANC in 1990, he returned to South Africa, and played an important role in ending political violence between the ANC and Inkatha Freedom Party. Zuma then rapidly ascended up the hierarchy of government; being elected National ANC Chairperson in 1994; Deputy ANC President in 1997; and Deputy President of South Africa in 1999. Viewed as a compassionate patriarch, Zuma is well-known as polygamist, who has married four wives and fathered eighteen children (SAPA 2008).

In 2003 the Directorate of Public Prosecutions investigated Zuma on charges of improper conduct in the arms deal. However, the chair of the National Prosecuting Authority, Bulelani Ngcuka, made an ambiguous statement, saying that 'there was *prima facie* evidence of corruption, but insufficient to win the case in court' (SAPA 2003). However, in June 2005 Zuma's financial advisor, Shabir Shaik, went on trial for arranging for a bidding company to pay Zuma R500,000 (€45,454) per annum, in exchange for assisting their efforts in relation to the arms deal. Shaik also allegedly spent lavishly on Zuma's residence in Nkandla. Shaik's defenders described these payments as 'gifts' to a struggle comrade, and claimed that his relationship with Zuma was one of 'reciprocal altruism' that transcend understanding in terms of blunt legal categories (SAPA 2006). Yet judge Hilary Squires sentenced Shaik to fifteen years imprisonment for bribery. The National Prosecuting Authority now laid a formal charge of corruption against Zuma, and President Thabo Mbeki dismissed him as South Africa's Deputy President.

---

[114] Feinstein (2007:295) sees a need to render political processes more apparent. He suggests that a mixed proportional representation, constituency system can ensure that politicians are beholden to constituents and not to party leaders. There is also a need, he argues, to disclose party funding, to separate state and party more clearly, and to established an adequately resources legal arm.

Only six months later, police charged Zuma with having raped the thirty-one year old daughter of a deceased comrade, who was HIV positive. During the trial Zuma admitted to having unprotected sex with his accuser, and claimed that he took a shower afterwards to 'cut the risk of contracting HIV'. Thousands of his supporters gathered outside the Johannesburg High Court, wearing T-shits with Zuma's face and with the slogans 'Innocent till proven Guilty!' and '100 % Zulu Boy'. During breaks in the court procedures, Zuma sang: 'My machine gun, my machine gun! Oh father! Please bring me my machine gun!' (*Umshini wami, Umshini wami. We Baba. Awuleth' umshini wami* in Zulu), and he danced with the crowd.[115] The supporters vilified his accuser, whilst a much smaller anti-rape group demonstrated on her behalf. Judge Van der Merwe found Zuma not guilty, but censured him for reckless behaviour (Skeen 2007).

These incidents have not dented Jacob Zuma's ambitions. He has remained extremely popular, especially amongst trade unionists, Zulu-speakers and members of the ANC Youth League – constituencies marginalized under Thabo Mbeki's rule. Loyalists argued that Zuma was a victim of conspiracy. They alleged that members from the inner circles of the ANC used South Africa's legal system to prevent his ascendency to president. Bulelani Ngcuka reportedly staged a private meeting with newspaper editors to enlist their support. Moreover, during the rape trial his accuser contacted South Africa's Minister of Intelligence, Ronnie Kasarils, before reporting the case to the police (Skeen 2007: 69–75). Zuma alleged that he was crucified by the press, and filed a series of defamation lawsuits against media outlets for besmirching his public profile. At the ANC's national conference in Polokwane during 2007, Zuma was elected ANC president, defeating Thabo Mbeki with 2,329 votes to 1,505.

But Jacob Zuma was not off the hook. In December 2007 the National Prosecuting Authority served him with an indictment to stand trial on numerous counts of racketeering, money laundering and fraud. Zuma's legal team effectively delayed proceedings. They succeeded in making critical evidence unavailable to the court, and in having the charges against him declared unlawful on procedural grounds. Judge Chris Nicholson found that the Directorate of Public Prosecutions had not given Zuma a chance to make representations before deciding to charge him. He added that he believed then President Thabo Mbeki and others had played a role in the decision to charge Zuma. In the aftermath of this finding, the ANC executive disbanded the National Prosecuting Agency, and forced Thabo Mbeki to resign from his duties as South African President. Kgalema Mothlante, a Zuma loyalist, was appointed caretaker president. The Youth League leader, Julius Malema, publically declared: 'Let me make it clear now: we are prepared to die for Zuma. Not only that, we are prepared to take up arms to kill for Zuma' (*History Matters* 2008).

However, on 12 January 2009, Deputy Judge President Harms overturned Judge Nicholson's rulings at the Supreme Court of Appeal, and decided that the National

---

[115] See L. Gunner (2009) an analysis of the song's deeper significance.

Prosecuting Authority was correct in having charged Zuma as it did. In response, Zuma's legal team lodged an application for a permanent stay of prosecution to the Constitutional Court. On 6 April, the National Prosecuting Authority dropped all charges against him, in the light of new revelations. Intercepted phone calls showed that its agent, Leonard McCarthy and Bulelani Ngcuka had conspired in the timing of the charges laid against Zuma, presumably to the advantage of his rival, President Thabo Mbeki.

The decision did not amount to an acquittal. But it did enable Zuma to lead the ANC to a resounding victory during the national elections of April 2009, polling almost 65.9 % of all votes cast (*News 24* 2009), and to be sworn in as South African President on 9 May 2009. These dramas surrounding Jacob Zuma's alleged involvement in rape and in fraud have had potent symbolic impact and have, as we shall see, informed interpretations of political events in more peripheral arenas of South African politics.

Dramaturgical Re-enactment: Murder in Bushbuckridge?

On the evening of Thursday 10 April 2008 a large police contingent arrested Milton Morema, the mayor of Bushbuckridge, Lakios Mosoma, regional manager of the Bushbuckridge municipality, and Erasmus Makhubele, another municipal official, whilst they were enjoying a barbeque (*braai*) with friends. Captain Leonard Hlathi, spokesperson for the Mpumalanga Police, was reticent when he addressed the media: 'Details cannot be released because doing so might interfere with our investigations at the moment' (Hlatshwayo 2008a).

A foremost local ANC activist, Milton Morema became involved in the anti-apartheid struggle whilst still at school. In 1986 he joined the Brooklyn Youth Organisation. This body challenged the management of local schools; launched consumer boycotts against white owned businesses, organized protest marches to demand the provision of infrastructure, and instigated rent boycotts, forcing Tribal Authorities to close. The organization also committed itself to eradicating evil. During a series of anti-witchcraft campaigns youth burnt more than a hundred homes, and killed at least 36 suspected witches (Niehaus 2001).

With the unbanning of liberation movements in 1990, ANC branches mushroomed throughout Bushbuckridge and effectively absorbed the Brooklyn Youth Organisation. Morema was elected chair of the Impalahoek ANC branch, and soon gained a reputation for hard work and for political astuteness.

In South Africa's first non-racial elections of 1994, the ANC gained 97 % of all votes cast in Bushbuckridge (Niehaus 2006:540). Through participation in these elections, local residents sought to achieve political being in the national centers of power, and saw African nationalism as eminently suitable for this purpose. This was realized when six local representatives were appointed to provincial governments or to the South African House of Provinces. Morema came to head the Transitional Local Government in Bushbuckridge North.

After the euphoria of the election had dissipated, the issue of service delivery became a major bone of contention, and Bushbuckridge became the scene of a violent border dispute. During the elections Bushbuckridge had formed part of Limpopo Province. But local leaders agitated that the region be ceded to the more prosperous Mpumalanga, and both provincial premiers brokered an agreement to facilitate such a transfer. However, in April 1997 government announced that Bushbuckridge would remain in Limpopo. Great fury followed. Villagers constituted a Border Crisis Committee that launched a 'rolling mass action campaign', including protest marches, school boycotts, strikes, and violent attacks of government vehicles and buildings (Niehaus 2005). President Mandela immediately appointed a task team to improve service delivery. Government launched new agricultural projects in Bushbuckridge, and constructed six clinics and at least three thousand three-roomed houses – fitted with electricity, sanitation and on site taps – for households earning less than R500 (€45) per month. It also introduced effective school feeding programs; and oversaw the distribution of food parcels, child maintenance grants, and vastly improved old age pensions. Yet, only in 2004, did government transfer Bushbuckridge to Mpumalanga Province.

Morema became the first mayor of Bushbuckridge municipality and played a central role in extending (neo) patrimonial politics. In the 2007/2008 financial year the municipality spent R379 million (€34 million) and distinguished itself as a significant source of lucrative construction and service provision contracts and of well remunerated jobs. Municipal contracts included those for the laying of electricity cables and water pipelines; constructing paved roads, public lights, taxi ranks and ventilated improved pit latrines; installing air-conditioners; catering; and destroying alien plants. The municipality employed a speaker, six full-time mayoral committee members, sixty part-time councilors, nine senior managers, and numerous other employees (Bushbuckridge Local Municipality 2008: 28). It recruited no fewer than four hundred people to work on a clay bricks project (Morema 2008).

The construction of new provincial and municipal governments, administrative inexperience, and hegemonic domination by the ANC has created an environment conducive to corruption. Several political representatives from Bushbuckridge have fallen foul of the law. An official enquiry found Jacques Modipane, MEC (Member of the Executive Council) for Finance in the Mpumalanga government, guilty of signing promissory notes worth R340 million (€30 million), which resulted into thirty-two game reserves being illegally used as collateral for offshore loans. He was relieved from his position. Luckson Mathebula, former MEC for Public Works and then Safety and Security, was charged with ordering the murder of his first wife, Aletta Mnisi. But his mistress, who was a key witness, retracted her statement and fled the province, allegedly after receiving death threats. In the absence of collaborating witnessed the state dropped all charges. In 2003 Mathebula was sentenced to ten years imprisonment for raping a teenage relative (Hlatswayo 2003). Patrick Mogale, a senator in the House of Provinces, was found guilty of statutory rape after he had impregnated a 12 year old girl, and refused to pay child maintenance (Maluleke 1995). In addition, the Commissioner for Women in Limpopo Province was also expelled for misappropriating funds and for employing relatives in non-existent posts (Mokgope 1998).

In the absence of transparency, talk about corruption has been extremely pervasive.[116] My informants complained that councilors only granted tenders to those who were already wealthy and capable of paying bribes of up to R60,000 (€5,454). A hospital worker expressed the following view to me:

'We see these businessmen and councilors together at Banda [a popular local tavern] at night. Sometimes a contractor will be in the mayor's company. They won't only be drinking. They will be having meetings. If you come close to them they will just say, 'Sit there! We are discussing!''

However, villagers felt compelled to participate in patrimonial politics. Many regarded ANC membership and appropriate political connections as necessary requirements for securing municipal contracts, services and jobs. They saw voting for the ANC as a strategy to ensure access to state-controlled resources.[117]

Allegations about Morema's possible involvement in corruption first arose in 2002, after his house burnt to the ground. Three men allegedly entered his yard in early morning hours and hid underneath the mango trees in his garden. The men then threw petrol bombs through the bedroom and dining-room windows. Morema told the police that he was at home, took his children outside, but could not see his wife in the smoke. National intelligence officers questioned some of Morema's opponents within the ANC. Different rumours circulated about the motives of his arsonists. Some claimed they were angered because Morema accepted bribes from scrap-yard owners involved in crime, or because he had evicted households from Dingleydale. Others speculated that Morema had actually spent the night elsewhere, and that he himself had sent the arsonists, so that he could claim R300,000 (€27,272) from his insurance to build a new, more luxurious house. One informant asked me, 'How else can he get a large, beautiful, new home like the one he has now?'

In 2003 a newspaper article appeared under the heading, *'Big-Spender Defies Parliament to Create Slush Fund'*. The article alleged that Morema allocated himself a discretionary fund of R160, 000 (€14,545) that he used to make donations to deserving causes. This is despite the fact that the Mpumalanga government had instructed all mayors to immediately stop the practice. Moreover, spokespeople for the Pan African Congress (PAC) were furious because Morema had been budgeting an additional R410, 000 (€37,272) for security of his home – the equivalent of nineteen RDP (Reconstruction and Development Program) houses (Samayende 2003).

---

[116] This is also the case in other postcolonial countries such as India. Parry (2000) observes that stories of corruption are told more often by men than any other genre of folklore.

[117] A household survey conducted amongst eighty-seven households in Impalahoek during 2003/2004 shows increased dependency on government: 44% of adults in the sample (214 of 482) were employed; and 30% (145) received old age pensions, disability, and/or child support grants. 23% (20) of the (87) households survived solely from social welfare (Niehaus 2006: 535,537).

The charges brought against Milton Morema, Lakios Mosoma and Erasmus Makhuleba, during April 2008, were of a far more serious nature. Police claimed that, five years previously, the three men hired Jeffrey Sedibe (Erasmus's nephew) and Calvin Mzimba to assassinate Abel Mashile. Abel was a senior teacher at the Impalahoek Primary School. On the evening that he was killed, friends saw Abel playing snooker with a Nigerian doctor at a local tavern. Three men reportedly followed him as he walked home, asked for money and then shot him at point blank range. Abel's son discovered his body the next morning whilst searching for a missing goat.

The assumed motive for the assassination was not immediately apparent. Newspapers claimed that Lakios Mosoma, who taught at the same school, had competed with Abel for the post of principal (Hlatswayo 2008a). But my informants at the school denied this, and argued that the two men were actually competing for the far more lucrative post of regional manager at the municipality. Though Abel Mashile had little political experience, he was frontrunner for the post. This is because he was better educated than his competitors and because his father, Matsikitsane Mashile, had been a founder of the ANC. Abel was sure he would get the post, and colleagues at school that he planned to resign from teaching. However, Milton Morema and Erasmus Makhubela reportedly wished to have Lakios Mosoma appointed. Mosoma was Morema's cousin, had supported his quest for the position of mayor, and the three men were members of the same ANC branch.

Police claimed that Morema and Mosoma had promised to pay Jeffrey Sedibe and Calvin Mzimba, who had previously worked as vigilantes for taxi associations, R17,000 (€1,545) each for the assassination. But when Sedibe received only R5,000 (€454), he started to behave irresponsibly, and threatened to spill the beans. Morema and Mosoma preempted this and sent Makhubela and Mzimba to kill Sedibe (Masinga 2009). (Makhubela once worked as Morema's body guard, and was now employed by the municipal roads department. His wife was the proprietor of a café where the ANC branch assembled after meetings to drink beer.) Mzimba subsequently became a state witness and agreed to testify against the murders. He led the police to a shallow grave in the Hazyview area, where they exhumed the remains of what they believed had been Sedibe's corpse (Masinga and Minsi 2008).

Jacob Zuma's trials provided Morema with a powerful script to defend and legitimize his own situation. Here the complex workings of 'mythopraxis' are clearly apparent. Sahlins (1985:58) uses this concept to denote the reenactment of historical myths in contemporary situations, notably in Polynesia where descendants emulate the deeds of mythical ancestors. In this way myths provide a model for understanding events and consecrate current arrangements.

On 10 April Morema remarked, "I've heard a rumour about being involved in murder and I went to the Acornhoek police station commissioner to ask him to investigate.' But Morema dismissed all charges, saying that he was a victim of political conspiracy. 'It is like something that happened to Jacob Zuma' (Hlatswayo 2008a). Paul Mbenyane, a spokesperson for the ANC in Mpumalanga, said Morema's arrest had 'come as a shock', but that he was 'innocent until proven guilty' (Masinga 2008a). (Supporters had used the same slogan to defend Jacob Zuma.)

Morema and Mosoma portrayed themselves as Zuma loyalists, victimized by Thabo Mbeki's supporters in Mpumalanga. In December 2007, Morema led a delegation from Bushbuckridge to vote for Jacob Zuma at the ANC's national conference in Polokwane. The delegation even refused to stay in the hotel paid for them by the ANC, because they did not wish to allow Mosiuoa Lekota to persuade them to vote for Mbeki. After the elections, Gwede Mantashe and Kgalema Mothlante, who had campaigned for Zuma, came to Bushbuckridge to thank the region for its support, and praised Morema as 'a true leader'.

Thabo Mbeki's supporters in Mpumalanga included Thabang Makwetla (the Premier), Fish Mahlalela (MEC for Safety and Security), Jacques Modipane (former MEC for Finance) and Gladys Nyathi (a councilor without portfolio). They reportedly conspired to remove Morema as mayor to secure a political foothold in Bushbuckridge. Gladys Nyathi allegedly arranged with her comrade, Sidney Mokgope, to have a love affair with Morema's estranged wife so that they could learn about his secrets. Fish Mahlalela sent eight policemen to detain Mokgope and question him at the Railway café in the nearby town of Hoedspruit. The police claimed that Morema had told them that he, Mokgope, had killed Jeffrey Sedibe and thrown the revolver into a dam. After one hour, Jacques Modipane came to the café and pleaded with Mokgope to help the police in their investigations. However, Mokgope remained uncooperative and later told Morema about the incident. In a secret report, Superintendent Rapelwana claimed that Fish Mahlelela and Jacques Modipane asked to see him in connection with the investigation against Morema (Rorke 2008).

Morema, Mosoma and Makhubela remained in police custody until 14 and 15 April, when they finally applied for bail at the Acornhoek periodical court. On 14 April Magistrate George Risimat became irate because the proceedings had started late, and because arguments between the organized crime unit and the defense team got out of hand. Members of the ANC Youth League also threatened journalists in court, and covered their cameras with blankets. He asked Morema and Mosoma not to plead to charges of murder, and ordered Makhubela to be taken for a medical assessment, because he claimed that a police officer had assaulted him to force a confession (Masinga and Mnisi 2008).

Nearly a thousand supporters waited outside the court on 15 April, wearing Jacob Zuma T-shirts, waving ANC flags, and holding placards proclaiming that the mayor was innocent. ANC councilors, Home Affairs officials and municipal employees led the demonstration. The crowd danced and enthusiastically sang the songs, including - 'Release him! This man is innocent' (*Moloko lleng: Mona ye ganamolato* in Northern Sotho, a hymn referring to the judgement of Jesus by Pontius Pilate) and 'Machine gun! Bring me my machine gun' (as popularized by Zuma). As in the case of Jacob Zuma's rape trail there were also smaller groups of opponents. They comprised supporters of opposition parties and members of Abel Mashile's family.'

Lawyer for the accused said their clients denied any knowledge of the charges, and denied that Mosoma had any relationship with the state witness. The magistrate set bail at R10, 000 (€909) for each of the accused, and ordered Morema and Mosoma to surrender their passports. Khazamula Gumede, one of Bushbuckridge's wealthiest businessmen, who had secured numerous lucrative municipal contracts in the past, posted bail for the three accused. An onlooker recalled hearing Gumede say outside the court: 'If he [the magistrate] wants bail I'll pay whatever he wants. If he wants R500, 000 (€44,454), I have it on me right now. If he wants R1 million (€90,909), I'll withdraw it from the bank.'

Morema's supporters were jubilant when they saw him coming out of the court, waving his fist like Mandela had done when he first came out of prison in 1990 (Mahlanga 2008). They carried him to the back of a van where he made a speech.[118] Morema said that he and his comrades were not killers, but that others had framed them. 'Some are ANC members! We know exactly who they are!' He then shouted, 'The power is ours' (*Matimba, iya hina* in XiTsonga) (Mhlanga 2008a). Supporters then followed Morema and Mosoma home. They celebrated and danced throughout the night to the sound of loud music. The Provincial Executive Committee of the ANC nonetheless asked Morema to step down from his post as mayor, with full pay, pending the outcome of the trial (Masinga 2008a).

On 27 May an even larger crowd assembled to listen to the trial. Municipal employees first met on the Impalahoek sports ground, from where they marched to the periodical court. Here other protesters joined them. Again, there were many allusions to Jacob Zuma's trail. The supporters wore black T-shits with '100 % Morema' on front, and 'Innocent until proven guilty' on the back, and bore ANC flags and placards.

A smaller group comprising members of the Mashile family and of the Bantu Apostolic Church, a congregation founded by Abel's father, demonstrated against the mayor. The church members beat drums, sang hymns, and waved placards proclaiming, 'GOD will never give power to the Killers.' Dressed in a church gown, Abel's brother, Julius, waved a placard, 'Though Shall Not Kill. Exodus 20 verse 13'. The opposition party members waved placards with more secular themes. Emotions ran high. Some of Morema's supporters removed opposition party placards, and burnt their flags. They also hit Riot Hlatswayo, a freelance journalist, and drove the Bantu Apostolic Church to the shopping centre, across the road, from where they continued their demonstration.

Inside the courtroom the noise of the singing, drums, and plastic bugals (*vuvuzelas*) grew louder and louder, disrupting the proceedings. The magistrate, George Risimati, asked, 'If there is anyone who can tell these people to be quiet let him do so'. With his

---

[118] At the end of each day's proceedings during his rape trail, Zuma often led his supporters outside the court in song, speech and dance (Skeen 2007:65).

lawyer's approval Milton Morema then went outside and told his supporters to calm down (Mhlanga 2008b).

Acting on behalf of the accused, Advocate Mpho Mashilwane, asked the court to postpone the case because the police docket had gone missing, and because police had failed to submit the results of DNA tests done on the suspected body of Jeffrey Sedibe. He also complained that because Milton Morema was a public figure, police had 'showcased the arrest..., arriving with thirty BMW sedans' (Mhlanga 2008b). Magistrate Risimati then struck the case off the roll due to insufficient evidence. He also expressed concern that the case was politically motivated, saying that it looked like a witch-hunt. 'I know nothing about politics, but I can tell you that this court is not a battlefield for politics' (Mhlanga 2008b). The magistrate ordered the bail money to be returned, and issued an interim interdict to prevent the police from re-arresting the accused.

Morema's supporters ululated and 'went crazy' outside the court. However, the Mashile family felt betrayed by the state. Julius Mashile, Abel's brother, said he no longer believed in the justice system of the country, but won't give up the fight. Many of my informants, too, were extremely skeptical of the judgment. They alleged that the magistrate was Morema's cousin and also that he was a neighbour and close friend of Morema's lawyer. There were also rumours that Morema had consulted Thabane, a well-known herbalist, who resides behind the police station. Thabane dispenses potions enabling criminals to escape heavy sentences.

Mpumalanga's organized crime unit continued to investigate the murders, and there has been growing resentment of the mayor, especially amongst those excluded from networks of patrimonial distribution. Supporters of the APC (African Congress Party) handed their headman a letter demanding that he expel Erasmus Makhubela from their village because they did want to reside amongst killers. On 4 July 2008 about 700 members of the APC and UDM (United Democratic Movement) marched to the Acornhoek police station, and handed the magistrate a memorandum, demanding that he reinstate the case. The protesters sang, 'We saw the Bones in the *Daily Sun*' (*Re bone mashapo ko Daily Sun*),[119] and held placards proclaiming, 'Your secret is our, Morema', '100 % for nothing', and 'Morema deserve to rott in jail'. Outside the station, they burnt a statue of planks made to look like Morema, wearing his 100 % T-shirt, and two trousers, 'blood' written in red on both legs (Mhlanga 2008c).

That very weekend, Morema's supporters abducted John Maboyi, an APC leader, from a tavern, tied his hands, and took him to the Inyaka dam, where they threatened to drown him. Police launched a manhunt in search of him, and an angry group of APC members congregated in front of Morema's gate, threatening to burn his home. Morema phoned the municipal manager, who was also at the dam, and asked him to bring Maboyi back. Maboyi returned that Sunday evening. He was alive, but had been

---

[119] Lyrics of the song refer to a photograph of Jeffrey Sedibe's remains, published in South Africa's popular tabloid newspaper, *The Daily Sun*.

brutally assaulted. Police immediately placed Maboyi on a witness protection program, and arrested the municipal manager on charges of kidnapping (SAPA 2008b).

On 16 August 2008 the Zuma loyalist, David 'Hurricane' Mabuza, was elected ANC chairperson in Mpumalanga. This strengthened Morema's position, and virtually destroyed the ambitions of Mbeki supporters. At a news conference in Nelspruit on 2 October 2008, Izaac Mahlangu, provincial secretary of the ANC Youth League, accused two MECs (Members of the Executive Councils) in the Mpumalanga government of trying to re-assert Morema. His public comments virtually echoed those made earlier by the national Youth League chair, Julius Malema, about Jacob Zuma.

> The two MECs whom we suspect have made the press a specialized division of the SAPS [South African Police Services] in their conquest to kill Comrade Milton Morema… Death be upon you. As for your stooges in the press and the SAPS – death be upon you! Since you have lived by the sword, you will die by the sword'. Your newspaper will be read by those ghosts who couldn't find their way to heaven (Masinga 2008).

Mahlangu defended his statement, saying he was not inciting violence against the MECs or against journalists, but was merely warning that they will 'reap what they sow'. Mahlangu declined to name the MECs.

The case against Morema and his co-accused has been smothered by legal procedure. Forensic tests failed to positively link the accused to the murder, and the office of South Africa's Safety and Security minister, Charles Ngcacula, issued an interdict to prevent the police from arresting them (Hlatswayo 2008b). Morema, Mosoma and Makhubela's final court appearance was in the Nelspruit circuit of the Pretoria High Court on Wednesday 18 March 2009. Like Magistrate Risimati, Judge Cynthia Pretorius struck the case from the roll after the state witness, Calvin Mzimba, claimed that police had forced him into agreeing to testify. Mzimba told journalists that the police had 'tortured' him and offered him R100, 000 (€9,909) in cash and also a house and a car to implicate the accused in murder (Hlatswayo 2009a). Addressing his supporters after the final court ruling, Morema again emphasized that he was the victim of a political conspiracy. "I have been treated like Msholozi [Jacob Zuma] and I am happy it is over. On Sunday I will use my last cents to buy and slaughter four cows to celebrate" (*African Eagle Eye News* 2009).

Conclusions

Historical and ethnographic evidence from South Africa points to different limitations of Olivier de Sardan's (1999) theory of a 'moral economy of corruption'. Here the obligation to render assistance to networks of kin, Comrades and friends, in a manner that transcends bureaucratic procedure was clearly related to allegations of corruption. Morema and Mosoma were cousins, as were Mosoma and Makhubela. They also resided in a common village section and were members of the same ANC branch. Olivier de Sardan's (1999) observations about expectations of redistributive accumulation and the acceptability of corruption are also pertinent to these dramas.

165

Certain of these limitations arise from a restricted conception of corruption. Olivier de Sardan's (1999) theory is more appropriate to everyday and routine forms of corruption, such as partisan access to government controlled resources and the demand of brides by officials; than to more serious forms of abuse of public office and authority, such as fraud, rape and murder, at the higher echelons of national and municipal government. Moreover, material from South Africa show that attempts to conceptualize corruption in terms of its legality inappropriately posit the law as an external yardstick, and deflect attention from police, lawyers and judges, as integral actors in these dramas. In these more dramatic cases, corruption is less likely to be accepted and its morality more likely to be contested.

The charges of murder against Morema by the police, and also explicit attempts by the accused to deny involvement, were at best uncertain bids with unpredictable outcomes. They were made in the context of hegemonic party system, where debate about policy and competition for office were internal matters of the ruling ANC, and took the form of conspiracy theories. Sanders and West (2003) remind us that in a world where transparency has become a political watchword, the existence of clandestine and hidden spaces, are especially conducive to allegations about conspiracies. Despite the absence of clear evidence, conspiracy theories have considerable force and can, in such contexts, lead to the deposition of presidents.

In his defense against the charge, Morema and his supporters invoked the authority of Jacob Zuma, and successfully attempted to draw parallels between their situations by claiming to be framed by Mbeki's loyalists, the police and the press. There is a complex interplay of dramas in the centre and periphery, apparent in numerous rhetorical and symbolic links. The demonstrators in support and against Morema at courts of law invoked images of Zuma's trials through the use of T-shirts, slogans, songs, and in addresses to the crowd. There were also parallels in the ambiguous pronouncements of Youth League leaders, promising death to their opponents, and in the inconclusive nature of the trials. Their claims to legitimacy did not rest on evidence of innocence, but rather on the exposing malevolent the motives of their accusers, police blunders, and breaches of legal procedure by the prosecution. In several important respects, therefore, Morema's trial was choreographed as being 'like something that happened to Jacob Zuma'.

Another perhaps less evident parallel is found in the replication of the materialistic aspects of solidarity networks and in political contestation. Much like the situation depicted in the Igbo-speaking areas of Nigeria described by Smith (2007), enthusiastic support for politicians embroiled in allegations of corruption by the subordinate, seems to be based on expectations of benefits in situations of (neo) patronage. Jacob Zuma's most vocal supporters were citizens who considered themselves to be marginalized under Thabo Mbeki's rule —and felt that a change of personnel within the highest echelons of the ANC government might being new opportunities. Those who demonstrated in favour of Morema were employees of the local municipality and recipients of municipal contracts and of social welfare – who were fearful of losing their positions and benefits should he be deposed. Morema's opponents were defeated factions within the ANC, excluded from spheres of influence, and opposition party members, excluded from benefits. These lines of contestation are apparent in settings where household survival increasingly depends upon access to redistributive networks of the state.

In our attempts to explain corruption it is essential to recognize that the sorts of 'moral economies' Olivier de Sardan (1999) identifies are closely tied to 'political economies'. Explanations cannot purely rest upon the explication of meaning. Ideological legitimation was crucial in the cases we examined. But it is far more inconsequential in the cases of post-communist Russia, where organized crime controlled certain businesses (Lovell 2005), and in the townships of Cape Town, where an oppressive mafia-style leadership controls houses documented for the poor (Bähre 2005).

THE CAPE VERDEAN NATIONAL IDENTITY: CULTURAL AND SOCIAL SOURCES (INCLUDING THE CZECH INSPIRATION)[120]

Jan Klíma
University of Hradec Králové

Within contemporary African states established forcibly during the era of colonialism, the strong and general national identity is mostly a serious problem. Ethnicity (Roosens 1989) or ethnic self-awareness is usually not identical with the nationality and individual nations may not feel belonging to the community of citizens to be designated as Nigerians, South Africans, etc. Moreover, the ethnic and national identity (Cerulo 1997) is a dynamic feature of social life, constantly evolving and changing. Among African nations, the Cape Verdean community can be characterized as a special and successful case as for the unambiguous, strong and clear nationality formed by means of cultural unification of extremely different sources.

It is mainly the difference in national identity feeling which juxtaposes the two nearby African countries belonging to the PALOP and CPLP groups. Compared to the instable neighbouring Guinea-Bissau, a country with identical colonial history and the same leadership of the anti-colonial resistance (Klíma 2005), the contemporary Republic of Cape Verde [121] is a stable democratic country. There are several causes of disorder and instability in Guinea-Bissau (AP 2009–02–03), the recent result of which was, on 2 March 2009, the assassination of the state president João Bernardo "Nino" Vieira (Howden 2009). Contrary to it is the stability of Cape Verde based on the *good governance* represented by the President Pedro Pires. However, the main reason for the new divergence is firmly rooted in history. The national identity of both West African countries formed in a different way during centuries.

From extremely different elements, a new nation is born

While various West African tribes were moving in permanent wars on the territory of the posterior Guinea-Bissau, two chains of the Cape Verde islands were discovered uninhabited in 1460 (Diffie and Winius 1977: 96–107) without any trace of African, Asian (Menzies 2004: 135, 137, 281) or European influence. The Portuguese colonization commenced in 1462 by building a settlement in Ribeira Grande (Grand Canyon) on the island of Santiago (Klíma 2002a). During the period of intensive explorations of the West African coastline and building fortresses in the resisting Morocco, it was extremely

---

[120] This chapter is a result of the research supported by the Specific Science Grant 2009 of the Faculty of Arts, the University of Hradec Králové.

[121] In the Czech language, three books on the evolution of Cape Verde exist as a result of the "Expedition Cape Verde 2002", organized by two lecturers of the University of Hradec Králové: Jan Klíma, Jan Vítek 2002, 2003; Jan Klíma: 2008.

difficult for the Portuguese to build a commercial base on Cape Verde. A handful of Portuguese slave traders, merchants from Castile and Holland, some Jews expelled from the Iberian Peninsula (Iria 1979) and "Moors", i. e. Muslims from Morocco, were forming, step by step, the "white" community. Black African imported as slaves from the interior of the continent resisted much better the difficult living conditions of the "insular Sahara". Members of many ethnic groups living originally between the commercial base (*feitoria*) Arguim at the coast of Mauritania and the region of Sierra Leone had to serve, after having been transported to the archipelago, as producers of food and fabric to be exchanged for more slaves later; they were, more frequently, submitted to the linguistic assimilation and obedience training before being sold to America later on. So, members of Balanta, Bijago, Mandingo, Nalu, Wolof and other African tribes had to spend a part or the whole of their lives on the islands (Carreira 2000: 385–507) while using the Portuguese language and respecting the regulations stipulated by the colonizers and slave traders.

During following centuries, the white minority used to abandon the archipelago to avoid pirate assaults, drought, starvation (Carreira 1985), illnesses, explosions of the Fogo volcano and other human and natural catastrophes. Only the African majority was able to survive under such unfavourable conditions. Meanwhile, the racial crossbreeding was under way when white proprietors, having many African women, co-created mixed population or even bequeathed their property to their mulatto descendants (Meintel 1984).

As late as after the abolition of the slave trade in 1836 and during the subsequent process of abolition of slavery in Portuguese colonies until 1869 (the last links between masters and slaves remaining until 1878) was it possible to take use of the insular isolation for creating a new nation from different racial components of the Cape Verdean society. To become aware of its special identity within the Portuguese colonial empire, the insular community needed intelligentsia, culture and language of its own.

Centre of education
In the mid-19th century, the competition of European powers in the conquest of Africa forced the Portuguese government to improve the hitherto neglected education in African colonies. As Lisbon controlled only coastlines of Angola, Mozambique and Guinea, the near Cape Verde islands were a safe basis for removing the handicap of bad colonial administration by establishing an educational centre of the future colonial intelligentsia.

On the archipelago, the public education began in 1817, but the basic school opened in Praia became extinct very soon. After reopening, in 1821, this school operated irregularly until 1840. During the school year of 1841–1842, only 12 basic schools existed on the whole archipelago, there were no higher schools (Anjos 2005: 19). In February 1845, the bishop of Cape Verde made an official report describing the educational conditions on the islands, demanding one basic school to be established on each island plus one central ecclesiastic seminar combined with a public grammar school to be founded for the whole archipelago. Based on the decree dated 23 November 1847, a higher school for 24 students, one half earmarked for the Catholic Church, the other half for the public or administrative sector, was to be established on the small island of Brava, where the significant portion of population was white. However, the geographical position of Brava at the south-western periphery of the archipelago was disadvantageous and the small community was not able to sustain the "Main School of Cape Verde" (*Escola Principal de Cabo Verde*). There were unfavorable conditions on other islands, too: landowners from the island Santo Antão used to protest – e. g. in 1850 – against the "literacy tax" which forced them to allocate some yields from the production of the sugar cane brandy (*grogue*) to the school subsidy. Thus, the higher school, which never operated properly, was transferred onto the most populated island of Santiago in 1860. New problems arose there: slaves and black lumpenproletarians as predominant part of the population had no interest in education. Meanwhile the handful of wealthy whites and mulattoes was not able to support the school. Therefore, the school worked a short time on Santiago.

In the meantime, the multiracial Cape Verdean community began to show traits of a new nation. Unfortunately, this society could not count with a cultured definition of its special nationality. The Portuguese folklore of whites as well as the African folklore of blacks (see e. g. Semedo and Turano s. d.) more divided than united the community. Thus, the enhancement of national consciousness depended mainly on active mulattoes (Carreira and Fyfe 1982).

José Luís Alves Feijó, bishop of Cape Verde from 12 November 1865, advocated and supported the ancient plan of establishing a seminar anywhere on the archipelago. Based on central decision dated 3 September 1866, the government established an "ecclesiastic seminar" with two programs: "preparatory studies" focused on general middle/grammar school education, while the "ecclesiastic studies" covered the professional instruction tailored for priests to work later in Portuguese overseas possessions.[122] For locating such a seminar, the small town of Ribeira Brava on the island of São Nicolau having nearly the same distance to other islands of Fogo, Santiago and São Vicente. Doctor Júlio José Dias donated his own spacious house at the end of one street to the new seminar (Silva 1890). At that time, São Nicolau was seat of the bishopric and there was no significant difference between the settlement on this island and other parts of the archipelago. The canon Manuel Correia de Figueiredo as the first school headmaster reached the port of Preguiça on the island of São Nicolau on 22 December 1866 and the "St. Joseph Seminar" started to operate on 16 January 1867. Next day, Correia de Figueiredo sent a report to the governor José Guedes de Carvalho e Meneses da Costa (1861–1869) where he declared main aims of the institution: taking use of the geographical position of Cape

---

[122] The most important Cape Verdean cultural review *Artiletra* published a special issue 59/60 in October 2004 dedicated to the seminar-grammar school. Among many documents, the review also reprints, on page 2, the mentioned Decree of the Secretary of (Portuguese) State for Navy and Overseas Possessions.

Verde for Portuguese and colonial students, the graduates were determined to "fertilize" all Portuguese colonies in Africa from the North to the Cape of Good Hope. The headmaster planned the posterior spreading of the "Christian civilization" by means of missions to be opened later in Guinea, São Tomé e Príncipe, Angola and Congo (*Artiletra* 59/60: 2).

Under hard conditions (*Artiletra* 59/60: 14–15), the *seminário-liceu* worked as a superstructure to raise the level of basic schools. The well-educated and democratic bishop José Luís Alves Feijó wrote to the governor Caetano Alexandre de Almeida de Albuquerque (1869–1876) in an extensive letter dated 15 September 1875:

> The basic education for both sexes deserves really the most serious attention and the highest care. It is the basis for the whole educational system and therefore it is important to undergo highest sacrifices in favour of its development and progress. I can not agree with the opinion of those functionaries who take for suitable to leave some social groups in ignorance and illiteracy. They are afraid that the people having a certain level of culture would be willing neither to be satisfied with their fate nor to accept the most brute work any more. Such an opinion contradicts fundamentally to the human dignity itself, as the man as an intelligent, sensible and free being spirit has the inalienable right of cultivating his spirit to be enhanced further on... (*Artiletra* 59/60: 13).

For appreciating duly such an opinion, let us take into consideration, that as late as 1866 special buildings for schools started to be erected in Portugal and the first Ministry of Education was established in Lisbon as late as in 1870 (Klíma 2007: 372, 374). No middle or higher schools existed in other Portuguese colonies, the neighbouring Portuguese Guinea, separated from the Cape Verde administratively in 1879, remained the country of "savages" struggling against the Portuguese more than posterior three decades.

In 1888, doctor Francisco Ferreira da Silva assumed functions of president of the administrative board and deputy headmaster of the seminar.Iin 1899 he published the book *Commentaries on the History of Diocesis Administration and Organization of the Seminary Grammar School of Cape Verde*, dedicated symptomatically to the "sons of Cape Verde". When applying to the governor for some blank forms for his school, on 24 April 1901, Ferreira da Silva noted that all documents should be kept "without any racial difference, which could be a little bit unfavorable for the nature of this establishment, as official statistics require such data." Thus, the *seminário-liceu* grew into the cradle of the Cape Verdean culture, when at the same time the colonial commanders like João Teixeira Pinto opened a series of military campaigns to control the nearby "savage" Guinea.

Pioneers of national intelligentsia
In the new spiritual atmosphere created by the Seminar, new cultural bodies arose. In 1867, the Dramatic Society of African Theater was founded in the capital city of Praia. Two years later, the Reader's Association (*Gabinete de Leitura da Praia*) came into existence. At the end of the 1860's, the society called *Ilustração Africana* was born even in the small port of Santa Maria on the island of Sal, stipulating its goals as follows: "to please

spirits, to divulge knowledge which is important for reading, and to strengthen social ties" (*Boletim Oficial de Cabo Verde* 1867, 1870, 1875).

Under hard conditions of drought, poor crops, erosion and emigration, educated people encouraged the burgeoning consciousness of a particular national identity by means of educational activities and press articles. After some exemplars of the newspaper *Independente,* founded in 1877, after *Correio de Cabo Verde* (1879) and *O Echo de Cabo Verde* (1880), the irregular periodical *A Justiça* started to be published in April 1881 "to instigate noble ideas within groups of intelligentsia, to set the sacred fire of love to the mother land to all hearts, to inform the people on their rights and obligations, to break the iron scepter, to free the consciousness from any oppression, to free the thinking from any gust of tyranny..." (*A Justiça* 1881). Although most newspapers and magazines ended with the first issue, the desire to read the printed word was perspicuous. Journalists were ready to fulfill their cultural and social task, many times as the voice of the population against the colonial authorities, which was demonstrated by the mere title of the newspaper *O Protesto,* 1883. In the most important periodical of that time called Cape Verde Review (*Revista de Cabo Verde*), Luís Loff de Vasconcelos thundered at "those figures who are moving around us with the aim of intimidating, weakening our spirit and leading us away from our little glorious struggle waged for the renovation and progress of this country" (Anjos 22).

For the second generation of pupils, the St. Joseph Seminary Grammar School in Ribeira Brava was a precious inspiration. The canon António Manuel da Costa Teixeira published, in 1894, a yearbook of contributions called *Almanach Luso-Africano,* where authors dealt with various problems of the archipelago from agriculture to history. Later on, he published an irregular periodical Hope (*Esperança*). Costa Teixeira, lecturer of the Seminary Grammar School of Ribeira Brava, even translated extracts from the Portuguese national epic *Lusíadas* by Luís de Camões into the commonly spoken insular language (*crioulo*). The year 1899 of the *Almanach Luso-Africano* reprinted, except for other documents, statutes of the Educational Association Hope, founded in 1895, with the following goal: "

In addition to the good education, the popular, practical and theoretical education for both sexes is to be organized by means of theoretical schools and practical apprenticeship establishments. This will lead the youth from the vice of loafing to the love to education, work and good (*Almanach Luso-Africano* 1899: 356).

In this way, the dream of higher culture emerged, many times on the basis of the local language (Duarte 2003) serving, besides the literary Portuguese, for artistic and journalistic purposes. Being aware of this new situation, the journalist José Lopes fired: "I wish I lived, even in the last moment of my life, the delight of seeing these poor islands independent and happy..." (*Revista de Cabo Verde* 1899).

Eugénio Tavares (1867–1930) assumed the most important task of confirming the special characteristics of the Cape Verdean national culture and feeling. A poor descendant of the Portuguese father and mother from the island of Fogo was being brought up in the family of his godmother on the island of Brava. Influenced by the rich library of his nanny's husband, Tavares published his first text in the *Almanac of Portuguese-Brazil Memorabilia* in the age of fifteen (*Artiletra* 34/35). When working on the cosmopolitan island of São Vicente and, later on, as a public functionary in Tarrafal, island of Santiago, he decided to be journalist and writer. Upon his flight before unjust accusation to New Bedford, New England (USA), Tavares published a periodical called *Alvorada* (Daybreak) for his countrymen in the USA. His article *Autonomy* expressed the general feeling of intellectuals of Cape Verde (Andrade 1998: 43) with following closing words: "We should have a Monroe of our own: Africa for Africans!"

After returning home, Tavares sent his articles to Lisbon and Porto, wrote for the domestic Cape Verde Magazine and satirical *Manduco* (Bludgeon). A generation of skilled journalists using both Portuguese and *crioulo* assembled round this national minstrel (Oliveira 1998). Tavares elevated the *crioulo* from the position of a disdained "negro dialect" onto the high level of the rich national literary language (Reis 1984). The collection of masterly poems *Mornas – Cantigas Crioulas* (published posthumously in 1932) became a basis for the whole national poetry. Tavares also wrote comical verses, excellent political commentaries, social references and interesting private letters.

Photograph1: Eugénio Tavares, national poet of Cape Verde

After the *Seminário-Liceu,* it was the work of intellectuals such as Eugénio Tavares, Pedro Cardoso with his pen-name *Afro* (Brito-Semedo and Morais 2008), Luís Loff de Vasconcelos and others which enabled the new nation to build its identity and political culture. After the Portuguese Republic has been proclaimed, Tavares appealed to central politicians in Lisbon to "disencumber the black race from its disgusting condition of slavery." At that time, the governor Pedro Vieira Júdice Biker (1911–1915) himself appreciated the insular *nativismo* (patriotism of natives) like "the love to homeland, love to freedom, desire for truth and justice, pains in enhancing the moral emancipation and higher civilization, hatred of racial prejudice and oppression." In 1915, at the same time, when Teixeira Pinto dominated last Guinean "savages", Pedro Cardoso published, in Praia, his first collection of poems called symptomatically *Caboverdeanas.*

During the general misery and anti-clerical campaign, the Portuguese Republic (since 1910) decided to close the Seminary Grammar School on 13 June 1917. The public school *Instituto Caboverdiano de Instrução,* established in the same town of Ribeira Brava, suffered from lack of experts and interest. After the Great War, the whole island of São Nicolau became a periphery of the insular social life. Finally, the central government closed this school in June 1931, transforming the building into a prison for democratic insurgents arrested after the rebellion in Madeira and Guinea.

Photograph 2: The Seminar-Grammar School in Ribeira Brava, São Nicolau

Sokols of Cape Verde

Drought, unemployment and maritime experiences forced the Cape Verdeans to emigrate to the United States of America during the whole 19th and 20th century. The community, with the center in New Bedford, New England, enhanced the skills of Cape Verdean musicians, priests, physicians and public activists. It was the well-educated mulatto population living round the *Porto Grande* in the town of Mindelo on the island of São Vicente, which maintained best relations to foreign commercial companies as well as to English culture and language. Through the English press mediation, the distant Czech inspiration appeared surprisingly in Mindelo.

Photograph 3: Júlio Bento de Oliveira, founder of the Cape Verdean Sokol

Júlio Bento de Oliveira, native of Paúl, Santo Antão and graduate of the Seminary Grammar School of Ribeira Brava, read an article on the Czechoslovak movement of Sokols (Falcons) in an English magazine. On 25 November 1932, he founded a civic movement in Mindelo aiming at "creating one big Cape Verdean family, expelling all evil, corruption and all factors of the national physical, moral and intellectual decadence from its bosom" (Ramos 1982).

Photograph 4: A Parade of Sokols in the Streets of Mindelo

Thanks to ideals of self-perfection, discipline and collectivism, the Sokol of Mindelo spread rapidly gaining popular sympathy and more and more members. J. Bento de Oliveira stressed the mission of the Czech model, which succeeded in achieving the national independence, in 1918, by means of self-organization and patriotism. Pursuing similar aims, the spontaneous civic association performed impressive gymnastic activities in Mindelo and gathered, under the photograph of the Czech Sokol founder Miroslav Tyrš, one fifth of the whole population of the island. New branch organizations were established, later on, on the islands of Santo Antão and Santiago. This civic association enriched the social life and that is why the governor Amadeu Gomes de Figueiredo did not obstruct its activities, changing only the denomination to *Falcões Portugueses de Cabo Verde*. Best insular intellectuals collaborated with the Sokol: Baltasar Lopes da Silva compiled the statutes of the organization (Lopes 1934), José Lopes da Silva wrote lyrics of the association's anthem.

Photograph 5: A rally of Sokols in Mindelo

The Sokol of Cape Verde was strictly non-political association. When hungry crowds around the leader Nhô Ambrósio plundered the Customs Office in Mindelo, on 4 June 1934, demanding support during the famine period, the local authorities asked Sokols to help in suppressing the unrest. Bento de Oliveira refused to act against the unsatisfied population. At that time, moral qualities of Sokols were generally acknowledged. Sokol members were often preferably employed as civil officers, clerks, teachers and responsible employees of domestic and foreign companies (particularly English company *Western Telegraph*). At the end of the 1930s, Sokol has various specialized departments (gymnastic, maritime and others), also organizing lectures and social meetings for its members.

Photograph 6: Sokols of Cape Verde

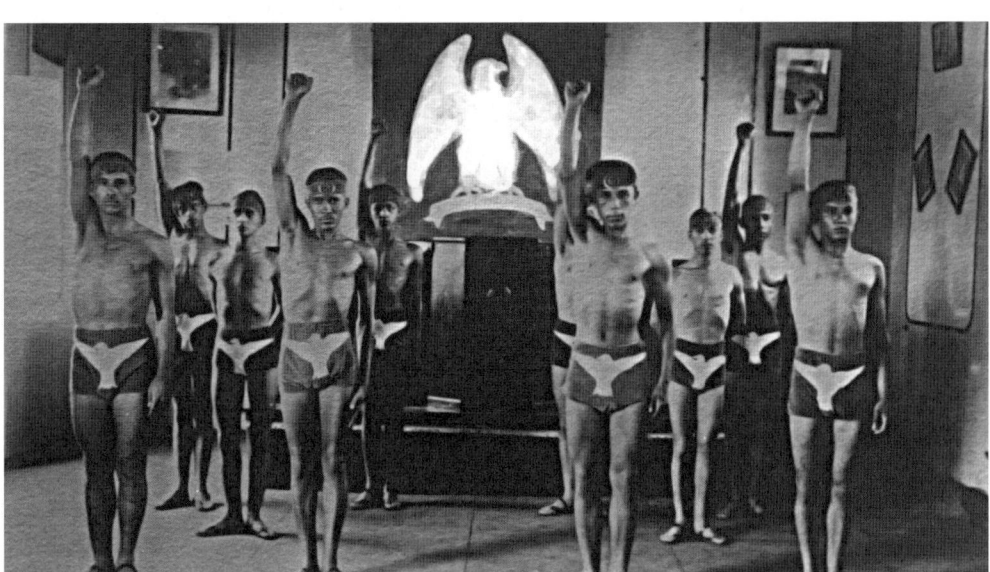

However, the civic spontaneity and slogan "Strength and Discipline" of the Cape Verdean Sokols (Reis 1933) was not welcome by the Salazar's regime after 1936, when the exclusive youth organization *Mocidade Portuguesa* (and *Mocidade Portuguesa Feminina* for girls) was established for all young people in Portugal and colonies (Klíma 2005a). Nevertheless, Sokol marches through Mindelo can be documented by photographs as late as in 1938. Later on, Sokols made their gymnastic show on the free space below the oldest residential quarter of the capital city of Praia called *Campo da Várzea* in 1939. On 24 June 1939, Sokols greeted the Portuguese President Carmona during his official visit to Cape Verde, acting probably for the last time in this way.

Júlio Bento de Oliveira rejected the official offer to unite Sokol with the Portuguese Youth. The Sokol episode was over, but its importance continued. Enthusiastic propagators of the Sokol ideas like Manuel Nascimento Ramos[123] or Félix Monteiro mentioned often the glory of their disciplined organization, the legacy of which gave an example to other independent groups of interest, including political ones. This is the reason of considering the Sokol of Cape Verde one of most important preludes of the posterior nationalist movement (Lopes 1996: 94–95).

---

[123] There are 24 precious photographs in the private archives of the Mr. Manuel Nascimento Ramos's family in Mindelo to document the history of the Cape Verdean Sokol between 1934–1939.

Photograph 7: A group of Sokols under the image of Miroslav Tyrš, Czech Sokol founder, with Czechoslovak flags

Besides the Czechoslovak support of the united Guinean and Cape Verdean resistance against Portugal in 1960–1974 (Zídek and Sieber 2007: 94–98, 115), the Sokol movement is one of few links between the Czech and Cape Verdean people. That is why it deserves attention from both Czech (Klíma 2002b, 2003) and Cape Verdean historians.

From *Claridade* to independence

Within the generation living in Cape Verde during the 1930s, the importance of both African and European source of identity was being discussed (Duarte 1999). The imperial idea stressed by the Portuguese "New State" as well as the reality of the intelligentsia mobility within the whole colonial empire[124] put also the question, whether the insular identity is more local than imperial Portuguese. However, the cultural endeavour accompanied by enhancing the literary *crioulo* of the 1930s contributed to an unambiguous final solution.

Young Cape Verdean writers, poets and journalists proved the richness of the national culture by editing five anthologies of poetry published between 1936 and 1947 as well

---

[124] Onésimo da Silveira, native of the island of São Vicente, can serve as an example of the all-imperial inspiration. He spent one part of his life on São Tomé, another part in Angola. In his poems and articles, he expressed a vigorous anti-colonial protest, but he was standing in the line of responsible and ideologically tolerant politicians after the independence had been proclaimed.

as the literary review called *Claridade* (Bright shine, Cleanness). In the work of *claridosos*, scenic landscapes of the island of São Nicolau frequently emerged to remember the Seminary Grammar School. Particularly Baltasar Lopes da Silva (1907–1989) liked using such motives, for example in his novel *Chiquinho* (1947). This generation already comprised the "fathers of foundation" of the insular independence and its youngest members became later politicians of the free Republic of Cape Verde.

Not by chance, Juvenal Cabral, teacher and casual writer (Cabral 1947) from Cape Verde, was the father of the Guinean guerrilla commander Amílcar Cabral (Chabal 2003). Along with this agricultural engineer, writers like Pedro Cousino Azevedo, Manuel Lopes, Gabriel Mariano and Ovídio Martins expressed their desire of independence based on the same language and culture. The armed resistance in Guinea in 1963–1973 was victorious thanks to the support of the Cape Verdean intellectuals and leaders (Tomás 2007). After the Portuguese "Carnation Revolution" on 25 April 1974, traditions of the local education and the well-developed national culture were the main reasons for the small nation to choose independence in 1975. Both a future coexistence with Portugal, and previously supposed union with ethnically diverse and culturally backward Guinea-Bissau were rejected (Chabal et al. 2002).

After the Guinean coup of 1980, Cape Verde strengthened its independence. On the contrary, Guinea-Bissau suffered from warlordism, instability and backwardness. Meanwhile the cultural and linguistic background guaranteed a favourable development of the Republic of Cape Verde, particularly after adopting the democratic multi-party political system in 1991.

Paradoxically, the Cape Verdean field commander of the Guinean PAIGC/FARP guerrilla Pedro Pires, the state president of Cape Verde, is a successful head of the democratic insular state. In contrast, his warfare colleague João Bernardo "Nino" Vieira has been shot dead during the recent coup in Guinea-Bissau. The explanation of the different evolution of the two brother countries rests in the force of the Cape Verdean identity. Another factor enhances the positive evolution in the Cape Verde. The archipelago remains open for foreigners and the emigration continues. The openness enables a new political mission of Cape Verde, that which corresponds with contemporary conditions of the globalized world: The Republic of Cape Verde, member of PALOP, CPLP and West African organizations, is now a connecting link between Europe and Africa, between Portuguese-speaking and French/English-speaking Africa, between Portugal and Brazil.

Thus, the problems of different sources of the Cape Verdean national identity was overcome by means of firm linguistic, educational and cultural foundations which have proved its importance for the present and future development of this extraordinary West African country.

Conclusion

The identification of the citizen with his African country remains a problem in such big continental countries like Mozambique, where many different cultural and linguistic groups live. This is not the case of Cape Verde. Definitions of identity concerning also human rights apply for continental African nations more than for historically new nations formed on uninhabited islands from various components. Partially, the definition of the World Bank could be valid for the Cape Verde case:

> Native groups/nations can be identified namely in the geographical sense on the basis of following characteristics: a) they have a close relation to the original territory and its natural resources, b) they are self-identified with the determined group, identifying other persons with another (different) cultural group, c) they use a native language, generally different from the official state language, d) they maintain traditional social and political institutions, e) they produce primarily for their own consumption only (Šavelková 2007: 225).

Other definitions and deliberations (Corntassel 2003) refer more to African continental natives and minorities in order to protect their identity and/or survival. As said above, the singular historical evolution of the Cape Verdean nationality was influenced by both geographical factors and by the use of the 'native' language, but Cape Verde possesses the identity of a modern nation with open and well-developed culture, economy and political relations. This is the main reason for the elevation of Cape Verde, a country without significant natural resources, from the level of less developed to medium developed countries recently. In comparison with the backward Guinea-Bissau, the use of human resources as unique resources available for enhancing the insular living standard is successfully based on cultural foundations of the Cape Verdean identity.

STILL WORKING ON THE STREET: POST WORKING CHILD TRANSITIONS IN KENYA

Philip L. Kilbride
Bryn Mawr College, Pensylvannia, U.S.A.

Introduction

Thus far little ethnographic data is available concerning adult post-street outcomes by boys and girls living and working on the world's streets. There are currently well over one hundred million worldwide defined as street children. Such children often live entirely on the streets whereas most are domiciled. Countries with street children are worldwide, for example, recent studies include: Haiti (Kovats-Bernat 2006), Venezuela (Marquez 1999), Mexico (Poniatowska 1999), United States (Taylor and Hickey 2001), Zimbabwe (Rurevo and Bourdillon 2003), and Vietnam (Burr 2006). Commonalities shared by children on the streets worldwide include, for example, the following characteristics:

1. Street children range in age from newborn to 20s
2. Proportion of boys to girls is 4 to 1
3. Child-like behaviours are often observed – sucking thumbs, crying, playing with toys
4. Sleeping on the streets (e.g. homelessness as de-domiciled)
5. Eating garbage and discarded food
6. Sniffing of glue (to keep warm and relieve stress)
7. Adult activities such as working in the informal economy, including begging for both boys and girls; street boys often take the label of their major occupation such as *khate* of Nepal (trash collector) or parking boys of Kenya
8. Girls frequently engaged in survival sex or prostitution
9. Because of all of the above, children on the streets are highly stigmatized, sometimes hunted for sport (Brazil) and in most nations are harassed by the police (good studies of this from India)

This paper reports recent research in Kenya following up on children first investigated a decade ago (Kilbride, Suda and Njeru 2001). The range of present adult activities of these former children on the streets is reported. Notably, labour on the street is still common such that a preliminary developmental typology assessing this labour is offered. Social class structure in Kenya significantly impacts children on the streets and their adult counterparts who are best understood as members of the working poor class "*jua kali*" (hot sun) labour.

Theoretical Objectives

Social class in Kenya is best understood historically taking into account first colonialism (1895–1963) and later post colonial concentration of power in the hands of ethnic elites

183

using increased post colonial presidential power and state authority to contract land and other resources through corruption, election rigging and neglect of public welfare (c.f. Leo 1984; Wrong 2009). Kenya remains among the top countries of the world having the most extreme income differences by social class (Holmquist et al 1994). Broadly, Kenya has a majority with a very young population living in cities and rural areas with small-scale agricultural activities for subsistence. Frequent famine is a recurring problem. The cities, especially Nairobi with about three million inhabitants, include what can be called the 'urban powerless' (Green 2001). The majority of those who live in slums are without employment or have "casual" labour or small scale occupations on the streets. Among these are thousands of children who live and work there. At the top of the class structure are the ethnic elites (big land owners and politicians) grading into a managerial professional class (wealthy professionals including some intellectuals). This class grades into a middle class of salaried workers with skills appropriate for the post industrial economy of today (e.g. educational, business middle men, computer workers, NGO workers, local and foreign companies personnel).

This chapter considers the extent to which street children experience any class 'mobility' as they become adults. We found that they cannot be upwardly mobile as they are not even on the ladder. Social class in Kenya must include gender as women are within each class at an economic disadvantage compared to men (Kilbride, Suda and Njeru 2001). We will see that street girls are very much at a disadvantage compared to boys working on the streets.

One main purpose of this paper, therefore, is to provide an ethnographic description of the working social context experienced by those labelled as street children in Kenya. This intention is to emphasize work of a certain kind, the informal economic sector wherein children and adults labour side by side as members of an analytical category we call "the working poor"(urban powerless). This term does not suggest strictly 'class consciousness', but here focuses on the street environment where unskilled Kenyans work side by side and sometimes compete with each other. Children as beggars, for instance, can be seen arguing with, for example, disabled Kenyans, over spaces thought to be advantages places for begging.

Another theoretical objective in this paper seeks to situate my research not only to those interested in social class, but also those anthropologists with an interest in cultural theory (cf. Ortner 2003, 2006). Allison James, speaking to anthropologists, for example, states, "Childhood research must now begin to engage more directly with core issues of social theory positioning children as social actors" (2007: 262). Presently, children remain as a neglected topic in the theoretical literature of anthropology (LeVine 2007). I return to this subject later.

Street Child as Problematic
In 2001, I, and my colleagues, published a book entitled *Street Children in Kenya: Voices of Children in Search of a Childhood* (Kilbride et al 2001). At that time the term street children

was standard whereas today there is growing tendency to conceptualize such children, not as street children, but by some broader category, such as children of the street (who live there), children on the street (who work there), survival sex workers, migrant to the city or, what I prefer now, "members of the working poor" or urban powerless (cf. Panter-Brick 2002). Street children are best understood in Africa and elsewhere as working poor who live and/or subsist on the world's streets. The label 'street child' is pejorative and understates the labour that children undertake as survival strategies. In Kenya, such work as collecting garbage, washing cars, running errands, carrying packages and guarding property are common among boys. Begging by boys and girls and survival sex for girls is significant (cf. Kilbride et al 2001).

In our research, for example, we found that 'street' boys and girls do accept the public label of street child, but rarely think of themselves as such most of the time. We found that they experience joys and sorrows, have nicknames, pets, aspirations, family connections, lovers, and dreams of life after the streets. This label of street child as an essentualized master status masks behavioural complexity and personality diversity. Most importantly most of these children in our study were not born on the streets, had a life before the streets and will, without exception, grow out of the label 'street child' as we are now attempting to better understand.

We now favour the term 'members of the working poor' as this term highlights what is most significant in the lives of children on the streets: their desire to work, and to receive formal and technical education so as to enhance their employment possibilities. This is the case not only in Kenya, but typical in the nations where over one hundred million children labelled as street children presently work and or live on the streets. Such children are often referred to by some word associated with a work activity, such as 'parking boy' in Kenya.

The label 'street child' is a temporary event in the lives of individuals. I will report here new material based on a revisit to Kenya in December 2007-January 2008 to locate and follow up with children first observed ten years ago for our book project as we reported above and to follow. The now adults to be considered here still attempt to survive, often still on the streets, but no longer as 'street children.' A preliminary typology will be suggested here concerning a social transition from child to adult for those still working on the streets. The question of class mobility in Kenya is at issue here.

African Children as Labourers: Not Only the Streets

Bass (2004: 3) has observed that "not all child labour is bad." Indeed, children perform important tasks in Africa outside of the labour market. She notes in Nigeria, not unlike Kenya, that activities among the Yoruba ethnic group involve useful work in preparation for adult work roles such as errands, fetching firewood and carrying water. Bass notes that girls help in the kitchen and in selling things in the market. Bass also states that child labour need not always be bad even when it violates cultural standards concerning proper labour practices for children, most often universal standards set by national and

185

international organizations (cf. Cheney 2007). I have observed children on the streets in Kenya who send remittances home, sometimes the only source of support for an impoverished rural family.

Bass also notes that the African continent has the highest proportion of the world's working children. At work on farms, as domestics, in industrial occupations, for example, Africa's children suffer the legacy of colonialism and post colonial poverty. In South African mines and farms and, for example, commercial farms in Zimbabwe there were exploitative colonial labour practices. The situation in Kenya was the same:

> In Kenya, the colonial past included oppressive labor practices for children. Kayongo-Male and Walji (1984) document conditions of forced child labor on plantations and in factories. They write, for example, 'In 1925 there were 11,315 children at work, mostly in the tea and coffee picking' (Kilbride et al. 2001).

Poverty, Tribal Clashes and Family Erosion

The post colonial legacy has only worsened the economic situation for children in Kenya since independence and the post colonial state since the 1960s. Kenya, today as noted above, has the most unequal income distribution in the world. "Imperial" state advantages have served to economically favour ethnic groups in power resulting in periodic tribal clashes and wealth disparities among ethnic groups. Overall, for example, Swadener et al have noted for Kenya:

> Forty-seven percent of the rural population lives in poverty and 29 % of Kenyans in urban areas are described as 'absolutely poor,' (Government of Kenya and UNICEF, 1998)" (2000).

Most of the children now working on Kenya's streets come from impoverished families and, as such, are importantly engaged in work activities instead of schooling where most desire to be. Others are children who have fled interethnic conflict over land rights which have flared up during election cycles in Kenya, first most dramatically in 1992 during the first multiparty elections when 300,000 people fled the Rift Valley.

Election violence erupted again in 2007 and 2008 when thousands of Kikuyu were killed or driven from the Rift Valley again including many children dislodged from their homes. Ethnic dispute concerns, for example, Kikuyu from elsewhere in Kenya who moved to the Rift Valley after independence with title deeds to land formerly held by Europeans. Indigenous groups such as the Kelenjin who the Europeans had replaced want their field lands back (cf. Kilbride 2008).

Elsewhere in Africa, of course, though not in Kenya, civil wars have broken out over ethnic disputes such that child soldiers are common among the continent's street population. HIV/AIDS has been a major cause of broken homes and displaced children, especially in Uganda previously and South Africa currently. Such AIDS orphans are known in Kenya but this is not a common cause there. Economic poverty is the most salient factor in Kenya and with it the erosion of family structures for economic and moral functions including child welfare. Suda (2007: 10) has remarked for Africa including Kenya:

Today, most of these socio-cultural values and moral standings are being eroded or distorted by the modernization process, resulting in moral decadence and the breakdown of traditional family life. Pre-marital pregnancies and divorce are increasingly common in contemporary Africa and public perceptions of them have changed drastically. There has also been a proliferation of single parents, the majority of whom are mothers who live in poverty and are becoming increasingly unable to provide adequate care and support for their families. The result has been premarital pregnancies, child abuse and neglect, increased numbers of street children, prostitution, and a tendency towards marital infidelity.

Bass (2004: 87) provides a useful overview of street children's work situation. She writes:

> The jobs of street children require few skills, offer little training, and may be dangerous and injurious to their health. Typical jobs are selling cigarettes, gum, candy, or newspapers; hauling garbage; guarding cars; washing windshields; and carrying luggage. Children who haul and scavenge for garbage often suffer cuts from shards of glass and metal. Further, street children are victims of unscrupulous adults who may abuse them, steal their earnings, or refuse to pay them.

Glassner (1994) writes about 'survival sex' by girls on the streets. This term is used instead of childhood prostitution so as to emphasize the lack of choice for children on the streets. In Kenya, we noted in our book (p. 123) that:

> Street girls are at the bottom of the status hierarchy on the street, if not in the entire Kenyan society. As such, their young, still developing bodies and childish smiles may not always immediately reveal what is privately a difficult life of pain and sorrow, one frequently including experiences of sexual exploitation. Certainly we observed many hazards encountered by these girls on a regular basis. We saw, for example, blister sores resulting from embers dropped on bare feet, painful foot lacerations due to stepping on nails, fever from untreated malaria or flu, and toothache. Suffering from harassment (or worse) by some police or internment in jail for extended periods of time, even while pregnant or already a mother with a child, is not uncommon. Middle-class men from the suburbs sometimes are a stressful threat to girls when they prostitute themselves. 'Going for the road,' their expression for survival sex, is nevertheless often a source of income in spite of the risks of diseases and beatings.

Many girls beg on the streets and this along with survival sex is a major source of their income. Sometimes girls, however, manage to acquire money by other means. One girl, who we befriended in 2008 in Nyeri at age 19, manages to rent her own room. She refers to herself as a street girl because she sniffs glue and hangs out at a roundabout seeking work. She washes clothes, washes glasses in a pub, and carries luggage and packages for market customers where we first met her. Although she does not beg, well-wishers do help her. She fears rape and has recently tested negative for HIV/AIDS. She hopes one day to be a hairdresser.

Children Working on the Streets of Nairobi
For most Kenyans and visitors alike, the glue bottle and begging symbolize the

187

public perception of the street child as a troublesome person or even a criminal. Police roundups of street children are common expressions of stigma and fear held by the public about them. Children in turn often express fear of the public, especially of the police, and sometimes casting doubt, for example, about the intentions of well-wishers whose gifts of food are suspected of containing poison. In our research we found that begging is indeed a major strategy for obtaining money, especially by boys under 14 who are still "innocent looking" and can be "easily pitied". Girls with babies can also be observed begging while holding their babies out with phrases such as "help the baby." Indeed in our survey of 400 boys and girls we found that about 45 % of them listed begging as their major means of gaining a livelihood. In the same survey, however, we found the following activities especially of boys which make up the majority occupations; collecting waste paper and scrap metal, cleaning vehicles, selling ground nuts, carrying goods for customers at stores and markets, watching parked vehicles, selling charcoal and roasting maize for sale (Kilbride et al 2001:72). Of these activities collecting waste paper, plastic items, scrap metals and tin is common, and was mentioned as their major occupations by 33 % of the sample. Significantly, watching parked cars was mentioned by 8 % of the children. The label 'parking boy' was the term first applied to street boys in Kenya in the 1960s at which time work watching cars was an overall positive perception of such children compared to more varied work activities presently, paradoxically widespread public stigma with little public awareness of their work activities. Currently, with a public image largely unaware that children work, child labour is largely invisible while images like sniffing glue dominate.

For girls survival sex is pronounced and is largely a night time activity on the streets, in cars and lodges and in the night clubs, thus beyond the gaze of most citizens of Kenya, who do not generally understand survival sex as necessary for survival but more simply as a morally negative choice to practice prostitution. For boys, their labour blends imperceptibly into the work activities of Kenyans who also work on the streets as the following description indicates.

> The observer is also struck not only by how the street child blends in with other street workers but also by the social complexity characterizing members of the general public going about their business among whom the street child is almost imperceptible among ... sounds of Kikuyu, Luo, Gujarati, Kiswahili, English, French ... against the backdrop of ... horns, racing engines, screeching tires ... smells such exhaust fumes, cooked foods, and garbage (2001:71).

Sharing the occupational street space with children guarding and parking cars, begging and collecting waste products for sale are, for example, "flower sellers, hawkers of radios, watches, flashlights, telephones, magazines, and fruits" (2001:71), in front of stalls with used clothes for sale and fresh fruits and vegetable stands with taxis and public buses loading and unloading passengers. In a word, observes of the child at work easily confirms him as a member of the working poor category in the jua kali outdoor informal economy.

The Enduring Street: Post Childhood Transitions

In December and January (2007–2008) I returned to Nairobi to locate our former research project children and others now on the streets. New research also included Nyeri, a regional city some 150 kilometres northeast of Nairobi. Election violence prevented me from fully following up work among street girls in Nairobi excepting one fortuitous observation reported below. Many, if not most children working on the streets somehow find their way into standard adult roles. There are even success stories such as one young man now attending a major university in America. For others fortunate encounters such as sponsorship in educational and technical programs in Kenya and abroad do occur. Some make and sell art products with sponsored programs, while many return to village farming activities. One we met is an "apostle" working for a church serving food to children on the streets. Others are employed in government agencies and NGOs which cater to children. Many former children working on the streets still work there as shoe shiners, sellers of newspapers and magazines, flowers and other small scale items.

The street, therefore, remains a significant occupational space for children after childhood. Among our previous informants we met a former girl now selling used clothing, itself a major adult street occupation for women. Some boys in our previous study now work as "touts", attached to public vans providing transport (*matatus*) with duties like collecting money from passengers and rounding up business at street stops and red lights. Others work as vendors of used clothing and jewelry at street stops while car passengers are waiting. We found that a prominent work activity, including some in our previous study, involves garbage collection but now as adults for some no longer as previously only as a collector of garbage.

Garbage Collection: A Typology

In my restudy I focused on garbage collection, the most economically rewarding occupation practiced by children in my previous research. Odegi-Awuondo, Namai and Mutsoto write for Nairobi:

> There is a connection between the toilet roll, exercise books, wrapping paper…envelopes in the groceries and the dirty, ill-clad garbage collectors in the streets of the city. The rubbish scavenged…is recycledto produce those items mentioned above (1994: 45).

They found that of 265 garbage collectors, 95 % were male; 50 % were married and ranged in age between 13 and 35. They also reported that "quite a number of them sleep on the streets in the open and…are therefore street children" (1994: 57).

In my follow up observations I found a number of boys who still collect garbage on a significant occupation. Two of them, however, represent different points in a transition process within this occupation. The first, called Jacob in our book, is still collecting garbage, to obtain money primarily to buy glue and food, and mixes garbage collecting with begging. He still sleeps on the streets without enough funds to rent a room. Now in his mid- twenties he as before when he was a child still sleeps on the streets and collects food to eat from dustbins. Little has changed from our previous description of Jacob as a boy, "with cuts, bruises, and one shoe, a broken — down watch secured by a string, and a badly town pair of trousers...who got burned with fire and nylon paper. I was warming myself by the fire; it was very cold last night" (Kilbride et al 2001: 101). We can think of Jacob as in an "arrested" occupational category, one that despite increased chronological age to adulthood is still the work of children on the streets in support of survival there.

For the second man we located however much has changed. We described Wamzee in our book as follows "Wamzee considers himself to be a street boy because he collects paper garbage for sale to middlemen for recycling. He is successful so he buys and cooks any good food" (2001: 80). We reported that Wamzee, about 20 years old and big physically was able to collect paper in bulk and with profits was a source for glue for other boys. He could afford cigarettes and regular bus fare to visit his girlfriend with some money to spare as pocket money. Like Jacob, however, Wamzee slept outside in a regular location with other boys.

Wamzee, now about 30, is married, rents a home in an urban slum and employs children to collect garbage for him which he now sells to recycling plants himself. He is now a middleman. Wamzee, moreover, buys directly metals from shops which he accumulates for resale. His work is made possible by his ownership of a weighing scale, and a (second hand) trolley push card for moving items rapidly and in bulk. Unlike Jacob, who is in an occupational child like activity, Wamzee has moved on developmentally into a fully adult occupational status which supports with marriage and a domicile as an adult status requires.

A transition stage between Jacob and Wamzee is observable among boys who no longer think of themselves as, or are not thought to be, street children. One such former street child now in his mid twenties (like Jacob) lives in a rented room with 3 other former street boys of the same age who once all were friends on the streets. They are not married, but share rent together and together rent a trolley for carrying waste paper, food produce and packages for customers from shops to their cars.

Street Girls and Labour: Wanjiru

In our book we described street girls, about 20 % of the children on the street, as at the bottom of the status hierarchy in Kenya. Like many women in Kenya, marriage remains the best option for upward mobility. Many had babies, sometimes by choice, to enhance sympathy while begging. The girls reported that pregnancy is most often not intentional as men won't use condoms and sex is a way to keep a boyfriend, but that there is frequent rape by street boys or members of the public. Moreover, most street girls compared to boys are worse off.

I expected in 2008 that street girls known by us would be less successful in moving beyond their limited opportunities outside of survival sex. Political circumstance prevented me some from a follow up. One day, however, I did unexpectedly meet one of several girls described in our book while on a major highway slowed by rush hour traffic. As we waited, a woman about 30 (but who looked much older), knocked on our window to beg. It was Wanjiru whom we had followed for several extended periods of time in the past. She greeted me, while after recognizing her; I was in a state of sadness and shock. Wanjiru was pregnant still again, held a baby in her arm, wore tattered clothes, but despite rotted teeth had the same big smile as previously. She said after greeting me that she no longer gets help from NGO's for her children as she is now "too old."

In our book we described Wanjiru, around 21, as a girl who scavenged for food, begged, and practiced survival sex. In those days, she had a three and a seven year old child. She was pregnant when we last spent time with her. Wanjiru wanted to leave the streets, especially for her children's sake, but had no options. She hoped that a successful marriage might be her best chance. Wanjiru was, and still is, extroverted, with a broad smile and easy laugh. She has had a hard life, especially with men who "just cause me to waste a lot of money."

Conclusion

In this paper we emphasize with new field work material the continuing significance of labour in the lives of children living on the streets of Nairobi and thereafter as adults. Although work is crucial for children in our research, I do not want to essentualize in such a way to overstate this focus. Children on the streets can be observed enjoying Sunday afternoons while the girls, for example, at church locations sing songs together and braid each other's hair. Boys play competitive games like football and also have nicknames, pets and romantic lives. Still, these children can be seen sucking their thumbs and crying like children everywhere. Life's challenges can be brutal too as indicated in the material above, with health problems at the forefront. Respiratory complaints (from cold rainy summers and truck fumes), gastronomic ailments (eating garbage) and HIV- AIDS for some, for example, remind us that these are children in need of our assistance, not to serve as the object of a public search for a scapegoat.

I suggest above some reasons why the label "street child" needs to be rethought among other reasons as it ignores the concept of social class. Other reasons would include:

1. Is a temporary status. Children are usually something before, although some are now born on the street;
2. Children now on the streets eventually, more or less, leave the streets (the focus here);
3. Such children do not think of themselves consistently as street children as a matter of their personal identity. In fact, in many ways they are culturally simply African children;

191

4. Most people do not know that they work, and work they do. As we have seen, terminologies about them should indicate this important fact;

5. Girls on the streets are at the bottom of the status hierarchy in the country of Kenya where girls, overall, are comparatively disadvantaged compared to boys in many areas of life. Therefore, a gender distinction is needed when referring to children on the streets apart from the street itself;

6. Efforts to rehabilitate street children by social programs rarely succeed, implying that other facts about their existence are more significant than the label street child.

Nevertheless, when all is said and done, children on the streets, although doing adult work, are still children. This fact remains in whatever human rights equation concerning their work is to be calculated concerning work.

We wrote in our book (Kilbride et al. 2000: 1):

> A child of ten years of age ran behind a small toy object made of wire, wood and maize cobs. The 'car' also had a wire passenger with head and arms in 'conversation' with the boy, whose dialogue could be inferred from his moving lips and focused attention on his 'car.' The street was crowded with late afternoon pedestrians who seemingly hardly noticed the street boy as he moved among them with an apparent clear sense of where he was heading. Following along behind him for a short time, I soon found myself at the boy's 'roundabout' destination. It was a grassy elevation surrounded by a circular highway around which rapidly moving vehicles of various sizes, shapes, and colors competed for entrance onto one of our highways for an opportunity to continue on their way to destinations distant and local. Just before his arrival at the peri-urban roundabout, other boys who were stretched out resting on the elevated terrain on which they ate and slept greeted the child. Just before crossing the road, circling the roundabout, the boy scooped his toy into his small hands as he dodged a car to reach the safety of his 'home,' the place where he sleeps and sometimes cooks scavenged potatoes and other vegetables with his cohorts. In the background could be heard noises from closely passing vehicles that emanated foul-smelling fumes, to which the children had become accustomed. His companions, about ten in number, dressed in torn clothing and barefooted, warmly greeted him. As he set down his toy he picked up a small bottle and joined the others in sniffing glue" (Kilbride field notes, 1995).

Gender differences were emphasized in the 2001 study. My attempts to follow up on this fully was not possible, although the life of Wanjiru would be one testimony to the likelihood that girls on the street fare worse than boys in the long run, if still on the street. More research is needed here, of course, and also for boys too in what is but a first effort here to investigate post childhood activities by me. It seems clear that the street provides for some boys an opportunity to make a transition from child to adult, and even to gain a decent livelihood in the process.

We emphasized previously the strong desire of boys and girls to be given opportunities to work, receive technical education, and to return to school. Government attempts to round up "street children" for confinement in camps, while well intended, have not succeeded. As in previous attempts, the children run back to the streets. A plan of confinement, punishment, and moral education misses the point that for many children the street is now "home" and offers freedom and a means of gaining a livelihood. These are children without a viable family support network like the majority of Kenyan children enjoy.

Concerning their work, it must be considered if work for wages is to be encouraged; this runs counter to child labour laws. What if a child (under 16) earns enough to support her/him and some family members? Is this acceptable when there are no options? Are there universal rights for children worldwide? What about cultural relativism? Should working children on the streets be organized into cooperatives to get a bigger share of the profits for the waste products they now collect? One advantage of no longer using the label "street child" is that attention could be better focused on the working element of their lives (cf. Kielland and Tovo 2006 concerning child labour in Africa for a consideration of the issues raised here). An emphasis on work, too, would soften current widespread public images worldwide of the street child as a glue addicted menace to society.

An important theoretical issue is pertinent to the material presented here that is the relative importance of structural constraints versus agency in human behaviour. In 2000, I contributed to a discussion in the Chronicle of Higher Education about how much agency do children really have in their lives and especially for those in stressful circumstances (such as children with terminal cancer, a cycle of never ending foster homes, a history of child battering). Such children often display striking resilience or agency in to their predicament. The term 'invulnerable child' is seen to be appropriate for some of these survivors as a psychological disposition. Children on the streets of Nairobi indeed have some considerable agency or room for self-help within the structural constraints that life circumstances impose on them. Despite the success of Wamzee, (was he an invulnerable child?) what are we to conclude about Jacob and Wanjiru? There are children worse off than them. Still, when all is said and done, I weigh in more on the side of structural circumstances, which calls attention to Kenya's post colonial state and all its limitations (e.g. marginal worldwide economical position, emphasis on exports, imports of key consumer items and of foreign products and dependence on donor nations approval along with foreign debt to them, (cf. Ogot and Ochieng 1996). Corruption in such circumstances is widespread and disrupts real efforts by Kenyans or others to assist children. In the main, the children in our research as the poorest of Kenyans are really more victims than agents in control of their own destiny.

The current status of working children on Nairobi's streets, especially girls, has implications for anthropological theory. Ortner (2003, 2006) has identified three theoretical components that interact dialectically and historically to account for social reproduction and social change. In brief, structural processes include social class constraints, among others, which shape how individuals act to address their own situation (e.g. agency or what Bourdieu calls "practice"). Interaction between structure and practice, for example, is mediated by cultural schemes (e.g. cultural models, cultural framed symbolic action). This theoretical framework works in Kenya to account for the socioeconomic situation of street girls as described in this paper. For example, there are now thousands of children living on the streets of Nairobi whereas in 1969 there were several hundred. This worldwide phenomena has recurring causes in various countries, but in Kenya, factors would include increased income inequality in the post colonial era due to excessive concentration of power and wealth in the hands of ethnic elders who, through control of government institutions, have amassed wealth at the expense of the majority of Kenyans who constitute the working poor or unemployed in both cities and rural areas. Children have migrated to Nairobi in increasingly larger numbers so as to obtain money in situations of poverty, child malnutrition, or garbage collectors, which the majority of street boys engage in for small sums of money.

Pre-colonial values (e.g. 1900), and still widely accepted, emphasize for females marriage and childbearing as the major means of prestige and income when in combination with agriculture, which the women do, constituting a cultural scheme whereby high fertility, marriage, and often life in plural marriage houses is desired by them. Today, however, while these values are still widespread, women now protest such practices as the levirate, co-wife status, and bride price as an intrusion on their sense of agency and power, especially those with western educations. What Foucault (1978) refers to as "sexuality for procreation" was elaborated in the past as a cultural system and as a cultural scheme for the basis of social action in religious, economic, marriage and family, and other social institutions. Street girls on the streets, however, engage in begging and survival sex in their position at the bottom of the gendered Kenyan class structure where gender inequality for women is the most acute for street girls. Sex is now for profit and includes for some getting pregnant so as to enhance begging through sympathy from tourists and Kenyans. Many street girls still hope for marriage to a successful man for social mobility off the streets. Many street boys do improve their situation through success in garbage collection and thereby accumulating small sums of capital, returning to the rural areas to farm or working in other domains such as hawking used clothing, washing cars and so on. Strikingly, girls first encountered in 1998 are all still on the streets with little evidence of improvement in their life styles – try as they might by having more children or seeking marital success.

My view, now reinforced with new fieldwork, is one where some children now adults by their efforts have made good progress but this is not the whole story, as was summarized in *The Chronicle* as follows:

> The Kenyan children in Mr. Kilbride's study…are clearly victims of the Kenyan political and social structure and don't have a lot of agency, but they have some, he says. Structure and agency must go hand in hand. That's why ethnography is so important. To understand how much agency children have, it's important to get out there and talk to them (Ruark 2000: 25).

HERITAGE, TOURISM, AND NATION-BUILDING IN POST-APARTHEID SOUTH AFRICA

Hana Horáková
Metropolitan University Prague

Introduction

In the current era of globalisation, localised concerns with national identity, politics of heritage, historical memory and collective belonging are assuming a new significance. They have come to play a crucial role in many multicultural societies, especially those in a state of transition that are commonly characterized of salience, fragility and uncertainty.

One of the underlying aims of the societies that undergo socio-political transition is, among others, the breakthrough from the problematic past, the (re)discovery and re-evaluation of previously denied or marginalised history, and the attempt to assert a new identity. Beyond it, there is a strong desire to tell the 'other' side of the story (Marschall 2004: 95).

There emerged new arenas through which processes of identity formation are being articulated – apart from the 'classic' ways (politics) it is the arenas of tourism and heritage that serve as an essential part of a planned process of economic and associated social and political reconstruction (Allen and Brennan 2004: 155). Tourism and heritage are used politically to legitimate state and nation, to articulate the so called 'real' nature of populations, which is the preferred vision held by or about a particular people (Hollinshead 2004: 25). In post-colonial – post-apartheid milieu, tourism, as well as heritage, are supposed to have a "pivotal role to play in helping subjugated populations come to realise for themselves what had seemed impossible, and to attain what had appeared only imaginable" (idem, p. 32).

The aim of the text is to explore the relationship between the politics of heritage and tourism on the one hand, and a wider project of nation-building and identity in South African post-apartheid society. It will empirically draw on my personal experience of being a tourist in South Africa while doing fieldwork on the South African culture in the making in various parts of the country between 2000 and 2004 (see Horáková 2007a). The observations will be contrasted and compared with diverse empirical studies on the politics of tourism and heritage *vis-à-vis* the nation-building process written by local (South African) and foreign social scientists from a wide range of academic fields (social anthropology, including anthropology of tourism, human geography, tourism studies, political science, etc.).

The first part of the text will look at the nature and background of major national political transformation project of post-apartheid South Africa – the universalist cultural experiment. It will raise the question whether a South African identity/culture can be engineered by state intervention, and whether governments could or should engineer a common South African nation and culture and then impose these by various ways on

195

their citizens (Venter 1998: 2).The second part will investigate the interlink between the process of nation-building and the politics of heritage and tourism. Two major approaches to fulfil the promulgated ideal of South African-ness will be discussed: the one stemming from the rhetoric of 'rainbow nation', and the other emerging from the discourse of 'Africanism'. The third part will present some of the counter-narratives to the dominant political cultural debate on nation-building that manifest themselves in the spheres of tourism and heritage.

1. South African Experiment

After 250 years of colonial rule followed by almost a century of racial segregation concluded by almost half a century of institutionalised apartheid, a new era based on the project of nation-building emerged (Fassin 2008). Leading politicians came up with an idea of the synthesis of cultural development that would overcome the legacy of the former regime which defined different cultures as exclusive enclaves. The emphasis on the entire cultural otherness[125] among different 'population groups' was replaced by a new political vision of building a single non-racial and non-sexist society with a single well-balanced culture respectful to a rich cultural mosaic. This ambitious cultural-emancipation process to build the 'imagined' community of the nation was launched by former President Nelson Mandela and his slogan of 'rainbow nation', which was to symbolise this universalist aspiration.

At a time when this political doctrine which inevitably requires an obligatory congruence between state and culture (Gellner 1997) is increasingly threatened both from the inside and outside of nation-states, South Africa with its immense cultural complexity and diversity adopted a policy whose theory and practical applications attract attention of social scientists. What are the threats social scientists (anthropologists) must inevitably predict in such a process of a universal cultural orientation? How can a national consciousness be forged? Will the call of 'rainbow nation' create the sort of modern nationalist community that the new South African government seems to want (Allen and Brennan 2004: 194)? So far it is obvious that the official proclamation of the unifying cultural project [126] is confronted with exclusivist and particularistic tendencies among different groups (e.g. the Zulu,[127] or Afrikaners) on the one hand and the policy of transformation in favour of the 'formerly historically disadvantaged' on the other hand.

---

[125] The belief in otherness embedded in the ideology of segregation which resulted in institutionalising the apartheid regime in South Africa was not, however, based on the biological concept of race but on the belief in separate *cultures* which were to develop apart (cf. Horáková 2007a; Horáková 2008).

[126] The ideal to 'build a nation' and to forge a national identity in South Africa by means of state intervention is part of the Preamble to the South African Constitution of 1996 „to build a united and democratic South Africa" (Venter 1998: 11).

[127] It is particularly Zulu cultural revivalism and its ethno-exclusivism, aiming to restore or prolong a privileged position within the South African society (cf. Horáková 2007b; Maré 1993).

Here are some general points of departure for further argumentation:

1) It seems to be beyond denial that the notion of culture is a political commodity and a resource for political and/or cultural representation. The appropriation of culture is an obvious political goal in today's world. If there is a lack of necessary history or tradition, or if it does not meet government's vision, those in power have to make it up, reform or rediscover. South Africa is facing a cardinal question on how to reconcile the demands of difference and national belonging, or, in other words, "how to allow for the multiplicity of identities while still maintaining some sense of national belonging, without which social reconstruction is doomed to failure" (Brown 2001: 763). As is self-evident, the rhetoric of 'unity in diversity' proclaimed in the Preamble to the South African Constitution of 1996 appears too simple and naive. Brown (2001) suggests the concept of a shared problematic of difference including global influences and affiliations, which could serve as the basis for national belonging, while Degenaar (1991) argues for the replacement of nationalism with constitutionalism, in which civic society allows difference within a common allegiance to constitutional justice. Is such a model of constitutional pluralist democracy based on a common citizenship with respect for different cultural traditions, deprived of the notion of national culture, viable? Can it meaningfully take the place of a common national identity?

2) A struggle for identity and its preservation is meaningful, for every human being is born into a situation which comprises culture. Elites cannot, however, dominate all the range of cultural production; ideological unity of majority is often overestimated, producers of cultural meanings can never fully control every situation as these meanings associate with people's different life experience. Yet, there have been and still are to be seen striking examples of socio-cultural engineering endeavour. From the history, we cannot but mention the case of Mao Ce-tung's cultural revolution, or an effort of the former communist rulers in the Soviet Union to create 'a new Soviet man' with its less pervasive reflection in one of its satellite countries, that of 'Czechoslovak culture'. A most illustrative case in point is self-evidently apartheid South Africa that 'excelled' in social engineering on an unprecedented scale; a well-known fact is that this form of state *dirigisme* influenced lives of South Africans 'from cradle to grave'. Moreover, contemporary debates within the European Union on creating European culture prove that endeavours to engineer social reality are not dead yet. Despite the common awareness of largely problematic or even malign outcomes of such state interventions into culture, there emerge other attempts to orchestrate cultural meanings, as if history did not really teach us a single lesson (Novotná 2002).

3) The concern of creating a new culture is associated with identifying common cultural denominators. Multi-ethnic states therefore have to solve the dilemma as to which of the constituent parts will contribute to the shared, national culture. By and large, new cultural symbols can be recruited either from already existing ethnic/tribal/cultural

197

particularities, or they can be made directly from scratch. The former option brings about a whole set of potential conflicts: within a certain number of distinctive cultural groups, it will be extremely difficult or even impossible to sustain a required balance in power. Moreover, such a fragile condition will inevitably be prone to be misused or abused not only in politics, but also in other social institutions such as media, NGOs, development aid and so forth. The latter choice resembles Hobsbawm's and Ranger's 'invention of tradition'. The major pretext lies in the fact that no culture is possible to be made literally from 'ground zero'. The cultural agents that would like to constitute entirely new cultural meanings will fall into a trap of tenacious old styles. From the two above mentioned extremes it is obvious that it is the state which will be a stable figurehead in such a process. The state and its cultural politics will be a decisive factor as to the range and level of its participation, intervention, and its differentiated support. The state will build an operation manual appraised by ones and condemned by the others. In the case of South Africa, the state will be an enthusiastic shaper of culture and heritage meanings in pursuit of its nation-building project (Hughes 2004).

2. Building a Nation through Tourism and Heritage

The first free democratic elections in South Africa, which were held in 1994, were accompanied by an upsurge in incoming tourism. Reasons for visiting post-apartheid South Africa by international tourists were manifold: value for money – South Africa has been labelled as a 'bargain' country (the weakness of the Rand against other currencies), all-year climate, sights and wilderness, a mix of adventure and exoticism, no jet-lag for the 90 per cent of visitors who come by air, and the opportunity to see the country after political change (Allen and Brennan 2004: 11). [128] Tourism received extremely positive sanctions from the new political dispensation; in fact, the ruling ANC decided to promote tourism in the new South Africa as the panacea of all social ills.[129] Tourism development was outlined in the Reconstruction and Development Programme (RDP)[130] of 1996 in

---

[128] The development of tourism in the new South Africa is seriously inhibited by an enormous crime rate. Public space is engulfed with news on frequent violence. The domestic media spread warnings about the risks of travelling in South Africa. Violence (murders, rapes, hijacking) has become a regular and frequent topic of conversation with respondents, many of whom have personal stories to tell of criminal attacks against themselves or their family members. Fears for personal safety among visitors are undoubtedly one of the most powerfully inhibiting factors in the development of tourism.

[129] There is a widely held belief that tourism development will bring the promised nirvana to both visitors and host populations. Though countless examples are available that tell how tourism development has created more costs than benefits, it is difficult to avoid tourism as a social activity in a world where tourism is a very popular pastime, a major employer and is 'media sexy' (Allen and Brennan 2004: 182).

[130] There was a widely held assumption that development would arise from the empowerment of the disadvantaged through their proactive involvement in all aspects of tourism projects. According to the proponents, "*tourism ... has the potential to achieve the objectives of the RDP of the new government...*" (DEAT 1996: 4). Thus, the agenda of empowerment as the main political procedure for realising significant social change has been replicated and reinforced by tourism industry (Allen and Brennan 2004: 207).

a belief that tourist expenditure can help to put right past inequities. Tourists, both the domestic affluent and any sort of international ones were attracted in order to alleviate poverty, to promote employment and kick off the economic growth and development (Marschall 2004). The emphasis was equally placed on empowerment and communal advancement, and on the humanitarian elements of democracy (Allen and Brennan 2004: 226). As South Africa embarked upon the universalist cultural project, tourism was recognized as a powerful vehicle for nation-building, for constructing a new identity, and presenting this identity to the outside. The interface between nation-building and economic development and tourism as one of its most important carriers was frequently addressed by the representatives of the ruling ANC. For instance, South African Minister of Environmental Affairs and Tourism, Valli Moosa, made the connection between heritage, tourism and economic development explicit when he referred to the country´s three newly created World Heritage sites[131] in South Africa declared in 1998 as to the 'symbols or icons' of national identity (cited in Marschall 2004: 97). He pointed out that the campaign to market South Africa to potential tourists cannot be separated from nation-building. In a similar vein, Thabo Mbeki viewed tourism–induced economic development as a central part of progress and reflected his conviction that economic growth is the means to racial peace (Sampson 1999).

Post-apartheid tourism industry found its major ally in cultural heritage[132] management. Likewise tourism, heritage is one of the key instruments in constructing and/or re-discovering collective identity particularly apparent in many societies in transition (post-colonial, post-apartheid, post-communist, post-conflict etc.). Thus, interlink between politics and heritage is unquestionable; ownership of heritage is an essential component of nation state. With the advent of new South Africa, commodification of 'heritage' has become part and parcel of the underlying socio-political transformation focused on nation-building. At present, South Africa is outright fascinated with the identification, celebration, and re-evaluation of 'heritage'. The rationale behind the prevailing fascination with heritage is the desire to create a new national identity "through a process of selective remembering, thereby simultaneously legitimating the present socio-political order" (Marschall 2004: 95-96). At the legislative level new laws and policies were adopted, e.g. the South African Heritage Resources Act from 1999; throughout the country new sites and events emerged in order to show 'new' aspects of national heritage. Let us mention at least some of the major forms: new museums, the annual celebration of Heritage Day (24 September); rituals, festivals, exhibitions; renaming streets, cities; the erection

---

[131] At present, South Africa is home to seven of the world´s official heritage sites, as determined by UNESCO´s World Heritage Committee– Robben Island, Greater St Lucia Wetland Park, uKhahlamba Drakensberg Park, Mapungubwe Cultural Landscape, Cape Floral Region, Vredefort Dome and the Cradle of Humankind at Sterkfontein (http://www.exploresouthafrica.net/worldheritagesites/).

[132] It would be useless to draw a boundary between culture and heritage in this paper as these areas of public life are very closely related when it comes to tourism policies.

of countless new monuments and memorials as the visual manifestations of the official interpretation of the past (cf. Marschall 2004).

In order to present a new South African identity outside, SATOUR – South African Tourism Authority – now re-badged as Tourism South Africa (www.satour.org) started to 'bring home tourists' (Rassool 2000). Though domestic tourism [133] plays a greater economic role than the overseas sector in South Africa, international tourism [134] has become one of the agents of social and cultural development in the post-apartheid society. To stimulate the international tourism market, diverse promotional campaigns ('South Africa Welcome Campaign', 'Discover South Africa, Rediscover Yourself', 'Explore South Africa – Culture – Hidden Heritage') have been launched heralding the 'rebirth' of South Africa, accompanied by new slogans – *Rainbow People, Multicultural Nation, One Nation – Many Cultures, Diversity in Unity, World in One Country*. Other promotional campaigns epitomize cultural battle over history, for instance the 'Ubuntu We Care' programme.

These campaigns do not only promise oceans and (pristine, even 'unexplored') landscapes but they also introduce a new dimension to the former 'Big Five package'[135], consisting of exotic peoples or cultures, under the umbrella term of rural tourism. The concept of rural tourism includes adventure tourism activities, cultural tourism and, lately, a new phenomenon in rural communities known as 'township tourism' (Briedenhann and Wickens 2004). Cultural/ethnic tourism ranks among new types of supposedly acceptable forms of tourism.[136] As Allen and Brennan argue, tourists have two options: either to respect (weak version), or celebrate (strong version) difference in culture while leaving things untouched by their presence in the other culture (2004: 181).

Who Owns the Past

The issue to whom belongs the past, that is who owns, controls and shapes the past in the present, appears to be legitimate in today´s world. Moreover, it is always contested. The emergence of a new political order goes hand in hand with the attempts of those with the power to control the construction of the past, and/or to rewrite the country´s history. There emerge two basic questions: *who* the stakeholders are in the process of

---

[133] SATOUR estimates that 16 million South Africans undertook at least one leisure trip involving at least one night away from home in 1996 (Allen and Brennan 2004: 21).

[134] As for the composition of international tourists to South Africa, tourists from the African continent make up over 70 per cent of South Africa´s international tourists. Majority arrive from neighbouring countries – Lesotho, Botswana, Mozambique, Zimbabwe, one quarter from the UK, while the third largest market is made by the USA, after Africa and Europe (Allen and Brennan 2004: 11)

[135] Originally used only by hunters, the term 'Big Five' refers to five of Africa's greatest wild animals - lion, leopard, elephant, buffalo and rhino (http://www.places.co.za/html/famousbig5.html).

[136] There is a whole host of terms that indicate a major shift from 'old', mass forms of tourism: 'alternative tourism' (de Kadt 1990), 'low impact tourism' (Lillywhite 1991), 'responsible tourism' (Wheeller 1991), 'progressive tourism' (Wheeler 1992), 'moral tourism' (Butcher 2007), or 'new tourism' (Poon 1994).

cultural battle over history and *what* is recognised as legacy in a country´s past, including the issue of *how* the past is being reappropriated and rewritten at the national level. The first question deals with the degree and intensity of the involvement in the process of negotiating the meaning of a country's past. It is legitimate to ask who the custodians of South Africa´s public memory, its producers and distributors are. Key players in this form of a 'cultural war' over the official symbolic representation of the new South African reality are politicians. It is not surprising given the fact that the past – as the force in shaping the present – has become the main political curriculum in South Africa (Allen and Brennan 2004: 191). Other interested parties are the heritage sector, tourism industry, as well as creators of public history, and representatives in the sphere of public education [137] who aspire to serve as gatekeepers of the 'true' version of the past. The involvement of all the above mentioned agents is equally contested. As Baines mentions, there has been a significant growth of the heritage sector accompanied by declining enrolments in university history departments. Thus, there remained substantial twin pressures of political expediency and the hegemony of the market to promote nation-building (Baines 2009).

The 'what – and – how' question is moulded by the stakeholders' desire to offer the 'true' account of 'what really happened' as opposed to the false history – in case of South Africa, the false history of the apartheid state and its ideologues. It is clearly illustrated in the following statement made by Luvuyo Mthimkhulu Dondolo, Amathole District Municipality Heritage Manager in East London:

> In a country like South Africa where places of cultural interest and institutions have been used by the previous regimes for their political agenda it is by no means surprising that the present political dispensation is trying to redress the former wrongs by similar procedures – redefining, reconfiguring and reconstructing the past. In this vein, [the new institutions] ought to also endorse the values and principles underpinning democracy, including cultural democracy, social cohesion, nation building, South African-ness, nationhood, unity in diversity, and [...] national consciousness. Those in power call for the reflection of the histories and heritages of all communities in 'proper' contexts (Dondolo, n.d.).

There is an ongoing debate over what should be included and what omitted (Hughes 2004). The urge to 'remember' salient incidents that were previously omitted from the official version of history develops simultaneously with the 'forgetting' of other incidents that are no longer part of the new official version of history. However, the situation is not so easy, as Didier Fassin shows in his article on the politics of memory in South Africa. He raises a question on what sort of historical truth is revealed in the present. He claims that the post-apartheid period is characterised by a 'dual relation to memory' (Fassin 2008: 312). On the one hand, there is the process of reconciliation, nation-

---

[137] In some instances, the initiative for the establishment of new heritage sites came from civil society or the private sector.

building and non-racialisation officially embarked upon by the new political dispensation aimed at making a final dot after the troubled past. On the other hand, there are lingering feelings of resentment that manifest itself through racism, inequalities and prejudices. This is what Fassin calls a 'paranoid style' (2008: 312) that shapes and affects politics of memory in South Africa. His article proves that the relation to historical truth is always complex and ambiguous; one cannot easily draw a clear frontier between 'reality' and 'fantasy'. The South African experience of history illustrates how uncertain and blurred such a frontier can be. Post-apartheid South Africa is an unfinished business, and the task 'how to make sense of history' remains the main political issue in South Africa (2008: 316).

An ambiguity in the approach to the 'true' version of the past in the present is also discussed in the article "The Politics of Public History in Post-Apartheid South Africa" by Gary Baines from Rhodes University (Baines 2009). The author claims that there is continuity in abusing history for ideological and political ends: the apartheid regime abused the past in the guise of nation-building, and in post-apartheid South Africa the ruling African National Congress (ANC) has been manipulating history in a similar way. Allen and Brennan confirm: "Social divisions and persecutions from the past are being turned into attractions of the present and future" (2004: 12). According to Baines, two competing discourses of the past in post-apartheid South Africa after 1994 can be traced down: so called **'rainbowism'** and **'Africanism'**. Let us 'borrow' these two terms from Baines and expand on them in order to reveal their degree of affiliation to or alienation from South Africa´s universalist project characterized by a whole host of key terms (nation-building, non-racialisation, reconciliation, multiculturalism) through the analysis of a number of tourist attractions. What do these two approaches have in common? Both of them have an ambivalent approach to the past; moreover, while endorsing the project of nation-building, they make use of the rhetoric of 'Otherness' derived from the multiculturalist discourse. Yet, there are certain differences between them. The first, historically earlier one, points to the ideal of South Africa´s common, shared history. As has already been mentioned, the founding father of this discourse is Nelson Mandela who took over the slogan of 'rainbow nation' from Archbishop Desmond Tutu. This attitude stressing reconciliation and toleration is embodied in the work of the Truth and Reconciliation Commission (TRC) which held its public hearings to investigate gross violations of human rights committed during the apartheid era. It was instrumental in the reconstruction of an official truth based on the testimonies of both the victims and the perpetrators. The key purpose of this 'collective exorcism' (Fassin 2008: 218) was to reconcile the South African nation and to turn towards its future. The TRC stressed the need to forge a co-operative future from the conflict-ridden past and suggested that a new civic ethic, based on extended boundaries of toleration, can be founded upon forgiveness (Allen and Brennan 2004: 268). The business of forgiveness as a specific South African means to progress is inseparable from the achievement of a non-racial, democratic and united nation (idem, p. 190).

The metaphor of rainbow nation represents resistance to the apartheid legacy of deeply divided society. How can 'rainbowism' with its emphasis on multiculturalism and the celebration of the cultural diversity, be reconciled with the national political project and its manifestations in the tourism and heritage sector? An illustrative example of 'rainbow' tourism is the project 'One City, Many Cultures' (1999)[138] in Cape Town which was to promote 'tolerance, integration and understanding', while celebrating the cultural diversity of the city. However, as Rassool claims, this 'new imagining of the nation in the city' tended to perpetuate timeless, ready-made, prefabricated categories such as Christian, Muslim, Jew, Hindu, or Xhosa (2000: 8). The analysis of the project proves that besides the ubiquitous rhetoric of 'rainbowism' the new multicultural/rainbow(like) discourse draws on ahistorical and exoticised notions of authentic traditional cultures that obscure both the hybridity and fluidity of African cultural identities (Robins 1999: 287). Some critics went even further. Baines argued that the discourse on difference which enabled atrocities committed during the apartheid era is now replicated in the new South Africa under the new name – multiculturalism – and its most powerful metaphor, that of the 'rainbow nation'.

Despite critical voices from the academe and other spheres of public life, this event has unleashed a process of vast commoditisation of culture that manifests itself in a number of products of 'new tourism'. The emphasis is put on cultural difference. As one of the SATOUR´s leaflets titled 'Why SA is unique' puts it,

> [T]here really is more to us than beasts and bush and beach. When you visit, do take the time to find out how we live and who we are. Visit our museums and villages, listen to our stories and dance to our music. When you visit South Africa, you´re not just visiting a place, you´re visiting a people (cited in Allen and Brennan 2004: 17).

Celebration of cultural diversity through cultural and heritage tourism takes many different forms – heritage sites, craft, dances, festivals, cultural or ethnic villages, etc. It reflects the recent world trend in defining heritage: a shift from tangible to intangible elements (languages, music, living cultures). The major demand for cultural tourism as a subcategory of rural tourism comes from organized groups of international tourists. How is 'Otherness' commodified by the tourism industry? There is a whole range of products from 'cultural/ethnic villages'[139] to 'township tours'. The former have mushroomed all over the country. Tourists can visit Xhosaville, Shakaland in KwaZulu-

---

[138] The project as a whole was launched by Nelson Mandela. In the course of twelve weeks, the local Cape Town daily newspaper, the *Cape Times*, explored „*how different religious and cultural groups relate to certain rites of passage and other important issues of life*" (www. inc.co.za). The campaign culminated in 'One City Festival' held in Cape Town on Heritage Day, September 24. Both the campaign and the festival were held within the 'static pre-ordained cultural framework' (Rassool 2000: 9).

[139] There are many interesting studies on cultural/ethnic villages carried out, *inter alia*, by Professor Keyan Tomaselli, Director of the Centre for Cultural and Media Studies at the University of Natal (www.und. ac.za/und/ccms/intro).

Natal, Lesedi cultural village near Johannesburg, the Shangaan village in Mpumalanga, the Kagga Kamma 'Bushman' village in the Cederberg, the Kalk Bay coloured fishing village, or the Malay Quarter in the Bo-kaap; in these sites the exotic 'other' ('living cultures') is packaged and transformed into a folkloric spectacle. At the heart of this 'recovered memory' is a conviction of ethnic uniqueness. As Hughes (2004) reminds us, the representatives of ethnic cultures aim to define themselves in competition with other ethnicities, through an emphasis on uniqueness, rather than revealing the features they share in common.

A cultural village is commonly sited near an established tourist route in a rural area, and consists of a homestead to show living arrangements, an arena for dance, music and other live cultural displays, including craft/souvenir outlet. The target market is international – cultural villages are very popular with foreign visitors. There are now around forty villages open for business across the country (Hughes 2004).

I remember visiting Shakaland, the pre-eminent cultural village in KwaZulu-Natal. Those who would expect the image and myth of Rousseau´s 'noble savage' would be dissatisfied. There were none. Despite the costumes, perfect ethnic dances and other manifestations of commodified Zuluness, one could encounter only streetwise young Africans glad to be at work – from nine to five – where they could have fun while simultaneously guiding and ridiculing the international tourists.

Township tourism or 'Dark Tourism' is a relatively new phenomenon that seeks to combine tourist desires for unique and authentic African experiences and the more mundane realities of township poverty (Robins 1999). A township tour usually includes a visit to *shebeens* (unlicensed bars or taverns), a cultural display, notable heritage/struggle sites, a crèche or welfare facility where visitors may make donations, and possibly a visit to someone's home (Hughes 2004). As such, township tours (e.g. to Soweto near Johannesburg, to Umlazi, Durban's biggest township, or the Cape Flats in Cape Town) seem to complicate the exotic/banal dichotomy by taking tourists to *shebeens, spaza* (township) shops, *sangoma* (faith healers), Mandela´s Soweto home and other places of political and cultural significance in poor coloured and black neighbourhood (Robins 1999: 282). The poverty of informal settlements and townships has been successfully transformed into a narrative of African resilience, vitality and creativity that appeals to international tourists. Such tours embody an archetypal, authentic Third Worlds encounter. The nature of township tours obviously differs. On the one hand, there are innovative attempts to avoid turning a township visit into a voyeuristic spectacle of poverty and paternalistic charity (Robins 1999: 290), and provide a politically sophisticated narrative of apartheid and commentary on the present situation of social life from the insider´s perspective – for a niche market of politically-inclined tourists. A number of operators offer a more dynamic, less essentialist view of culture and heritage, for example the Durban or Cape Town tourism authorities that have developed some of the themed tours that challenge old divisions. Others, on the other hand, absorbed entirely by the discourse of otherness, tend to focus on the 'unique ethnic character' and exotic, timeless features of the place while, in the name of an imagined rainbow city and exotic culture, continuing to obscure the legacy of racialised inequality and social polarisation, and thus help to reproduce the apartheid legacies. What is eventually incorporated into a canon of popular culture and heritage in township tours largely depends on the operators who are able to assert themselves in a highly competitive milieu (see Hughes 2004).

Despite the manifold criticisms aimed at 'ghettoisation' of townships and perpetuating the sense of spatial division, central to apartheid, township tours in many ways subvert the 'pastoral paradigm' of cultural villages. Most also explicitly stress ethnic diversity (Hughes 2004).

The second discourse called 'Africanism' emerged when Thabo Mbeki came to power after 1999. He initiated a profound change in the relation of the South African society to its past. As Fassin (2008: 318) mentions, most of Mbeki's speeches are based on the evocation of history, evident for instance in his famous address of 1998 entitled *South Africa: Two Nations* in which he clearly stated that "the objective of national reconciliation is not being realised" because there remained truths which admitted no reconciliation (http://www.go.za). His appeal was quite certain: the past does not pass so easily, especially for those who have suffered from it. Another address of his – *I am an African*– kicked off an indigenisation process in South Africa and a subsequent discourse of African Renaissance (see Horáková 2006).

Unlike the former perspective of 'rainbowism', though equally approving nation-building, this version of the past is exclusivist, even an ANC-centred as it proclaims *African* leadership of the national liberation struggle and in government. It is epitomised by Mbeki's 'Peoples' History' project which seeks to construct an official history in which the liberation struggle becomes the master narrative of South African national history (cf. Baines 2009). As Hughes (2004) states the freedom struggle itself has been the most urgent and in many ways least problematic subject for the ANC government's nation-building efforts. The flagship project has been the Robben Island Museum. Since 1994 numerous 'new sites of memory' have been commissioned with the aim to celebrate aspects of South Africa's reconfigured past. These 'new' historical sites – places of political struggle – now feature strongly as sites of visitation. These include national, local and community-based public history projects (memorials, monuments, public holidays, national symbols, commemorative events and civic rituals). Dominant cultural debate (Rassool 2000) on struggle history is reflected in a number of projects such as the Legacy Project which include building new national monuments and museums emphasising topics such as struggle, democracy, and nation-building. Others include 'History Trail of Slave Resistance in the Western Cape', 'In the Footsteps of Gandhi', 'The Long Walk to Freedom: the Mandela Trail', or township tours. New heroes of the nation emerged, which has led to the renaming of streets and other public places after the icons of the struggle – Nelson Mandela, Chris Hani, Oliver Tambo, and Steve Biko. Others celebrate ethnic-nationalist history. Still others focus on telling the stories of local communities but have inserted these within the master narrative of struggle history.

As is evident, the politics of history pays tribute to heroes of South Africa's struggle for freedom. However, the choice of the 'proper' heroes is far from smooth and unambiguous as proves a recent project of the Freedom Park, the country´s leading post-apartheid monument built outside Pretoria worth R350 million (Marschall 2004). This project which includes a Garden of Remembrance where the pantheon of heroes of the liberation struggle is to be memorialised has recently sparked controversy about who exactly should be honoured in its precincts. The construction and sharing of a common history is itself a form of manipulating the past to serve a political purpose. The question of whose version of history gets disseminated and institutionalized is, after all, a political one.

Blending the discourses

As has been emphasized, calls for Africanisation and the discourse of African Renaissance in all spheres of South African culture come alongside with a global discourse of multiculturalism. Thus, various ethnic tourist villages and township tours emerge and flourish in various parts of the country within the multiculturalist milieu (Robins 1999). How are national identities formulated in and through the tourist sites? How is the past commodified? A need to transform the past in general and the heritage sector in particular includes the focus on African 'sacred spaces'; for instance in Cape Town, as Robins observed, a focus of urban planners is placed on Xhosa initiation sites instead of identifying the more mundane and banal socio-economic realities of racialised poverty and the spatial legacies of the post-apartheid city. Thus, it tends to obscure class differentiation and poverty while disguising the absence of fundamental social transformation in the country (Robins 1999: 286).

The project of ethnic tourist villages where international tourists photograph semi-clad Zulu and 'bushmen', though originally planned as a manifestation of the 'new South African multi-cultural tourism' (Robins 1999: 287), tends to come under the rubric of 'Africanism'.

Perhaps the best example to illustrate the intermingling of the two dominant discourses is the icon of South Africa´s success story – former President Mandela – that makes the strongest recent and current image of the country. Nelson Mandela is South Africa's premier cultural tourism attraction which mixes up ingredients derived from 'rainbowism' such as of reconciliation and nation-building, with elements based on 'Africanism', namely, African resistance and struggle. This ambiguity can be revealed in a number of projects, such as the 'Mandela Trail' and the 'Mandela Library' on Constitution Hill in Gauteng (a Legacy Project), the Robben Island Museum with its central feature Cell No 5 in Block B, or travelling exhibit under the name 'Long Walk to Freedom'[140] which tells in part, the life story of Mandela and how this intersected with the resistance struggle against apartheid.

---

[140] The project derives its title from Mandela's autobiography (co-authored by Richard Stingle).

By and large, what prevails both within the discourses of 'rainbowism' and 'Africanism' is the narrative in which African culture is being exoticised through multicultural discourses that reify and homogenise cultural difference. Is there a possibility to escape the trap of these two extremes – cultural essentialism and the denial of difference?

3. Nation-Building and Counter-narratives

The idea of a past that all South Africans can share is chimerical. On the one hand, there are projects that seek to validate or confer legitimacy on politically correct versions of the past (Baines 2009). On the other, there is also a counter-perspective in the form of competing claims to the ownership of the past. Let us use again the who, how and what questions: *Who* endangers the dominant political-cultural debate embedded in the nation-building project? *How* do particularist histories and memories proliferate on the scene? *What* do they propose?

As for the first question, alternative stakeholders and cultural brokers come from a variety of political persuasions and communities. These are representatives of cultural, ethnic, linguistic, religious, regional and other particularist identities that are seeking their own 'sites of memory'. A case in point is the Sarah Baartman memorial erected by the Khoisan community (see Baines 2009). Other 'parallel, ambivalent discourses' (Rassool 2000) or 'counter-narratives' (Hollinshead 2004) include, for instance, 'Robben Island: Cell Stories Exhibition and Archive' which transcends the fixed cultural framework of resistance and reconciliation by challenging the idea of a homogeneous prisoner community, or District Six Museum in Cape Town which focuses on forced removals[141]. By emphasising unity between Africans and Coloureds, the museum exhibits draw attention to the mundane banality of apartheid´s devastating Group Areas removals (Robins 1999).

Counter-memory usually exists in opposition to the official (hi)story. These memories are 'subaltern' and serve as a potentially threatening undercurrent to the social order (Baines 2009). If ordinary voices do not fit the dominant narrative they are silenced and exit the space of public memory – a case in point is the Red Location Cultural Museum project in the century-old township of New Brighton in Port Elizabeth. The public memory of New Brighton's past privileges the experiences of political activists over those of ordinary people. The stories of their everyday lives have been subsumed by the triumphalism of the liberation struggle. As the liberation struggle becomes the dominant narrative of South African national history, the stories of smaller communities are subordinated to this meta-narrative. So New Brighton is remembered as a 'site of resistance' and a 'stronghold of the African National Congress'. This is typified in reminiscences published in books, journals, web sites and local newspapers that glorify both living and deceased 'heroes of the struggle' who happened to have lived in the township (cf. Baines 2009).

---

[141] The multicultural neighbourhood of District Six, characterised by the unity between Africans and Coloureds, was entirely demolished in the 1970s due to the apartheid Group Areas Act.

However, the two narratives do not have to necessarily exhibit any sharp borderline. Official and vernacular cultural expressions are often intersected. For instance, official memory cultural brokers or authorities operate in local and regional government departments, bureaucracies, and educational institutions. However, it is nearly impossible to reach a consensus on the interpretation of historical events such as a museum exhibit, war memorial, or commemorative ceremony.

Conclusion

The South African government has set itself the task of deconstructing the old politics of apartheid and establishing a new politics of democracy. A significant role in accomplishing the task of nation-building was assigned to international tourism and the heritage sector. The text revealed a substantial discrepancy between the promulgated ideal of nation-building, envisaged by the post-apartheid political dispensation and the way this alleged 'unity in diversity' is conceptualized by current cultural and heritage tourism. It was shown that neither 'rainbowism', nor 'Africanism' can substantially help in this effort. On the contrary, many 'subversive' aspects within these two discourses (such as cultural exclusivism and particularism stemming from a reified concept of culture used by tourism and heritage planners, or an excessive stress on the one-sided interpretation of South African past in the present – the master narrative of struggle) may counteract the political-cultural universalist aspiration. Moreover, the existence of parallel discourses can equally undermine the project of forging South African-ness from above. It is clear that the quest to achieve South African unity is endangered by the 'saboteurs' who have been initially – and perhaps naively – envisaged as allies. The supposedly automatic interlink between the politics of nation-building and the politics of heritage/tourism have been seriously undermined.

NEGOTIATING MANHOOD IN POST-APARTHEID SOUTH AFRICA: PRECARIOUS TRANSFORMATIONS OF TSHIVENDA-SPEAKING LABOUR MIGRANTS INTO RELIGIOUS LEADERS

Vendula Řezáčová[142]
Charles University, Prague

The case

The idiom of 'Venda' ancestor spirit possession, *malombo*, has provided a trenchant commentary of the engagement of men in rural-urban labour migration instituted in colonial and apartheid South Africa, and continuing to shape post-apartheid realities and identities. This commentary, however, has not been static. Until the 1980s, men have been excluded from the ancestor cult by virtue of their urban experience. The bodies of men active in labour migration were deemed as polluted through congress with customs and women of non-Venda groups in the urban hub of Gauteng which was supposed to render them unsuitable abodes for ancestor spirits. Ancestor possession had been a domain of primarily women in the rural areas seen to abide by the precepts of 'proper Venda morality'. In the past decade, however, the thrust of this moral commentary has radically shifted. Rather than excluding men from discourses affirming 'Venda morality' embodied in ancestor possession on account of their urban experience, it has put them at their very centre.

This paper aims to contextualize the socio-cultural dynamics of this change against the background of transformations of the regime of labour migration – and, jointly, of gender relations - in de-industrializing, post-apartheid South Africa. It asserts that the idiom of 'illness' and ancestor possession has been mobilized to articulate and redress the diminishment of social power of men which these transformations have engendered. Concentrating on a case study of ritual undertaken on behalf of a 'possessed' man, Athiambi, it will also address the ambiguities and contestations which men, as labour migrants returning to the rural area, have faced when seeking empowerment through the symbolic resources of a cult which has remained dominated by women. Furthermore, the paper will examine the complex intertwining of personal concerns of individual identity and collective concerns of 'Venda' cultural identity in the context of the post-apartheid dispensation.

Historical background: labour migration and gender identities

Until the 1980s, 'Venda' had been a typical labour reserve of the apartheid political-economy of South Africa. The regime of labour migration and remittances had demarcated the role

---

[142] The author is a PhD candidate in sociology/social anthropology at the Faculty of Social Sciences, Charles University of Prague, Czech Republic. She conducted fieldwork in north-eastern Transvaal ('Venda') in South Africa between 2004-6.

of able-bodied men as underpaid urban workers in the Gauteng industries (ideally) sending major part of their income to stay-at-home wives in the rural areas to support families of dependants. This coercive model had been subsumed within the cultural notions of 'Venda' masculinity and femininity – 'it is our culture' (*ndi mvelele yashu*), explained my informants, 'that the man works in the city and sends money for the bag of corn flour (*saga a mugayo*) to the wife in the Venda countryside'. In the context of these cultural precepts which have accommodated the experience of political-economic subjugation of the 'Venda reserve', work in the city, *tshikuani* ('place of the whites'), or *tsheledeni* ('place of money') has not only been a matter of economic necessity for adult men, but of living up to society's expectations and of achieving prestige and a sense of self-worth.

However, in the same period the regime of labour migrations, and concomitantly the notions of gender identities, had begun to undergo major transformations. By the end of the 1980s, the apartheid dispensation had run into major political and economic difficulties. This period was marked by increasing returns of migrant workers to rural areas, partly as the result of influx controls, partly of the sharpening political conflict and violence in the cities. The former had largely been a measure with which the apartheid government hoped to solve the over-saturation of urban industrial and service economies with cheap labour force in the period of economic recession, and contain political resistance to its rule. The institution of the 'Bantustans', including 'Venda' in the 1979, associated with forced misappropriation of arable land and population relocations, dealt with the rural end of the forced urban-rural migrations. Aiming to reorient urbanization to the rural areas under the guise of 'development', these measures, together with processes which had resulted in the extension of employment opportunities within the cash economy into the Venda homeland itself – in government bureaucracies and state-provided services such as schools, hospitals and infrastructure, in trade and cash-based agricultural projects – were to substantially transform the social position and experiences of men as migrant workers.

By the 1980s, labour migration had ceased to be the most viable option for men, and most men worked in commuting distance from their homes in Venda for diminishing wages (Seekings, Nattras 2006: 230). At the same time they began to compete with women who had entered the labour market and the monetary economy in increasing numbers, although initially at its lower rungs – as nurses, primary school teachers, secretaries, or raised income outside of it in street vending, beer-brewing, crafts etc. The predicament of labour migrants especially those with little skill has been further exacerbated in the 1980's by incipient stratification processes engendered in the developing skill economy. The achievement of educational qualification has began to draw the dividing line between those with a foot in the door of the labour market and those without, the haves and the have-nots, ever more sharply. While until the 1970s the migrant worker returning to the rural area after a spell of urban employment as a miner, bus driver or house servant inspired respect of the community, since the 1980s he has seen not only a diminishment of work opportunities, but also a rapid deterioration of status and prestige in relation to the growing numbers of well-salaried government employees, civil servants, police officers, attorneys and businessmen – and in relation to women.

The absence from households of men as breadwinners or as absconders under the regime of labour migration has led women to assume roles as de facto household heads, resulting in increasing numbers of female-headed households. Not infrequently, a single woman's income has supported a three-generational family composed of grandmother, mother, daughter and their children. During my fieldwork, substantial changes of value-orientations have been set in train with regard to gender relations, reflecting both the assumption of responsibility for economic and social reproduction of households by women, and the loss of power of men in this sphere. Women informants of all generations often relegated men to the role of progenitors and occasional lovers whom a woman was wisely advised not to marry and rely on. 'Work is your husband' (*munna yanu ndi mushumo*) was a set phrase which elder women used to motivate younger women to achieve economic autonomy and abandon prospects of a successful and emotionally fulfilling marriage, seen by the former as utterly unrealistic and undesirable. Men, on the other hand, complained: 'the women today, they became clever; they only want a man to give them a child (*vhasadzi vha namusi vho thanyela, vha sokou toda vho fhiwa nwana*); they only look for the money' (*vha sedza tshelede fhedzi*). Acquiring set forms, such sayings have contributed to the construction of men as 'the others' of women-dominated female networks which have assumed a great deal of responsibility for economic and social reproduction of households in rural 'Venda'.

It is these two historical strains – crisis of the regime of labour migration engendered in the economic recession and restructuring, and changing gender roles and identities, which have challenged the grounds of men's social power in the 'Venda' context (similar processes have been observed in the Lowveld; Niehaus, personal communication). While the ideal of urban employment has been upheld for young men in particular, it has become increasingly difficult to live up to due to the reduction of employment opportunities in the cities – in particular for low-skilled labour force, the larger portion of 'Venda' men. Since the fulfilment of other men's roles in society – as husbands, fathers, sons, respected members of the community – have hinged on access to cash, diminishment of economic power has led to a thoroughgoing social marginalization of unemployed men, or men with only itinerant work, *piece jobo*. This marginalization has been further highlighted vis-í-vis women's increasing economic and social autonomy. One of the sources of livelihood for unemployed men, especially young, have been grandmothers' elderly pensions and mothers' or sisters' income-raising activities. The other option of lifestyle which many unemployed men have chosen, associated with the beer house (shebeen) and often petty crime, has straddled the bounds of legality.

The 'sickness of the city'

It is against this background that the 'illness' to which men have in ever greater numbers succumbed in the urban centres of Gauteng, and the processes of 'healing' through the domains of the ancestor possession cult, must be seen. The men reported to have suffered from severe pains in different parts of their bodies, head, neck, shoulders and arms which biomedicine failed to both diagnose and alleviate. Recently, medical anthropologists have identified such symptoms as chronic pain or neurasthenia (Kleinman, Good 1985) and explained them as having a psychosomatic or sociosomatic origin, associated with oppressive social situations in a range of world's societies. In these oppressive contexts, idioms of somatic distress have been interpreted as the last resort, often unconscious, for persons who have not possessed other means to voice discontent with their situations – due to political or structural constraints, cultural norms of propriety or relations of authority; usually all of these in conjunction.

While the psychosomatic mechanisms of such syndromes have remained a matter of much contention among medical anthropologists, their association with situations of disempowerment has brought the impact of social and political factors on experiences and perceptions of 'health' and 'illness' to the fore. Such a perspective helps to widen the understanding of a state of 'illness' beyond objective physiological causes by placing it in the midst of social pressures and power struggles which such a state, although of great costs to the actor, helps to articulate and even redress. It also helps to illuminate the complex concerns, some of them socially disapproved of, which 'Venda' men have addressed through the condition of 'sickness', *u lwala*, when faced with the dilemmas of labour migration in the cities under conditions of economic recession and diminishment of employment opportunities.

Invariably, the men's narratives associated the symptoms of debilitating pain, disorientation and chronic fatigue with periods of stress at work or unemployment. Most of the 'sick' men had been involved at the lowest rungs of the urban labour market where remuneration has been meagre and guarantees of obtaining it absent, employers unreliable and work insecure. The possibility of leaving the city and returning to 'Venda' had occurred to them when facing such difficulties but they dismissed it as inappropriate for it would mean a personal failure. As men, they were supposed to stay in the city and earn cash to be able to build a house in the rural area, *u fhatha mudi*, and support a wife, children and families of origin. The masculine ideal of urban employment has been upheld by both the sufferers and their relatives who regarded their 'illness' as malingering and disapproved of the men leaving urban employment, however insecure. The symptoms of chronic pain from which the men suffered were closely related to a situation of disempowerment – while faced with own inability to cope with the growing demands of work and life of social isolation in the city, the ideals of masculinity and authority of relatives did not allow the men to evade these without losing self-respect and support of kin.

Negotiating the 'ancestral gift'

The analysis of symbols associated with ancestor possession which the men drew upon to interpret their condition and through which they sought 'cure' reveals a complex interface between concerns of personal identity of the individual men, and of collective concerns with cultural identity. The ancestor spirit was identified as the agent causing the men's difficulties at work and their 'sickness', conditioning 'cure' by the men's return to the rural area and taking up of the ancestral call to become 'traditional healers', *nanga*, in rural 'Venda'. In their biographical narratives which had a standardized form, the 'possessed' men have frequently stressed that their life in the city lacked a sense of purpose. All the money which they had earned, they also spent – on luxuries, alcohol and women without having any left over to send to wife or relatives in the rural area; they lacked 'happiness', *dakalo*, they said. The interpretation of socially condemned behaviour as being caused by ancestor spirits had allowed the narrator to construct himself not as an agent of such behaviour, but as its passive sufferer. It has also enabled him to isolate the period spent in the city from the rest of the biographical narrative as virtually a time of 'non-being', death, *lufuni*. By undergoing this culturally constructed amnesia, he had achieved exoneration from responsibility for socially disapproved behaviour.

However, by reinterpreting own experience in the city as overly negative and morally suspect, the 'possessed' men have also participated in more widely shared discourses which had constructed the 'cities', *tshikuani*, as places of utter immorality and lawlessness, antithetical to 'Venda' cultural values associated with the rural area. Such value-laden dichotomy between the 'city' and 'Venda' has had a long history in providing conceptual categories through which the experiences of forceful incorporation into the colonial and apartheid political economy of 'Venda' have been reflected. By associating the 'cities' with a much desired source of income – *tsheledeni*, 'the place of money', these discourses have highlighted dependence of 'Venda' on urban economies. At the same time, they have denied the 'cities' a place in constructions of cultural identity and belonging to 'Venda' – the 'cities' have been assigned the role of the immoral 'Other' in such constructions of 'moral', 'Venda' Self.

Through the idiom of ancestor possession, the men have been able to redefine their position of marginality into one of empowerment, and to contest hegemonic models of masculinity associating men with the 'city' – the sphere 'outside' and income-generating employment. Moreover, the 'sick' bodies of 'possessed' men have been 'good to think with' in reflections on the changing relations of the 'city' and the 'countryside'- '*tshikuani*' ('place of the whites') and 'Venda' as a result of the faltering regime of labour migration. They have become sites through which concerns over boundaries between social worlds have been dramatized. By becoming persons endowed with the ancestral gift, *mpho*, the men have become localized subjects, bound to rural 'Venda' and the household sphere. The idiom of 'sickness' from which they reported to have suffered if they stayed in the 'cities' for more than several days after their initiation into the ancestor cult, portrayed the rural-urban dichotomy in dramatic terms.

For the 'possessed' men returning to the rural area has been as much a source of stress as the experiences of inequitable conditions of employment and social isolation in the cities. They have faced disapproval and rejection of their families for which they have now become a further strain on already tenuous household resources. Their sense of personal failure has often been highlighted by dependence on support of female relatives – grandmothers, mothers, and sisters. However, the symbols of ancestor possession have allowed them to redefine their social placement and identity, and relations to relatives, although not without having their claims to relations with the ancestors contested. The possession ritual has been the principal arena in which these complex negotiations have been taking place. I will concentrate on a case study of a possession ritual which had been undertaken in eastern Venda on behalf of a man in his thirties, Athiambi. In many senses this case study can be seen as exemplary of the nine rituals which I had the opportunity to observe during my fieldwork. It points to issues of conflict and power struggles, of empowerment and contestation, impinging on the efficacy of contemporary rituals due to their shifting social embeddedness with regard to gender.

Ritual efficacy: The ambiguities of ancestor possession

In actors' terms, the purpose of the possession ritual is described as 'healing', *u lafha*, and as 'releasing people', *u bvisa/ u vhsisa vhathu*. 'Healing' is believed to be achieved by making the afflicting ancestor spirit enter the adept's body through sequences of dance and song performed by the adept and the gathered audience. These are carried out in an area ritually sealed off with care from potential threats from evil people – 'witches', *muloi*; it is usually a hut or a house-room in the initiating healer's household. The state of possession is marked by the adept falling on the ground, *u wa*, trembling and issuing a buzzing sound. By adepts it is described as the moment when they feel most 'empowered' – energized, immune to pain or fatigue, and boundless, 'free'. The achievement of this state is preceded by a long effort of the audience playing the rattles, tshele, and signing, and the adept dancing in a painful posture while kneeling down – posture explicitly associated with women's behaviour.

After the ancestor spirit descends, which is usually in the small hours of the morning after a night-long ritual activity, it speaks in Khalanga language to demand ancestor cloths and paraphernalia – salempores *nzheti* and *palu*, ceremonial stick and axe, *thonga* and *mapfumo*. The adept now held to be possessed is taken out of the ritual arena to get dressed in the proper ancestral manner and returns to be greeted as honorific ally Vhakhalanga ('Khalanga') or *vhomakhulu* ('elder') by the participants. The same greeting gesture, *u losha*, as is used in everyday interactions to connote respect of the junior to the senior, is used by the adept and other participants, representing the 'ancestor spirit' and 'living humans' respectively. The ritual proceedings continue with singing and dancing, with sometimes more already initiated persons becoming possessed, for hours or even days until the spirits have been satisfied and left their descendants. Such consumption of ritual activity is held to have been successful in establishing amicable relations with the ancestors and thereby converting their evil influence into sympathy and support.

The identity ascribed to the ancestor spirits – as both the dead forebear of the 'sick' men and as Khalanga, points to the close intertwining between constructions of personal

214

and group descent and history. The significance of Khalanga identity of the possessing spirits must be seen in the context of the folk model of Venda origin which holds that VhaVenda are related to the Khalanga through lineage descent. Although still source of some controversy among historians, this folk model has allowed the VhaVenda to lay symbolic claims to the prestige of royal clans of Great Zimbabwe. It has recently become one of the building stones of incipient Venda nationalism also on the level of state-funded discourse of African renaissance. Within the domains of the ancestor possession cult, the recourse to the powerful Other – VhaKhalanga – serves not only as an element of historical consciousness and group identity, but also as a means to status elevation of particular individuals contesting their social marginalization. The domains of the Venda possession cult, however, also aim to appropriate the power of historical 'insiders' – the chiefs, *musanda, khosi*. The assumption of ceremonial paraphernalia of historical chieftainship (the stick and the axe) by the possessed, and references to the ritual space as 'chiefly kraal', *musanda*, and the royal court, *khoro* – the central political event in the historical chiefdom – are symbolic acts which, by reference to an imagined past, resignify the ritual arena as the socio-political centre of local affairs in the present.

The image of timeless social order depicted in the reincarnation of dead forebears in their living descendants, constructs the order of social relations as inert. Moreover, it identifies the asymmetrical relationship between the senior and the junior as the main principle of this social order which persists beyond the cycle of birth, maturation and death. This symbolic construction, however, is depicted through ritually mediated interactions among participants which are by no means immune to contingent social processes and power struggles. The sense of confidence and agency which actors are able to gain through participation in the possession ritual – which empowers them as representatives of 'the royalty of the past' (*vhathu vhahulu vha kale*), however, is not achieved by all categories of participants to equal degrees. Men in particular have faced difficulties in achieving the state of possession and in having it recognized as 'genuine' due to difficulties in appropriating female cultural styles and domains. It is to this issue of social efficacy of ritual that I will now turn in the analysis of ritual proceedings which had been undertaken on behalf of Athiambi.

When the ritual was organized for him, Athiambi was a man in his 30s. He recently returned from Johannesburg where he was supposed to commence study at the Technicon but soon dropped out due to lack of funds to pay for the tuition. Subsequently he took up odd employment, 'piece jobs', marked by frequent dismissals – as a cook, house servant, cleaner, and eventually as a miner. Throughout his stay in the city he suffered from severe headaches, pains in the shoulders and back and swollen legs. During his employment in the mine which he explicitly stated to have disliked very much – in particular resenting the authority of the head of his work unit – these symptoms worsened. He was no longer able to continue mine work and returned to the rural area, to the 'location' settlement (*lokishini*) where he and his sisters were raised by their mother's sister, *mme muhulu*, after the mother's death. His return met with resentment on the part of the women in his

215

family. His sense of failure was in sharp contrast to the success of his elder sisters – one married to a Zulu man living in Johannesburg, raising her own income as a fashion designer; another studying at Technicon in the local urban centre of 'Venda'. It was the *mme muhulu* and the sisters who paid for his initiation and the ritual, further stressing his dependence on the women in the family.

Athiambi perceived his inadequacy in relation to his sisters and often commented on his marginal status. His sisters corroborated such view of himself by their reluctance to show any sympathy for Athiambi´s pains, regarding them as malingering. They had been hard-pressed to provide financial support for the initiation processes of their brother to become a 'traditional' healer. Furthermore, the interactions with his initiating 'mother', the other female adepts and women from the neighbourhood of the initiating healer's household, did little to change his self-image. The 'mother' regarded him as a slow-learner (which later proved inaccurate), the other women as clumsy and fat, and certainly inadequate when enacting the female postures and tasks appropriate for a person with the 'ancestral gift', *mpho*.

Ahtiambi's uncertain social standing in relation to the women in his family and his female co-initiates projected into disruptions during the ritual proceedings. The tensions and animosities in their mutual relationships came to a head when after several long hours of playing the rattles, singing and dancing the spirit had not yet been enticed to enter Athiambi´s body. Athiambi´s lack of self-confidence showed in his shy and inadequate dancing. For this he attracted open criticism from the women in the audience who at several points in the ritual performance refused to continue to sing and play the rattles. During an intermission Athiambi complained to the initiating 'mother' and the other adepts in a separate room which served as a 'backstage' about the women's backbiting. He had not been kneeling for thirty years of his life like the women had, he said, his knees were swollen, and everyone had come in vain because no spirit would ever come to him. In the main room, the women in the audience mimicked Athiambi´s ungainly movements, criticizing the new generation and the men in particular for being useless compared to the elder generation of women.

At this point the ritual performance became stalled for over an hour during which the initiating 'mother' encouraged Athiambi, made him ingest more medicines, and reprimanded the women in the audience. Subsequently, Athiambi´s movements became more confident and persuasive, the audience showed more support and attention. The sisters became anxious that it might be them who had been preventing the spirit from coming, inviting ancestral disapproval by their unsupportive attitude towards their brother. The eldest sister broke into a litany of wrongs which she committed towards her brother, promising support and money in the future. Shortly afterwards Athiambi 'fell with the spirit' to a sigh of relief of all the participants.

Commentary
Rituals, by taking participants beyond their everyday routines, provide a space in which

mundane identities can be suspended and new possibilities of self-understanding and social relations can be imagined. The possession ritual undertaken to 'heal' Athiambi has revealed an initial reluctance to explore such potentialities of ritual, pointing to salient conflicts among the participants which only the authority of the initiating healer and a common interest to 'please the ancestors' and assure their blessing for all concerned, and Athiambi in particular, had been able to override. While at first highlighting animosities between Athiambi as a man and the women-dominated audience, and between him and his relatives, the ritual allowed their expression and eventual resolution. The possession ritual proved to be a principal arena through which Athiambi had been able to negotiate his return to the rural area from unsuccessful spell of work in the city, and gain acceptance for his new identity as a 'traditional healer' from his relatives and other cult members. In order to draw on the symbolic resources of empowerment embodied in ancestor possession, however, Athiambi had to appropriate styles of dress and behaviour proper to women.

Conclusion

Although drawing on powerful symbols of the past, ancestor possession must be seen as a contemporary strategy through which groups and individuals have been able to imagine new solutions for their contemporary problems and experiences of social marginalization, and act on them. The entrance into the ancestor cult of a new category – men who have engaged in labour migration, has reflected wider transformations of the political-economy of post-apartheid South Africa and of gender relations through which the social power of men from lower socio-economic strata has been diminished. The domains of the ancestor cult have offered highly ambivalent options of empowerment for these men. While on the one hand assigning them the prestigious task of embodying the values of 'Venda' morality through which they could wield influence in the rural area, it has also required a degree of their emasculation and submission to the authority of women by virtue of the latter's superior ritual skill and knowledge.

SOCIOCULTURAL ASPECTS OF THE SOUTH AFRICAN MICROCREDIT INDUSTRY: AN EXPLORATORY ANTHROPOLOGICAL STUDY

Stephné Herselman
University of South Africa

Introduction

The conventional economic view of poverty, the ***achievement model of income determination,*** suggests that with effort, ability and strength of character, a person should be able to escape from poverty's clutches, and that those who do not make the effort will never escape (Bowles et al. 2006: 1). This might be true in a perfect world, but not in one characterised by inequality, exploitation, and the impact of institutions that are a barrier to productive activity. Amartya Sen, winner of the 1998 Nobel Prize in Economic Science, defines poverty "as the deprivation of basic capabilities rather than merely as lowness of incomes, which is the standard criterion of identification of poverty" (Sen 1999: 87). With this, for the purpose of this paper, the 'poor' encompasses people with limited, or no access to resources, and who are consistently challenged to adapt and survive in an environment of chronic social and economic uncertainty.

The demands of poor people for financial services are unique but they are beyond the interests of conventional commercial banks which regard the poor as unprofitable and as too great a financial risk (cf. Robinson 2001: 9). While the sums that would be involved are small, administration costs would be as high as they are for larger loans (Todaro 2000: 664). Many poor people lack collateral to secure credit, and are unbanked with limited access to credit – indeed if they lack a regular income, they have no access to credit at all. As Rutherford (2000: 15) states, poor people's needs for money often far exceed what they can immediately access. Yet, they need credit to empower themselves, improve household management, smooth income flows and consumption costs, for life-cycle needs, and to alleviate their poverty (cf. Fisher and Sriram 2002: 23; Moyo et al. 2002: 5). Besides borrowing money from relatives or employers, their usual recourse to credit is from money lenders, but this usually entails extremely high cost. Entrepreneurship that could produce an income flow is also beyond their reach. Strategies to provide the poor with capital or resources such as housing, schooling and health services might be forms of poverty relief (Robinson 2001: 19), but they do not necessarily translate into security.

Explanations for persistent poverty in terms of economic theory do not, or only inadequately, address behavioural issues (cf. Bowles et al. 2006: 4). What influences the lives of the poor and entraps them in persistent poverty? How do they cope and what values underpin their borrowing behaviour? What options do they have to access credit? What might anthropology have to say about this? Drawing on available literature and a multisite ethnographic approach that entailed participant observation and in-depth interviews with a range of stakeholders – from service and credit providers to borrowers

– I attempt to answer these and similar questions with reference to the demand for and repayment of credit among some of South Africa's chronically poor, and do so against the background of the country's political and economic situation.

Contextualisation: political and economic factors that shape the life-style of the poor

In 1994 the democratically elected African National Congress government in South Africa inherited a society characterised by high levels of economic inequality as well as pervasive poverty (Adato et al. 2006: 226). To address the poverty and former injustices, the government introduced the poor-friendly Reconstruction and Development Programme (RDP) as a cornerstone of its macro-economic policy (Moyo et al. 2002: 2), providing homes, access to fresh water, electricity, and primary health care to millions of poor people. In 1999, facing the quandary of meeting the needs of the poor and retaining long-term growth and stability, the ANC government under President Thabo Mbeki accepted the principles of neoliberalism and the free market system as solutions to poverty, and replaced the RDP with GEAR (Growth, Employment and Reconstruction) (Ramphele 2008: 151–152). Since then, South Africa has had a long period of unprecedented economic growth. However, its benefits have been skewered. On the one hand, sectors of the black population in particular, have benefited from this upward movement of wealth as a result of legislative requirements of employment equity and affirmative action, and from Broad-based Black Economic Empowerment that has benefited a few people, many of whom have connections with the ruling party (Horwitz 2001: 349). Together they have contributed to the development of an elite black middle class (Ramphele 2008: 152–154), the so-called 'Black Diamonds'. By 2008 the incomes of the richest families – those with a combined income of over R26 000 (approx. $2 600) per month – had risen by a third (*Sunday Times* 16, 2008:8).

On the other hand, increasing unemployment, inequality and poverty, and a widening gap between rich and poor (Schwabe 2004: 1; Adato et al. 2006: 226; Klein 2007: 215) continue to plague the majority of South Africans. To address the poverty, the government introduced a comprehensive social grant system in 1999, initially for 2,5 million people, but by 2007 this figure had grown to approximately 12 milllion (Appel 2008). This system, which the government calls 'social relief', has supposedly almost doubled the incomes of the poorest families – 10–20 % of the population – over the past five years, but the social grants consisting of pensions, child maintenance and disability grants have done little to empower the poor, representing instead passive delivery of political goods rather than a contribution to sustainability. In fact the grants have been interpreted as creating a 'culture of dependency' (Ramphele 2008: 154) and millions of South Africans remain as marginalised as they were under apartheid in a post-democratic economic system that might be regarded as a joint economy. Indeed, in 2000 President Mbeki described South Africa as 'economically [being in] two worlds' (Adato et al. 2006: 226; Klein 2007: 215).

According to a recent survey, more than half the households in the country (a total of 25,7 million people or 57 % of the population) – on average consisting of 5 people – live on a combined income of less than R2000 per month (approx. $200) (Schwabe 2004: 1; Statistics South Africa National Treasury: 2007; *Sunday Times* 16, 2008:8). The poorest 10 % (approx 4.5 million people) survive on R360 (approx. $36 per month) per family, well below the 2006 poverty line of R431 per person, making a life of dignity impossible. People in rural areas are worse off than urban dwellers: 51 % of the total rural population fall below the poverty line (cf. Carter and May 1999: 3).

Evidence of the unrestrained neoliberal economic policies of the past decade is conspicuous throughout South Africa. Shopping malls offering goods in line with the best in the world, new vehicles, many of which are status symbols of wealth, and upmarket residential areas are now common. Black people who before 1994 lacked resources and opportunities are now exposed to western commercialism at its best (cf. Herselman and Van Heerden 2003). The overall increased incomes have brought many goods and services marginally within their reach, thereby stimulating a demand for credit which has resulted in increasing numbers of people landing in financial difficulties. Directly alongside the affluence are pockets of insular poverty, the consequences of structural factors such as those mentioned previously, with concomitant values and behaviour which seem to hinder economic and social progress. They might also suggest the disadvantages of proximity to others, specifically in terms of the 'haves' versus the 'have nots'. The information is inconclusive, but such spatial concentration and associated social influences have been associated with persistent poverty (Sobel 2006: 209–217), an idea supported by an informant who said that although the government has 'opened people's eyes' by freeing them from the restrictions of apartheid, they lack the means to support the type of lifestyle they now see around them. He compared them with a herd of cattle breaking free and running wildly in all directions. Spatial concentration seems to matter, but it is likely to be difficult to identify the precise behavioural patterns that emerge from it (cf. Bowles et al. 2006: 9).

Flowing from spatial concentration is the matter of peer group effect. South African schools are desegregated, but the inequalities of the former education system remain (Ramphele 2008: 171–176). Theoretically learners can attend any school, but in practice this is impossible and the majority of children attend dysfunctional township or rural schools. Poor parents also want the best for their children though, and if possible send them to former whites-only schools. In a type of peer group or role model effect, they borrow money at exorbitant rates to pay for clothing for matriculation functions, school tours and learning programmes to ensure that their children compare favourably with children from wealthy homes.

Since 2008, higher than expected inflation figures resulting from food, fuel and energy price increases, and the meltdown in the global economy which South Africa has not escaped, have exacerbated the situation, and in 2008 an estimated 70 000 people across all sectors of society faced legal action for being in arrears in debt repayments. The poor segments of society are most vulnerable, and have no option but to spend increasing portions of whatever income they might have on subsistence. Anything else must either be done without or bought on credit.

The microcredit industry: Overview

The expansive microcredit industry in South Africa has roots in the country's mining industry where miners loaned money to others at exorbitant interest rates. Historically, problematic access to loans and credit, a lack of access to formal banking, and irresponsible lending all promoted the demand for credit and stimulated the establishment of alternative financial service providers, particularly money lenders (Black Sash Report 1999, quoted in Mohane et al. 2002). The problem of usurious interest, amongst others, has plagued the industry since its origin. In 1992, the previous government amended the Usury Act to allow lenders to offer loans under R6000 at any interest but subject to particular rules, and in 1999 this was increased to R10 000 but only for lenders who were registered with the Microfinance Regulatory Council. In this way the government intended to open up the market for small borrowers to have access to credit. This in turn, led to the establishment of cash loan shops across the country. By 2000 the industry had grown into a multibillion-rand enterprise (Mohane et al. 2002).

To regulate the industry, the Government introduced the new National Credit Act, Act 34, 2005, with the first phase of implementation in 2006. For the microlending industry phase three of the Act, which capped interest rates and introduced new and improved consumer rights from June 1, 2007, is particularly important.

> The purposes of the Act are to promote and advance the social and economic welfare of South Africans, promote a fair, transparent, competitive, sustainable, responsible, efficient, effective and accessible credit market and industry, and to protect consumers ... (Republic of South Africa 2006:30).

The Act aims to protect the poor, restrict credit and curb inflation, and significantly, to empower people to be responsible for their own well-being. Through the National Credit Regulator (NCR) it sets the criteria for qualification for a loan, offers clients protection from unscrupulous lenders; requires lenders to conduct affordability checks on new clients; prohibits them from lending clients more than they can afford, and caps administration fees associated with lending. The Usury Act prohibits any microlender from holding a client's identity document, bankcard or pin number. Nonetheless, the microcredit industry continues to have a bad reputation. Reports in the local press emphasise unethical practices such as wreckless lending, exploitation, levying exorbitant interest rates, or retaining clients' bankcards and identity documents.

Access to credit continues to vary. People in lower income categories with a stable income, who are reasonably adequately nourished and are not destitute, the so-called 'economically active poor' (Robinson 2001: 18), have access to credit through institutions such as rotating savings and credit associations, and registered and unregistered credit providers. They earn too little to qualify for credit from institutions in the formal sector. The extremely poor include the unemployed and the underemployed whose work is so poorly remunerated that malnutrition is unavoidable (Robinson 2001: 18). They have no access to credit and live below the minimum subsistence level.

The implications of the new Act for South African society fall outside the scope of this paper, except to say that for the poor its effects have been limited. By capping interest rates without providing other means of finance, the government effectively harms those they intended to protect. There are then no incentives to increase the number of loans available which, in turn, will mean a shortage in the supply of loans (Mohane et al. 2002). In an environment of poverty, a state pension of R940, a child social grant of approximately R220, or a domestic wage of R1000 per month does not go far. People use incomes to pay their debt, and then immediately borrow against future income to sustain themselves. The poor work or bide their time until they are able to repay the loans that financed past consumption, becoming trapped in a cycle of debt out of which few people ever escape, a situation similar to the economic concept of a poverty trap defined as '[a] mechanism[s] that could cause poverty to persist' (Bowles et al. 2006: 2). Such poverty traps are prevalent in societies with joint economies. Living on credit becomes a way of life, and promotes the development of a 'credit culture' or a *leenkultuur,* a culture of borrowing as research participants commented. To deal with this situation, the government introduced a sophisticated electronic system of channelling social grants to institutions from which the poor can obtain their money or make purchases by means of either a debit card or a so-called smart card. The government's intention with this system of, what it calls social relief, is to empower people to stop borrowing, and to spend their money on food, health care and education, rather than on unnecessary items such as alcohol. However, this might also be construed as attempts to control what poor people do with credit, which as Johnson et al. (2005: 292) comment, is often futile and the poor should rather be given the opportunity to adapt their activities themselves than be forced to do so by others.

Microlending organisations

Microlending organisations are roughly distinguished into three categories. First are the *cash loan stores, microlenders or retail stores* that are registered with the National Credit Regulator, and manage their business in terms of the National Credit Act. They are obliged to display the logo of the National Credit Regulator prominently. To obtain credit, a client must provide documentary evidence of a stable income such as a salary advice or bank statement. Borrowing from a microlender is a form of budgeting since a borrower cannot borrow more than what is allowed in terms of the Act. All clients are subject to an affordability check. Even so, the cost of repayment is high because of the addition of interest, an initiation fee, administration fee and VAT to the capital amount borrowed.

Second are the *semi-formal unregistered microlenders* who operate randomly outside the National Credit Act. Some hold people's bankcards and pin numbers, although unscrupulous registered microlenders do the same. They do not conduct affordability checks, and lend clients whatever they insist they can afford because it is in their interest to do so, although they are likely to have a maximum amount that they will lend. By holding bankcards and pin numbers, they ensure future transactions with the owners. Moreover, they are paid before anyone else if they illegally withdraw money from clients' accounts the moment they are credited, despite this being a criminal offence carrying a R25 000 fine or 3-year prison sentence. Certainly, they have an advantage over registered microlenders who operate in terms of the National Credit Act. Many of them have stores in back streets or close to poor communities but unlike the microlenders, they do not display the logo of the National Credit Regulator. Ironically the registered microlenders are most vulnerable to action by the NCR because their activities can be monitored.

The third category are the **loan sharks** (*amashonisa*, translated from Zulu as 'being out in a dark hole', *skoppers* [lit.: kickers in Afrikaans because they are known to assault non-paying clients], or 'camels' [a camel kneels down to allow a person to get on its back, but once it stands up, getting off is impossible]. They operate outside the law and keep borrowers' identity documents and bankcards, but they provide easy access to credit because they usually live among their clients. They do not keep records of their clients and cannot divulge personal details to any one; they make quick decisions about loans, do not require documentation, and provide money when it is needed most (Moyo et al 2002: 10), all of which contribute to their popularity. Interest is usually levied at a flat rate of up to 50 % (repayment of a 'rand for a rand' was also mentioned) on the original balance. If small amounts are repaid at a time, the original interest payable is added to the balance, and eventually the total interest can outstrip the amount borrowed. However, when people are desperate for money, the amount of interest they are charged is immaterial. Once a loan has been repaid, or is about to be repaid, borrowers are offered another loan and people fall into a trap of never-ending debt. Loan sharks do not question how much debt a person might have. Their only interest is whether a borrower is theoretically able to repay. Defaulters can be treated ruthlessly: physical attacks and raids on homes to remove possessions such as televisions, radios, and clothing to be sold to recover debt are not uncommon, and two cases of suicide by debtors unable to repay a loan were mentioned to me. Some loan sharks employ 'debt collectors' to recover outstanding loan repayments, thereby retaining a level of respectability. Loan sharks or their 'debt collectors' sometimes accompany a borrower to a bank or cash loan store on pension day and wait, sometimes inside the building, until they receive the money owing to them. I observed two debt collectors meet a client who handed over money – assumedly debt repayment – in the main entrance of a commercial bank in the main street of a town in the Eastern Cape. Although people fear the loan sharks, they turn to them when they need money, often in the middle of the month when no other option of obtaining money is available. Such behaviour and the exorbitant interests rates they charge are similar to the behaviour of individuals or groups that economic theorists call 'parasites', or unproductive enterprises that feed on productive endeavours. Like 'parasites', loan sharks lock the poor into reinforcing patterns of beliefs and behaviour that result in persistent poverty (Mehlum et al 2006: 79, 80).

Like all the other microlenders, loan sharks do not lend money to the unemployed. People often borrow money from a microlender to repay their debt to a loan shark, although the reverse also occurs, again reinforcing the vicious cycle of debt mentioned previously. As among the microcredit providers, clients of loan sharks range from recipients of a state pension or social grant to teachers, nurses, police, prison warders and other government officials, that is ostensibly people who can be regarded as 'middle-income' and thus not 'poor'. One of my informants described the pattern of borrowing from one provider to repay another as 'borrowing from Jack to pay Jackson'. He also interpreted the behaviour of chronic borrowers as the result of

> life being too fast; people want to live the high life, but their salaries prohibit them from doing so. There is no increase in the quality of life – it is only about material existence; people live other peoples' lives; they do not have a life of their own because they are always indebted to others. Their lives are fake, a fantasy … and they are never in charge of their own destiny.

The household and interpersonal relationships

The collectivist spirit emerging from the importance of community and the notion of *ubuntu* (lit: a person becomes a person through other people; cf. Mbigi 1992: 24) are manifest in principles of interdependence and participation by all the members of a group in activities that affect it. Historically kinship systems have depended upon an elaborate set of social sanctions that enforced and sustained mutual assistance. Poor households faced with chronic risk and without insurance and credit facilities often met, and still meet, in social and economic groups to provide mutual economic assistance. The value of the kinship system as an institution thus lies in its ability to provide essential goods and security when such services from other sources are unavailable. Ideally, it forms a type of social contract of mutual assistance between relatives and an instrument of progress to help members to adapt to changing social and economic circumstances. Sanctions for those who shirk the obligation of the kin system include economic consequences such as loss of employment or accommodation, and stigma.

In many of South Africa's poor communities mutual economic assistance and security involves not only the nuclear family of husband, wife and children, but also the extended family of parents, uncles and aunts, nieces and nephews, or other people who are relatives by birth, marriage and/or ethnicity (cf. Hoff and Sen 2006: 95, 97). The individual is subordinate to the immediate group and people are obliged to try to meet the needs of relatives. A state pension is often the only stable source of income in such a household and the pensioner supports all its members. This situation often presents itself in very large households. One person I interviewed was a member of a household of twenty people, stretching across four generations, and occupying a municipal house with three bedrooms. The female household head, a pensioner, was the main breadwinner, although one daughter was employed and the other adult members contributed to the household economy when they were able to find work. Children in such households are entitled to a maintenance grant of R220. The government's social welfare policy requires that such a grant be used for the child's food, clothing and schooling, but on closer examination this appeared not always to be the case and the money is either used by the parent of grandparent who receives the money or it is added to the household economy. If a pensioner is illiterate, the chances of understanding the intricacies of contractual obligations to meet loan repayments are not good. Hence, a daughter, granddaughter or some other trusted relative accompanies the pensioner to a lender. There is also fear of being accosted, and the presence of a younger person is a security measure during the walk home. As a further security measure, in such cases a client might only borrow small sums of money, but this adds to the total cost of the borrowing because of the administration fee attached to each loan.

Religious beliefs also enforce social obligations. The importance of ancestor worship that dominates African religious beliefs is evident in funerals. They are interpreted as honorary rights for the deceased and are characterised by high mortuary costs, extravagant feasts, new clothing for the chief mourners, an elaborate coffin befitting the real or assumed status of the deceased, a tombstone and the high expenses involved in unveiling it. These are costly but essential features of a 'decent' funeral (Herselman and Van Heerden 2003). Even the lowliest pensioners set aside a portion of their monthly incomes to pay for a 'funeral policy' or membership of a burial 'society'. If the deceased was not a member of such a society, relatives borrow from microlenders to help pay for the funeral, which can cost R15 000 or often more, thereby placing themselves in massive debt. Ironically, a funeral is one of the few occasions when microlenders lend money beyond what is legally permitted, but only on receipt of a death certificate. This is often in addition to other debt, and it becomes increasingly difficult for borrowers to repay their loans. By implication, placing kin in a situation where their behaviour constitutes a set of control mechanisms suggests that the kin system can also be dysfunctional (Hoff and Sen 2006: 96, 97), and constitutes an instrument of stagnation that prevents its members from benefiting from accumulating wealth and economic progress.

By tradition, women are nurturers and homemakers, and continue to play a far greater role in family and community maintenance than men. To their traditional roles has been added recognition of their reliability in credit transactions. Consequently, women are more prominent in such transactions than men, and are the preferred clients of credit providers, although this is because of their reliability or efficiency and not out of concern for their empowerment. However, the degree of control that women have over the use of a loan is affected by factors grounded in conventionality, not least of which is the fact that they are often considered as minors and possessions of their patriarchal families, despite the importance of gender equality in the South African Bill of Rights (Ramphele 2008: 75). Few women can use the money in a way that could help them to increase their incomes and repay their debt sooner, for example, by establishing a vegetable garden to sell vegetables, or by buying sugar or tobacco to sell it in small quantities in the middle of the month when people have little money. Their money must be shared among large numbers of people and is 'eaten', as it were. What I did discern however, was that elderly female pensioners who are head of multigenerational households generally maintain control over distribution of their money and of the goods that they purchase with it.

Exploitation also occurs in the kin system and comments about parents sending their children to their grandparents to be cared for and about children demanding unaffordable clothing from their grandparents are common. This links with the idea that an economically successful person is often confronted with demands from less successful relatives. There is increasing evidence both in the literature (cf. Ramphele 2008: 154) and from input from informants involved in social services that teenage girls deliberately have children to access child grants. The government denies this, but what has not been denied is misuse of the grants by parents and grandparents to repay their debts to loan sharks.

On the other hand: all borrowing on credit is relationship-based. Clients, who meet their obligations, and those in need of some form of social security, establish relationships with their creditors and are thus assured of future assistance or the means to cope with unexpected crises and hardship. In this sense credit is provided in the context of interlinked transactions with the lender also being the borrower's supplier of various resources (cf. Robinson 2001: 16). It is about more than just the availability of money (Johnson et al. 2005: 277). For instance, cash loan stores have the benefit of being able to buy large quantities of good and supplies at discounted prices which are then packed into hampers for sale to clients. The hampers, which consist of sufficient food, washing, lighting and cooking materials, and basic medication to last a month, are sold to clients at prices which they would not be able to afford themselves if they bought the same goods from a retail store.

Reciprocity

As suggested, the provision of credit offers the poor far more than just loans. It enables them to establish social relationships with others which help them cope with crises and hardship (Johnson et al. 2005: 278). This implies that credit contracts between poor people, friends, relatives, employers or credit providers are reciprocal because they are embedded in social relationships which are often long-term, based on trust and from which both parties benefit.

The poor offer lenders a means for economic opportunity and a source of employment for themselves and for the assistants that they employ. Fixed repayment dates replace collateral for the lender. For the poor, credit reduces risk, offers security besides access to money, and is a means of empowerment. It also constitute a safety valve for the broader community since people who can sustain themselves are more likely to be stable citizens than those who cannot (Robinson 2001: 117). Cash loan stores are usually located within a specific geographical area from which they draw their clients who then form a steady and familiar client base. Many borrowers insist that their local stores retain their bankcards for safekeeping. The cash loan stores usually only lend to a small number of borrowers who are known to them. The links that are thereby established reduce the risk of default on payment, and also constitute information flows. A lender's best advertisers are satisfied clients. Assistants are also recruited from the area, i.e. people who are familiar with the community. A cash lender that I visited sells hampers of different sizes, and clients who buy them get a lift home thereby saving the money they would otherwise have to spend on a taxi. In this sense the lender is also the client's supplier and it would seem, benefactor. The owners also hold Christmas parties for their clients where they receive refreshments and small gifts, but from this lesson can also be learned. One year, clients received a baseball cap with the name of the store printed on it. This was not a good idea however, because it identified the wearer as someone who lives on credit. Although outwardly parties and gifts are gestures of goodwill, they are probably also a means of retaining a loyal client base.

In a perverse way, a similar relationship exists between loan sharks and their borrowers. The latter become dependent upon them, are loyal to them and while they might know that leaving their bankcards and documents with them is illegal, they continue to do so. The control the loan sharks have over them also prevents the latter from reporting abuses to the police. Although people fear the loan sharks, they might need them in the middle of the month when other sources of credit have run dry, and people default on other debt repayments but not on meeting their obligations to a loan shark.

Conclusions

By drawing on an ethnographic enquiry, I have commented on the nature and extent of the demand for microcredit in the context of the current political and economic situation in South Africa, but with due regard for the persistence of poverty as a result of politico-economic circumstances introduced by the former government. I suggest that persistent poverty is the result of structural factors such as unemployment, lack of access to credit, and spatial distribution, and also of values and behaviour that hinder economic and social advance. Obviously the two are linked. Over the last two decades the microcredit industry in South Africa has developed into a multibillion-rand industry, fuelled by commercialisation, increased incomes and the government's system of social relief for the extremely poor. On the one hand, the industry is a survival strategy, offering economically active poor people at least some security. The government is also using it as an instrument to give the poorest of the poor some access to credit. On the other hand, it acts as a poverty trap out of which people are unlikely to emerge even when money is borrowed from a registered cash lender. Such access to credit does not help poor people to work their way out of poverty, neither does it contribute to sustainability. It is merely a survival strategy. With millions of poor still lacking access to credit, there is clearly a need for the provision of micro-financial intervention on a mass scale and this can only be achieved through actions that lead to sustainability. More money or greater salaries are unlikely to make a difference because people increase their spending in proportion to their incomes. Once borrowing becomes a way of life, people continue to borrow, behaviour that was likened with alcoholism and gambling by various respondents. Often though, it is the only possibility available for survival, but of concern is the use of credit to support habit-forming consumption. In this way poverty becomes self-reinforcing. For the desperately poor who fall outside the safety net of access to credit, other strategies of poverty relief are required – feeding schemes, job creation, access to proper health care and education for children, infrastructural development, and numeracy for women who are keen to start petty trading could be considered.

Post-apartheid South Africa allows people to make choices about education, effort, where to live, and exposes people to a wide variety of goods and services, but access to them is in theory only since the material and social poverty of the poor restrict them from making any real choices. Furthermore, people cannot choose among institutions and social norms. No one can move out of the broader kin system. While this system, and in particular the extended household, have conventionally constituted safety valves, social circumstances such as unemployment, lack of housing and crowded living conditions, teenage pregnancies, the addition of a third and sometimes a fourth generation, the need to spend money on elaborate funerals, and the lure of commercial goods sometimes render the system dysfunctional, and people are trapped in a cycle of poverty.

Economists and statisticians explain poverty in terms of theories, models, trends and figures. All provide essential information on poverty, but my concern has been with poor people themselves. I hesitate to use the concept of 'poverty trap' as defined in the economic literature, but my experience has shown that poor people are indeed trapped, not only by structural impositions on their lives, but also by values imposed by their conventional lifestyles. Similarly, I am not convinced that the government's social relief policy is the way to go. It might relieve people's plight in the short term, but it does not introduce sustainability or stability into their lives. The xenophobic violence that erupted in South Africa in May 2008 (Sichone 2008a, 2008b) and ongoing tensions in townships seem to attest to this fact. Anomalies are also apparent in the industry. On the one hand the kinship system ensures a person's wellbeing, but it also has dysfunctional consequences; borrowing from a loan shark might meet critical needs, but future consequences could be dire. Understanding and addressing poverty are indeed complex matters and I would hesitate to embark too far on a situation of 'blaming the victim'. Dealing with poverty's pervasiveness and it implications on people's lives calls for a comprehensive investigation beyond what would be offered by a single theoretical paradigm.

VOCATIONAL TRAINING IN THE 'INFORMAL SECTOR' IN BENIN: PROBLEMS OF QUALITY AND QUANTITY

Daniel Künzler
University of Fribourg, Switzerland

The educational system in Benin today is still organized according to the model used by the former colonial power (Künzler 2007, 2008): the secondary level is comprised of a general academic track (*enseignement secondaire général*) and a track which is orientated towards vocational training (*enseignement secondaire technique*). The latter is comparatively small (11 % of all pupils starting on the secondary level)[143] and is mostly provided by the private sector. This training costs almost three-quarters more than academic secondary education (see Adeye 2000). The greater part of the budget is used for salaries and stipends, little money is left for the creation and maintenance of school infrastructure. The quality of teaching is low, and this is reinforced by the lack of qualified teaching and training staff.

The practical orientation of vocational-technical secondary education has changed since the national conference in 1990; previously employment in public administration was the main goal, but in the meantime – completely in accordance with international trends – self-employment is now to the fore (World Bank 1994; Oke 1999: 33; Hountondji 2000: 249). Even if the responsible ministry claims that the relation to practice is not missing, in 2004 the majority of state vocational schools nevertheless reported that neither legal nor economic aspects of self-employment appear on their curricula (METFP 2004: 12, A–8). Out of the twelve regional state vocational schools, which are unevenly distributed, only two can give information about the employment of previous graduates („tracer studies"), while the others have details of only a few individual cases (Hyle and Bosio 2002: 2; METFP 2004: A–34).[144] The information available indicates that formal state vocational education mainly leads the way to further educational opportunities. This phenomenon is also well-known in other countries, like Togo and Cameroon (Paul 1990: 406). For a minority (10–30 %), vocational training in Benin does lead to employment in an occupation, but only rarely to self-employment.[145] Even if the desire to enter a certain occupation is there, the problem that the knowledge acquired does not correspond to the needs of the labour market often arises. The vocational schools themselves do indeed see the necessity to adjust the curricula to the requirements of the labour market (METFP

---

[143] This portion is somewhat higher than in 1985; this is in contrast to the assumption by Middleton et al. (1993: 44f.), which was refuted by other data too, that vocational secondary education in developing countries will lose in importance in comparison to the academic secondary education. In comparison with other African countries, the share of formal vocational training lies in Benin in mid-range.

[144] It is well-known from other contexts (Gerhards 2002: 237) that, for various reasons, those responsible content themselves with recording only the number of apprentices.

[145] In Mali, lower figures for starting an occupation are reported (Kail 2003: 282).

2004: A 11). While for some occupations the supply exceeds demand, for others training is completely lacking despite demand. Nevertheless, the individual vocational schools wish to provide the same education as other schools and do not wish to give up any courses (METFP 2004: S. A–5/A–6).

State subsidization of vocational training would be justified particularly if social equality and equal opportunities for the lower social classes can be achieved. It cannot be denied, however, that state vocational training does not attract the poorest section of the population. In addition, the portion of women is lower in vocational training than in academic education, which also increases inequalities. According to newspaper reports, this was also the view of the Minister for Vocational Training at the time, Léa Hounkpé. It is, therefore, astonishing that the well-known path continues to be followed by the government in Benin, in cooperation with Western partners, and that even "more of the same" is being planned. Yet the World Bank, which normally presses for a reduction in the budget for vocational-technical secondary education (World Bank 1994), has not succeeded in realizing this priority in Benin. After approval of the credit, the portion of the budget for vocational education rose from 2 % (before 1994) to 4 % (1997) (Adeye 2000).

Various parties, and particularly the World Bank (1995), support the opinion that vocational training is best provided "on the job" by the employer. One of the arguments which apparently support this view is the higher social return on investment of general education (Psacharopoulos 1994: 1327). There are indications that this does not apply for Benin (Fourcade et al. 1994: 739), although more up-to-date research is necessary. This contribution aims to examine the question of whether or not private vocational education is indeed better adjusted to the requirements of the labour market and to discuss this using the example of craft or manual trade apprenticeships in the informal economic sector. This work is based on research in Benin and on the relevant local and international literature on this topic and it describes the situation at the end of Mathieu Kérékou's government (2006).[146]

The private "informal sector" in Benin

The 2002 census showed that 95 % of the population over 10 years of age is employed in the informal sector (MPPD/INSAE 2003). The remaining 5 % is divided between public administration, 2.6 %, and the formal private sector, 2.4 %. "Informal" is, however, an unfortunate description, because this sector does have many formalized elements and thus cannot always be distinguished from the formal sector. Because of its wide use, this term will continue to be employed here. In addition to agriculture, the informal sector consists particularly of the urban informal sector, which is still gaining in importance

---

[146] The fieldwork in Benin was funded by the Swiss National Science Foundation and the Emil Boral Foundation for Postgraduates.

through the increasing urbanisation. Apart from general trade or commerce and other services, like transport and the catering business, the crafts and manual trades occupy an important place.

In the informal sector there is a wide band of non-formal training courses, which are provided by various kinds of establishments. Although very varied, a few general characteristics of the apprenticeships can be distinguished, but these are not found in each individual case. Charmes and Oudin (1994) differentiate between two models of vocational education in West Africa: The 'Coastal model' and the 'Sahel model'. In the 'Sahel model' the apprenticeship is based more on familial, or quasi-familial, relationships between the apprentice and the employer (this term has been chosen to mean the person giving on-the-job training, usually a workshop owner with our without a certified apprenticeship).[147] In the 'Coastal model' these relationships are less close. Furthermore, the apprenticeship does not last as long as in the 'Sahel model', but the beginning and ending is more strongly formalized. Completion of the apprenticeship is also more often confirmed by a certificate, which – according to general usage – is the prerequisite for opening one's own workshop. The status of the apprentice is in the 'Sahel model' not so linked with the status of the family worker. The work of Devauges (1982) on the Congo shows at that time a picture similar to the 'Coastal model', particularly with regard to the increasing distance between the apprenticeship and family relationships. Senegal too appears to follow the 'Coastal model' more (Naumann and Wolf 2002). According to Reuter (1994) the apprenticeship is at that time less well-known in eastern and southern Africa. His description of the apprenticeship in Zimbabwe corresponds in many ways more to the 'Sahel model'. The main aspects of the apprenticeship in Benin correspond to the 'Coastal model', but in contrast to this model, the duration of the apprenticeship is seldom fixed from the beginning, even if it is approximately known for each occupation. Moreover, a written contract is not usual. In the following, the main emphasis lies on the apprenticeship in informal crafts and manual trades in Benin, to which the hairdresser can also be counted. The information is based particularly on Hounyè (1997), Ligan (1997) and Adeye (2000), as well as on discussions between the author and various actors in this sector during a two-year research stay.

A few figures will help to demonstrate the importance of the apprenticeship in Benin. Of all the workers in the non-itinerant informal sector, the number of skilled workers is insignificant. While the employers make up 31.4 %, the apprentices are the largest group with a percentage of 42.2 % of all workers (Maldonado 1998). In some other countries this portion is even higher, for example in Dakar, where it reaches four-fifths (Naumann and Wolf 2002). The manual trade sector in Benin in 2000 consisted of 78,000 enterprises, which employed approximately 300,000 people. Of these 170,000 were apprentices, 75,000 employers and 55,000 family employees, who are paid very little.

---

[147] In French, this person is called 'patron'.

Here too the lack of skilled workers is apparent. In addition, it is clear that employers have several apprentices on average.

Beginning an apprenticeship in a craft or manual trade

In some African countries there are occupations which are linked to a certain sex, or to one's affiliation to a particular family, ethnic group or nation state. The growing urbanization and the emergence of 'modern' occupations have undermined these limitations (Duval-Arnould and Martinot-Lagarde 1994; Ligan 1997, Kail 2001, Meunier 2001). In the old kingdom of Abomey, an area which is part of Benin today, there were families who specialized in certain occupations, for instance, the Hountondji in leather goods or the Djimadjč in carpet weaving (Ligan 1997). In principle, any occupation can be chosen in Benin today, as long as the parents and the employer are in agreement. This arrangement is made by means of a verbal contract. Written contracts have been rare up to now. Sometimes there are family relationships with the employer, who is then also under familial pressure to accept apprentices. These relationships are, however, not as prevalent as in the 'Sahel model'. At the beginning of the apprenticeship, the employer may receive a present or very often money, whereby the amount varies according to the occupation, the relationship between employer and apprentice, and the location. The sum lies somewhere between CFA 20,000 (a little more than €30) and CFA 150,000 (almost €230) and in some cases it can even be as high as CFA 350,000 (€534).[148] The majority of apprenticeships probably cost between CFA 40,000 (€61) and CFA 60,000 (€91). An apprenticeship in Northern Benin costs less than one in the densely populated coastal area with the cities Cotonou and Porto-Novo. In comparison to the direct and indirect costs of several years of schooling, the apprenticeship is an economical option. It must be pointed out, however, that the costs of an apprenticeship have increased considerably in the last few years.

While in some cases talent and inclination are certainly decisive, an apprenticeship is often started in the urban informal sector due to the lack of alternatives. Often a premature end to the school career is the reason, be it because exams were not passed and there was no possibility of going to the next school level, or because the parents could, or would, no longer pay the school fees. Thus, the aspirations for social advancement via an educational career and employment in public administration are, as a rule, shattered. Some apprentices begin the apprenticeship in Benin as soon as they fail the primary school exams, that is, before the legal minimum age of 14 years. In this group, girls are represented particularly frequently. A second wave of apprentices reaches the labour market between the ages of 15 and 20 years. In general, no minimal school level is required. Access to the apprenticeship is, therefore, quite open, even if some trade associations are trying to standardize the apprenticeship, i.e. to fix acceptance criteria,

---

[148] The average income, adjusted for purchasing power, lies at around €834 per year.

duration, costs at the beginning and completion and to formalize the apprenticeship contracts.

The pedagogy of the apprenticeship

The employer takes on responsibility for the apprentice, but this responsibility refers more and more purely to professional aspects and less to a comprehensive responsibility for education. It still includes the partial payment of food costs, transport and lodging for the apprentice. Through the apprenticeship, the apprentice also learns certain values, like respect for the employer, obedience to older apprentices as well as punctuality and discipline. It is not unusual for apprentices who arrive too late, steal or make mistakes, to be beaten. The apprentices are also subject to health risks, low work security and a lack of social insurances, as well as working hours that often go beyond legal regulations. The teaching of occupation-specific knowledge takes place during work in a rather unstructured way. The employer sees her- or himself often as the only source of professional knowledge and this consists of experience-related practical know-how and seldom theoretical knowledge. This orientation of the apprenticeship is explained – at least partially – by the fact that the employers themselves often received a limited education and have no theoretical knowledge. A significant portion of the employers can neither read nor write.

The prevailing pedagogy of the apprenticeship – not only in Benin – is based on the apprentice quietly observing the work of the employer or older apprentice and remembering occupation-specific actions without any theoretical explanation or teaching aids (see also METFP 2004). It is not usual for an apprentice to ask questions. More and more the apprentice can help with the work and then carry out work independently, by imitating occupation-specific actions. There is no curriculum for the apprenticeship and the apprentice learns the work that is currently demanded by the customers. Progress depends, therefore, to a great extent on his or her ability to observe patiently and to carry out increasingly complex work. Often there is a kind of 'hierarchy' in the work involved and during the course of the apprenticeship the apprentice 'rises up' through this. Nevertheless, use of the actions observed is limited, because the theoretical understanding is missing. In addition, the employer's knowledge is also sometimes limited, particularly in occupations which are exposed to technological development (e.g. car repairs, electric appliances). The apprentice can, therefore, only acquire limited knowledge.

Completion of the apprenticeship

The duration of an apprenticeship depends only partially on the apprentice's age at the beginning and the knowledge gained. It can vary between three and seven years – or even more – according to the occupation. The estimated average of five years is counter to the legal framework of regulations. The employer often mentions relatively vague criteria for the end of the apprenticeship, like for instance that "everything to be shown has been shown". The length of the apprenticeship often depends not on the difficulties of the occupation, but rather on the goodwill of the employer and the financial situation of the parents. The latter is linked by the fact that towards the end of the apprenticeship – sometimes after successful completion of the final examination – an 'apprenticeship diploma' is issued. Theoretically, the state has fixed the price for this diploma at CFA 20,000 (a little more than €30), but in practice this rule is seldom respected. Even though some trade associations try to avoid misuse, many apprentices have no choice but to pay these large sums as a kind of "release fee". This can range from several tens of thousands up to CFA 200,000 (just over €300). For this the French description "*dot de liberation*" is widely used in the francophone states on the Gulf of Guinea. "*Libération*" is a word which was also used in connection with the relation between slaveholders and slaves (Hounyè 1997: 66). The employer grants leave to the apprentices, so that these can do small jobs in order to raise the necessary money. These jobs cover anything from pursuing one's occupation as an itinerant worker to prostitution. This 'release fee' was once more of a symbolic nature, but it is becoming more and more important. With the 'apprenticeship diploma', the apprentice becomes a master craftsman according to common practice. Without this diploma, the opening of one's own workshop will scarcely be accepted by the other craftspeople. The Ministry responsible introduced new diplomas at the end of the research period. The apprentices now receive the CQP (*Certificat de Qualification de Professionnel*). Furthermore, there is also the CQM (*Certificat de Qualification de Métier*), which is issued to craftsmen and -women who pass the examination, of which 80 % is based on practical work. The increasing efforts to achieve formalization of the apprenticeships are causing mistrust among the people in crafts and manual trades in Benin. As findings in the Côte d'Ivoire (Labazée et al 2000b) and Sierra Leone (University of Sierra Leone 1991) have suggested, the actors in the informal sectors are fearful of growing state interference (taxation, authorization, controls, keeping within the law, etc.).

In the apprenticeship, a certain process of selection takes place, for instance, by breaking off the apprenticeship. This can occur due to lack of money for completion of the apprenticeship, or for women due to pregnancy. Selection is not carried out based on the specialized knowledge of the apprentice, even though some trade associations have begun to organize the final apprenticeship examinations. The qualification function of the apprenticeship remains limited, because the qualification of the employers themselves is already limited and often does not keep in step with technological change. In this system, the capacity for innovation is therefore restricted (Middleton et al 1993; Charmes and Oudin 1994). These observations put into relative terms the apparent coherence between the private provision of apprenticeships and the requirements of the market, which is assumed by the World Bank to exist (Psacharopoulos 1987). Moreover, the employers sometimes try to keep certain 'professional secrets' from the apprentices, because they fear the (potential) competition. In particular, contact with the customers is often monopolized by the employers, in order to ensure that their custom remains with the workshop.

False incentives for the employers

The great majority of the employers did an apprenticeship themselves (Charmes and Oudin 1994; Adeye 2000). Although their level of education has increased in the past few years, it remains under that of the formal sector (Middleton et al. 1993; Adeye 2000). This finding also applies outside Benin in the Subregion (Maldonado 1998; Labazée et al. 2000a; Meunier 2001). The proportion of illiterate employer is significant, but varies from region to region. In contrast to the usual inequalities in the educational system (Künzler 2007, 2008), Adeye (2000) found that there was a slightly higher educational level for employers in the north of Benin than in the south of the country. The average educational level of the apprentices is as a rule higher than that of the employers and seems to be increasing further. But even after several years of schooling, the ability to read and write remains limited and is probably below the national average. As already mentioned, many are not able to continue their educational career. State employees are over-represented among the apprentices' parents; according to Adeye (2000: 130f.) they make up almost 20 %. For these young people, the apprenticeship is evidence of the failed aspirations to maintain the familial status with an educational career. One consequence of the expansion of education is that social positions like that of the apprentice are taken by people whose educational level is constantly increasing ('credential inflation').

The income of an employer is often higher than that of state teaching staff. From the viewpoint of many employers though, this income is not sufficient for one to survive and, therefore, in some cases they fall back on other sources of income like transport, commerce and agriculture. Apart from this additional income, the apprenticeship fees and the release fees are the main source of income. The employers also profit from the cheap labour of their apprentices, who sometimes have to do jobs that have nothing to do with their occupation. Thus for the employers, there are strong incentives to employ as many apprentices as possible. As already mentioned, skilled workers are often lacking, while most employers have several apprentices, often up to 14 and, in rare cases, over 30. The workshops are thus transformed into informal training centres, which train apprentices badly and this in numbers which far exceed the labour market's capacity for absorption (Charmes and Oudin 1994; Hounyè 1997; Maldonado 1998; Adeye 2000). The idea that vocational training should be left to private actors instead of providing it in state institutions is, therefore, not unproblematic. It is based mainly on economic considerations, which demand a reduction in state expenditure (Psacharopoulos 1987; Middleton et al. 1993). In the private sector there can be incentives for the employer – like the apprenticeship fees and the release fees – which bring a surplus of badly trained apprentices onto the labour market.

The argument that the incentive to employ as many apprentices as possible is compensated for by the fear of the emerging competition is true only to a certain degree. The opening of one's own workshop represents a big problem for many after their apprenticeship. Joint workshops are rare, the goal is to open one's own workshop. Various difficulties present themselves here, similar to those mentioned in Fauré and

Labazée (2000). Apart from getting established in a market with already stable relations between the other craftspeople and their customers, the search for a suitable location and the problematic relationship with the public administration, there is another large problem, namely the financing of the investment. The necessary sums vary according to the occupation, but they quickly amount to several times the average annual income. As the position 'skilled worker' is not usual in the crafts or manual trades, this intermediary status between apprentice and self-employment is missing.[149] It is, therefore, seldom possible for these workers to save the necessary capital from their wages.

Loans are also rarely a realistic alternative. For those in commerce, there are more loan possibilities, as here more guarantees (the goods) are available; in addition the necessary amounts are relatively modest and they can be paid back within shorter periods. In this sector, therefore, the supply of loans is developing, even if there are often complaints about the high interest. With short loan periods and limited capital, no-one can equip a workshop. For craftspeople in the informal sector, guarantees are lacking. Here there is neither land nor a house which could serve as a guarantee. The wages of relatives who are salaried employees or collective guarantees from trade associations are only partially available as guarantees. The need for credit is highest exactly at that time when it is most difficult to find guarantees and, thus, to obtain a loan. The only remaining way remains family help, which is more difficult during an economic crisis. So after the apprenticeship, many struggle on in the informal sector (transport, commerce) or work as itinerant craftsmen or craftswomen in the hope of finding the necessary financial means to become self-employed. The popular saying that the gift of a fish provides food for a day, but teaching someone to fish provides food for ever is a half-truth. If fishing is to be successful, one needs not only knowledge but also the necessary equipment, access to fishing grounds with potential, the certainty that nobody will take the fish away by force and finally also ability to market the fish, in short the right basic conditions. To ensure such conditions, the need is not for minimal government, but rather for effective government, which is unfortunately seldom found in sub-Saharan Africa (Künzler 2004).

Conclusions and future outlook

The apprenticeship places the main emphasis on the socialization of the apprentices and on their embeddedness in a professional environment, but less on social integration. After an apprenticeship in the informal area, one is indeed prepared for the conditions prevailing in the informal sector, but there is often no possibility of changing to the formal sector. Only in a few cases are the chances of employment with informal vocational training better, for instance when the minimal wage for employees with diplomas from

---

[149] While in Benin most enterprises fall back on family workers, in neighbouring Niger the position of skilled worker is more usual (Meunier 2001).

formal vocational training is to be avoided or practical ability is important (Paul 1990: 406; Fourcade et al. 1994: 740; Paul and Vernières 1994: 207f.). In general the allocation function of vocational training in the informal sector is targeted to this sector. Because of the limited employment possibilities in the formal sector, the graduates of formal vocational training are increasingly forcing their way into the informal sector, for which however they are less well prepared.

For children from wealthy families, the apprenticeship has become more a way of limiting social decline after failing in school than of reproducing social status. The apprenticeship is becoming less and less a means of integrating the children of craftspeople and farmers into the urban economy. Thus, the possibilities for the lower social classes are reduced, resulting in a growing problem of legitimation. This applies for the whole educational system and is not a characteristic of the apprenticeship in the informal sector only.

It is therefore important not to overestimate the capacity of the informal sectors to create jobs and absorb the growing number of human resources. The informal sector too suffers from economic crises and from the dwindling purchasing power of the urban population, particularly the salaried employees. It is to these that the manual trade sector is particularly linked.[150] Even the growing demand for repairs cannot make up the loss in purchasing power. Informal vocational training will, though, continue to play an important role in Benin, as is shown by the efforts of the Administration as well as international development cooperation. The latter has invested a lot to support the trade associations of the crafts and manual trades. Some projects try to build a bridge between purely informal and formal vocational training by initiating dual apprenticeships. In the present situation, however, private vocational training is adjusted to the needs of the labour market only to a limited degree, as there are strong incentives to train too many workers who cannot be absorbed by the labour market and who, in addition, often lack sufficient theoretical knowledge.

---

[150] Only a few sectors in the crafts and manual trades are directed to any considerable extent towards the non-African population in Benin or tourists. Nevertheless, there is one specialty: in the public administration, the sector of crafts/manual trade is not under the control of the Ministries for the Economy or Labour, but of this for Culture and Tourism.

DATING IN PORT HARCOURT, NIGERIA

Jana Bayerlová
University of Pardubice

Introduction

This contribution should examine opinions of young urban Nigerians on marriage, relationships and dating with their spouses. Nigeria as a very religious country with still persisting customary law, is a space where young people have to negotiate between tradition and modernity (Para-Mallam 2006). But this contradiction does not really exist. This study will show how they are able to integrate critically the values originating in Christian religion, Western influence, and popular notion of how "cool" relationship should look like, into one but always individual model. Respondents were mostly university students or young working people from the middle class. All of them were living in the surroundings of Port Harcourt, number one oil city of Nigeria, formerly known as the Mecca of party life. Now, however, the city has become rather infamous for the highest number of AK47 you can see on the street in a day. There reigns an atmosphere of insecurity that exerts surely not a marginal influence on human relationships.

Main goal of the paper is to introduce new attitudes of young Nigerians toward dating and marriage. When couple date and sometimes live together for several years without formal acknowledgment of their parents, when people date every month someone else, when they do that for the money or when they condemn such a behavior at all, they still have to deal with few questions. How do they feel about gender equality and gender roles in relationship?. What is desirable on the partner? Is premarital abstinence valuable? How big importance should be ascribed to romantic love? Does fidelity matter? Or in other words, what to pick up form the church and what from Carrie Bradshaw. Quite simple questions, but answers on them implied attitudes which people have toward male and female relationship. And at the same time these questions create prevalent discourse among young people.

Presentation will also use my experience from Czech universities. I could not completely cancel my own pre-understanding of society where sex before marriage and a beer is the biggest sin. Therefore I shall try to show my prejudices about Nigerians and on the other hand their opinions about my life as the example of "Western" life style.

Methodology

I have spent six months in Port Harcourt. I arrived there as a member of student organization AIESEC and lived with one of the member's family. My closest friend was a daughter of the family. She was a student of history, but above all, she was an enthusiastic fashion designer. I have worked as a volunteer with disabled children for Catholic Compassion Centre.

Practical problems of the research were obvious from the beginning, but there was no chance how to prepare for them from the distance of my home. Everything started just after my arrival to Nigeria. Primarily, it was broken English as a lingua franca of the area. Broken is one of the fastest developing languages in the world. It is based on a playful approach, when official English is modified in everyday life, for both, practical and echoic purpose. As a non-native English speaker, it was quite difficult for a while to understand, but on the other hand, learning the language was a good way how to get closer to people and start a conversation. Second biggest complication was the orientation in the city space compounded with movement restrictions. Port Harcourt has two millions inhabitants, no public transport and no official map, in spite of that the chaos-system works very well. Finally, I found out that orientation is just the matter of time and restrictions are more in my head than anywhere else. Of course, I had to behave according my gender role plus be careful because of security situation, but when I travelled alone, I could feel that people deal with me in much more equal way. Most of the white persons travelled with police security guards. Paradoxically, they were in bigger danger than me as they gave a proof that they had money and connection to oil business. I have realized that position of a student and a volunteer, staying with a Nigerian family was the safest foundation for the research I could imagine.

Under Nigerian circumstances, my attention was mainly attracted by oil politics, vigilantes and strategies how common people deal with such a situation. My research about gender relationships of young Nigerians has accrued quite unwittingly. Almost every time I tried to interview a person how they feel about government and Shell, the discussion topic turned to relationships, sooner or later. Usually, it was the point when the roles of researcher and respondent have switched. The status of unmarried young girl from Europe in Niger Delta aroused almost anthropological curiosity among most of the people I have met. It seemed to me fair to answer their questions, even when they were often very same, often with a second meaning. Top two: Are you married? And what do you think about premarital sex? But we start to talk and lots of times it was very open interesting discussion. Another valuable access to gender information was my stay with the Nigerian family. It was there, in everyday practical life that I started to understand origins of values connected with male and female relationships, gender roles and importance of family.

Old Times

For a better understanding of today's gender relationships I will try to outline how they looked like in the past. I do not claim there is some direct continuance or impact on contemporary young generation, because they are often not aware of old habits, but certainly the old ways help to create set of values which prevail till now. For my purpose I will mostly use an ethnographic research of Professor Otonti Nduka about Rebisi Kingdom of Port Harcourt. Prof Otonti Nduka is an Ikwerre man and the Ikwerre people are regarded as one of the autochthonous groups of the city.

Not only the Ikwerre, but most of the Niger Delta ethnic groups were segmentary societies with highly egalitarian political ethos together with highly valued ethos of warrior (Wolpe 1973). This ethos should not imply a simple-minded sense of a proclivity for violence. Rather it starts from the recognition that physical courage and the figure of the warrior are deeply etched in a history and culture of bravado, war, and resistance (Watts et al. 2008: 41). Example of that are not only inter tribal wars, but also widespread phenomenon of wrestling, when strong men take pride in showing off their prowess and physique. Wrestling season follows the planting one and it was a big festival where young men and women could socialize. Successful wrestlers were regarded as very desirable among young girls. And it was clearly one of the characteristics important for a good man. Other expectation was signs of responsibility. A man should have a house of his own and be engaged in a viable occupation such as farming, hunting and fishing. Good moral standing, wealth, health and family reputation were not of less importance. The same is applicable to bride. She should also show noticeable signs of responsibility and decency. Woman was expected to be dutiful and seen to have a cheerful, fertile and resourceful disposition. Above all she would continue to maintain her virginity till she is married (Nduka 2006: 29).

Before a couple could get married there was a long period of negotiations. After suitability and compatibility was ascertained, the family of the suitor initiated contacts with that of the bride. The first visit was *omahia-oro*, enabling the suitor's family to visit the prospective bride's home with gin and jar of palm wine for presentation to her father. The second visit was *osikwa nwerhe* to formally ask the woman's hand in marriage, again with bottle of gin and jar of palm wine. Father usually requests the suitor to allow him some time to consult with his daughter, what could take sometimes several weeks. Another two visits followed with gin and palm oil before *nne nu nda wonru manya* and *okwu onuekhwu*, when the bride price was settled. Then there was a big event of bride's open acceptance before both families to marry the man. The last ceremony was oath called *ogba-onu*. The hosts entertained their new in-laws lavishly and the bride enacted a dramatic search in the midst of the large crowd to identify her husband with whom she would publicly share a cup of wine. That was the climax of it all. After ceremonies there was a grand festival, when father ordered his daughter to be escorted to her new home and she was accompanied by a large group of dancers and relatives. She carried along a full range of domestic items and sometimes was accompanied even by a maid (Nduka 2006: 31–32).

All the communities in Niger Delta were very patriarchal. Female sexuality was guarded and restrained. There is an old story about king Rebisi and his daughter. She was much loved, but one day she was caught by her father flirting with one of his slaves and Rebisi ordered her to be beheaded as a punishment. But it doesn't mean that women were powerless. Second daughter of Rebisi was not forced to get married and she remained as the hostess of his kingdom with responsibility to preside over the sharing of booties among her brothers (Nduka 2006: 9–10). Women were indispensable not only as moral teachers who carry the tradition from one generation to another, but also as part of village economy. Farming was done actively by both men and women during the planting and harvest season, but it was only the women who cultivated the fields all around the year. Main products were the yams. And it was in yams that wealth of man was measured (Nduka 2006: 35) Women played important role in business and diplomatic relations too. As they married to another village they still kept the contacts with women from their home community. Exogamy then worked like cement binding the villages together, or like a consolidating network which had to some extent made trading between communities possible (Wolpe 1973: 35). Women unions as institutions exist mostly among the Ibo people, but as a tool they function among most of Niger Delta ethnic groups.

My goal was to show the roots of patriarchal nature of the Nigerian society, but equally stress the importance of African family and woman as a central figure in it. Therefore I will start from the family in the next capture again.

Dating

Once we watched documentary about Beyoncé. My friend shrugged with her arms saying, you see how white people support their children. It was when parents of Beyoncé put her into the dancing school. Young Nigerian generation is very well aware of differences between African and European upbringing and they hope to use the best from both. Most of the contemporary families still teach their children to respect elders, fear God and keep unity of the family. I have known a guy, who recently graduated, plus he created a successful design company, but his family never said a word that how they are proud of him. In their eyes he was an ungrateful son who did not respect his parents. The reason was that he did not visit them very often. There was another boy, living just with his mother and sister, the rest of polygamous family living separately. In spite of that he was in the conviction that he will graduate and feed the whole because it is the benefit of the whole family what is important not the benefit of the individuals. It is the love in form of respect and is expressed through the support of one's family. Young people are formed by these values, but in the same time they have problems to stand up to them. Most of them have a plan to be friend to their children, to bring up successful individuals, but still preserve traditional values.

Family is also a model for gender roles. I would not even say that there is such a big generation gap between parents and children in understanding of male and female roles. It more depends on the situation. When you date, it is a guy who takes care of a girl, when you get married it is a woman who takes care of the whole family. There are three main influences which create a picture of how should ideal man and ideal woman look like. It is African family tradition, Christian religion in its Pentecostal version, and the notion of romantic love. Young Nigerians look for a partner who will give them true love, but their expectations are quite practical. Fidelity and honesty are highly valued, on the other hand girls were often willing to forgive unfaithful guy (not vice versa). Some of them even condemn those women who leave partner because he was cheating. Favourite saying: jealousy is from devil. You should fight for your man/family. However same tough girls dream about beautiful weddings, big houses, expensive cars and I wondered how they are going to pay for it. Probably they will not have to, because it is the man, who is supposed to feed the family. But it is not the material goods what is important (well, that is not entirely true), it is the ability of a man to provide them, his ability to be successful. That's how he earns respect. Woman is the soul of the house and the moral teacher (Suda 2007). But today, she stands in front of the contradictory demands on her person. She needs to be obedient wife, but at the same time an outspoken one; she is supposed to be gentle and shy, but still party going; virtuous, but to have a sex-appeal. I don't know how it is possible, but Nigerians girls are able to stand the challenge and be everything. That's how they earn the love.

Is there any equality between these roles? Equality has different dimensions in different parts of world. For Western culture all members of society are equal. Same equality is between young and older people, or between man and woman. Of course, that you have different attitude to different people, you greet older person in different way than younger, and gender equality is in question at all, but equality is a value. Western societies judge themselves according how equal they are. Nigerian society is not necessarily less equal than the Czech one, but no one in Nigeria would admit that a son could be equal with his father. It doesn't mean they don't have close relationship, but both of them have different roles. Children respect their parents and parents love their children. There is similar proverb on gender issue. *Man should love his wife and woman should respect her husband.* When we speak about gender equality, this Nigerian widespread opinion explains a lot. No one would ask what is more valuable, love or respect, because equality doesn't mean the sameness. All Nigerians told me, that there is no equality between man and woman. On the other hand, I have seen lots of inequalities in everyday life, but most of them were connected with poverty, social injustice and corrupted political power, not primarily with gender. Gender relationships seemed to me more as a fragile, often violated, but equilibrium. You can hear in church that woman should be submitted to husband. My little bit bored friend replied that someone should do the statistic and count how many times you have in the bible that woman should obey and how many times there is written that man should love her. Female submission is an accepted symbol, but in reality women rule the house and educate children. We always asked mum for decisions, she was the one checking if we went to church and while daddy read newspapers, she read the books and spiritual literature.

Young generation has a possibility to try the marriage roles in advance. However, my experience is that dating is more a game on relationship, than a real one. There are several reasons. Total importance of marriage excludes any other type of commitment. Parents, if they don't forbid dating at all, they at least don't want to know. They are just interested in future wife or husband. Couple usually doesn't have a place to meet in private, so the dates are more like hanging out with friends. But there are definite advantages, too. Dating is a cool game, which brings prestige for both girls and boys. As a girl you have certain access to your boyfriend's resources. You need to prove that you can treat yourself, but in a sober way and give a man an opportunity to take care of you. As a boy, your prestige in the group originates from how well can your girlfriend represent you. Premarital sex is very ambivalent issue in the young relationships. It is something what is equally forbidden by church and African tradition, but what was always present. In contemporary Nigeria, we have to add the problem of HIV and the official propaganda telling that: the best protection is not a condom, but no sex. There is no surprise that sex in general has become a taboo topic. Even a girl who is not married and sleeps with her boyfriend will not miss a chance to give you a lecture about how sinful a premarital sex is. When young people advocate abstinence they give several reasons. One of them is a strong will. Celibacy is form of asceticism, which makes a person stronger. For girls it is usually their virtue they need to protect. Interesting moment is the negotiation when it is appropriate to have sex. This negotiation is a power game. Girls can wear very sexy dresses, they dance in an erotic way, boys try to seduce them, they tempt each other, but the winner is the one who can refrain. The power is coming from a moment when you are totally vulnerable but still able to say no. This 'no' is the female source of power. Safest way how to sustain this source is to keep your virginity till wedding. That's why premarital sex is much more risky game for girls. They hazard with their reputation. They act on the background of social control that is expressed through rumours and stereotyped stories. For example, the story of a girl who falls in love and sleep with a boy. But the guy is just using her. He laughs behind her back, spreads a rumour and destroys her reputation after. There are no such stories to frighten the guys.

What applied to both genders in the same way was the curiosity about my relationships back home and a total non-understanding of the fact that I did not want to get married. Later I have made small cross-cultural translation for myself. When someone asked me if I want to get married, I translated it as 'possible commitment' in my head and replied with clear consciousness yes. That meant yes, I am normal. Stereotypes about gender relationships of white people are little bit contradictory. At the end of my stay when I felt as a proper young Nigerian (Sunday church, no beer, no sex), a cousin from Jamaica came to our family. She was sent to learn how to sew, but more importantly for re-education. Just then I have realized how different measure applies to me and her. My behaviour was accepted just because I was from Europe and Europeans have different morality. And I thought I was the only cultural relativist in the house. In spite of condemning liberal attitudes on sex and marriage, lots of Nigerians confess they like to marry a white person. I thought they wanted to get out of Nigeria, but the case was that white people are believed to be faithful and to keep their word. What they are not able is to keep abreast with fashion. Their terrible taste in fashion is famous. It was the first thing I had to do, to go shopping; otherwise they would not let me step into church. Last thing, we are impolite. We can't greet properly and we don't respect elders. In brief, we are barbarian. I did my best to destroy as many stereotypes as was possible.

REFERENCES

Abebe, Z. (2004): Ethnic Politics and the Question of Cultural Right and Participatory Development in Siltie, Ethiopia: Some Preliminary Hypotheses. *Ethiopian Journal of the Social Sciences and Humanities* 2 (1): 123–139.

Abraham, A. (1975): The Pattern of Warfare and Settlement among the Mende of Sierra Leone in the Second Half of the Nineteenth Century. *Kroniek van Afrika* 2 (5): 121–40.

Adam, H. and Ford, R. (1998): *Removing Barricades in Somalia: Option for peace and Rehabilitation.* Washington D.C.: United States Institute for Peace.

Adam, M. H. (1983): Language, National Consciousness and Identity – the Somali experience. In: Lewis, I.M. (ed.): *Nationalism & Self-Determination in the Horn of Africa.* London: Ithaca Press.

Adams, T. K. (1999): The New Mercenaries and the Privatization of Conflict. *Parameters* (Summer 1999): 103–16.

Adato, M.; Carter, M.R. and May, J. (2006): Exploring Poverty Traps and Social Exclusion in South Africa using Qualitative and Quantitative Data. *Journal of Development Studies* 42 (2): 226–247.

Adebajo, A. (2002): *Building Peace in West Africa: Liberia, Sierra Leone, and Guinea-Bissau.* Boulder: Lynne Rienner.

Adeye, M.O. (2000): *Gestaltung einer angepassten Berufsausbildung, Klein(st)gewerbe- und Handwerksförderung für die westafrikanischen frankophonen Länder am Beispiel des „Quartier Latin" Afrikas: Die Republik Benin.* Kassel: Verlag Institut für Arbeitswissenschaft Kassel Universität – Gesamthochschule Kassel.

African Eye News Service (2009): 'Murder Charges Don't Stick', *News 24* (18 March). Online: http://www.news24.com/News24v2/Components/Generic?News24v2 (20 March 2009).

Ahmed, I. I. and Green, R. H. (1999): The heritage of war and the state collapse in Somalia and Somaliland: local-level effects, external interventions and reconstructions. *Third World Quarterly* 20 (1): 113–127.

Aidoo, A. A. (1977): Order and Conflict in the Asante Empire: A Study in Interest Group Relations. *African Studies Review* 20 (1): 4–36.

al-Azmeh, Aziz [' Azòmah, ' Azīz]. (2003): *Ibn Khaldūn: an Essay in Reinterpretation.* Budapest: CEU Press.

Alie, J.A.D. (2008): Reconciliation and traditional justice: tradition-based practices of the Kpaa Mende in Sierra Leone. In: Huyse, L. and Salter, M.: *Traditional Justice and Reconciliation After Violent Conflict: Learning from African Experiences.* Stockholm: International Institute for Democracy and Electoral Assistance. Online: http://www.idea.int/publications/traditional_justice/upload/Traditional_Justice_and_Reconciliation_after_Violent_Conflict.pdf (18 April 2009)

Allen, G. and Brennan, F. (2004): *Tourism in the New South Africa: Social Responsibility and the Tourist Experience.* London & New York: I. B. Tauris.

Allen, T. (2006): *Trial Justice: The International Criminal Court and the Lord's Resistance Army* London: Zed Books.

Almanach Luso-Africano, Anuário Ultramarino, year 1899, Paris-Lisbon-Cape Verde

Andrade, M. Pinto de (1998): *Origens do Nacionalismo Africano.* Lisbon: Dom Quixote.

Anjos, J. C. dos (2005): O nascimento da tradição cabo-verdiana e de sua cultura política sob enfoque sociológico. *Revista de Estudos Cabo-verdianos,* No.0, Praia: Universidade de Cabo Verde.

AP – Associated Press (March 2, 2009): A look at Guinea-Bissau's history of instability.

Apollos, F. M. and A. A. Yakubu (1999): Revitalizing Traditional African Approaches to Peacebuilding and Reconciliation during Armed Conflict. A panel discussion paper at the All Africa Conference on African Principles of Peace and Reconciliation. Addis Ababa: United Nations Conference Centre.

Appel, M. (2008): *Poverty in South Africa 'is declining'.* Online: http://www.sarpn.org.za/ documents/d0000990/ (18 April 2009).

Apter, A. (2003): IBB+419. Nigerian Democracy and the Politics of Illusion. In: J.L. Comaroff and J. Comaroff (eds.) *Civil Society and the Political Imagination in Africa,* pp.267–308. Chicago: University of Chicago Press.

Apter, D. (1955): *The Gold Coast in Transition.* Princeton, Princeton University Press.

Apter, D. (1961): *The Political Kingdom in Uganda: A Study in Bureaucratic Nationalism.* Princeton: Princeton University Press.

Apter, D. (1963): *Ghana in Transition.* New York: Athenaeum.

Apter, D. (1965): *The Politics of Modernization.* Chicago: Chicago University Press.

Apter, D. (1966): Ghana. In: Coleman, James S., Rosberg, Carl G. (eds.), *Political Parties and National Integration in Tropical* Africa, pp. 259–315. Berkeley and Los Angeles: University of California Press.

Armond, L. De. (1951): Justo Sierra O'Reilly and Yucatecan-United States Relations, 1847–1848. *Hispanic American Historical Review* 31: 420–436.

Armstrong, M. (2007): Private Military Companies. In: Weber, J.A. and Eliasson, J. (eds.): *Handbook of Military Administration,* pp. 161–190. London: CRC Press.

Artiletra, year 9, No. 34/35, Praia, June-July 2000; year 13, No. 59/60, Praia, October 2004.

Asante, R. (2006): Local Factors that Shapes the 2004 General Elections in the Ejura-Sekyeumase, Mampong and Effiduase-Asokore Constituencies. In: Boafo-Arthur, K. (ed.): *Voting for Democracy in Ghana: the 2004 Elections in Perspective vol. 2,* pp. 331–356. Accra: Freedom Publications.

Asante, R. and Gymiah-Boadi, E. (2004): *Ethnic Structure, Inequality and Governance of the Public Sector in Ghana.* UNRISD.

Atmore, A. and Marks, S. (1974): The Imperial Factor in South Africa in the Nineteenth Century: Towards a Reassessment. *Journal of Imperial and Commonwealth History* 3 (1).

Avant, D. (2000): From Mercenary to Citizen Armies. *International Organization* 54 (1): 41–72.

Ayenew, M. (2007): A Rapid Assessment of Wereda Decentralization in Ethiopia. In: Assefa, T. and Gebre-Egziabher, T. (eds.): *Decentralization in Ethiopia*, pp. 69–102. Addis Ababa: Forum for Social Studies.

Azikiwe, N. (1957): *The Development of Political Parties in Nigeria.* London.

Bagley, R. (ed.) (2001): *Ancient Sichuan: Treasures from a Lost Civilization.* Princeton, NJ: Seattle Art Museum and Princeton University Press.

Bähre, E. (2005): How to Ignore Corruption: Reporting Shortcomings of Development in South Africa. *Current Anthropology* 46 (1): 107–120.

Baines, E. (2005): *Roco Wat I Acoli: Restoring Relationships in Acholi-land: Traditional Approaches to Justice and Reintegration.* Liu Institute for Global Issues, Gulu District NGO Forum and Ker Kwaro Acholi. Online: http://www.ligi.ubc.ca/?p2=modules/liu/publications/view.jsp&id=16 (18 April 2009).

Baines, G. (2009): *The Politics of Public History in Post-Apartheid South Africa.* Online: http://academic.sun.ac.za/history/news/baines_g.pdf (4 April 2009).

Bakewell, P.J. (2004): *A History of Latin America: c. 1450 to the Present*, 2nd ed. London: Blackwell Publishing.

Balsvik, R.R. (2003): The quest for expression: The state and University in Ethiopia under three regimes, 1952–2002. International Conference on Ethiopian Studies, University of Hamburg, July 20–25.

Bass, L. (2004): *Child Labor in Sub-Saharan Africa.* Boulder: Lynne Rienner Publishers.

Batibo, H. M. (2005): *Language Decline and Death in Africa. Causes, Consequences and Challenges.* Clevedon: Multilingual Matters Ltd.

Bayart, J.-F. (1993): *The State in Africa. The Politics of the Belly.* Harlow: Longman.

Bayart, J.-F., Ellis, S. and Hibou, B. (1998): *The Criminalization of the State in Africa.* Oxford: James Currey for the International African Institute.

Bayly, C. A. (1990): *Indian Society and the Making of the British Empire.* Cambridge: Cambridge University Press.

Behrend, H. and Luig, U. (eds.) (1999): *Spirit Possession: Modernity and Power in Africa.* Madison: University of Wisconsin Press.

Bennett, E. (ed.) (1999): *Child soldiers in Southern Africa.* ISS Monograph Series No. 37. Pretoria: Institute for Security Studies. Online: http://www.iss.co.za/index.php?link_id=3&slink_id=491&link_type=12&slink_type=12&tmpl_id=3 (18 April 2009)

Bennett, G. (1957): The Development of Political Organisations in Kenya. *Political Studies* 2 (5): 415–433.

Bergère, Marie-Claire. (1998): *Sun Yat-sen*, trans. Janet Lloyd. Stanford, CA: Stanford University Press.

Berhanu, K. (2007): Decentralization, Local Government and Federalism in Ethiopia. In: Berhanu, K.; Olika, T.; Kefale, A. and Erega, J. (eds.): *Electoral Politics, Decentralized Governance and Constitutionalism in Ethiopia*, pp. 33–65. Addis Ababa: Addis Ababa University.

Bernales, E. B. (1997): *Report on the Question of the Use of Mercenaries as a Means of Violating*

Human Rights and Impeding the Exercise of the Right of Peoples to Self-determination. Geneva: United Nations.

Beshir, M. O. (1972): *The Mercenaries and Africa.* Khartoum, Sudan: Khartoum University Press.

Beyme, K. von (1985): *Political Parties in Western Democracies.* Gower: Aldershot.

Blacking, J. and Byron, R. (eds.) (1995): *Music, Culture and Experience: Selected Papers of John Blacking.* Chicago: University of Chicago Press.

Blondel, J. (1978): *Political Parties: A Genuine Case for Discontent.* London: Wildwood House.

Blum, W. (2004): Killing *Hope: US Military and CIA Interventions Since World War II.* London: Zed Books.

Boafo-Arthur, Kwame (2001): Chieftaincy and Politics in Ghana since 1982. *West Africa Review* 3, 1.

Boddy, J. (1989): *Wombs and Alien Spirits: Women, Men and the Zar Cult in Northern Sudan.* University of Wisconsin Press: Milwaukee.

Boege, V. (2006): Traditional Approaches to Conflict Transformation – Potentials and Limits, in Bloomfield, D.; M. Fischer and B. Schmelzle (eds.): *The Berghof Handbook for Conflict Transformation.* Berghof Research Center for Constructive Conflict Management. Online: http://www.berghof-handbook.net/uploads/download/boege_handbook.pdf (16 August 2006).

Boesche, R. (2002): *The First Great Political Realist: Kautilya and his Arthashastra.* Lanham, MD: Lexington Books.

Boletim Oficial de Cabo Verde, No. 26 dated 29 June 1867; No. 4 dated 22 January 1870; No. 15 dated 10 April 1875.

Bowles, S.; Durlauf, S.N. and Hoff, K. (2006): *Poverty Traps.* New York: Russell Sage Foundation.

Bradbury, M. Yusuf, A. and Yusuf, H. A. (2003): Somaliland: Choosing Politics over Violence. *Review of African Political Economy* 30 (September): 462–473.

Bradshaw, R. (2007): Mercenaries: 1750–2000. In: Sterns, P. (ed.): *Encyclopedia of Modern World History.* Oxford: Oxford University Press.

Bradshaw, R. and Ndzesop I. (2008): African Armies and Warfare, 1750–1914. In: Overfield, J.H. (ed.): *World History Encyclopedia, Vol. 15: Age of Revolutions.* Santa Barbara, CA: ABC-Clio.

Bradshaw, R. and Ndzesop I. (n. d.): *Mercenaries, Military Manpower and State-Building in Precolonial Africa.* Forthcoming.

Bratton, M. and Van de Walle, N. (1997): *Democratic Experiments in Africa.* Cambridge: Cambridge University Press.

Briedenhann, J. and Wickens, E. (2004): Rural tourism – meeting the challenges of the new South Africa. *International Journal of Tourism Research* 6 (3): 189–203.

Briggs, L.P. (1949): The Appearance and Historical Usage of the Terms Tai, Thai, Siamese and Lao. *Journal of the American Oriental Society* 69 (2): 60–73.

Brito-Semedo, M. and Morais, J. (eds.) (2008): *Pedro Cardoso. Textos jornalísticos e literários. Parte I,* Praia: Instituto da Biblioteca Nacional e do Livro.

Brooks, S. (2005): Images of 'Wild Africa': nature tourism and the (re)creation of Hluhluwe game reserve, 1930–1945. *Journal of Historical Geography* 31 (2): 220–240.

Brown, Duncan (2001): National Belonging and Cultural Difference. South Africa and the Global Imaginary. *Journal of Southern African Studies* 27(4): 758–769.

Brown, M. (2007): *Adventuring through Spanish Colonies: Simón Bolívar, Foreign Mercenaries and the Birth of New Nations.* Liverpool: Liverpool University Press.

Bulcha, M. (1988): *Flight and Integration: Causes and Mass Exodus from Ethiopia and Problem of Integration in the Sudan.* Uppsala: Scandinavian Institute of African Studies.

Burr, R. (2006): *Vietnam's Children in a Changing World.* New Brunswick, NJ: Rutgers University Press.

Burton, W. L. (1998): *Melting Pot Soldiers: the Union's Ethnic Regiments.* New York: Fordham University Press.

Butcher, J. (2007): *The Moralisation of Tourism: Sun, Sand Saving the the World?* Taylor and Francis eBook.

Cabral, J. (1947): *Memórias e Reflexões,* Praia: s.e.

Cady, J.F. (1964): *Southeast Asia: Its Historical Development.* New York: McGraw Hill.

Callaway, B. (1974): National-Local Linkages in Ghana. *The African Review* (Nairobi) 4 (3): 407–421.

Carr, C. (1995): *The Devil Soldier: The American Soldier of Fortune Who Became a God in China.* New York: Random House.

Carreira A. and Fyfe, Ch. (1982): *The People of Cape Verde Islands: Exploitation and Emigration.* London: C. Hurst & Co.

Carreira, A. (1985): Secas e fomes em Cabo Verde (Achegas para o estudo das Ilhas de 1845–1846 e 1889–1890), *Revista da História Económica e Social,* Lisboa, No.15, p. 135–150.

Carreira, A. (2000): *Cabo Verde. Formação e extinção de uma Sociedade Escravocrata (1460–1878).* Praia: Estudos e Ensaios.

Carter, G. (ed.) (1962). *African One-Party States.* Ithaca: Cornell University Press.

Carter, M.R., May, J. (1999): Poverty, Livelihood and Class in Rural South Africa. *World Development* 27 (1): 1–20.

Cassanelli, L. V. (1982): *The Shaping of Somali Society. Reconstructing the History of Pastoral Peoples, 1600–1900.* Philadelphia: University of Pennsylvania.

Cerulo, K. A. (1997): Identity Construction: New Issues, New Directions. *Annual Review of Sociology* 23: 385–409.

Chabal, P. (2003): *Amílcar Cabral. Revolutionary Leadership and People's War.* 2nd edition. Lawrenceville: Africa World Press.

Chabal, P. (2009): Africa. *The Politics of Suffering and Smiling.* London: Zed Books.

Chabal, P. et al. (2002): *A History of Postcolonial Lusophone Africa.* London: Hurst & Company.

Chabal, P. et al. (2002): *A History of Postcolonial Lusophone Africa.* Bloomington: Indiana University Press.

Chabal, P. and Daloz, J.-P. (1999): *Africa Works. Disorder as Political Instrument.* Oxford: James Currey for the International African Institute.

Chabal, P., Feinman, G. and Skalník, P. (2004): Beyond States and Empires: Chiefdoms and Informal Politics. *Social Evolution and History* 3 (1): 22–40.

Charmes, J. and Oudin, X. (1994): Formation sur le tas dans le secteur informel. In: Hugon, P.; Gaud, M. and Penouil, M. (dir.): *Crises de l'éducation en Afrique. Afrique contemporaine, numéro spécial* 172: 230–237.

Cheney, K. (2007): *Pillars of the Nation: Child Citizens and Ugandan National Development.* Chicago: University of Chicago Press.

Chilcote, R. H. (1973): *Emerging Nationalism in Portuguese Africa. Documents.*

Coleman, J. (1958): *Nigeria, Background to Nationalism.* Los Angeles: University of California.

Coleman, J. S. and Rosberg, C. G. (eds.) (1966): *Political Parties and National Integration in Tropical Africa.* Berkeley and Los Angeles: University of California Press.

Comaroff, J. and Comaroff, J. (eds.) (1993): *Modernity and Its Malcontents: Ritual and Power in Postcolonial Africa.* Chicago: University of Chicago Press.

Contini, P. (1971): The Evolution of Blood-Money for Homicide in Somalia. *Journal of African Law* 15 (1): 77–84.

Corntassel, J. J. (2003): Who is Indigenous? "Peoplehood" and Ethnonationalist Approaches to Rearticulating Indigenous Identity. *Nationalism and Ethnic Politics,* 9 (1), p.75–100

Curtin, P.; Feierman S.; Thompson L., and Vansina J. (1978): *African History.* London: Longman.

Dagafa, A. (2008): *The Scope of Rights of National Minorities under the Constitution of the Federal Democratic Republic of Ethiopia.* Addis Ababa: Addis Ababa University.

Dahl, R. (1971): *Polyarchy: Participation and Opposition..* New Haven, Conn.: Yale University Press.

Dahl, R. (1995): *Demokracie a její kritici.* Praha: Victoria Publishing.

de Kadt, E. (1990): *Making the Alternative Sustainable. Lessons from Development for Tourism.* Institute of Development Studies, Discussion Paper 272. University of Sussex.

Degennar, J. (1991): Nations and Nationalism: The Myth of a South African Nation. *IDASA Occasional Paper* 40.

Dempsey, G. (2002): *Napoleon's Mercenaries: Foreign Units in the French Army under the Consulate and the Empire, 1799–1814.* London: Greenhill Books.

Denov, M. (2007): *Is the Culture Always Right? The Dangers of Reproducing Gender Stereotypes and Inequalities.* Coalition to Stop the Use of Child Soldiers Website. Online: http:// www.child-soldiers.org/psycho-social/Gender_stereotypes_and_inequalities_2007. pdf (16 August 2006).

Department of Economic Affairs and Tourism (1996): *White Paper on the Development and*

252

Promotion of Tourism in South Africa. Pretoria.

Devauges, R. (1982): Le neveu et l'apprenti. In: Deblé, I. and Hugon, P. (dir.): *Vivre et survire dans les villes africaines*, pp. 208–217. Paris: Presses Universitaires de France, Paris.

Diffie, B. W. and Winius, G. D. (1977): *Foundations of the Portuguese Empire, 1415–1850*. Minneapolis: University of Minnesota Press.

Dirar, U. C. (2000): The Issue of Nationalities in Eritrean and Ethiopian Constitutions: a Historical Perspective. In: Piergigli, V. and Taddia, I. (eds.): *International Conference on African Constitutions*, pp. 223–246. Torino: G. Giappichelli Editore.

Docherty, P. (2008): *The Khyber Pass: A History of Empire and Invasion*. New York: Union Square Press.

Dondolo, Mthimkhulu, L. (n. d.): *Democratization of Museums in Post-Apartheid South Africa: A Case Study of Three Museums in South Africa*. Online: http://www.maltwood.uvic. ca/cam/activities/past_conferences/Papers_pdf/Dondolo.bio.abst2(2).pdf (4 April 2009).

Doorne, S.; Ateljevic I. and Bai, Z. (2003): Representing Identities Through Tourism: Encounters of Ethnic Minorities in Dali, Yunnan Province, People's Republic of China. *International Journal of Tourism Research* 5(1): 1–11.

Dougherty, B. K. (2004): Searching for Answers: Sierra Leone's Truth & Reconciliation Commission, *African Studies Quarterly* 8 (1): 39–56. Online: http://web.africa.ufl.edu/ asq/v8/v8i1a3.htm (18 April 2009).

Duarte, D. A. (2003): *Bilinguismo ou diglossia?*. Praia: Spleen Edições.

Duarte, M. (1999): *Caboverdianidade e Africanidade*. Praia: Spleen Edições.

Dunlay, T. W. (1982): *Wolves for the Blue Soldiers: Indian Scouts and Auxiliaries with the United States Army, 1860–90*. Lincoln: University of Nebraska Press.

Dunn, J. P. (1996): *Neo-Mamluks: Mercenary Talent and the Failure of Leadership in the Army of Khedive Ismail (1863–1879)*. Ph.D. Dissertation. University of Florida.

Dunn, J. P. (2005): *Khedive Ismail's Army*. New York: Taylor & Francis.

Dunnigan, J. (2008): Russian Mercenaries over Africa. *Strategy Page* (21 June 2008). Online: http://www.strategypage.com.

Duval-Arnould, C. and Martinot-Lagarde, P. (1994): Apprentis des villes africains. *Études* 380 (5): 601–610.

Duverger, M. (1978): *Political Parties. Their Organization and Activity in the Modern State*. Translated by Barbara and Robert North with a Foreword by D. G. Brogan. London, Methuen & Co Ltd.

Dvořáková, V. and Kunc, J. (1994): *O přechodech k demokracii*. Praha: Sociologické nakladatelství.

Dvořáková, V. and Kunc, J. (1996): *Rozštěp historika a politologa*. In: Acta Universitatis Carolinae – Philosophica et Historica 3, pp.133–145. East, Roger, Joseph, Tany (eds.) (1993): *Political Parties of Africa and the Middle East*. Essex: Longmann Group, U.K

Echenberg, M. J. (1991): *Colonial Conscripts: the Tirailleurs Sénégalais in French West Africa*,

1857–1960. Portsmouth, NH: Heinemann; London: J. Currey.

Edgerton, R. B. (2002): *Africa's Armies: from Honor to Infamy: a History from 1791 to the Present.* Boulder, CO: Westview Press.

Ellis, S. (1999): The New Frontier of Crime in South Africa. In: Bayart, J.-F. Ellis, S. and Hibou, B.: *The Criminalization of the State in Africa,* pp. 49–68. Oxford: James Currey.

Englund, H. (2002): Winning Elections, Losing Legitimacy: Multi-Partyism and the neo-liberal state in Malawi. In: M. Cowan and L. Laaso (eds.) *Multi-Party Elections in Africa,* pp.172–186. Oxford: James Currey.

Epstein, L.D. (1967): *Political Parties in Western Democracies.* London: Pall Mall Press.

Eriksen, T. H. (2002): *Ethnicity and Nationalism. Anthropological Perspectives.* Second Edition. London: Pluto Press.

Ezera, Kalu (1960): *Constitutional Development in Nigeria.* Cambridge: Cambridge University Press.

Fambul Tok (2008): *Fambul Tok. Community Healing in Sierra Leone. Project Summary.* Unpublished Document.

Farah, D. (1997): Mercenaries at Work for Mexico's Drug Families; Traffickers Hire Foreigners to Train Private Militias in Face of Reform Efforts, Officials Say. *The Washington Post* (30 October 1997).

Farwell, B. (1989): *Armies of the Raj from the Great Indian Mutiny to Independence: 1858–1947.* New York: W.W. Norton & Co.

Fassin, D. (2008): The Embodied Past. From Paranoid Style to Politics of Memory in South Africa. *Social Anthropology* 16(3): 312–28.

Faure, G. O. (2000): Traditional Conflict Management in Africa and China. In: Zartman, W.I. (ed.): *Traditional Cures for Modern Conflicts: African Conflict "Medicine",* pp.153 – 165. Boulder: Lynne Rienner.

Fauré, Y.-A. and Labazée, P. (2000): Le Petit Entrepreneuriat tel qu'en lui-même. Caractéristiques d'ensemble, dynamiques de création et de diversification. In: Fauré, Y.A. and Labazée, P. (dir.): *Petits patrons africains. Entre l'assistance et le marché,* pp. 249–299. Paris: Éditions Karthala.

Feinstein, A. (2007): *After the Party: A Personal and Political Journey Inside the ANC.* Johannesburg: Jonathan Ball Publishers.

Ferguson, J. (1999): *Expectations of Modernity: Myths and Meanings of Urban Life on the Zambian Copperbelt.* University of California Press: Berkley and Los Angeles.

Fiala, P. and Strmiska, M. (1998): *Teorie politických stran.* Brno: Barrister & Principal.

Fiala, V. (1984): *Dějiny portugalských kolonii v Africe.* Unpublished M.A. thesis. Olomouc, Filozofická fakulta.

Fiala, V. (1987): *Některé otázky formování avantgardních stran pracujících (MPLA-PT, Strana Frelimo, WPE.)* In: *Vědecká zasedání a zprávy z výzkumu,* pp. 59–97. Vol. 3, Praha: Orientální ústav ČSAV.

Fiala, V. (1989a): The Countries with Socialist Orientation: Sub-Saharan Africa. Some Critical Remarks on Bourgeois Political Science. In: *Current Problems in Africa,* pp.

7–32. Prague: Oriental Institute.

Fiala, V. (1989b): Ideologie MPLA a FRELIMO v období boje za nezávislost (1956–1975). *Nový Orient* 44 (3): 1–8 (supplement).

Fiala, V. (1989c): *Formování avantgardních stran pracujících v Angole, Mosambiku a Etiopii.* Unpublished CSc. Dissertation. Praha: Orientální ústav ČSAV.

Fiseha, A. (2006): Theory versus Practice in the Implementation of Ethiopia's Ethnic Federalism. In: Turton, D. (ed.): *Ethnic Federalism. The Ethiopian Experience in Comparative Perspective*, pp. 131–164. Oxford: James Currey.

Fiseha, A. (2007): *Federalism and the Accommodation of Diversity in Ethiopia. A Comparative Study.* Revised Edition. Nijmegen: Wolf Legal Publishers.

Fisher, T. and Sriram, M.S. (2002): *Beyond Microcredit: Putting Development back into Microfinance.* New Delhi: Vistaar Publications; Oxford: Oxfam Publishing.

Fisiy, C.F. (1995): Chieftaincy in the Modern State: An Institution at the Crossroads of Democratic Change. *Paideuma* 41: 49–62.

Fokwang, J. (2005): Tribal Innovators? Traditional Leadership and Development in Africa. *Codesria Bulletin* 3–4: 41–43.

Fokwang, J. (2009): *Mediating Legitimacy: Chieftaincy and Democratization in Two African Chiefdoms.* Bamenda: Langaa RPCIG.

Forrest, A. (1989): *Conscripts and Deserters: The Army and French Society during the Revolution and Empire.* Oxford: Oxford University Press.

Forrest, A. (2008) : L'armée de l'an ii: la Levée en Masse et la Création d'un Mythe Républicaine. *Annales Historiques de la Révolution Française* 335: 1–11. Online: http://ahrf.revues.org.

Foucault, M. (1978): *History of Sexuality.* New York: Penguin.

Fourcade, B.; Paul, J.-J. and Verničres, M. (1994): L'insertion professionnelle dans les pays en développement: concepts, résultats, problčmes méthodologiques. *Revue Tiers Monde* 35 (140): 725–750.

Francis, D. J. (ed.) (2005): *Civil Militia: Africa's Intractable Security Menace?* Burlington, VT: Ashgate.

Frempong, A. K. D. (2001): Ghana's Election 2000: The Ethnic Undercurrents. In: Ayee, J. R. A. (ed.): *Deepening Democracy in Ghana: Politics of the 2000 Elections,* pp. 141—159. Accra: Freedom Publications Ltd.

Frempong, A. K. D. (2006): Etnicity, Democracy and Ghana's Election 2004. In: Boafo-Arthur, K. (ed.): *Voting for Democracy in Ghana: the 2004 Elections in Perspective vol. 1.* pp. 157–186. Accra: Freedom Publications.

Frempong, A. K. D. (2007): Political Conflict and Elite Consensus in the Liberal State. In: Boafo-Arthur, K. (ed.): *Ghana: One Decade of the Liberal State,* pp. 128–164. London: Zed Books.

Gat, A. (2006): *War in Human Civilization.* Oxford: Oxford University Press.

Gbla, O. (2003): Conflict and Postwar Trauma Among Child Soldiers in Liberia and Sierra Leone. In: Sesay, A. (ed.): *Civil Wars, Child Soldiers and Post Conflict Peace Building in West Africa.* College Press Publishers.

Geertz, C. (1983): Centres, Kings and Charisma: Reflections on the Symbolics of Power. In: Geertz, C., *Local Knowledge. Further Essays in Interpretive Anthropology,* pp.121–146. New York: Basic Books.

Gellner, E. (1997): *Nationalism.* London: Weidenfeld & Nicolson.

Gerhards, T. (2002): Difficulties and Prospects of Vocational Education in Africa – MISEREOR's Experiences. In: Imunde, L. (ed.): *Visionen für das Bildungssystem in Afrika. Reflections on Education Systems in Africa,* pp. 235–256. Rehburg-Loccum: Evangelische Akademie Loccum.

Gernet, J. (1996): *A History of Chinese Civilization.* Cambridge: Cambridge University Press.

Glasser, I. (1994): *Homelessness in Global Perspective.* New York: G.K. Hall.

Gommans, J. L. J. (1995): *Horse-traders, Mercenaries and Princes: the Formation of the Indo-Afghan empire in the Eighteenth century.* Leiden; New York: E.J. Brill.

Gommans, J. L. J. (1999): *The Rise of the Indo-Afghan Empire, c. 1710–1780.* Delhi: Oxford University Press.

Good, K. (1997): Accountable to Themselves: Predominance in Southern Africa. *Journal of Modern African Studies* 35 (4): 547–573.

Gordin, J. (2008): *Zuma: A Biography.* Johannesburg: Jonathan Ball.

Gordon (1969): Scarf and Sword: Thugs, Marauders and State Formation in Eighteenth Century Malwa. *Indian Economic and Social History Review* 6: 403–430.

Gould, R. (1995): *Mercenaries of the Napoleonic Wars.* Brighton: Tom Donovan Publishing.

Graff, D. A. and Higham R.D.S. (2002): *A Military History of China.* Boulder, CO: Westview Press.

Green, C. (2001): *Manufacturing Powerlessness in the Black Diaspora.* Walnut Creek: AltaMira Press.

Gudina, M. (2006): Contradictory Implementations of Ethiopian History: the Need for a New Consensus. In: Turton, D. (ed.): *Ethnic Federalism. The Ethiopian Experience in Comparative Perspective,* pp. 119–130. Oxford: James Currey.

Gudina, M. (2009a): interview, Addis Ababa, 30 Jan 2009.

Gudina, M. (2009b): interview, Addis Ababa, 5 Sep 2009.

Gunner, L. (2009): Jacob Zuma, the Social Body and the Unruly Power of Song. *African Affairs* 1008 (430): 27–48.

Gupta, A. (1995): Blurred Boundaries: The Discourse of Corruption, the Culture of Politics and the Imagined State, *American Ethnologist* 22 (2): 375–402.

Gyebi, E. (2009): NPP ministers are a bunch of thieves – JJ. *Ghanaian Chronicle* 7 April 2009. Online: http://www.modernghana.com/news/210183/1/npp-ministers-are-a-bunch-of-thieves-jj.html (15 April 2009)

Gyimah-Boadi, E. (ed.) (2004): *Democratic Reform in Africa. The Quality of Progress.* Boulder and London: Lynne Rienner Publisher.

Hack, K. and T. Rettig. (2006): Demography and Domination in Southeast Asia. In:

Hack K. and T. Rettig (eds.): *Colonial Armies in Southeast Asia,* pp. 39–73. London: Routledge.

Hall, D.G.E. (1958): *A History of Southeast Asia.* London: Macmillan.

Hall, M. C. and Tucker, H. (2004): Tourism and Postcolonialism. An Introduction. In: Hall, M. C. and Tucker, H. (eds.) *Tourism and Postcolonialism.* London and New York: Routledge, p. 1–24.

Hall, M. C. and Tucker, H. (eds.) (2004): *Tourism and Postcolonialism.* London and New York: Routledge.

Haller, D. and Shore, C. (2006): Introduction. In: Haller, D. and Shore, C. (eds.), *Corruption: Anthropological Perspectives,* pp. 1–26. London: Pluto.

Haller, D. and Shore, C. (eds.) (2006): *Corruption: Anthropological Perspectives.* London: Pluto.

Halpern, B. (2001): *David's Secret Demons: Messiah, Murderer, Traitor, King.* Grand Rapids, MI: William B. Eeerdmans.

Hamilton, N. L. (1975): Mexico: The Limits of State Autonomy. *Latin American Perspectives* 2 (2): 81–108.

Hamilton-Merritt, J. (1993): *Tragic Mountains: The Hmong, the Americans, and the Secret Wars for Laos, 1942–1992.* Bloomington: Indiana University Press.

Harry J. L. (1990): Lineage Feuding in Southern Fujian and Eastern Guangdong under Qing Rule. In: Lipman J.N. and Albany H.S. (eds.): *Violence in China: Essays in Culture and Counterculture,* pp. 71–64. State University of New York Press.

Hasbrouck, A. (1969): *Foreign Legionaries in the Liberation of South America.* New York: Octagon Books.

Haskin, J. M. (2005): *The Tragic State of the Congo. From Decolonization to Dictatorship.* New York: Algora Publishing.

Henze, P. B. L. (2001): *Layers of Times: A History of Ethiopia.* London: Hurst& Company.

Herselman, S. and Van Heerden, M.E. (2003): *'Getting the job done': Work performance and related issues of selected members of [an insurance company].* Pretoria: Unpublished Research Report.

Hess R. L. (1964): The 'Mad Mullah' and the Northern Somalia. *Journal of African History* 3 (1): 415–433.

Hill, R. A. (ed.) (1987): *The Marcus Garvey and Universal Negro Improvement Association Papers, Volume V, September 1922–August 1924.* Berkeley: University of California Press.

Hill, R. and Hogg P. (1994): *A Black Corps d'Elite. An Egyptian-Sudanese Battalion with the French Army in Mexico, 1863–1867.* East Lansing, MI: Michigan State University Press.

History Matters (2008): 'Julius Malema is a Child of the ANC', *History Matters* (20 June 2008). Online: http://historymatters.co.za/2008/06/20/ julius-malema-is-a-child-of-the-anc (4 May 2009).

Hlatswayo, R. (2003): 'Rapist Politician to Learn His Fate', *Africa Eye News Service* (7 July).

Online: http://www.accessmylibrary.com/cosite5/bin/aml-landingtt.pl?purchase-type+ITM&it (7 May 2009).

Hlatswayo, R. (2008): 'Mayor held for two murders', *The Sowetan* (11 April). Online: http://www.sowetan.co.za/News/Article.aspx?id=746150 (8 May 2009).

Hlatswayo, R. (2009): 'Cops Forced Me to Implicate Mayor', *The Sowetan* (25 March).

Hloušek, V. and Kopeček L. (eds.) (2004): *Demokracie. Teorie, modely, osobnosti, podmínky, nepřátelé a perspektivy demokracie.* Brno: Mezinárodní politologický ústav Masarykovy univerzity.

Hobsbawm, E. and T. Ranger (eds.) (1983): *The Invention of Tradition.* Cambridge: Cambridge University Press.

Hodgkin, T. (1961): *African Political Parties. An Introductory Guide.* Baltimore: Penguin Books Ltd.

Hoehne, M. V. (2007): *Puntland and Somaliland clashing in Northern Somalia: Who cuts the Gordian Knot?* New York: Social Science Research Council.

Hoff, K. and Sen, A. (2006): The Kin System as a Poverty Trap. In: Bowles, S.; Durlauf, S.N. and Hoff, K. (eds.): *Poverty Traps,* pp. 95–115. New York: Russell Sage Foundation.

Hoffman, D. (2003): Like Beasts in the Bush: Synonyms of Childhood and Youth in Sierra Leone. *Postcolonial Studies* 6 (3): 295–308.

Hoffman, E. (2008): Reconciliation in Sierra Leone: Local Processes Yield Global Lessons. *The Fletcher Forum of World Affairs* 32 (2): 129–141.

Højbjerg, C. K. (2007): *Resisting State Iconoclasm among the Loma of Guinea.* Durham, NC: Carolina Academic Press.

Hollinshead, K. (2004): Tourism and new sense. Wordmaking and the enunciative value of tourism. In Hall, M. C. and Tucker, H. (eds.): *Tourism and Postcolonialism,* pp. 25–42. London and New York: Routledge.

Holmquist, F.; Weaver, F. and Ford, M. (1994): The Structural Development of Kenya's Political Economy. *African Studies Review* 31: 69–107.

Honwana, A. (2006): *Child Soldiers in Africa.* Philadelphia: University of Pennsylvania Press.

Hooper, N. and Bennett, M. (eds.) (1995): *The Cambridge Illustrated Atlas of Warfare.* New York: Cambridge University Press.

Horáková, H. (2002): *Predicament of Culture in the New South Africa.* Unpublished paper presented at the 7th Biennial Conference of the European Association of Social Anthropologists, Copenhagen 14–17 August 2002.

Horáková, H. (2006): Africká renesance – mýtus nebo realita? In: Machalík, T. and Záhořík, J. (eds.): *Viva Africa 2006,* pp. 113–128. Plzeň: Dryada.

Horáková, H. (2007a): *Národ, kultura a etnicita v postapartheidní Jižní Africe.* Hradec Králové: Gaudeamus.

Horáková, H. (2007b): Zulu Nation: Ethnicity and Politics. In Machalík, T. and Záhořík, J. (eds.): *Viva Africa 2007,* pp. 113–125. Plzeň: Dryada.

Horáková, H. (2008): „Rasa" a rasismus v Jižní Africe. *Sociální studia* 4/2007: 113–129.

Horowitz, D. L. (2000): *Ethnic Groups in Conflict*. Berkeley: University of California Press.

Horton, M. C. and Middleton J. (2000): *The Swahili: the Social Landscape of a Mercantile Society*. Oxford, UK; Malden, Mass.: Blackwell Publishers.

Horwitz, R.B. (2001): *Communication and Democratic Reform in South Africa*. Cambridge: Cambridge University Press.

Hountondji, P.J. (2000): Construire l'Autosuffisance. L'économie béninoise, d'hier à demain. In: Hountondji, P.J. (dir.): *Économie et société au Bénin. D'hier à demain*, pp. 181–253. Paris/Montréal: L'Harmattan.

Hounyè, E.D. (1997): *Les Contraintes de l'Apprentissage en Milieu Urbain: Cas des Coiffeuses à Cotonou*. Mémoire de Maîtrise de Socio-Anthropologie. Faculté des Lettres, Arts et Sciences Humaines (FLASH), Département de Philosophie et de Socio-Anthropologie. Abomey-Calavi: Université Nationale du Bénin.

Howden, D. (3 March 2009): President shot dead in palace as rebel troops take revenge. *Independent*.
http://www.independent.co.uk/news/world/africa/president-shot-dead-in-palace-as-rebel-troops-take-revenge-1635904.html

Hubbell, A. (2001): A View of the Slave Trade from the Margin: Souroudougou in the Late Nineteenth Century Slave Trade of the Niger Bend. *Journal of African History* 42: 24–47.

Hughes, A. and Perfect, D. (2008): *Historical Dictionary of Gambia*. Lanham, MD: Scarecrow Press.

Hughes, H. (2004): *What is remembered and what forgotten: a decade of redefining culture and heritage for tourism in South Africa*. The paper presented at the Conference on Developing Cultural Tourism, the University of Nottingham, December 2003. Online: http://www.nottingham.ac.uk/ttri/pdf/conference/Heather %20Hughes.pdf (4 April 2009).

Huntington, S. (1991): *The Third Wave: Democratisation in the Late Twentieth Century*. Norman: Oklahoma University Press.

Huntington, S. (2001): *Střet civilizací. Boj kultur a proměna světového řádu*. Přeložili Michael Žantovský a Ladislav Nagy. Praha: Rybka Publishers, Stanford: Hoover Institution Press.

Hyle, M. and Bosio, J.-L. (2002): L'enseignement technique agricole au Bénin: histoire, actualité et perspectives. *Agridoc* 3. Online: http://www.agropolis.fr/formation/pdf/2002_Bosio_Hyle_Agridoc_3.pdf (27 February 2009).

Iliffe, J. (2005): *Honor in African History*. New York: Cambridge University Press.

International Crisis Group (2003): *Somaliland: Democratization and its Discontents*. Brussels: IGC. Online: http://www.crisisgroup.org/home/index.cfm?id=1682&l=1

International Crisis Group, Africa Report No. 153, *Ethiopia: Ethnic Federalism and Its Discontents*, 4 September 2009.

Irchin, J. (1981): Efiopiya: na puti k sozdaniyu avantgardnoy partii trudiashchikhsya.

Afrika i Aziya Segodnya 6: 60–61.

Iria, A. (1979): *Judeus em Moçambique, Angola e Cabo Verde: epigrafia e história.* Lisboa s.e.

Isaacman, A. and Isaacman, B. (1977): Resistance and Collaboration in Southern and Central Africa, c. 1850–1920. *The International Journal of African Historical Studies* 10 (1): 31–62.

Isaacman, A. and Rosenthal, A. (1984): War, Slaves and Economy: the Nineteenth-century Chikunda Expansion in South Central Africa. *Cultures et Développement* 16 (3–4): 639–670.

Ismagilova, R. (2000): Ethnicity in Africa and the Principles of Solving Ethnic Problems in the Constitutions. In: Piergigli, V. and Taddia, I. (eds.): *International Conference on African Constitutions,* pp. 205–219. Torino: G. Giappichelli Editore.

James, A. (2007): Giving Voice to Children's Voices: Practices and Problems, Pitfalls and Potentials. *American Anthropologist* 109 (2): 261–272.

Johnson, S.; Hulme, D. and Ruthven, O. (2005): Finance and Poor People's Livelihoods. In: Green, C.J.; Kirkpatrick, C.H. and Murinde, V. (2005): *Finance and Development: Surveys of Theory, Evidence and Policy,* pp. 277–303. Cheltenham, UK, Northhampton MA Edward Elgar.

Kail, B. (2003): Une sélection insidieuse: les savoirs scolaires dans l'apprentissage f Bamako. *Cahiers d'Études Africaines* XLIII (1–2): 279–298.

Kaplan, S. (2008): The Remarkable Story of Somaliland. *Journal of Democracy.*4 (1): 143–157.

Katz, R. S. (2001): The Problem of Candidate Selection and Models of Party Democracy. *Party Politics* 7: (3): 277–296.

Keen, D. (2005): *Conflict and Collusion in Sierra Leone.* Oxford: Palgrave Macmillan.

Kefale, A. (2003): Federalism and Self-Determination: Some Observations on the Ethiopian Experience. In: Olika, T.; Arsano, Y. and Aaland, O. (eds.): *Topics in Contemporary Political Development in Ethiopia. Towards Research Agenda in the Framework of DPSIR-NIHR Research Programme (1998–2003),* pp. 1–22. Addis Ababa: Addis Ababa University.

Keller, E. J. and Rothchild, D. (1987): *Afro-Marxist Regimes. Ideology and Public Policy.* Boulder & London: Lynne Rienner Publisher.

Kelsall, T. (2005): Truth, Lies and Ritual: Preliminary Reflections on the Truth and Reconciliation Commission in Sierra Leone. *Human Rights Quarterly* 27: 361–391.

Khalidi, O. (1997): The Hadhrami Role in the Politics and Society of Colonial India, 1750s to 1950s. In: Clarence-Smith, W.G. and Freitag, U. (eds.): *Hadhrami Traders, Scholars, and Statesmen in the Indian Ocean, 1750s–1960s,* pp. 67–81. Leiden: Brill.

Kielland, A. and Tovo, M. (2006): *Children at Work: Child Labor Practices in Africa.* London: Lynne Rienner.

Kilbride, P. (November 2008): Kenya Elections: Local Level Observations from the Field. American Anthropological Association Annual Meeting, San Francisco, CA.

Kilbride, P.; Suda, C. and Njeru, E. (2001): *Street Children in Kenya: Voices of Children in*

Search of a Childhood. Westport, CT: Bergin and Garvey.

Killingray, D. and Omissi, D. (eds.) (1999): *Guardians of Empire: The Armed Forces of the Colonial Powers c. 1700–1964*. New York: Manchester University Press.

Kleeman, T. F. (2002): Ethnic Identify and Daoist Identity in Traditional China. In: Kohn, L. (ed.): *Daoist Identity: History, Lineage, and Ritual*, pp. 23–38. Honolulu: University of Hawaii Press.

Klein, M. A. (1972): Social and Economic Factors in the Muslim Revolution in Senegambia. *The Journal of African History* 13 (3): 419–441.

Klein, N. (2007): *The Shock Doctrine*. London: Penguin Books.

Kleinman, A. and Good, B. (1985): *Culture and Depression: Studies in the Anthropology and Cross-Cultural Psychiatry of Affect and Disorder*. Berkeley: University of California Press.

Klíma, J. (2002a): Sláva a úpadek Ribeiry Grande (Splendor and Decay of Ribeira Grande). *Historický obzor*, No. 9–10, Praha, p. 215–219.

Klíma, J. (2002b): Kapverdští sokolové ve 30. letech 20. století, *Východočeské listy historické*, Hradec Králové: Gaudeamus, No.19–20, p. 225–242.

Klíma, J. (2003): Sokols de Cabo Verde nos anos trinta do século XX. *Ibero-Americana Pragensia*, ano XXXVI – 2002, p.185–198.

Klíma, J. (2005): *Guinea-Bissau*. Praha: Libri (Stručná historie států).

Klíma, J. (2005a): *Salazar tichý diktátor*. Praha: Aleš Skřivan ml.

Klíma, J. (2007): *Dějiny Portugalska v datech*. Praha: Libri

Klíma, J. (2008): *Kapverdské ostrovy. Svatý Tomáš a Princův ostrov*. Praha: Libri (Stručná historie států).

Klíma, J. and Vítek, J. (2002): *Kapverdy znovu objevené*. Hradec Králové: Paradise Studio.

Klíma, J. and Vítek, J. (2003): *Kapverdské ostrovy. Historie a georeliéf*. Hradec Králové: Gaudeamus.

Koknar, A. (2003): Russian Mercenaries at War in the Balkans. *Bosnian Institute*, 14 July 2003.

Kolff, D. H. (2002): *Naukar, Rajput & Sepoy: the Ethnohistory of the Military Labour Market in Hindustan, 1450–1850*. Cambridge: Cambridge University Press.

Koliopoulos, J. (1987): *Brigands with a Course: Brigandage and Irredentism in Modern Greece, 1821–1912*. Oxford: Clarendon Press.

Kovats-Bernat, J. Ch. (2006): *Sleeping Rough in Port-au-Prince: An Ethnography of Street Children and Violence in Haiti*. Gainesville, FL: University of Florida Press.

Kümmel, G. (2006): A Soldier is a Soldier is a Soldier! The Military and Its Soldiers in the Era of Globalization. In: Caforio, G. (ed.): *The Handbook of the Sociology of the Military*, pp. 417–436. New York, NY: Kluwer Academic/Plenum Publishers.

Kumsa, A. (2006): Přehled socio-politického vývoje Etiopie od poloviny 19. století do současnosti. In: Machalík, T. and Záhořík, J. (eds.): *Viva Africa 2006. Sborník příspěvků z konference věnované Africe*, pp. 21–30. Ústí nad Labem: Dryada.

Künzler, D. (2004): *Wo die Elefanten tanzen, leidet das Gras. Staat und Entwicklung in Afrika*.

Münster: Lit Verlag.

Künzler, D. (2007): *L'éducation pour quelques-uns? Enseignement et mobilité sociale en Afrique au temps de la privatisation: le cas du Bénin.* Paris: L'Harmattan.

Künzler, D. (2008): "The State Has Resigned." Transformations in the Educational System of Benin, West Africa. In: Machalík, T.; Mildnerová, K. and Záhořík, J. (eds.): *Viva Africa 2008. Proceedings of the IIIrd International Conference on African Studies,* pp. 251–262. Plzeň: ADELA Publishing.

Kuper, A. (1999): *Culture: The Anthropologists' Account.* Cambridge, Mass: Harvard University Press.

L'Estrange, W.D. (1884): *Under Fourteen Flags: the Life and Adventures of Brigadier-General MacIver, A Soldier Of Fortune.* 2 Vols. London: Tinsley; reprinted 2008 by Kessinger Publishing Company.

Labazée, P.; Akaffou, D.I. and Gnamien, G. (2000a): Situation et tendances du secteur privé. Mutations ivoiriennes. In: Fauré, Y.-A. and Labazée, P. (dir.): *Petits patrons africains. Entre l'assistance et le marché,* pp. 77–126. Paris: Éditions Karthala.

Labazée, P.; Guichaoua, Y. and Niango, A. (2000b): Les dispositions d'appui au secteur privé ivoirien. Configuration d'ensemble. In: Fauré, Y.-A. and Labazée, P. (dir.): *Petits patrons africains. Entre l'assistance et le marché,* pp. 177–244. Paris: Éditions Karthala.

Lamphear, J. (2005): Sub-Saharan African Warfare. In: Black, J. (ed.): *War in the Modern World Since 1815,* pp. 169–191. London: Routledge.

Lamphear, J. (ed.) (2007): *African Military History.* Burlington: Ashgate.

LaPalombara, J. and Weiner, M. (eds.) (1966): *Political Parties and Political Development.* Princeton: Princeton University Press.

Lapping, B. (1989): *Apartheid: A History.* George Braziller: New York.

Le Mon, Ch. J. (2007): Rwanda's Troubled Gacaca Courts. *Human Rights Brief* 14 (2): 16–20. Online: http://www.wcl.american.edu/hrbrief/14/2lemon.pdf?rd=1 (18 April 2009)

Le Vine, V. T. (1964): *The Cameroon: From Mandate to Independence.* Berkeley and Los Angeles: University of California Press.

Le Vine, V. T. (2004): *Politics in Francophone Africa.* Boulder, London: Lynne Rienner Publishers.

Lechner, J. C. (1990): *Textos y Documentos: 46 Congreso Internacional de Americanistas Amsterdam Holanda 1988.* Amsterdam: Centre for Latin American Research and Documentation.

Lederach, J.P. (1997): *Building Peace. Sustainable Reconciliation in Divided Societies.* United States Institute of Peace Press.

Lee, M. A. (1999): *The Beast Reawakens: Fascism's Resurgence from Hitler's Spymasters to Today's Neo-Nazi Groups and Right-Wing Extremists.* London: Routledge.

Leo, C. (1984): *Land and Class in Kenya.* Toronto: University of Toronto Press.

Lepp, A. and Harris, J. (2008): Tourism and National Identity in Uganda. *International Journal of Tourism Research* 10 (6): 525–536.

Levine, D. (1974): *Greater Ethiopia. The Evolution of Multi-Ethnic Society.* Chicago: The University of Chicago Press.

LeVine, R. (2007): Ethnographic Studies of Childhood: A Historical Overview. *American Anthropologist* 109 (2): 247–261.

Lewis, G. (1981): *The Day of Shining Red: An Essay on Understanding Ritual.* Cambridge: Cambridge University Press.

Lewis, H. S. (2001): *Jimma Abba Jifar: An Oromo Monarchy.* Lawrenceville, NJ: Red Sea Press.

Lewis, I. M. (1958): Modern Political Movements in Somaliland. *Africa* 28 (3–4): 344–363.

Lewis, I. M. (1999): *A Pastoral Democracy. A Study of Pastoralism and Politics among the Northern Somali of the Horn of Africa.* London: James Currey Publishers.

Lewis, I. M. (2002): *A Modern History of the Somali Revised.* Oxford: James Currey.

Lewis, S. H. (1966): The Origins of the Gala and Somali. *The Journal of African History* VII (1): 27–46.

Liebenow, J. G. (1986): *African Politics. Crisis and Challenges.* Bloomington: Indiana University Press.

Ligan, A.A.F. (1997): *Un exemple de petit métier urbain: la coiffure à Cotonou.* Mémoire de Maîtrise. Faculté des Lettres, Arts et Sciences Humaines (FLASH), Département de Géographie et d'Aménagement du Territoire. Abomey-Calavi: Université Nationale du Bénin.

Lillywhite, M. (1991): *Low Impact Tourism on a Strategy for Sustaining Natural and Cultural Resources in Sub-Saharan Africa.* Washington D.C: USAID.

Lindberg, S. I. (2008): *The Rise and Decline of Parliament of Ghana.* University of Florida.

Linek, L. and Outlý, J. (2005): Výběr kandidátů do Evropského parlamentu v hlavních českých politických stranách. *Politologický časopis* 12 (1): 3–26.

Linz, J. (2000): *Totalitarian and Authoritarian Regimes. With a Major New Introduction.* Boulder & London: Lynne Rienner Publisher.

Lipset, S. M. and Rokkan, S. (1967): *Party System and Voters Alignments: Cross-National Perspectives.* New York: The Free Press

Lloyd, Peter (1955): The Development of Political Parties in Western Nigeria. *American Political Science Review* 48 (3): 693–707.

Lomnitz, C. (1995): Ritual, Rumour and Corruption in the Constitution of Polity in Mexico. *Journal of Latin American Anthropology* 1 (1): 20–40.

Lonsdale, J. (1985): The European Scramble and Conquest in African History. In: Oliver, R. and Sanderson, G.N. (eds.): *The Cambridge History of Africa from 1870 to 1905.* Cambridge Histories Online: Cambridge University Press.

Lopes, J. V. (1996): *Cabo Verde. Os bastidores da independência,* Praia-Mindelo: Spleen Edições.

Lovejoy, P. E. (2000): *Transformations in Slavery: A History of Slavery in Africa.* Cambridge, UK; New York: Cambridge University Press.

Lovell, D. (2005): Corruption as a Transitional Phenomenon: Understanding Endemic Corruption in Post-Communist States. In: Haller, D. and Shore, C. (eds.), *Corruption: Anthropological* Perspectives, pp. 65–82. London: Pluto.

Low, D. A. (1962): *Political Parties in Uganda, 1949–1962*. London: Athlone Press.

Low, D.A. (1975): Warbands and Ground-level Imperialism in Uganda, 1870–1900. *Australian Historical Studies* 16 (65): 584–597.

Lynch, J. (2006): *Simon Bolívar: A Life*. New Haven, CT: Yale University Press.

MacCarthy, F. (2002): *Byron: Life and Legend*. London: John Murray.

Mackenzie, S. P. (1997): *Revolutionary Armies in the Modern Era: A Revisionist Approach*. London: Routledge.

Mainwaring, S. and Scully, T. R. (1995): *Building Democratic Institutions. Party Systems in Latin America*. Stanford University Press.

Maldonado, C. (1998): *Secteur Informel: Fonctions macro-économiques et politiques gouvernementales. Le cas du Bénin*. Document de recherche S-INF-1-18. Genève: Organisation Internationale du Travail.

Málek, J. (1992): *In the Shadow of the Pyramids: Egypt during the Old Kingdom*. Norman: University of Oklahoma Press, pp. 98–99.

Maluleke, E. (1995): Sex Scandal: Girl Speaks. *City Press* (27 August).

Mamdani, M. (2001): *When Victims Become Killers. Colonialism, Nativism, and the Genocide in Rwanda*. Oxford: James Currey.

Manifesto 99 (2002): Traditional Methods of Conflict Management/Resolution of Possible Complementary Value to the Proposed Sierra Leone Truth and Reconciliation Commission. Unpublished Report for the OHCHR in Sierra Leone.

Marcum, J. (1969): *The Angolan Revolution. Volume 1. The Anatomy of an Explosion (1950– 1962)*. Cambridge, Massachusetts, and London: The M.I.T. Press.

Marcum, J. (1978): *Angolan Revolution. Volume 2. Exile Politics and Guerrila Warfare (1962– 1976)*. Cambridge, Massachusetts, and London: The M.I.T. Press.

Maré, G. (1993): *Ethnicity and Politics in South Africa*. London: Zed Books.

Markakis, J. (1987): *National and Class Conflict in the Horn of Africa*. Cambridge: Cambridge University Press.

Markakis, J. (2006): *Ethiopia. Anatomy of a Traditional Polity*. Addis Ababa: Shama Books.

Marks, S. (1985): Southern Africa, 1867–1886. In: Oliver, R. A.; Fage, J. D. and Sanderson, G. N. (eds.): *The Cambridge History of Africa, Volume 6: from 1870–1905*, pp. 359–421. Cambridge: Cambridge University Press.

Marquez, P (1999): *The Street is My Home: Youth and Violence in Caracas*. Stanford, CA: Stanford University Press.

Marschall, S. (2004): Commodifying Heritage: Post-apartheid Monuments and Cultural Tourism in South Africa. In: Hall, M. C. and Tucker, H. (eds.): *Tourism and Postcolonialism*, pp. 95–112. London and New York: Routledge.

Masinga, S. (2008a) 'Murder: Mayor to Stand Down', *African Eye News* (22 April). Online: http://www.news24.com/News24/South_Africa/News/0,,2-7-1442_2310441,00.

html (28 April 2008).

Masinga, S. (2008b) 'Death be upon you!-ANCL' (2 October) *SAShopper*. Online: http://www.sashopper.iblog.60.3a/2008/10/02/death-be-upon-you-ancyl (4 May 2009).

Masinga, S. and Mnisi, O. (2008): 'Bail hearing gets out of hand' *African Eye* (14 April). Online: http.www. news24.com/News24/South_Africa/News/0,,2-7-1442_2305814,00.html (16 April 2008).

Mavhunga, C. (2003): Firearms Diffusion, Exotic and Indigenous Knowledge Systems in the Lowveld Frontier, South Eastern Zimbabwe 1870-1920. *Comparative Technology Transfer and Society* 1 (2): 201–231.

May, R.E. (1991): Young American Males and Filibustering in the Age of Manifest Destiny: The United States Army as a Cultural Mirror. *The Journal of American History* 78 (3): 857–886.

May, R.E. (2002): *Manifest Destiny's Underworld: Filibustering in Antebellum America*. Chapel Hill: University of North Carolina Press.

Mazrui, Ali A. (1975): The Resurrection of the Warrior Tradition in African Political Culture. *The Journal of Modern African Studies* 13 (1): 67–84.

Mbigi, L. (1992): Unhu or ubuntu: The Basis for Effective HR Management. *People Dynamics*: 20–26.

McCord, E. A. (1993): *The Power of the Gun: The Emergence of Modern Chinese Warlordism*. Berkeley: University of California Press.

McFarland, A. D. (1887): The Employment of Indian Auxiliaries in the American War. *The English Historical Review* 2 (8): 709–728.

Mehlum, H.; Moene, K. and Torvik, R. (2006): Parasites. In: Bowles, S.; Durlauf, S.N. and Hoff, K. (2006): *Poverty Traps,* pp.95–115. New York: Russell Sage Foundation.

Meintel, D. (1984): *Race, Culture and Portuguese Colonialism in Cape Verde*. New York: Syracuse University Press.

Meixel, R. (2006): American Exceptionalism in Colonial Forces? In: Karl, H. and Rettig T. (eds.): *Colonial Armies in Southeast Asia,* pp. 171–194. London: Routledge.

Mendonsa, E.L. (2002): *West Africa: An Introduction to its History, Civilization and Contemporary Situation*. Durham, NC: Carolina Academic Press.

Mennasemay, M. (2003): Federalism, Ethnicity, and the Transition to Democracy. *Horn of Africa* 21: 88–114.

Menzies, G. (2004): *1421 – the Year China Discovered America*. New York: Harper, Perennial.

Meunier, O. (2001): *Formation, organisation du travail et maintenance dans les entreprises en Afrique subsaharienne. Anthropologie des techniques dans les P.M.I./P.M.E. du Niger*. Paris et al.: L'Harmattan.

Mhlanga, B. (2008a): 'The Mayor's Skeletal Closet'. *The Amazwi Villager* (5 May). Online: http://issuu.com/amazwi_villager/docs/issue05/3?mode=a_p (4 April 2009).

Mhlanga, B. (2008b) 'The Mayor's Skeletal Closet closed, to be opened again', *The Amazwi Villager* (6 June). Online: http://issuu.com/amazwi_villager/docs/

issue06?mode=a_p (4 April 2009).

Mhlanga, B. (2008c) 'An Anti-Morema March'. *The Amazwi Villager* (15 August). Online:http://amazwivillager.org/?p=166 (5 May 2009).

Middleton, J.; Zidermann, A. and Van Adams, A. (1993): *Skills for Productivity: Vocational Education and Training in Developing Countries*. Oxford et al.: Oxford University Press.

Mockler, A. (1987): *The New Mercenaries: The History of the Hired Soldier from the Congo to the Seychelles*. New York: Paragon House Publishers.

Mohamed, A. (2008): *The Human Rights Provisions of the FDRE Constitution in Light of the Theoretical Foundations of Human Rights*. Addis Ababa: Addis Ababa University.

Mohane, H.; Coetzee, G. and Grant, W. (2002): The Effects of the Interest Rate Ceilings on the Micro Lending Market in South Africa. Working Paper: 2002: 2. Pretoria: University of Pretoria, Department of Agricultural Economics, Extension and Rural Development.

Mokgope, K. (1998): *Rural Women and Politics: The Case of Rooiboklaagte B, Northern Province, South Africa*. Unpublished MA thesis. Durban: Department of Social Anthropology: University of Durban-Westville.

Mondlane, E. (1983): *Struggle for Mozambique*. 2nd Edition. London: Zed Press.

Moran, D. (2003): Introduction: The Legend of the Levée En Masse. In: Moran, D. and Waldron, A. (eds.): *The People in Arms: Military, Myth and National Mobilization since the French Revolution*, pp. 1–7. Cambridge: Cambridge University Press.

Morema, M.J. (2008): *Speech for the Official Opening of Bushbuckridge Local Municipality Council*. Online: http://www.bushbuckridge.gov.za (4 May 2009).

Morgenthau, R. S. (1964): *Political Parties in French-Speaking West Africa*. Oxford: Clarendon Press.

Morse, R. M. (Ed.) (1965): *The Bandeirantes: The Historical Role of the Brazilian Pathfinders*. New York: Knoft.

Morton, W.S. and Lewis, C.M. (2005): *China: Its History and Culture*. New York: McGraw-Hill Professional.

Moyo, S.; Musona, D.; Mbhele, W.T. and Coetzee, G. (2002): Use and Impact of Savings Services among Low Income People in South Africa. *Micro-Save Africa*. Nairobi: 1–24.

Musah, A-F and Fayemi, J. (2000): *Mercenaries: an African Security Dilemma*. London: Pluto Press.

Naumann, J. and Wolf, P. (2002): Formale und informelle Formen beruflicher Bildung in Senegal. In: Wiegelmann, U. (ed.): *Afrikanisch – europäisch – islamisch? Entwicklungsdynamik des Erziehungswesens in Senegal,* pp. 249–279. Frankfurt a.M.: IKO – Verlag für Interkulturelle Kommunikation.

Nduka, O. (2006): Rebisi Kingdom of Port Harcourt. Port Harcourt: Nduks Printing Limited

Nduru, M. (2004): The Age of Mercenaries Not Over in Africa. *Inter Press Service* (15 September 2004), pp.1–3, *Antiwar.com*, www.antiwar.com.

Negussie, S. (2008): *Fiscal Federalism in the Ethiopian Ethnic-based Federal System*. Revised Edition. Nijmegen: Wolf Legal Publishers.

Ness, G.D. and Stahl, W. (1977): Western Imperialist Armies in Asia. *Comparative Studies in Society and History* 19 (1): 2–29.

Neumann, S. (ed.) (1956): *Modern Political Parties. Approaches to Comparative Politics*. Chicago: University Press

Newitt, M. D. D. (2004): *A History of Portuguese Overseas Expansion, 1400–1668*. London: Routledge.

News 24. (2009) *Special Elections Report*. Online: http://www.news24.com/News24/Elections/Home (5 May 2009).

Ngwane, G. (1996): *Settling Disputes in Africa. Traditional Bases for Conflict Resolution*. Yaounde: Bumakor.

Nicolini, B. (2006): The Makran-Baluch-African Network in Zanzibar and East Africa during the XIXth Century. *African & Asian Studies* 5 (3–4): 347–370.

Niehaus, I. (2005): Violence and the Boundaries of Belonging: Comparing Two Border Disputes in the South African Lowveld. In: Vigdis Broch-Due (ed.), *Violence and Belonging: The Quest for Identity in Post-colonial* Africa, pp. 91–111. London and New York: Routledge.

Niehaus, I. (2006): Doing Politics in Bushbuckridge: Work, Welfare and the South African Elections of 2004. *Africa* 76 (4): 521–548.

Niehaus, I. with Mohlala, E. and Shokane, K. (2001): *Witchcraft, Power and Politics: Exploring the Occult in the South African Lowveld*. London: Pluto.

Norris, E. G. and Heine, P. (1982): Genealogical Manipulations and Social Identity in Sansanne Mango, Northern Togo: an 'Imâm'-List and the Qasîda of ar-Ra 'îs Bâdîs. *Bulletin of the School of Oriental and African Studies, University of London* 45 (1): 118–137.

Novák, M. (1997): *Systémy politických stran. Úvod do jejich srovnávacího studia*. Praha: Sociologické nakladatelství.

Ntahombaye, P.; A. Ntabona; J. Gahama and L. Kagabo, (eds.) (1999): *The Bashingantahe Institution in Burundi. A Pluridisciplinary Study*. Bujumbura: University of Burundi.

Nugent, P. (2001): Winners, Losers and Also Rans: Money, Moral Authority and Voting Patterns in the Ghana 2000 Elections. *African Affairs* 100: 405–428.

Nugent, P. (2004): *Africa since Independence*. New York: Palgrave Macmillan.

O'Donnell, G. (1994): Defective Democracy. *Journal of Democracy* 5 (1): 55–69.

Obeyesekere, G. (1981): *Medusa's Hair*. Chicago: University of Chicago Press.

Odegi-Awuondo, C.; Namai, H. and Mutsotso, B. (1994): *Masters of Survival*. Nairobi: Basic Books.

Ogot, B.A. and Ochieng, W. R. (1996): *Decolonization and Independence in Kenya, 1940–93*. Athens, Ohio: Ohio University Press.

Öhman, M. (2004): *Heart and Soul of the Party Candidate Selection in Ghana and Africa*. Uppsala: Uppsala University Press.

Oke, E.A.S. (1999): *L'enseignement au Bénin: Les réformes et leur impact sur la formation des jeunes de 1960 à 1990.* Mémoire de Maîtrise. Département d'Histoire et d'Archéologie. Abomey-Calavi: Université Nationale du Bénin.

Oliveira, J. Nobre de (1998): *A Imprensa Cabo-Verdiana,* Praia: s.e.

Oliver, R. (1963): Discernable Developments in the Interior c. 1500–1840. In: Oliver, R. and Gervase, M. (eds.): *History of East Africa, Vol. 1*, pp. 209–221. Oxford: Oxford University Press.

Olivier de Sardan, J.P. (1999): A Moral Economy of Corruption in Africa? *Journal of Modern African Studies* 37 (1): 25–52.

Olukoshi, A. O. (ed.): *The Politics of Opposition in Contemporary Africa.* Uppsala: Nordiska Afrinainstitutet.

Ortner, S. (2003): *New Jersey Dreaming: Capital, Culture and the Class of '58.* Durham, NC: Duke University Press.

Ortner, S. (2006): *Anthropology and Social Theory: Culture, Power, and the Acting Subject.* Durham, NC: Duke University Press.

Osaghae, E. (2000): Applying Traditional Methods to Modern Conflict: Possibilities and Limits, In: Zartman, W.I. (ed.): *Traditional Cures for Modern Conflicts: African Conflict "Medicine",* pp. 201–217. Boulder: Lynne Rienner.

Ottaway, D. and Ottaway, M. (1981): *Afrocommunism.* New York, Africana Publishing Co.

Panter-Brick, C. (2002): Street Children, Human Rights, and Public Health: A Critique and Future Directions. *Annual Reviews Anthropology* 31: 147–171.

Para-Mallam, O. J. (2006): Faith, gender and development agendas in Nigeria: conflicts, challenges, and opportunities. *Gender & Development* 14 (3): 409–421

Parry, J. (2000): The 'crisis of corruption' and 'the idea of India': A worm's eye view. In: I. Pardo (ed.), *The Morals of* Legitimacy, pp.27–35. New York: Berghahn Books.

Parsons, T. H. (1996): *East African Soldiers in Britain's Colonial Army: a Social History, 1902–1964.* Ph.D. Dissertation. Johns Hopkins University.

Paul, J.-J. (1990): Technical Secondary Education in Togo and Cameroon. *Economics of Education Review* 9 (4): 405–409.

Paul, J.-J. and Vernières, M. (1994): L'insertion professionnelle et la formation en cours d'emploi. In: Hugon, P.; Gaud, M. and Penouil, M. (dir.): *Crises de l'éducation en Afrique. Afrique contemporaine, numéro spécial* 172: 203–215.

Pearce, S.; Spiro A.G. and Buckley, P.E. (2001): Introduction. In: Pearce, S.; Spiro A.G. and Buckley, P.E. (eds.): *Culture and Power in the Reconstitution of the Chinese Realm, 200-60,* pp. 1–32. Cambridge, MA: Harvard University Asia Center.

Peers, C.J. and McBride A. (1990): *Ancient Chinese Armies 1500-200 BC.* Oxford: Osprey Publishing.

Pellow, D. and Chazan, N. (1986): *Ghana: Coping with Uncertainity.* Westview: Builder, CO.

Percy, S. (2007): *Mercenaries. The History of a Norm in International Relations.* New York: Oxford University Press.

Person, Y. (1985): Western Africa, 1870–1866. In: Oliver, R. A.; Fage, J. D. and Sanderson, G. N. (eds.): *The Cambridge History of Africa, Volume 6: c. 1870- c. 1905*, pp. 208–256. Cambridge: Cambridge University Press.

Poniatowska, E. (1999): *El Nino: Children of the Streets, Mexico City*. New York: Syracuse University Press.

Poon, A. (1994): The New Tourism Revolution. *Tourism management* 15 (2): 91–2.

Porch, D. (1991): *The French Foreign Legion*. New York: Harper Collins.

Posen, B. R. (1993): Nationalism, the Mass Army, and Military Power. *International Security* 18 (2): 80–124.

Praeg, B. (2006): *Ethiopia and Political Renaissance in Africa*. New York: Nova Science Publishers, Inc.

Price, R. (2005): *A Concise History of France*, 2nd ed. Cambridge: Cambridge University Press.

Prunier, G. (1995): *Somalia: Civil War, Intervention and Withdrawal 1990–1995*. London: REFWORLD.

Psacharopoulos, G. (1987): To Vocationalize or Not to Vocationalize? That is the Curriculum Question. In: *International Review of Education* 33 (2): 187–211.

Psacharopoulos, G. (1994): Returns to Investment in Education: A Global Update. In *World Development* 22 (9): 1325–1343.

Puntland Development Research Center (PDRC). (2002): *Pastoral Justice: A Participatory Action Research Project on Harmonization of Somali Legal Traditions*. Garowe: PDRC.

Quincy, K. (2000): *Harvesting Pa Chay's Wheat: The Hmong and America's Secret War in Laos*. Spokane: Eastern Washington University.

Rahat, G. and Hazan, R. Y. (2001): Candidate Selection Methods: An Analytical Framework. *Party Politics* 7 (3): 297–322.

Ramos, M. do Nascimento (1982): Recordar é viver. Os 50 anos dos Sokols de Cabo Verde. *Terra Nova,* 8th year, 88, S. Vicente (i. e. Mindelo), November 1982, p. 8.

Ramphele, M. (2008): *Laying Ghosts to Rest: Dilemmas of the Transformation in South Africa*. Cape Town: Tafelberg.

Randal V. and Svasand, L. (2002): Political Parties and Democratic Consolidation in Africa. *Democratization* 9 (3): 30–52.

Randall, V. (1988): *Political Parties in the Third World*. London: Sage Publications

Rasheed, M. al (1992): Durable and Non-Durable Dynasties: The Rashidis and Sa'udis in Central Arabia. *British Journal of Middle Eastern Studies* 19 (2): 144–158.

Rassool, C. (2000): The Rise of Heritage and Reconstruction of History in South Africa. *Kronos* 26: 1–22.

Raugh, H. E. (2004): *The Victorians at War, 1815–1914: An Encyclopedia of British Military History*. Santa Barbara: ABC-CLIO.

Reid, J.J. (2000): *Crisis of the Ottoman Empire: Prelude to Collapse, 1839–1878*. Stuttgart: Franz Steiner Verlag.

Reis, J. Alves dos (1984): Subsídios para o estudo da Morna, *Raízes,* No. 21, Praia

Reis, M. G. dos (1933): Os Sockols de S. Vicente, *Notícias de Cabo Verde,* Mindelo, 5 August 1933, p. 2.

Reno, W. (1995): *Corruption and State Politics in Sierra Leone.* Cambridge: Cambridge University Press.

Reuter, Dieter (1994): *Ansätze situationskonformer beruflicher Bildung in Simbabwe. Der Beitrag neuer Berufsbildungsvorhaben im unabhängigen Simbabwe zur Entwicklung angemessener Formen beruflicher Bildung.* Frankfurt a.M. et al.: Peter Lang.

Revista de Cabo Verde, No.14, Praia, September 1899

Richter, L. and Morrell, R. (2006): *Baba: Men and Fatherhood in South Africa.* Human Sciences Research Council.

Roberts, A. (2006): *The Wonga Coup: Guns, Thugs, and a Ruthless Determination to Create Mayhem in an Oil-rich Corner of Africa.* New York: Public Affairs.

Robins, S. (1999): Spicing up the Multicultural (Post-) Apartheid City. *Kronos* 25: 280–293.

Robinson, M.S. (2001): *The Microfinance Revolution: Sustainable Finance for the Poor.* Washington: The International Bank for Reconstruction and Development/The World Bank.

Rodriquez, M.E. (2006): *Freedom's Mercenaries: British Volunteers in the Wars of Independence in Latin America.* 2 vols. Lanham MD: Hamilton Books.

Rokkan, S. (1970): *Citizens, Elections, Parties.* Oslo: Universitetsforlaget.

Roosens, E. E. (1989): *Creating Ethnicity. The Process of Ethnogenesis.* Newbury Park, CA: SAGE Publications, Inc.

Rorke, D. (2008): 'MEC on Warpath'. *Lowvelder Online* (3 November). Online: http://www.lowvelder.co.za/show-story.asp?storyid=10834 (6 November 2008).

Rosberg C. G. and Callaghy T. M. (eds.) (1979): *Socialism in Sub-Saharan Africa. A New Assesment.* Berkeley: University of California Press.

Rosenfeld, H. (1965): The Social Composition of the Military in the Process of State Formation in the Arabian Desert, Part II. *The Journal of the Royal Anthropological Institute of Great Britain and Ireland* 95 (2): 174–194.

Rouveroy van Nieuwaal, E.A.B. van (2000): *L'Etat en Afrique face à la chefferie: le cas du Togo.* Paris: Karthala.

Royer, Ş. and Royer, P. (2001): *West African Challenge to Empire: Culture and History in the Volta-Bani Anticolonial War.* Athens, OH: Ohio University Press; Oxford, GB: James Currey.

Ruark, J. (2000): Seeing Children and Hearing Them, Too. *Chronicle of Higher Education,* Nov. 17, pp. 24–25.

Rurevo, R. and Bourdillon, M. (2003): *Girls on the Street.* Harare, Zimbabwe: Weaver Press.

Rustow, D. (1970): Transitions to Democracy: Towards a Dynamic Model. *Comparative Politics* 2 (3): 337–363

Rutherford, S. (2000): *The Poor and their Money. New Delhi:* Oxford University Press

Sage, Le A. (2005): *Report: Stateless justice in Somalia. Formal and Informal Rule of Law*

Initiatives. Geneva: Center for Humanitarian Dialogue.

Sahlins, M. (1985): *Islands of History*. Chicago: University of Chicago Press.

Saler, B. (1993): *Conceptualizing Religion: Immanent Anthropologists, Transcendent Natives and Unbound Categories*. E.J. Brill: Leiden.

Salih, M. M. A. (ed.) (2004): *African Political Parties. Evolution, Institutionalisation and Governance*. London: Pluto Press

Salim, A.I. (1984): The East African Coast and Hinterland 1800–1845. In: Ajayi, A. A. (ed.): *UNESCO General History of Africa, The Nineteenth Century until 1880*. Paris: UNESCO.

Samayende, S. (2003): 'Big Spender Defies Parliament to Create Slush Fund', *Africa Eye News* (7 July). Online: http://www.accessmylibrary.com/coms2/summary_0286-23742542-ITM (5 May 2009).

Sampson, A. (1999): *Mandela: The Authorized Biography*. London: Harper Collins.

Sandbrook, R. (1996): Transitions without Consolidation: Democratization in Six African States. *Third World Quarterly* 17 (1): 69–87.

Sanders, T. and West, H. (2003): Power Revealed and Concealed in the New World Order. In: H. West and T. Sanders (eds.), *Transparency and Conspiracy: Ethnographies of Suspicion in the New World* Order, pp.1–37. Durham: Duke University Press.

SarDesai, D.R. (1997): *Southeast Asia: Past and Present*. Boulder, CO: Westview Press.

Sartori, G. (1976): *Parties and Party Systems: A Framework for Analysis*. New York: Cambridge University Press.

Sartori, G. (1993): *Teória demokracie*. Bratislava: Archa.

Šavelková, L. (2007): Globalizace a původní, domorodí obyvatelé světa. In: Tomeš, J.; Festa, D.; Novotný, J. et al.: *Konflikt světů a svět konfliktů*. Praha: P3K

Saw, S.H. (1988): *The Population of Peninsular Malaysia*. Singapore: Singapore University Press.

Schapera, I. (1970): *Tribal Innovators: Tswana Chiefs and Social Change, 1795–1940*. London School of Economics Monographs on Social Anthropology no 43. London: Athlone Press.

Scheina, R.L. (2003): *Latin America's Wars: The Age of the Caudillo, 1791–1899*. Washington, DC: Brassey's.

Schlee, G. (1994): *Identities on the Move. Clanship and Pastoralism in Northern Kenya*. Nairobi: Gideon S. Wese Press.

Schraeder, P. J. (1999): *African Politics and Society*. Boston and New York: Bedford/ St. Martin's.

Schwabe, C. (2004): *Fact Sheet: Poverty in South Africa*. Online: http://www.southafrica. info/about/social/poverty-021008.htm. (18 April 2009).

Seekings, J. and Nattrass, N. (2005): *Class, Race and Inequality in South Africa*. Yale University Press.

Segal, R. (1961): *Political Africa: A Who's Who of Personalities and Parties*. New York: Praeger.

Segell, G. (1998): *Stability and Intervention in Sub-Sahara Africa.* London: G. Segell Publishers.

Semedo, J. M. and Turano, M. R. (s.d.): *Cabo Verde. O ciclo ritual das festividades da Tabanca.* Praia: Spleen Edições

Sen, A. (1999): *Development as Freedom.* New York: Alfred. A. Knopf.

Shillington, K. (1985): *The Colonisation of the Southern Tswana.* Johannesburg: Ravan Press.

Sibthorpe, A. B. C. (1906): *The History of Sierra Leone,* 3rd ed. London: Elliot Stock.

Sichone, O. (2008a): 'Xenophobia' in Shepherd, Nick and Robins, Steven (eds.) *New South African Keywords.* Johannesburg: Jacana/Athens: Ohio University Press

Sichone, O. (2008b): 'Xenophobia and xenophilia in South Africa' in Werbner, Pnina (ed.) *Anthropology and the New Cosmopolitanism.* Oxford: Berg

Silva, B. Lopes da (1934): *Estatutos dos Falcões Portugueses de Cabo Verde,* Praia: Imprensa Nacional.

Silva, F. Lopes da (1890): Júlio José da Silva. *Notícias de Cabo Verde,* Praia, 1 May 1890.

Skalník, P. (1978): Early States in the Voltaic Basin. In: Claessen, H.J.M. and Skalník, P. (eds.), *The Early State,* pp. 469–494. The Hague: Mouton Publishers.

Skalník, P. (1981): The Role of the State in the Dismantling of Ghanaian Rural Economy. *Journal of Legal Pluralism and Unofficial Law* 19: 177–188.

Skalník, P. (1983): Questioning the Concept of the State in Indigenous Africa. *Social Dynamics* 9 (2): 11–28.

Skalník, P. (1986): Nanumba Chieftaincy Facing the Ghanaian State and Konkomba 'Tribesmen': An Interpretation of the Nanumba-Konkomba War of 1981. In: Binsbergen, W. van, Reyntjens, F. and Hesseling, G. (eds.), *State and Local Community in Africa,* pp. 89–109. Bruxelles/Brussel: CEDAF/ASDOC.

Skalník, P. (1987): On the Inadequacy of the Concept of the 'Traditional State'. Illustrated with Ethnographic Material on Nanun, Ghana. *Journal of Legal Pluralism and Unofficial Law* 25 & 26: 301–325.

Skalník, P. (1988): Tribe as Colonial Category. In: Boonzaier, E. and Sharp, J. (eds.): *South African Keywords: The Uses and Abuses of Political Concept,* pp. 68–78. Cape Town: David Philip.

Skalník, P. (1989): Outwitting Ghana: Pluralism of Political Culture in Nanun. In: Skalník, P. (ed.): *Outwitting the State,* pp. 145–168. Political Anthropology 7. New Brunswick: Transaction Publishers.

Skalník, P. (1992a): Why Ghana is Not a Nation-state. *Africa Insight* 22 (1): 66–72.

Skalník, P. (1992b): Economic Parameters of an Archaic Polity: Nanun, Northern Ghana. In: De Soto, H. (ed.): *Culture and Contradiction. Dialectics of Wealth, Power, and Symbol* (Festschrift for Aidan Southall), pp. 193–199. San Francisco: Mellen Research University Press.

Skalník, P. (1996a): Authority versus Power: Democracy in Africa Must Include Original African Institutions. In: Special issue edited by E.A.B. van Rouveroy van Nieuwaal and D.I. Ray of *Journal of Legal Pluralism and Unofficial Law* 37 & 38: 109–121.

Skalník, P. (1986b): Ideological and Symbolic Authority: Political Culture in Nanun, Northern Ghana. In: Claessen, H.J.M. and Ooosten, J.G. (eds.): *Ideology and the Formation of Early States*, pp. 84–98. Leiden: Brill.

Skalník, P. (2001): Explaining the state in Africa: Bayart, Chabal and other options. In Kropáček, L and Skalník, P. (eds): *Africa 2000. Forty Year of African Studies in Prague*, pp. 145–155. Prague: Set Out

Skalník, P. (2002): The State and Local Ethnopolitical Identities (the case of community conflicts in northern Ghana). *Nouveaux Mondes* (Geneva) No.10: 141–166.

Skalník, P. (2003): Nanumba versus Konkomba: An Assessment of a Troubled Coexistence. In: Binsbergen, W. van (ed.), *The Dynamics of Power and the Rule of Law. Essays on Africa and Beyond in Honour of Emile Adriaan B. van Rouveroy van Nieuwaal*, pp. 69–78. Münster and Leiden: LIT and African Studies Centre.

Skalník, P. (2004): Chiefdom: a universal political formation? *Focaal. European Journal of Anthropology* 43: 76–98.

Skalník, P. (2007): African Political Leadership: Any Alternatives? In: Machalík, T. and Zahořík, J. (eds.): *Viva Africa 2007. Proceedings of the 2nd International Conference on African Studies*, pp. 165–176. Ústí nad Labem: Dryada.

Skalník, P. (2008): Rethinking Chiefdoms. In: Bellagamba, A. and Klute, G. (eds.): *Beside the State. Emergent Powers in Contemporary Africa*, pp. 183–192. Köln: Köppe.

Skeen, E. (2007): *The Rape Trail of Jacob Zuma: AIDS, Conspiracy and Tribalism in Neo-liberal South Africa*. Unpublished BA thesis. Department of Anthropology: Princeton University.

Sklar, R. (2004): *Nigerian Political Parties: Power in an Emergent African Nation*. New York: Africa World Press.

Sleeman, W.H. (1841): *On the Spirit of Military Discipline in our Native Indian Army*. Calcutta: Bishop's College Press.

Smith, D. (2007): *A Culture of Corruption: Everyday Deception and Popular Discontent in Nigeria*. Princeton: Princeton University Press.

Smith, K. (1983): *Alfred Aylward: The Tireless Agitator*. Johannesburg: Ad. Donker.

Smith, R. A. (1999): *Borderlander: the Life of James Kirker, 1793–1852*. Norman: University of Oklahoma Press.

Smith, R. S. (1989): *Warfare and Diplomacy in Precolonial West Africa*. Madison: University of Wisconsin Press.

Sobel, M.E. (2006): Spatial Concentration and Social Stratification. In: Bowles, S.; Durlauf, S.N. and Hoff, K. (2006): *Poverty Traps,* pp. 204–229. New York: Russell Sage Foundation.

Solodovnikov V. G., Letnev, A. B., Mancha P.I. (1970): *Politicheskie partii Afriki*. Moskva: Izdatelstvo Nauka.

South African Press Agency (SAPA) (2003): 'Ngcuka Spoke in Riddles-Expert.' *News 24* (25 October). Online: http://www.news24.com/News24/South_Africa/

Politics/0,,2-7-12_1406870,00.html (4 May2009).

South African Press Agency (SAPA) (2006): 'Shaik's desperate move to clear his name'. *Independent Online* (18 November). Online: http://www.iol.co.za/general/news/ newsprint.php?art-d=iol1163842802214B263&sf= (5 May 2009).

South African Press Agency (SAPA) (2008a): 'Zuma may take Fifth Wife. *News 24*. (10 October). Online: http://www.news24.com/News24/South_Africa/ Politics/0,,2_7_12_2772263,00.html. (4 May 2009).

South African Press Agency (SAPA) (2008b): 'Municipal manager nabbed for kidnapping'. *Pretoria News* (19 September). Online: http://www.pretorianews.co.za/? fSectionId=&f ArticleId=w20080919060255177 C329210. (28 September 2008).

Spalinger, A. J. (1974): Warfare in Ancient Egypt. In: Spitzer, L. (ed.): *A Companion to the Ancient Near East. The Creoles of Sierra Leone: Responses to Colonialism, 1870–1940.* Madison: University of Wisconsin Press.

Spitzer, L. (ed.): *A Companion to the Ancient Near East. The Creoles of Sierra Leone: Responses to Colonialism, 1870–1940.* Madison: University of Wisconsin Press.

Stark, L. (2006): Cleansing the Wounds of War: an Examination of Traditional Healing, Psychosocial Health and Reintegration in Sierra Leone. *Intervention* 4 (3): 206–218.

Statesman (15 May 2009): NPP choose flag-bearer: At National Congress in April? Online: http://www.modernghana.com/news/216558/1/npp-choose-flagbearerat-national-congress-in-april.html (17 May 2009).

Stovel, L. (2006): *Long Road Home: Building Reconciliation and Trust in Post-War Sierra Leone.* Unpublished Doctoral Dissertation. Department of Sociology and Anthropology. Simon Fraser University.

Stovel, L. (2008): 'There's No Bad Bush to Throw Away a Bad Child': Tradition-Inspired Reintegration in Post-War Sierra Leone. *Journal of Modern African Studies* 46 (2): 305–324.

Streek, B. and Wicksteed, R. (1981): *Render Unto Kaiser: A Transkei Dossier.* Johannesburg: Ravan Press.

Suda, C. A. (2007): *Formal Monogamy and Informal Polygyny in Parallel: African Family Traditions in Transition.* Inaugural Lecture.

Suda, C. A. (2007): *Formal Monogamy and Informal Polygyny in Parallel.* Nairobi: University of Nairobi Press

Sunday Times 16, (2008):8.

Swadener, B., Kabiru, M. and Njenga, A. (2000): *Does the Village Still Raise the Child?* New York: State University of New York.

Tafesse, T. (2007): *The Migration, Environment and Conflict Nexus in Ethiopia. A Case Study of Amhara Migrant-settlers in East Wollega Zone.* Addis Ababa: Organisation for Social Science Research in Eastern and Southern Africa.

Taylor, L. and Hickey, M. (2001): *Tunnel Kids.* Arizona: University of Arizona Press.

Taylor, R.M. (1995): Warriors, Tributaries, Blood Money and Political Transformation in Nineteenth-Century Mauritania. *The Journal of African History* 36 (3): 419–441.

Taylor, L. D. (1986): The Great Adventure: Mercenaries in the Mexican Revolution, 1910–1915. *The Americas* 43 (1): 25–45.

Tegenu, T. (2006): *Evaluation of the Operation and Performance of Ethnic Decentralization System in Ethiopia. A Case Study of the Gurage People, 1992–2000.* Addis Ababa: Addis Ababa University.

Teshome, W. and Záhořík, J. (2008): Federalism in Africa: Ethnic-Based Federalism in Ethiopia. *International Journal of Human Sciences* 5: 2–39.

The Miami Herald. http://www.miamiherald.com/news/world/AP/story/928307.htm

The Open Society Initiative for West Africa and AfriMap (2007): *Ghana: Democracy and Political Participation.* Johannesburg: The Open Society Initiative for West Africa.

Thomas, G. S. (1984): *Mercenary Troops in Modern Africa.* Boulder, CO: Westview Press.

Thomson, J. E. (1996): *Mercenaries, Pirates, and Sovereigns: State-Building and Extraterritorial Violence in Early Modern Europe.* Princeton: Princeton University Press.

Thornton, J. K. (1996): The African Background to American Colonization. In: Engerman, S. M. and Gallman, R. E. (eds.): *The Cambridge Economic History of the United States,* pp. 53–94. Cambridge: Cambridge University Press.

Thornton, J. K. (1999): *Warfare in Atlantic Africa, 1500–1800.* New York: Routledge and London: UCL Press.

Todaro, M.P. (2000): *Economic Development* 7th edition. Harlow: Pearson Education.

Tomás, A. (2007): *O Fazedor de Utopias. Uma biografia de Amílcar Cabral,* Lisboa: Tinta da China.

Tong, J. W. (1991): *Disorder under Heaven: Collective Violence in the Ming Dynasty.* Stanford, CA: Stanford University Press.

Topik, S. C. (1998): Mercenaries in the Theatre of War: Publicity, Technology and the Illusion of Power during the Brazilian Naval Revolt of 1893. In: Joseph, G. M.; LeGrand, C. and Donato R. S. (eds.): *Close Encounters of Empire: Writing the Cultural History of U.S.-Latin American Relations (2nd edition),* pp. 173–207. Durham, NC: Duke University Press.

Touval, S. (1963): *Somali Nationalism. International Politics and the drive for unity in the Horn of Africa.* Cambridge, Massachusetts: Harvard University press.

University of Sierra Leone in cooperation with the German Adult Education Association DVV (1991): Training Opportunities in the Informal sector of Freetown in Sierra Leone. A Research Study. *Supplement to Adult Education and Development* 37.

Urban, W. (2007): *Bayonets for Hire: Mercenaries at War 1550–1789.* London: Greenhill Books.

Uyar, M. and Erickson, E. J. (2009): *A Military History of the Ottomans: From Osman to Ataturk.* Santa Barbara: Praeger Security International/ABC-CLIO.

Van der Beken, C. (2003): *The Ethiopian Federal State Structure and the Accommodation of Ethnic Diversity: a View from the Southern Nations, Nationalities and Peoples Region.* Gent: Gent University.

Vandervort, B. (1998): *Wars of Imperial Conquest in Africa, 1830–1914.* Bloomington:

Indiana University Press.

Vansina, J. (1990): *Paths in the Rainforest: Toward a History of Political Tradition in Equatorial Africa.* Madison: University of Wisconsin Press.

Venter, A. (1998): Questions of National Identity in Post-Apartheid South Africa. *Occasional Papers.* Johannesburg: Konrad-Adenauer-Stiftung.

Venter, A. (2006): *War Dog: Fighting other People's Wars -The Modern Mercenary in Combat.* Havertown, PA: Casemate.

Verdirame, G. (2000): Human Rights and African Constitutions: Some Observations. In: Piergigli, V. and Taddia, I. (eds.): *International Conference on African Constitutions,* pp. 109–118. Torino: G. Giappichelli Editore.

Vysockaja, N.I., Geveling, L.V. and Kosuchin, N.D. (eds.) (1998): *Politicheskie partii sovremennoy Afriki.* Moscow: Vostočnaja literatura RAN.

Ware, A. (1996): *Political Parties and Party Systems.* Oxford: Oxford University Press

Watts, M. (2008): Sweet and Sour. In: Watts, M. and Kashi, E. (eds.): *Curse of the Black Gold,* pp. 37–47. New York: PowerHouse Books

Werner, C. (2000): Gifts, Bribes and Development in Post-Soviet Kazakhstan. *Human Organisation* 59 (1): 11–22.

Wesseling, H.L. (2004): *The European Colonial Empires 1815–1919.* Harlow, UK: Pearson Education.

Wheeller, B. (1991): Tourism's Troubled Times. Responsible Tourism is not the Answer. *Tourism Management* 12 (2): 91–96.

Wheeller, B. (1992): Is Progressive Tourism Appropriate? *Tourism Management* 13 (1): 104–5.

Whitehead, L. (1990): Carib Ethnic Soldiering in Venezuela, the Guianas, and the Antilles, 1492–1820. *Ethnohistory* 37 (4): 357–385.

Wienia, M. (2008): Daring to Tackle: Calm and Insecurity in Northern Ghana. In Machalík, T.; Mildnerová, K. and Zahořík, J. (eds.): *Viva Africa 2008. Proceedings of the 3rd International Conference on African Studies,* pp. 203–218. Plzeň: Adela Publishing.

Willcox, W. (2006): Transnationalism and Multiethnicity in the Early Nguyễn Áhn Gia Long Period. In: Tran, N. T. and Reid A. (eds.): *Viêt Nam Borderless Histories,* pp. 194–256. J.S. Madison: The University of Wisconsin Press.

Williamson, J. (2006): The Disarmament, Demobilization and Reintegration of Child Soldiers: Social and Psychological Transformation in Sierra Leone. *Intervention* 4 (3): 185–205.

Williamson, J. and L. Cripe (2002): *Assessment of DCOF-Supported Child Demobilization and Reintegration Activities in Sierra Leone.* Online: www.forcedmigration.org/psychosocial/papers/WiderPapers/williamson_cripe_sierraleone.pdf (18 April 2009).

Willis, J. R. (ed.) (1979): *The Cultivators of Islam. Vol. I of Studies in West African Islamic History.* London: Frank Cass Publishers.

Wolpe, H. (1973): *Urban politics in Nigeria: A study of Port Harcourt.* London: University of California Press

World Bank (1994): *Republic of Benin. Education Development Project (Third Education Project)*. Cotonou: World Bank.

World Bank (1995): *Priorities and Strategies for Education. A World Bank Review*. Washington: World Bank.

Wright, D. (2004): *The World and a Very Small Place in Africa: A History of Globalization in Niumi, The Gambia* (2nd edition). Armonk, NY: M.E. Sharpe.

Wrong, M. (2009): *It's Our Turn to Eat: The Story of a Kenyan Whistle-Blower*. New York: HarperCollins Publishing.

Wylie, K. (1969): Innovation and Change in Mende Chieftaincy, 1880–1986. *Journal of African History* 10 (2): 295–309.

Zacks, R. (2005): *The Pirate Coast: Thomas Jefferson, the First Marines, and the Secret Mission of 1805*. New York: Hyperion.

Záhořík, J. and Kumsa, A. (2008): Ethiopian Federalism and the Question of Self-Determination of Nations. In: Siwek, T. and Baar, V. (eds.): *Globalisation and Its Impacts on Localities*, pp. 48–57. Ostrava: University of Ostrava.

Zakaria, F. (1997): The Rise of Illiberal Democracy. *Foreign Affairs* 76 (6): 22–43.

Zartman, W.I. (ed.) (2000): *Traditional Cures for Modern Conflicts: African Conflict "Medicine"*. Boulder: Lynne Rienner.

Zídek, P. and Sieber, K. (2007): *Československo a subsaharská Afrika v letech 1948–1989*. Praha: Ústav mezinárodních vztahů.

Zolberg, A. R. (1966): *Creating Political Order. The Party-States of West Africa*. Chicago.

Zolberg, A. R. (1969): *One-Party Government in the Ivory Coast*. Revised Edition. Princeton, Princeton University Press.

Zotov, N.M. (1985): *Angola, borba prodolzhaetsya. Ot natsionalnogo fronta k avantgardnoy partii*. Moskva: Nauka.

SOURCES

A Justiça, No.1, 17 April 1881.

Afrobarometr (2005): *Sustained Support for Democracy in Ghana*. Afrobarometer Briefing Paper 18, Afrobarometr. Online: http://www.afrobarometer.org/papers/AfrobriefNo18.pdf (20th April 2009).

Bushbuckridge Local Municipality (2008): *Annual Financial Statements for the Year Ended 30 June 2008*.Online: http://www.bushbuckridge.gov.za (4 May 2009)

Electoral Commission of Ghana. 2007. *Political Parties' Elections Results*. Online: http://www.ec.gov.gh/political_parties (14th April 2009)

Electoral Commission of Ghana. *http://www.ec.gov.gh*

Ghana Daily Graphic. http://www.graphicghana.com

Ghanian Times. http://www.newtimesonline.com/

Government of Ghana (1992): *The 1992 Constitution of the Republic of Ghana*. Accra: Assembly Press.

Government of Ghana (2000): *Political parties act, 2000 Act 574*. Online: http://ghana.gov.gh/ghana/political_parties_act_2000_act_574.jsp (22nd April 2009)

Lomé Peace Agreement (1999): Peace Agreement between the Government of Sierra Leone and the Revolutionary United Front of Sierra Leone. Online: http://www.sierra-leone.org/lomeaccord.html (18 April 2009)

METFP (Ministère de l'Enseignement Technique et de la Formation Professionnelle) (2004): *Enquête sur l'état de mise en oeuvre des stratégies de la Réforme de l'ETFP dans les établissements publics du METFP. Interrogation de 12 établissements publics du METFP (juillet – août 2004)*. Cotonou: METFP.

MPPD/INSAE (Ministère chargé du Plan, de la Prospective et du Développement, Institut National de la Statistique et de l'Analyse Économique) (2003): *Troisième Recensement Général de la Population et de l'Habitation, Février 2002. Synthèse des Résultats*. Cotonou: INSAE.

National Democratic Congress (2002): Constitution of the National Democratic Congress. Accra: NDC.

National Democratic Congress (2008): *Manifesto for a Better Ghana 2008*. Accra: NDC.

New Patriotic Party NPP (1998): *Constitution of the New Patriotic Party*. Accra: NPP.

OAU (2000): Rwanda: The Preventable Genocide. Special Report of The International Panel of Eminent Personalities to investigate the genocide in Rwanda and its surrounding events. Online: http://www.africa-union.org/Official_documents/reports/Report_rowanda_genocide.pdf (18 April 2009)

OHCHR (2003): Annual Report. Online:www.ohchr.org/Documents/AboutUs/annualreport2003.pdf (18 April 2009)

Republic of South Africa. (2006): *Government Gazette* vol.489. Act No. 34 of 2005: National Credit Act. Cape Town.

Statistics South Africa National Treasury. (2007) *A National Poverty Line for South Africa*. Online: http://www.treasury.gov.za/publications/other/povertyline/Treasury %20 StatsSA %20poverty %20line %20discussion %20paper.pdf. (18 April 2009).

The African Executive. http://www.africanexecutive.com

The Constitution of the Federal Democratic Republic of Ethiopia. Addis Ababa, 1995.

The Imperial Constitution of 1931. http://www.angelfire.com/ny/ethiocrown/Constitution.html

Think Ghana. http://news.thinkghana.com

Truth and Reconciliation Commission (2004): The TRC Final Report. Online: http://www.trcsierraleone.org/drwebsite/publish/index.shtml (18 April 2009)

Truth and Reconciliation Commission Act (2000). Online: http://www.usip.org/library/tc/doc/charters/tc_sierra_leone_02102000.html (18 April 2009)

United States Congress, House Committee on International Relations, Special Committee on Investigations. (1976): *Mercenaries in Africa: Hearing before the Special Subcommittee on Investigations of the Committee on International Relations*. House of Representatives. Ninety-fourth Congress, Second Session, August 9, 1976.

UNODC/SAG. (2003): *Country Corruption Assessment Report.* Online: http://www.gov.za/
    reports/2003/corruption.pdf. (7 May 2009).
www. inc.co.za
www.exploresouthafrica.net/worldheritagesites/
www.go.za
www.places.co.za/html/famousbig5.html
www.satour.org
www.und.ac.za/und/ccms/intro

INDEX